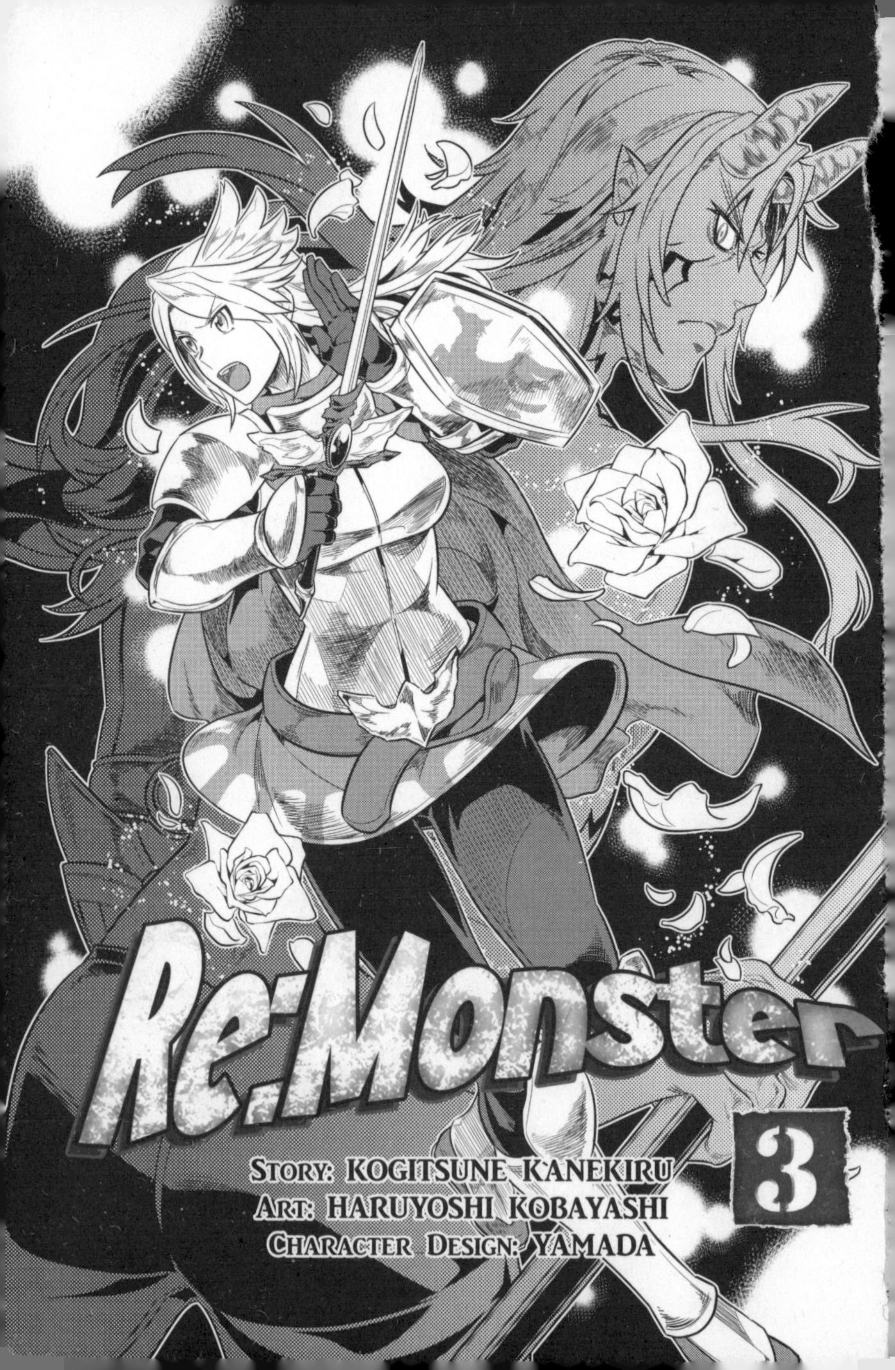
Re:Monster
3
STORY: KOGITSUNE KANEKIRU
ART: HARUYOSHI KOBAYASHI
CHARACTER DESIGN: YAMADA

SEVEN SEAS ENTERTAINMENT PRESENTS

Re:Monster vol. 3

story by **KOGITSUNE KANEKIRU**   art by **HARUYOSHI KOBAYAKAWA**

TRANSLATION
Wesley Bridges

ADAPTATION
Rebecca Spinner

LETTERING AND RETOUCH
Meaghan Tucker

ENGLISH COVER DESIGN
Nicky Lim

PROOFREADER
Janet Houck
Tim Roddy

ASSISTANT EDITOR
Jenn Grunigen

PRODUCTION ASSISTANT
CK Russell

PRODUCTION MANAGER
Lissa Pattillo

EDITOR-IN-CHIEF
Adam Arnold

PUBLISHER
Jason DeAngelis

RE:MONSTER VOL. 3
© KOGITSUNE KANEKIRU, HARUYOSHI KOBAYAKAWA 2017.
First published in Japan in 2017 by KOGITSUNE KANEKIRU and
HARUYOSHI KOBAYAKAWA.
English translation rights arranged with AlphaPolis.
Book design by ansyyqdesign.

Seven Seas books may be purchased in bulk for promotional, educational, or
business use. Please contact your local bookseller or the Macmillan Corporate
and Premium Sales Department at 1-800-221-7945, extension 5442, or by
e-mail at MacmillanSpecialMarkets@macmillan.com.

Seven Seas and the Seven Seas logo are trademarks of
Seven Seas Entertainment, LLC. All rights reserved.

ISBN: 978-1-626924-82-6

Printed in Canada

First Printing: November 2017

10 9 8 7 6 5 4 3 2

FOLLOW US ONLINE: *www.gomanga.com*

READING DIRECTIONS

This book reads from *right to left*, Japanese style.
If this is your first time reading manga, you start
reading from the top right panel on each page and
take it from there. If you get lost, just follow the
numbered diagram here. It may seem backwards at
first, but you'll get the hang of it! Have fun!!

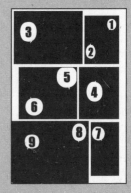

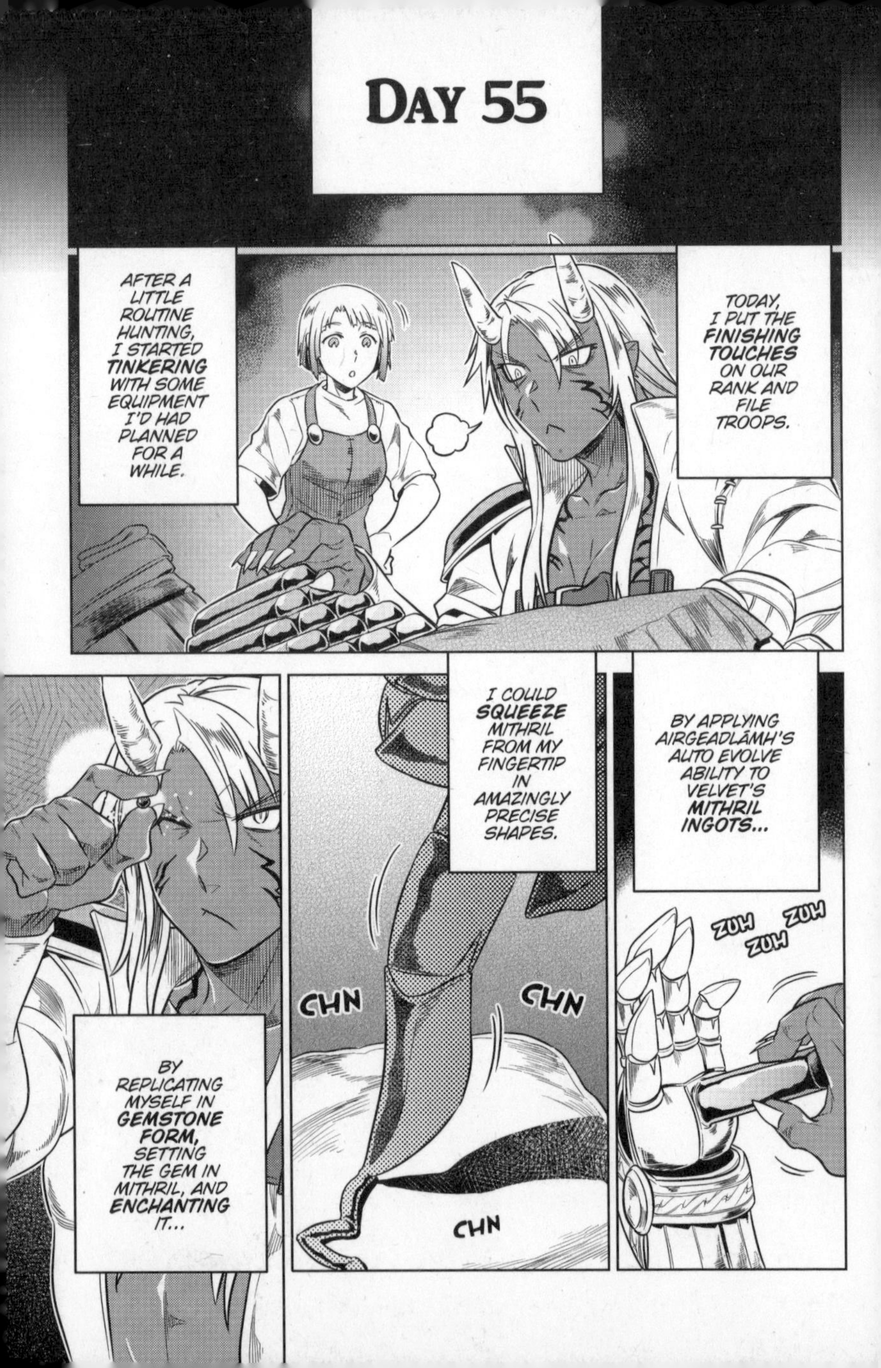
DAY 55
TODAY, I PUT THE FINISHING TOUCHES ON OUR RANK AND FILE TROOPS.
AFTER A LITTLE ROUTINE HUNTING, I STARTED TINKERING WITH SOME EQUIPMENT I'D HAD PLANNED FOR A WHILE.
BY APPLYING AIRGEADLÁMH'S AUTO EVOLVE ABILITY TO VELVET'S MITHRIL INGOTS...
ZUH
ZUH
ZUH
I COULD SQUEEZE MITHRIL FROM MY FINGERTIP IN AMAZINGLY PRECISE SHAPES.
CHN
CHN
CHN
BY REPLICATING MYSELF IN GEMSTONE FORM, SETTING THE GEM IN MITHRIL, AND ENCHANTING IT...

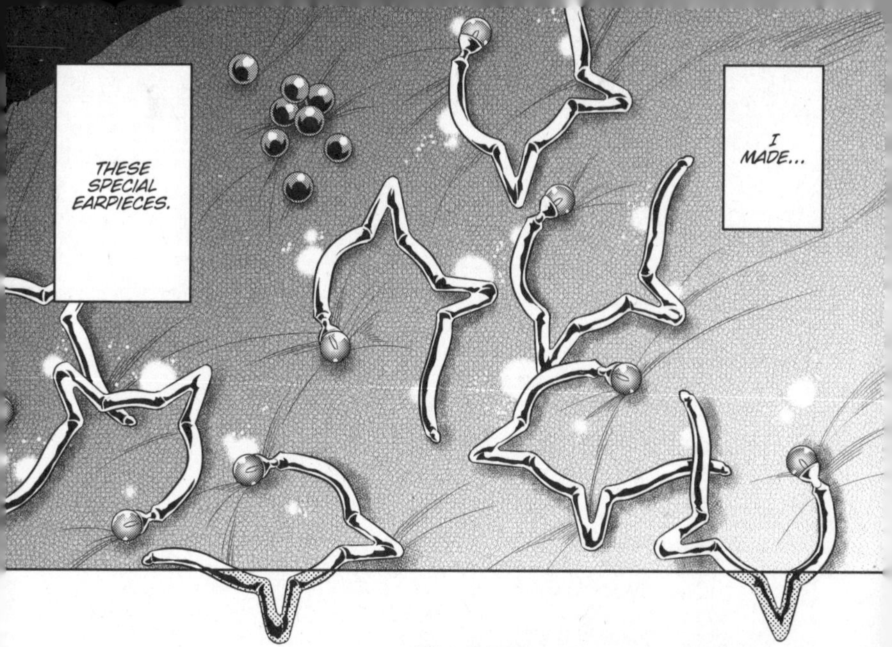
I MADE...
THESE SPECIAL EARPIECES.

CHAPTER 20

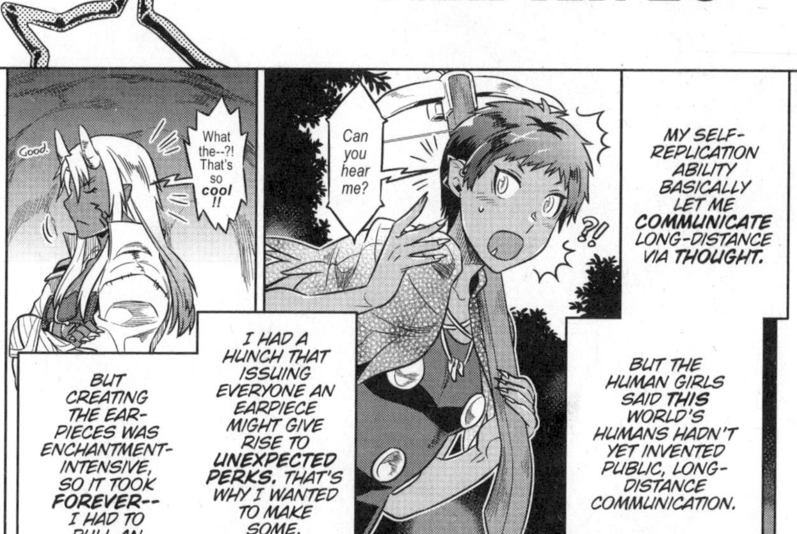
MY SELF-REPLICATION ABILITY BASICALLY LET ME COMMUNICATE LONG-DISTANCE VIA THOUGHT.
BUT THE HUMAN GIRLS SAID THIS WORLD'S HUMANS HADN'T YET INVENTED PUBLIC, LONG-DISTANCE COMMUNICATION.
Can you hear me?
?!
I HAD A HUNCH THAT ISSUING EVERYONE AN EARPIECE MIGHT GIVE RISE TO UNEXPECTED PERKS. THAT'S WHY I WANTED TO MAKE SOME.
What the--?! That's so cool!!
Good.
BUT CREATING THE EAR-PIECES WAS ENCHANTMENT-INTENSIVE, SO IT TOOK FOREVER-- I HAD TO PULL AN ALLNIGHTER.

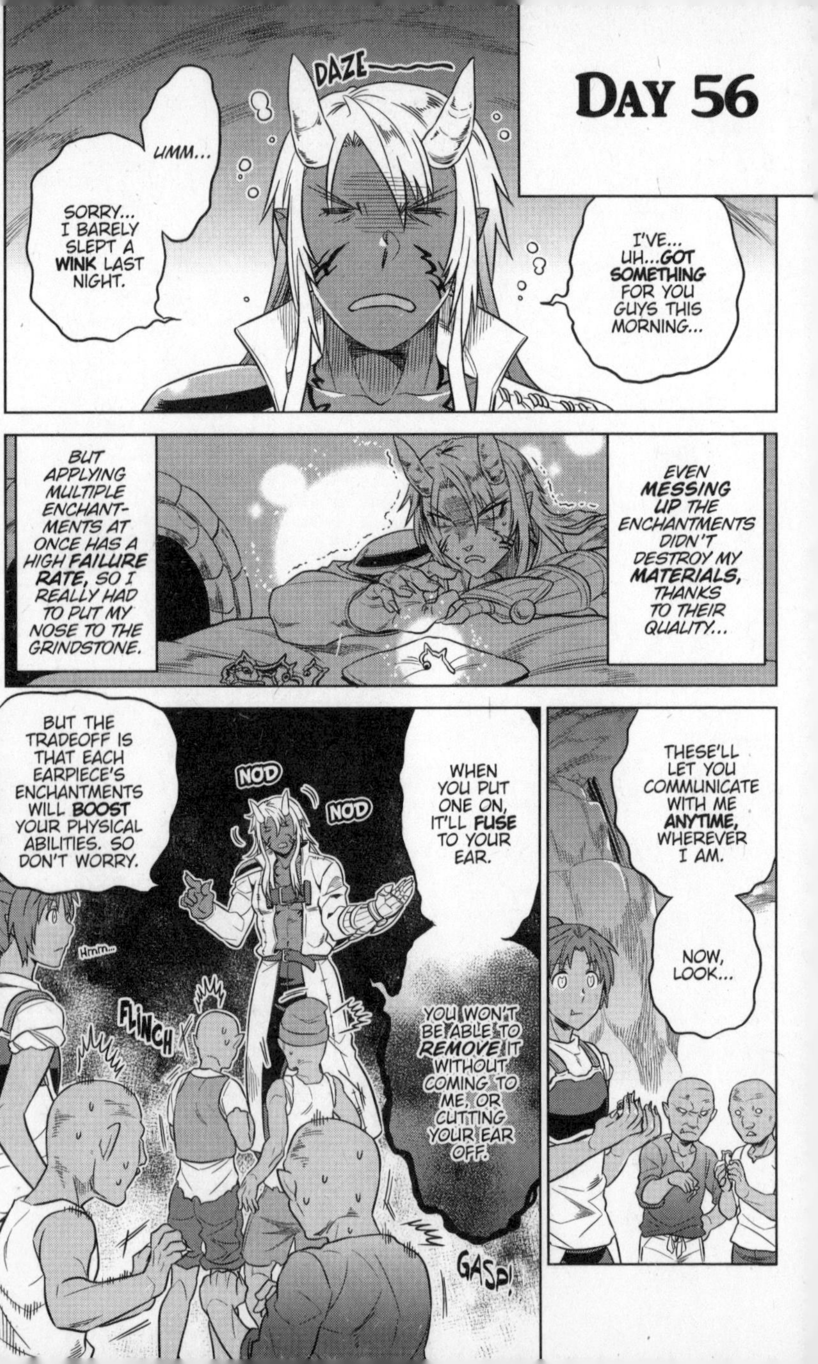
DAY 56
DAZE
I'VE... UH...GOT SOMETHING FOR YOU GUYS THIS MORNING...
UMM...
SORRY... I BARELY SLEPT A WINK LAST NIGHT.
EVEN MESSING UP THE ENCHANTMENTS DIDN'T DESTROY MY MATERIALS, THANKS TO THEIR QUALITY...
BUT APPLYING MULTIPLE ENCHANT-MENTS AT ONCE HAS A HIGH FAILURE RATE, SO I REALLY HAD TO PUT MY NOSE TO THE GRINDSTONE.
THESE'LL LET YOU COMMUNICATE WITH ME ANYTIME, WHEREVER I AM.
NOW, LOOK...
WHEN YOU PUT ONE ON, IT'LL FUSE TO YOUR EAR.
NOD
NOD
YOU WON'T BE ABLE TO REMOVE IT WITHOUT COMING TO ME, OR CUTTING YOUR EAR OFF.
BUT THE TRADEOFF IS THAT EACH EARPIECE'S ENCHANTMENTS WILL BOOST YOUR PHYSICAL ABILITIES. SO DON'T WORRY.
Hmm...
FLINCH
GASP!

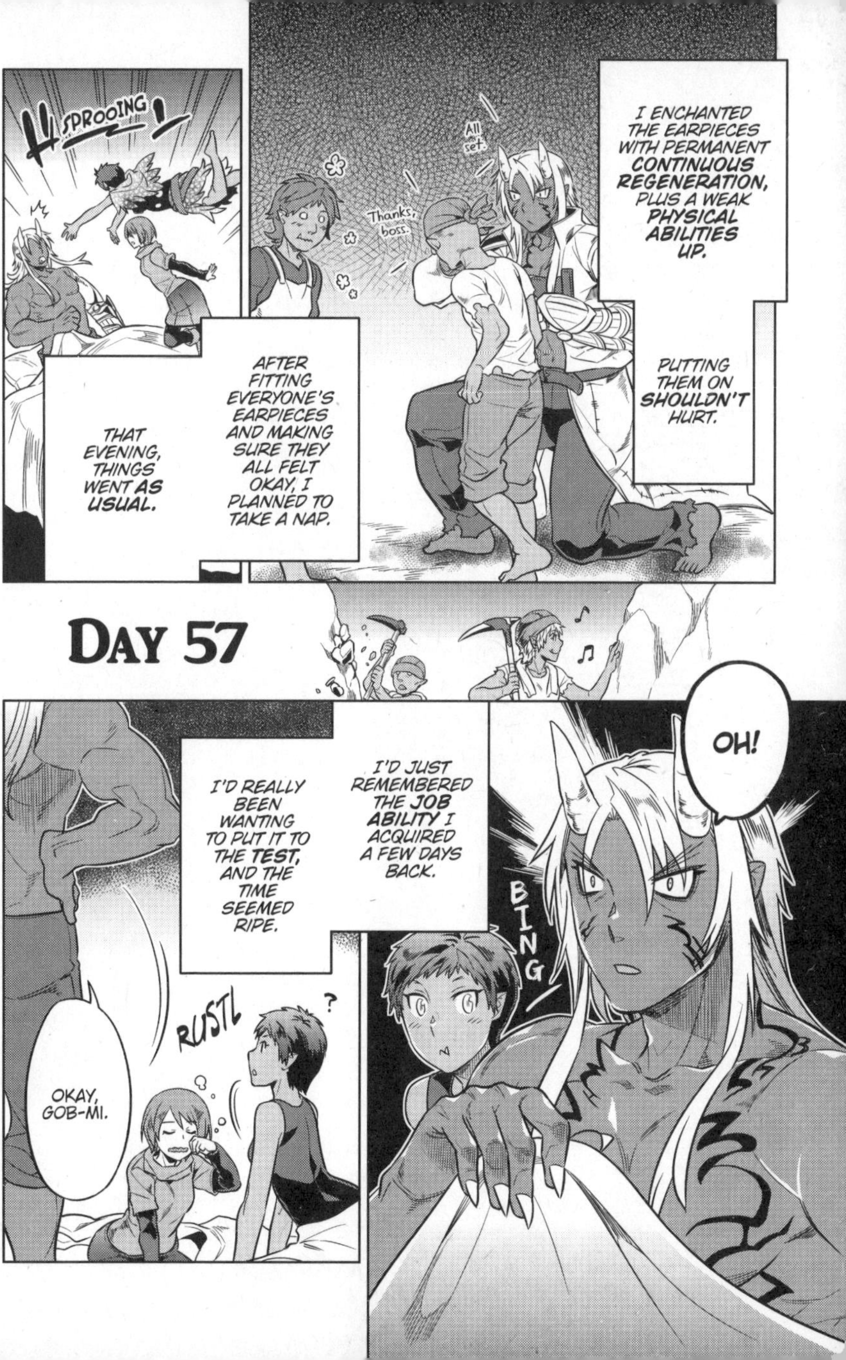
I ENCHANTED THE EARPIECES WITH PERMANENT CONTINUOUS REGENERATION, PLUS A WEAK PHYSICAL ABILITIES UP.
All set.
Thanks, boss.
PUTTING THEM ON SHOULDN'T HURT.
SPROOING
AFTER FITTING EVERYONE'S EARPIECES AND MAKING SURE THEY ALL FELT OKAY, I PLANNED TO TAKE A NAP.
THAT EVENING, THINGS WENT AS USUAL.
DAY 57
OH!
BING
I'D JUST REMEMBERED THE JOB ABILITY I ACQUIRED A FEW DAYS BACK.
I'D REALLY BEEN WANTING TO PUT IT TO THE TEST, AND THE TIME SEEMED RIPE.
?
RUSTL
OKAY, GOB-MI.

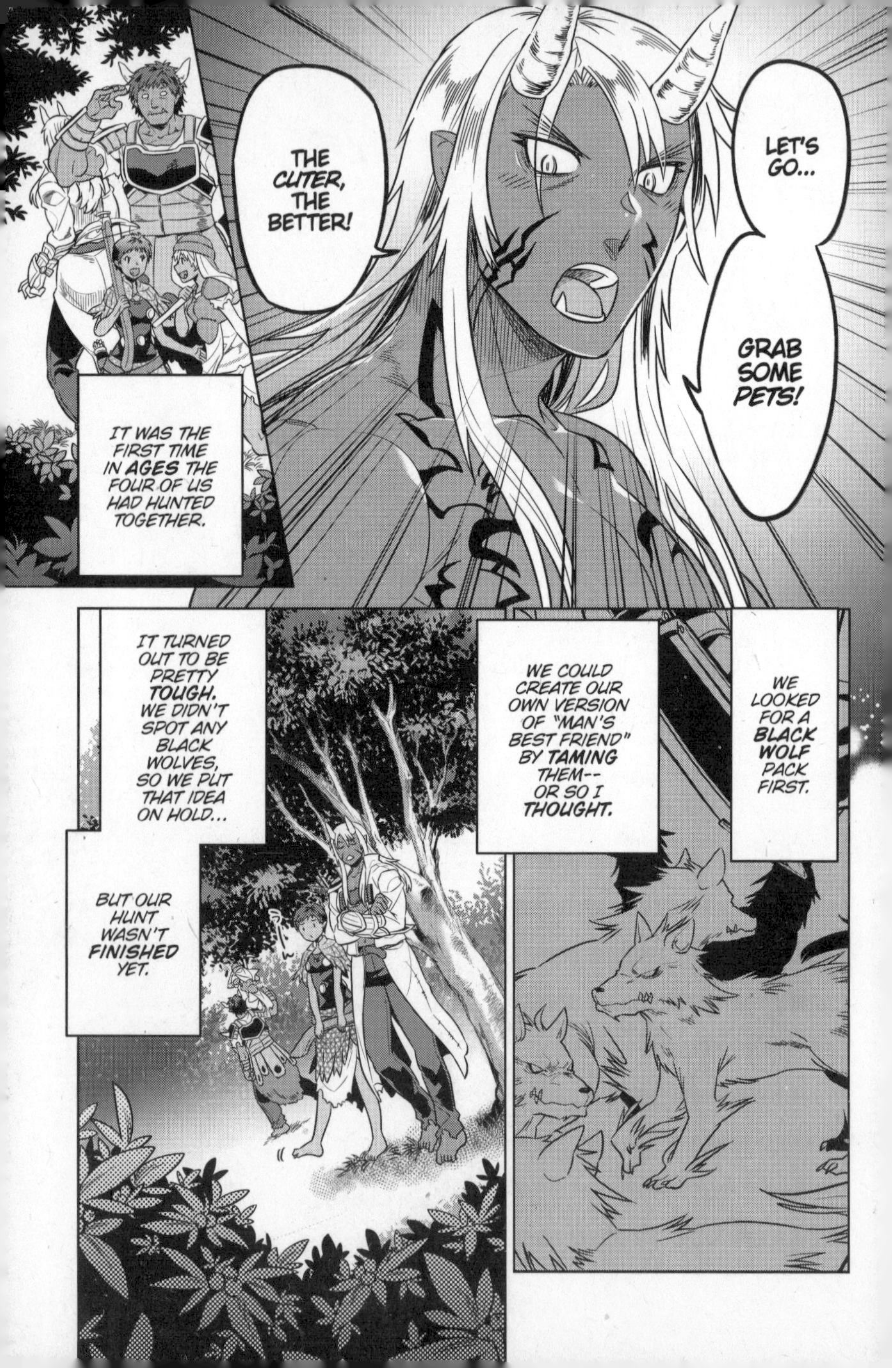
LET'S GO...
GRAB SOME PETS!
THE CUTER, THE BETTER!
IT WAS THE FIRST TIME IN AGES THE FOUR OF US HAD HUNTED TOGETHER.
WE LOOKED FOR A BLACK WOLF PACK FIRST.
WE COULD CREATE OUR OWN VERSION OF "MAN'S BEST FRIEND" BY TAMING THEM-- OR SO I THOUGHT.
IT TURNED OUT TO BE PRETTY TOUGH. WE DIDN'T SPOT ANY BLACK WOLVES, SO WE PUT THAT IDEA ON HOLD...
BUT OUR HUNT WASN'T FINISHED YET.

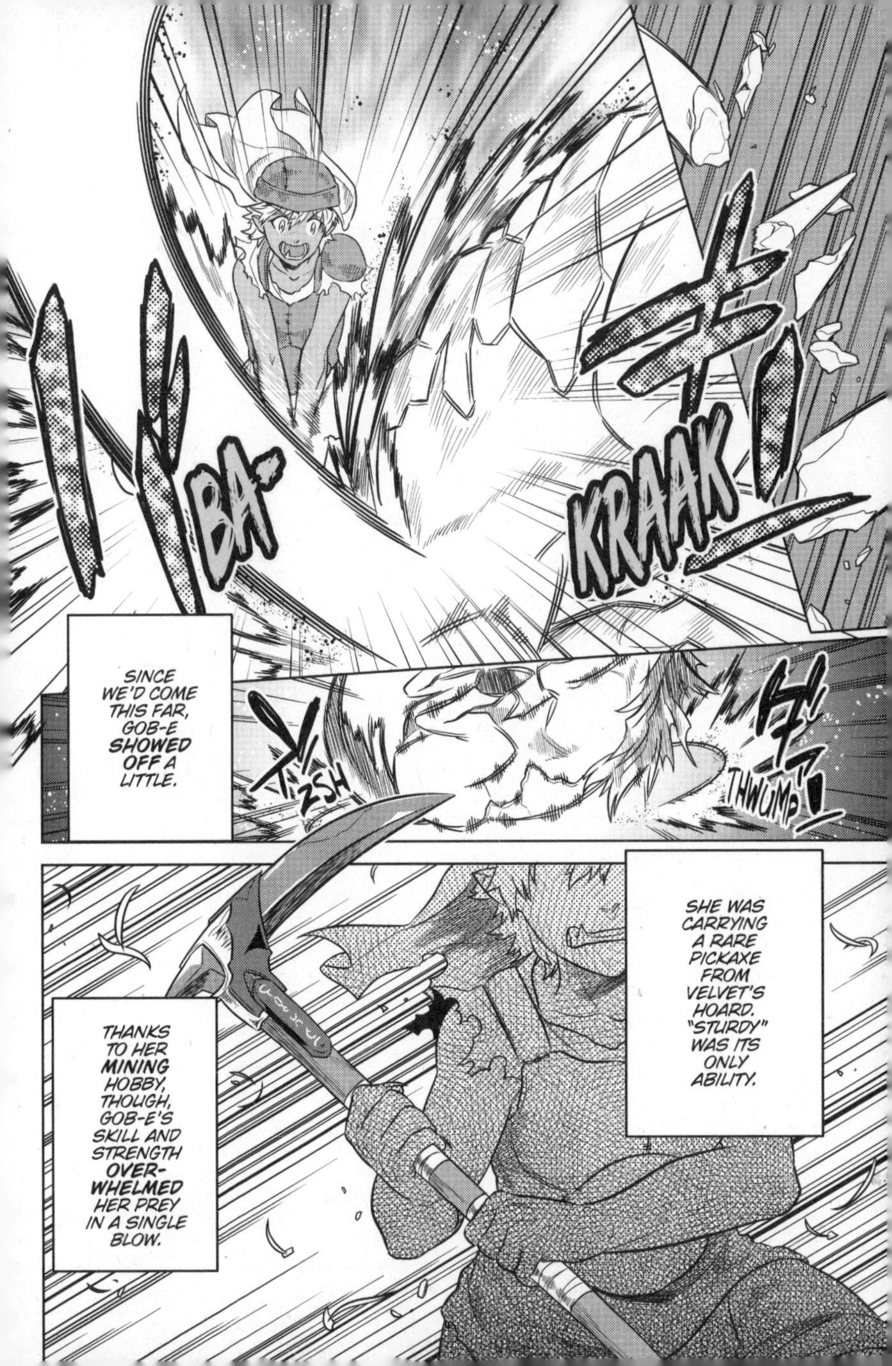
KRAAK!
BA
SINCE WE'D COME THIS FAR, GOB-E SHOWED OFF A LITTLE.
THWUMP!
ZSH
SHE WAS CARRYING A RARE PICKAXE FROM VELVET'S HOARD. "STURDY" WAS ITS ONLY ABILITY.
THANKS TO HER MINING HOBBY, THOUGH, GOB-E'S SKILL AND STRENGTH OVER-WHELMED HER PREY IN A SINGLE BLOW.

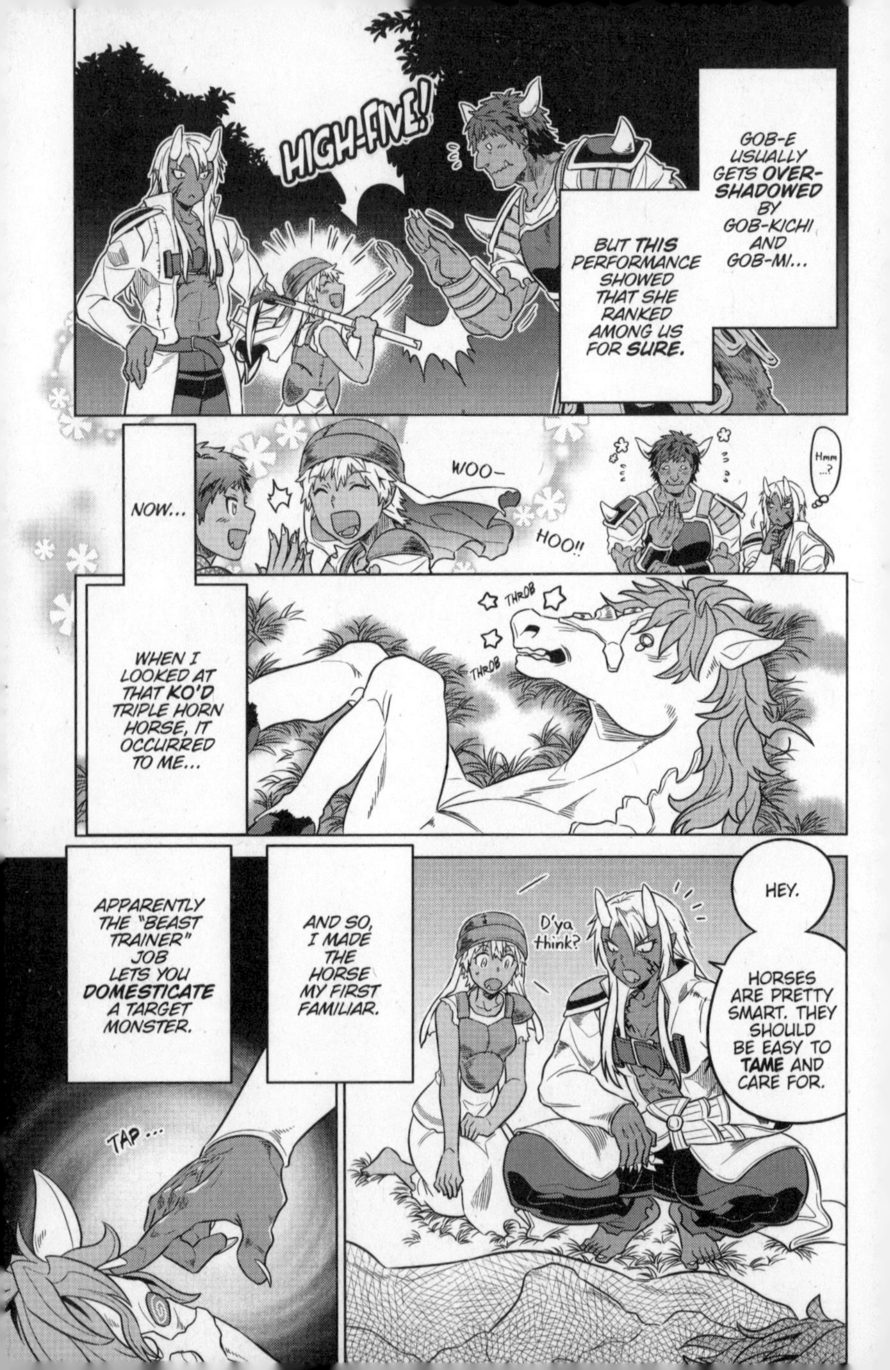
GOB-E USUALLY GETS OVER-SHADOWED BY GOB-KICHI AND GOB-MI...
BUT THIS PERFORMANCE SHOWED THAT SHE RANKED AMONG US FOR SURE.
HIGH-FIVE!
Hmm ...?
WOO-
HOO!!
NOW...
THROB
THROB
WHEN I LOOKED AT THAT KO'D TRIPLE HORN HORSE, IT OCCURRED TO ME...
HEY.
HORSES ARE PRETTY SMART. THEY SHOULD BE EASY TO TAME AND CARE FOR.
D'ya think?
AND SO, I MADE THE HORSE MY FIRST FAMILIAR.
APPARENTLY THE "BEAST TRAINER" JOB LETS YOU DOMESTICATE A TARGET MONSTER.
TAP ...

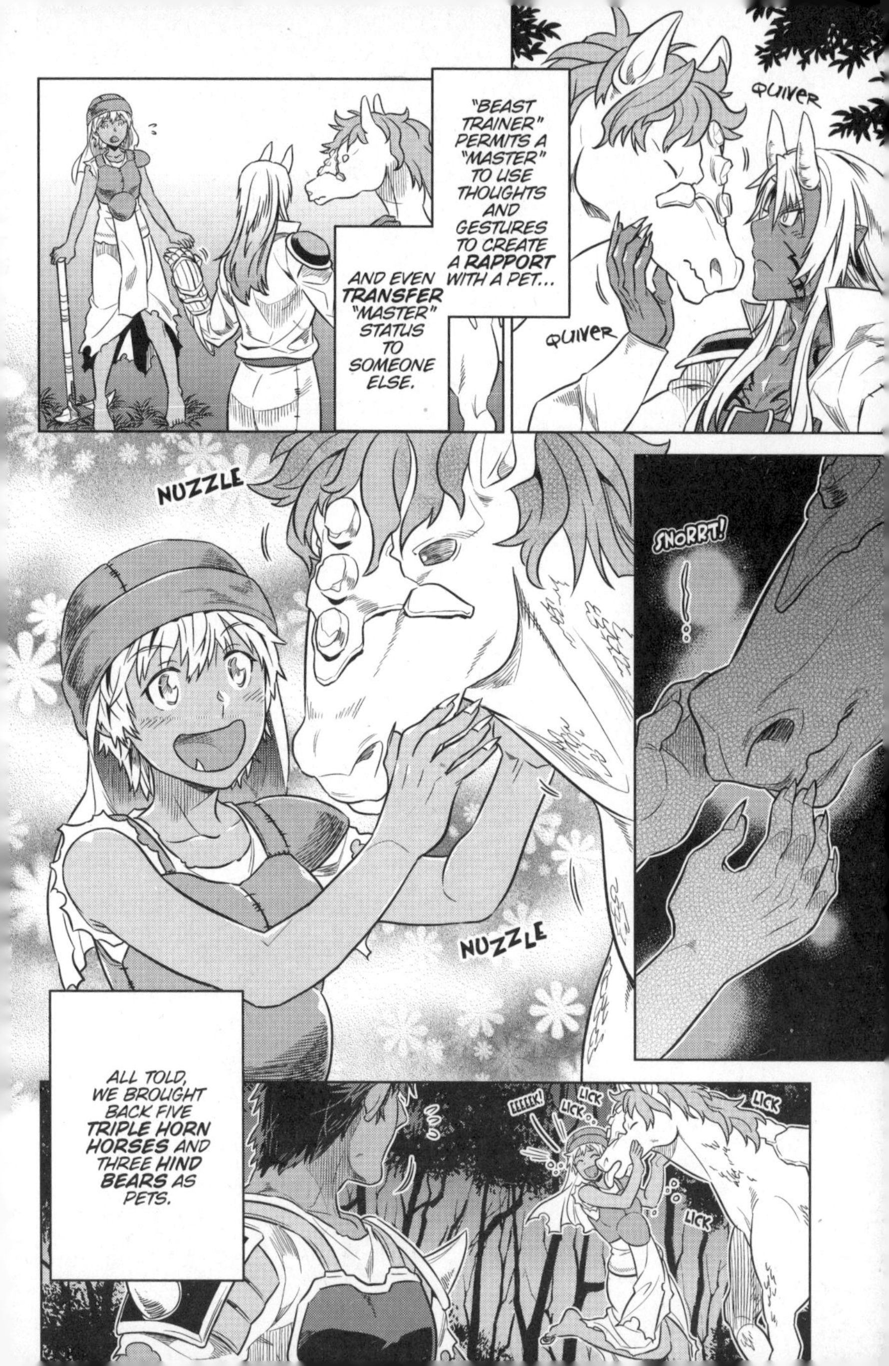
QUIVER
QUIVER
"BEAST TRAINER" PERMITS A "MASTER" TO USE THOUGHTS AND GESTURES TO CREATE A RAPPORT WITH A PET...
AND EVEN TRANSFER "MASTER" STATUS TO SOMEONE ELSE.
SNORRT!
!
NUZZLE
NUZZLE
ALL TOLD, WE BROUGHT BACK FIVE TRIPLE HORN HORSES AND THREE HIND BEARS AS PETS.
LICK
LICK
EEEEEK!
LICK
LICK

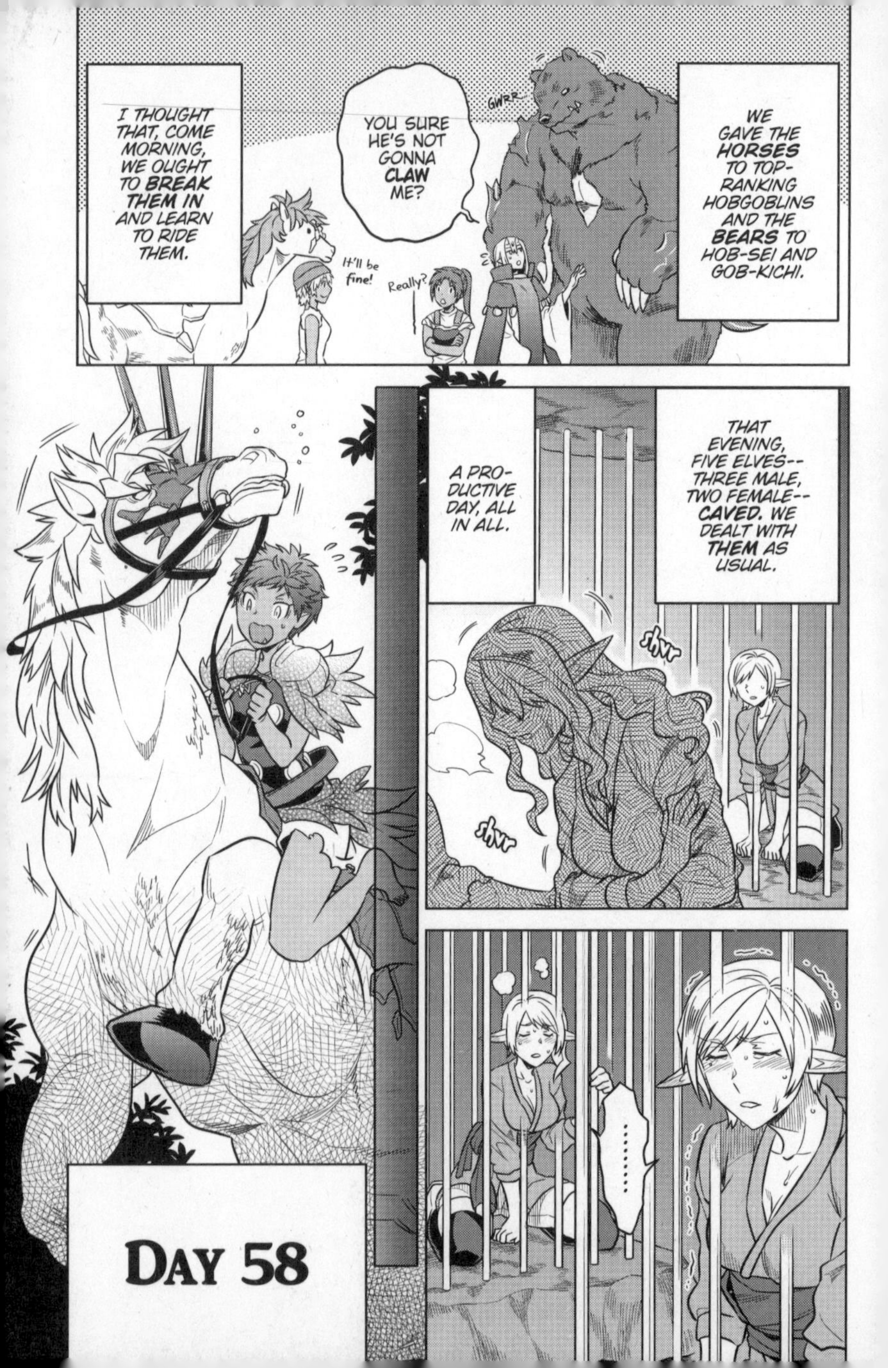
WE GAVE THE **HORSES** TO TOP-RANKING HOBGOBLINS AND THE **BEARS** TO HOB-SEI AND GOB-KICHI.
GWRR
YOU SURE HE'S NOT GONNA **CLAW** ME?
It'll be **fine**!
Really?
I THOUGHT THAT, COME MORNING, WE OUGHT TO **BREAK THEM IN** AND LEARN TO RIDE THEM.
THAT EVENING, FIVE ELVES--THREE MALE, TWO FEMALE--**CAVED.** WE DEALT WITH **THEM** AS USUAL.
A PRODUCTIVE DAY, ALL IN ALL.
shvr
shvr
......
DAY 58

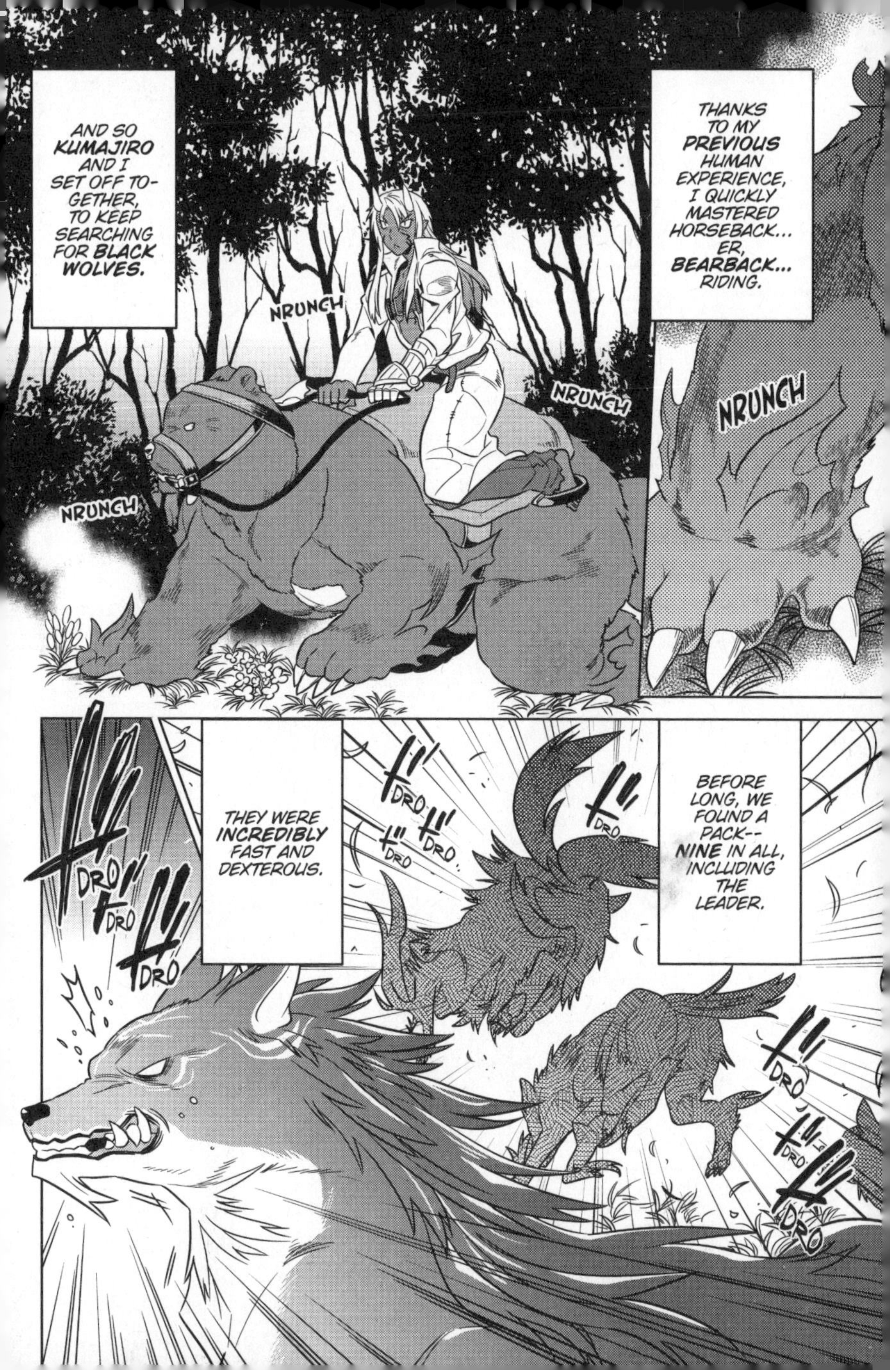
THANKS TO MY PREVIOUS HUMAN EXPERIENCE, I QUICKLY MASTERED HORSEBACK... ER, BEARBACK... RIDING.
NRUNCH
AND SO KUMAJIRO AND I SET OFF TO-GETHER, TO KEEP SEARCHING FOR BLACK WOLVES.
NRUNCH
NRUNCH
NRUNCH
BEFORE LONG, WE FOUND A PACK-- NINE IN ALL, INCLUDING THE LEADER.
DRO
DRO
DRO
DRO
DRO
THEY WERE INCREDIBLY FAST AND DEXTEROUS.
DRO
DRO
DRO
DRO
DRO
DRO

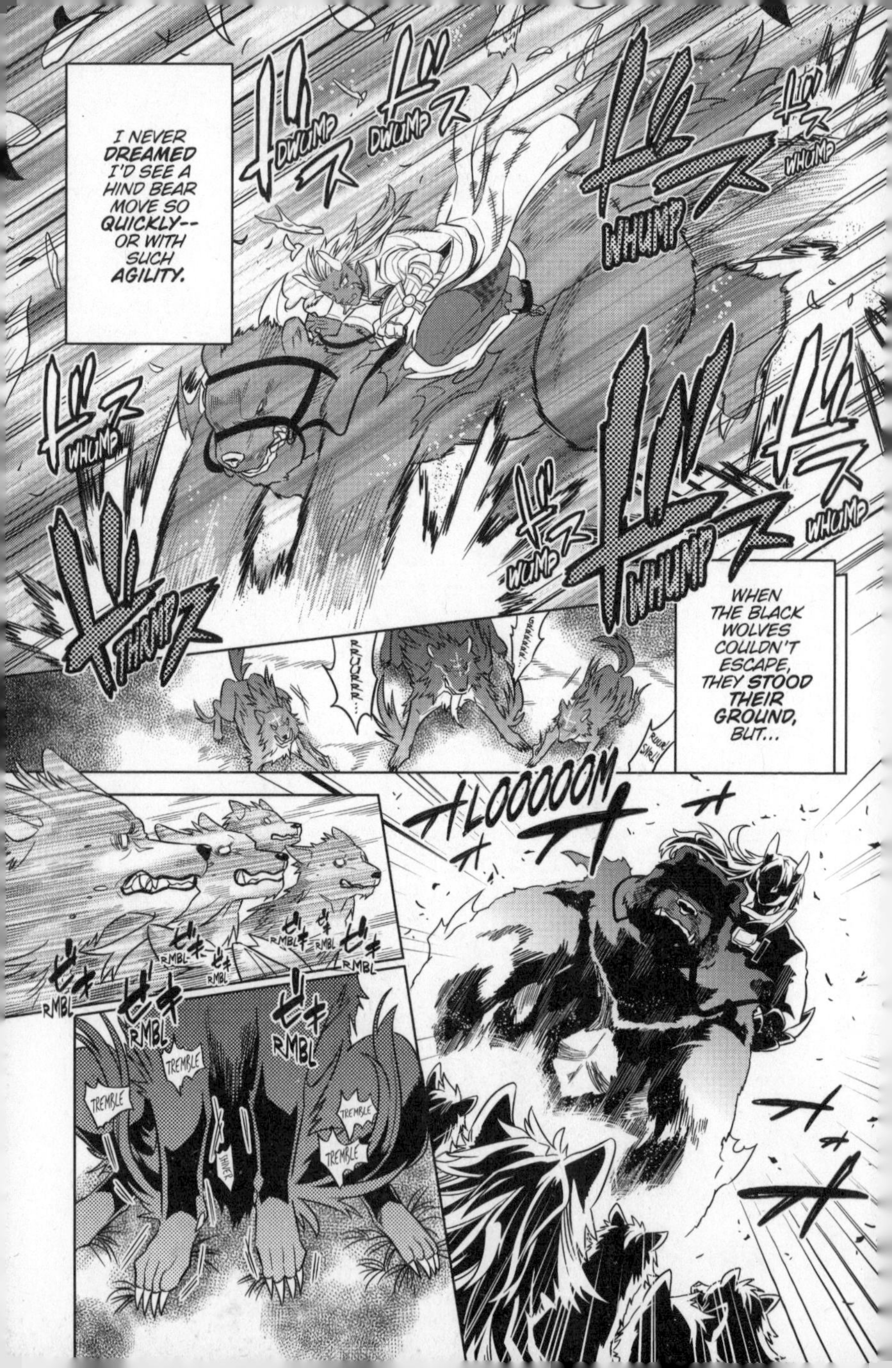
WHUMP
WHUMP
DWUMP
DWUMP
I NEVER DREAMED I'D SEE A HIND BEAR MOVE SO QUICKLY-- OR WITH SUCH AGILITY.
WHUMP
WHUMP
WUMP
WHUMP
THUMP
WHEN THE BLACK WOLVES COULDN'T ESCAPE, THEY STOOD THEIR GROUND, BUT...
RUUR SNRL
GRRRRR...
RRUURRR...
HLOOOOOM
RMBL
RMBL
RMBL
RMBL
RMBL
RMBL
RMBL
TREMBLE
TREMBLE
TREMBLE
TREMBLE
SHIVER

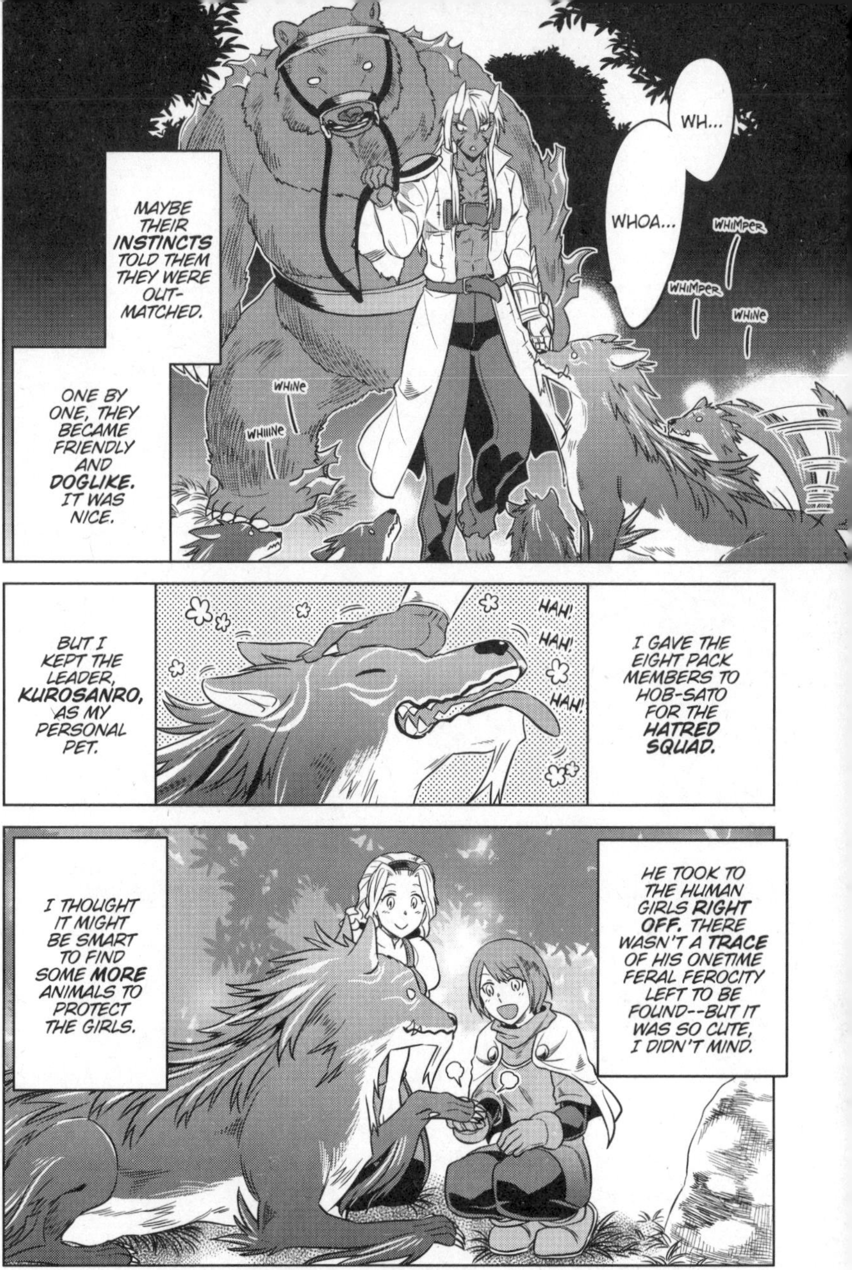
WH...
WHOA...
WHIMPER
WHIMPER
WHINE
MAYBE THEIR INSTINCTS TOLD THEM THEY WERE OUT-MATCHED.
ONE BY ONE, THEY BECAME FRIENDLY AND DOGLIKE. IT WAS NICE.
WHINE
WHIIINE
I GAVE THE EIGHT PACK MEMBERS TO HOB-SATO FOR THE HATRED SQUAD.
HAH!
HAH!
HAH!
BUT I KEPT THE LEADER, KUROSANRO, AS MY PERSONAL PET.
HE TOOK TO THE HUMAN GIRLS RIGHT OFF. THERE WASN'T A TRACE OF HIS ONETIME FERAL FEROCITY LEFT TO BE FOUND--BUT IT WAS SO CUTE, I DIDN'T MIND.
I THOUGHT IT MIGHT BE SMART TO FIND SOME MORE ANIMALS TO PROTECT THE GIRLS.

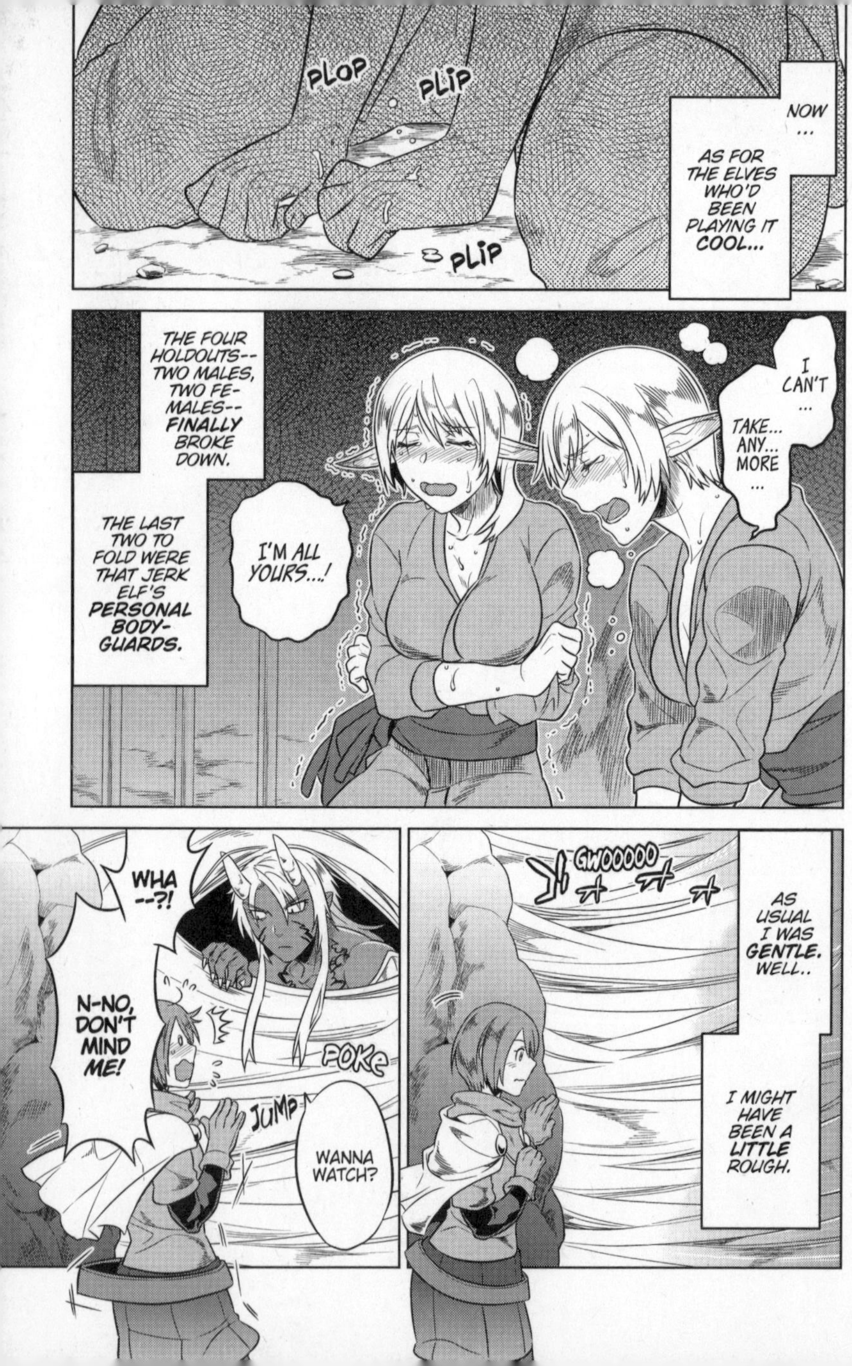
NOW... AS FOR THE ELVES WHO'D BEEN PLAYING IT COOL...
PLOP
PLIP
PLIP
I CAN'T... TAKE... ANY... MORE...
THE FOUR HOLDOUTS--TWO MALES, TWO FE-MALES--FINALLY BROKE DOWN.
I'M ALL YOURS...!
THE LAST TWO TO FOLD WERE THAT JERK ELF'S PERSONAL BODY-GUARDS.
GWOOOOO
AS USUAL I WAS GENTLE. WELL..
I MIGHT HAVE BEEN A LITTLE ROUGH.
WHA--?!
POKE
N-NO, DON'T MIND ME!
JUMP
WANNA WATCH?

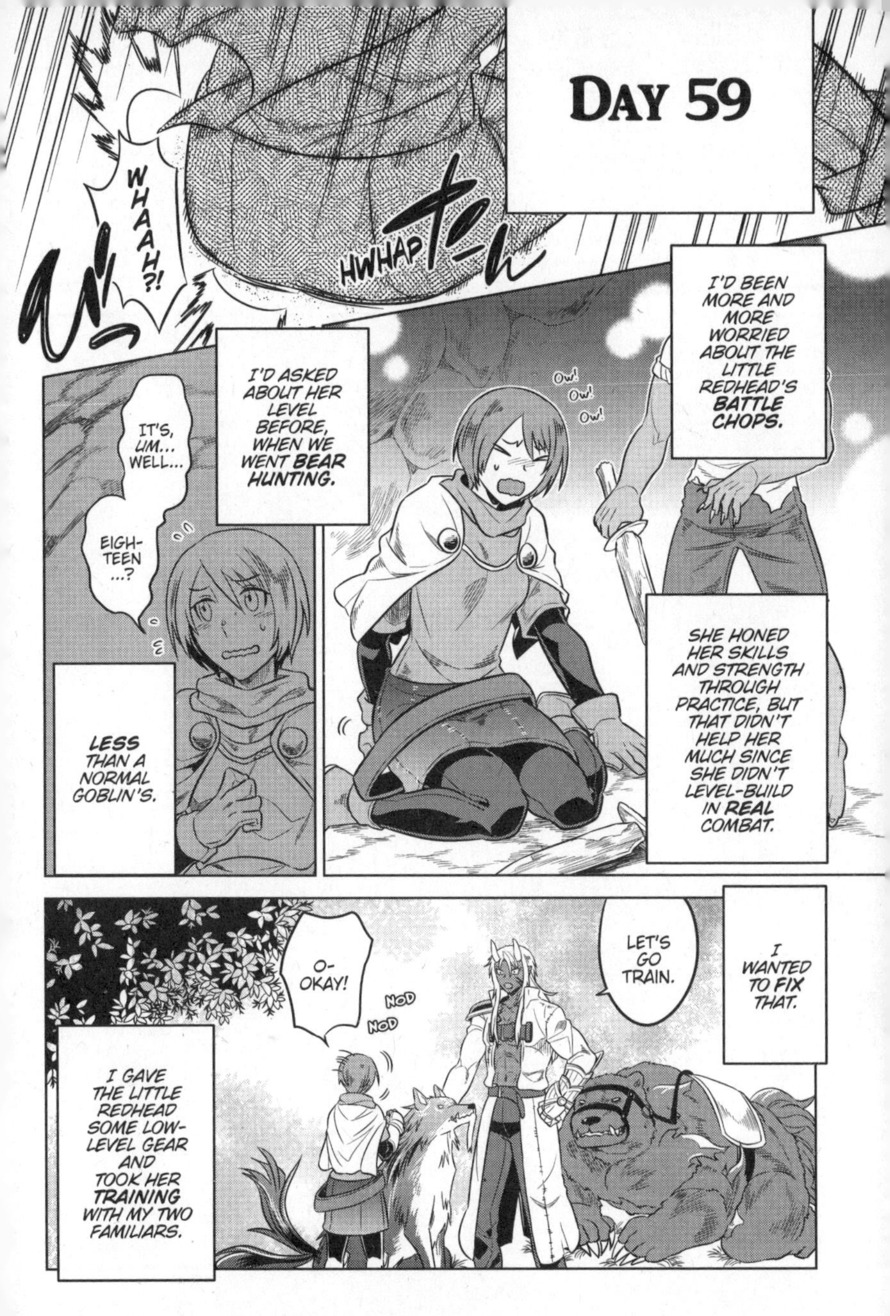
DAY 59
HWHAP
WHAAAH?!
I'D BEEN MORE AND MORE WORRIED ABOUT THE LITTLE REDHEAD'S BATTLE CHOPS.
Ow! Ow! Ow!
SHE HONED HER SKILLS AND STRENGTH THROUGH PRACTICE, BUT THAT DIDN'T HELP HER MUCH SINCE SHE DIDN'T LEVEL-BUILD IN REAL COMBAT.
I'D ASKED ABOUT HER LEVEL BEFORE, WHEN WE WENT BEAR HUNTING.
IT'S, UM... WELL...
EIGHTEEN...?
LESS THAN A NORMAL GOBLIN'S.
I WANTED TO FIX THAT.
LET'S GO TRAIN.
O-OKAY!
NOD
NOD
I GAVE THE LITTLE REDHEAD SOME LOW-LEVEL GEAR AND TOOK HER TRAINING WITH MY TWO FAMILIARS.

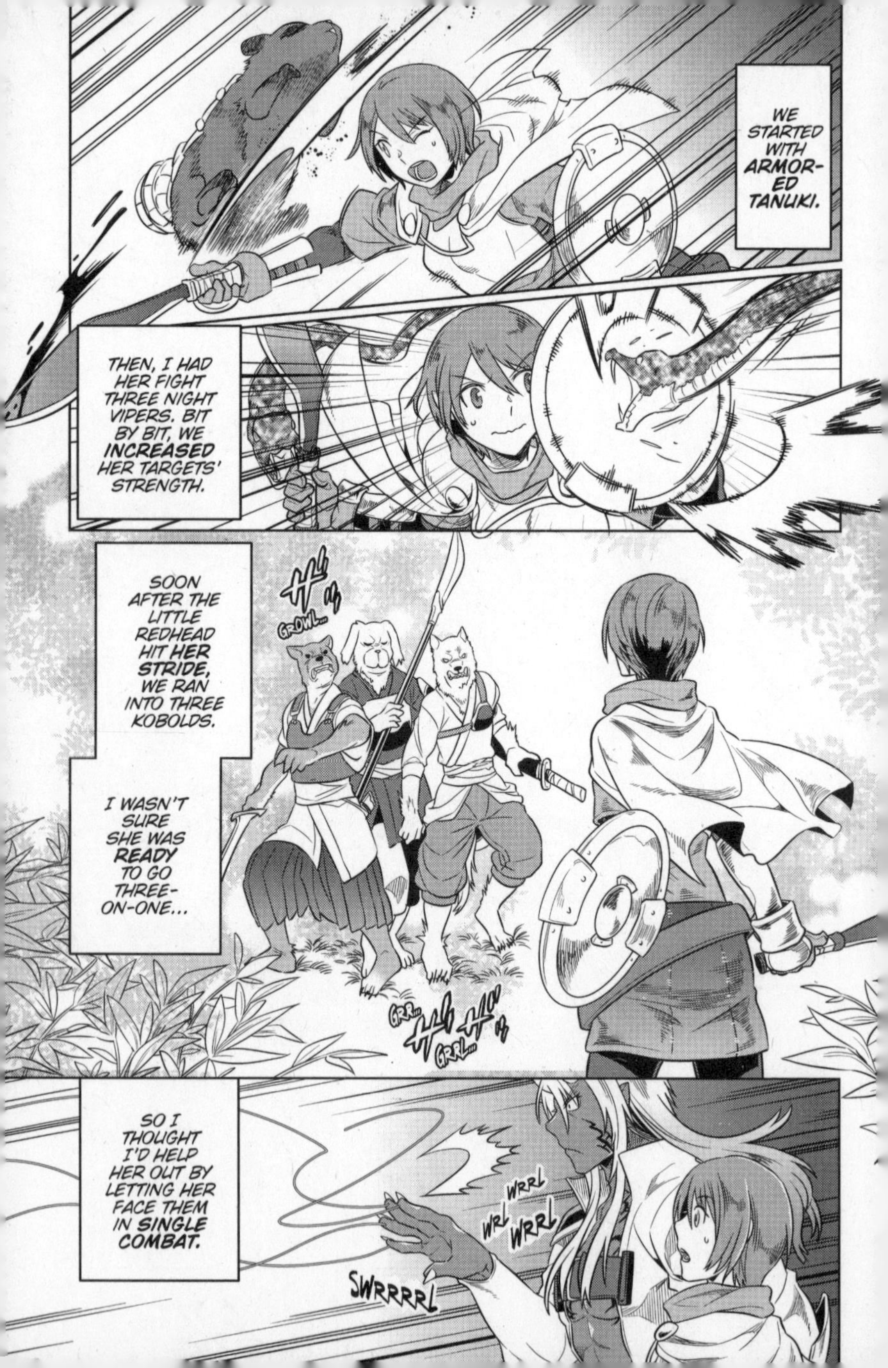
WE STARTED WITH ARMORED TANUKI.
THEN, I HAD HER FIGHT THREE NIGHT VIPERS. BIT BY BIT, WE INCREASED HER TARGETS' STRENGTH.
SOON AFTER THE LITTLE REDHEAD HIT HER STRIDE, WE RAN INTO THREE KOBOLDS.
HF
GROWL...
I WASN'T SURE SHE WAS READY TO GO THREE-ON-ONE...
HF
GRR...
HF
GRRL...
SO I THOUGHT I'D HELP HER OUT BY LETTING HER FACE THEM IN SINGLE COMBAT.
WRRL
WRL
WRRL
SWRRRRL

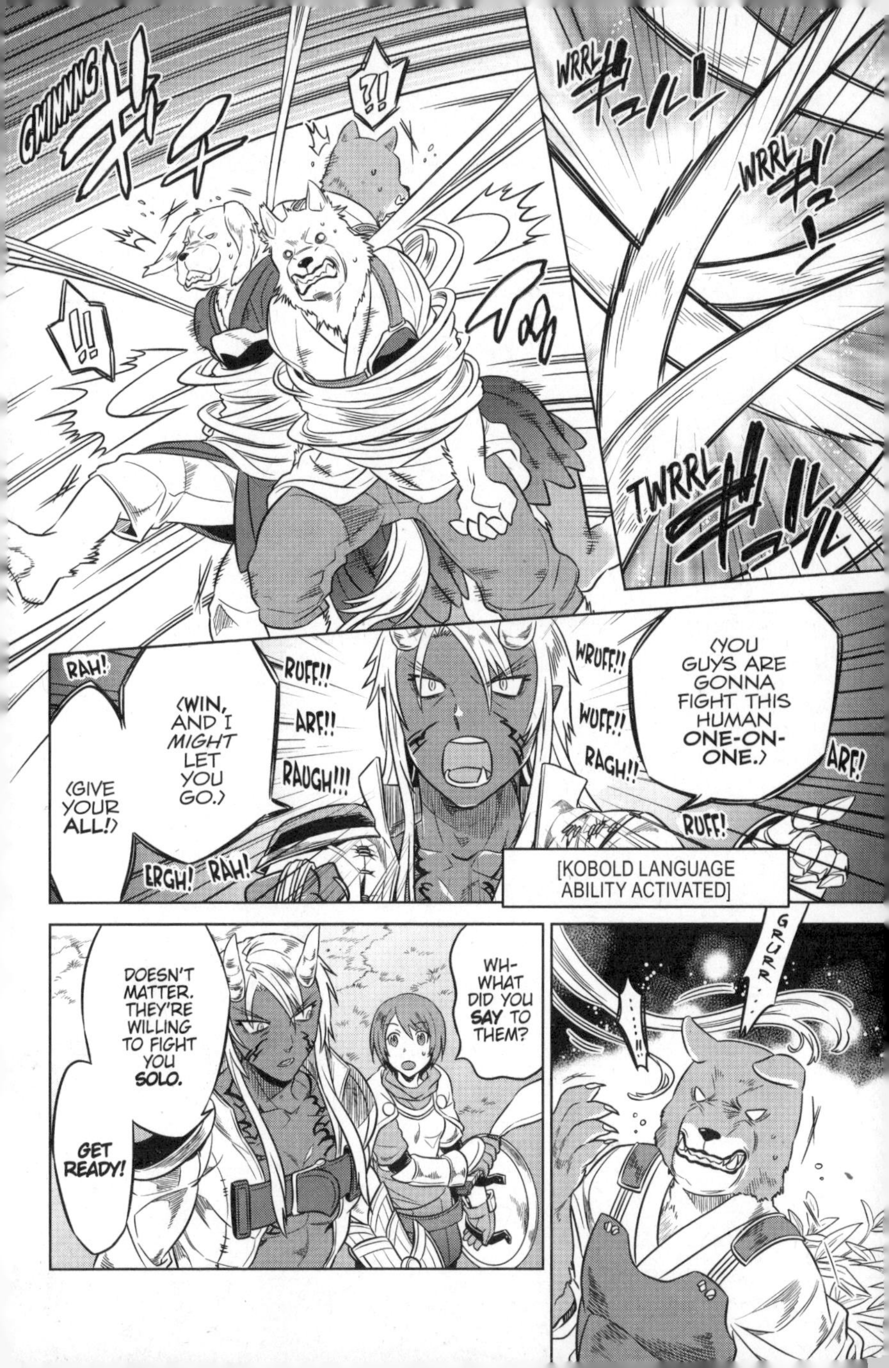
WRRL ギュル!
WRRL ギュ!
TWRRL ギュルル
GWINNNG ギチ
?!!
!!
⟨YOU GUYS ARE GONNA FIGHT THIS HUMAN ONE-ON-ONE.⟩
WRUFF!!
WUFF!!
RAGH!!
ARF!
RUFF!
[KOBOLD LANGUAGE ABILITY ACTIVATED]
⟨WIN, AND I MIGHT LET YOU GO.⟩
RUFF!!
ARF!!
RAUGH!!!
RAH!
⟨GIVE YOUR ALL!⟩
ERGH!
RAH!
GRURR...
!!
WH-WHAT DID YOU SAY TO THEM?
DOESN'T MATTER. THEY'RE WILLING TO FIGHT YOU SOLO.
GET READY!

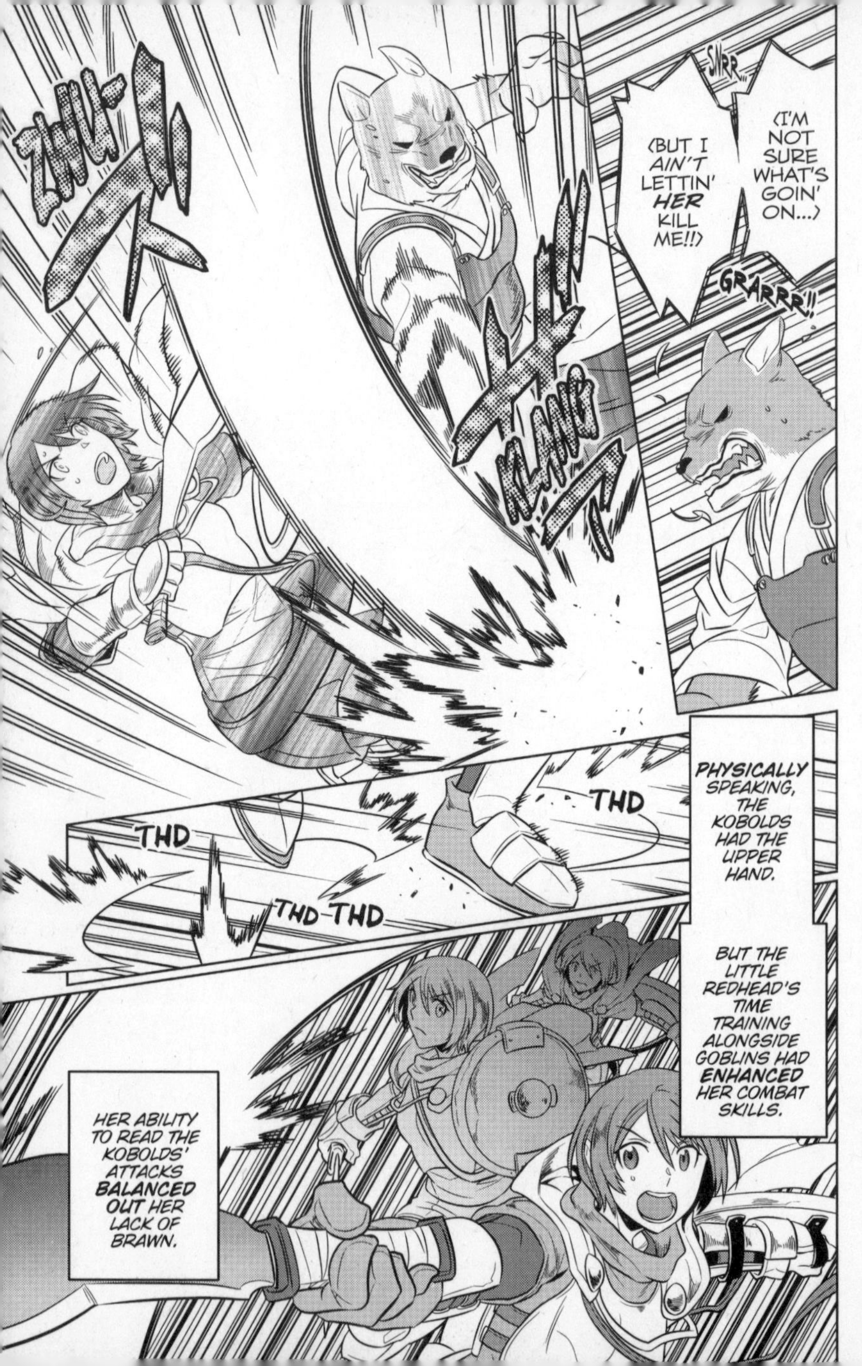
SNRR...
‹I'M NOT SURE WHAT'S GOIN' ON...›
‹BUT I AIN'T LETTIN' **HER** KILL ME!!›
GRARRR!!
KLANG
ZWU-
PHYSICALLY SPEAKING, THE KOBOLDS HAD THE UPPER HAND.
THD
THD
THD THD
BUT THE LITTLE REDHEAD'S TIME TRAINING ALONGSIDE GOBLINS HAD **ENHANCED** HER COMBAT SKILLS.
HER ABILITY TO READ THE KOBOLDS' ATTACKS **BALANCED OUT** HER LACK OF BRAWN.

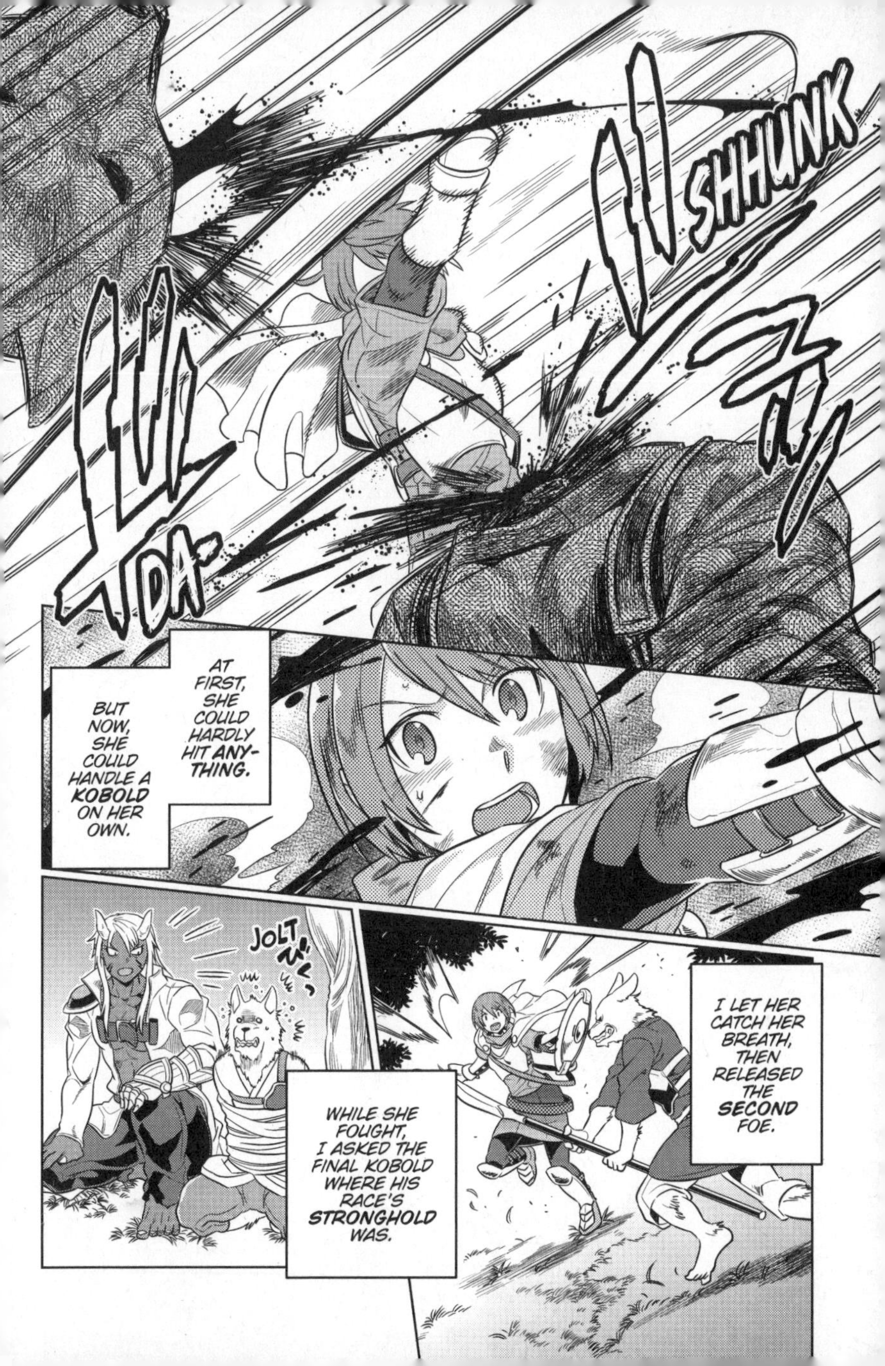
SHHUNK
DA-
AT FIRST, SHE COULD HARDLY HIT ANYTHING.
BUT NOW, SHE COULD HANDLE A KOBOLD ON HER OWN.
I LET HER CATCH HER BREATH, THEN RELEASED THE SECOND FOE.
JOLT
WHILE SHE FOUGHT, I ASKED THE FINAL KOBOLD WHERE HIS RACE'S STRONGHOLD WAS.

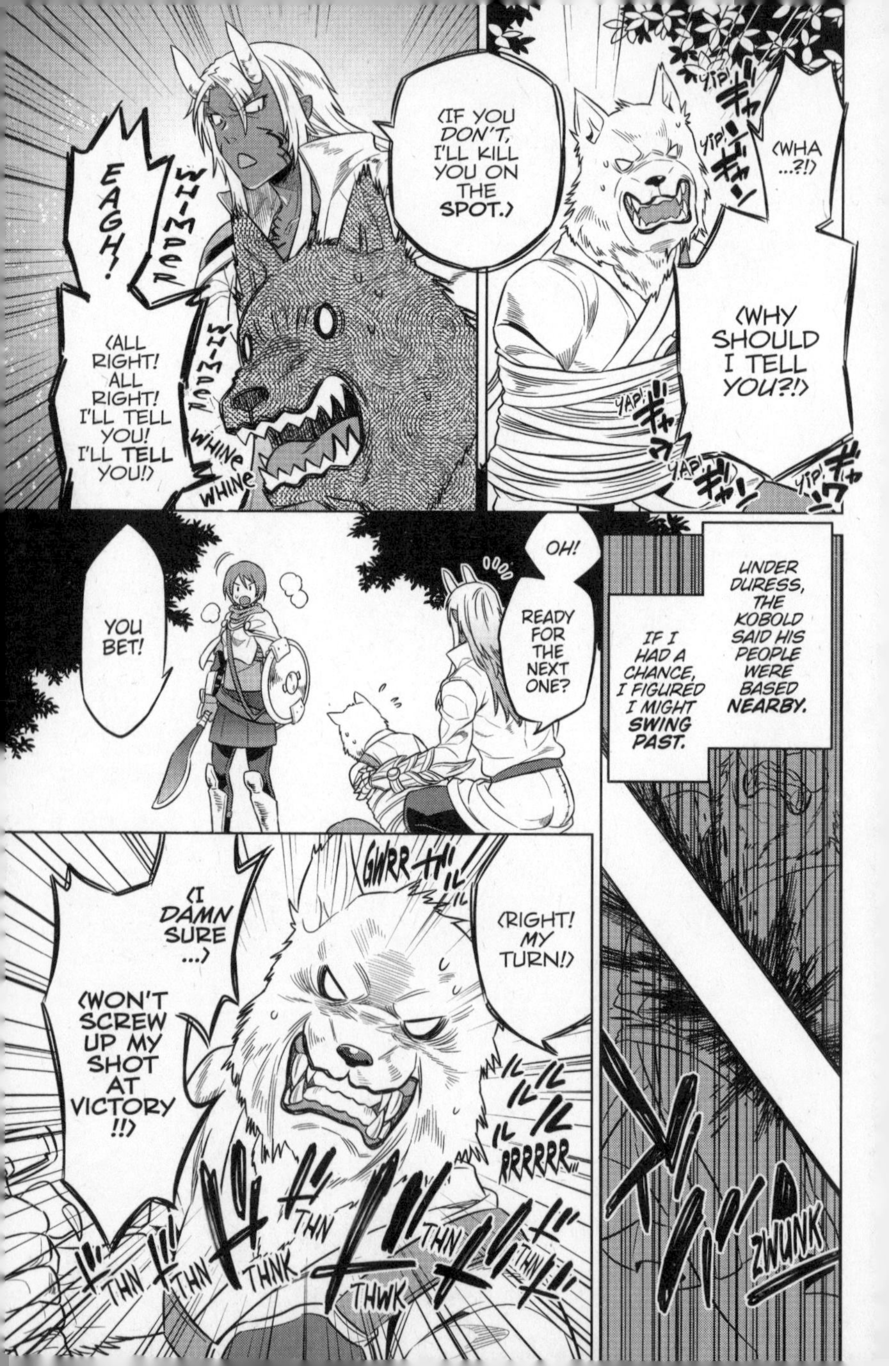

YIP!
YIP!
〈WHA...?!〉
〈WHY SHOULD I TELL YOU?!〉
YAP!
YAP!
YIP!
〈IF YOU DON'T, I'LL KILL YOU ON THE SPOT.〉
WHIMPER
EAGH!
WHIMPER
〈ALL RIGHT! ALL RIGHT! I'LL TELL YOU! I'LL TELL YOU!〉
WHINE
WHINE
UNDER DURESS, THE KOBOLD SAID HIS PEOPLE WERE BASED NEARBY.
IF I HAD A CHANCE, I FIGURED I MIGHT SWING PAST.
OH!
READY FOR THE NEXT ONE?
YOU BET!
ZWUNK
GRRR
〈RIGHT! MY TURN!〉
〈I DAMN SURE...〉
〈WON'T SCREW UP MY SHOT AT VICTORY!!〉
RRRRRR
THN
THN
THN
THNK
THN
THWK
THN

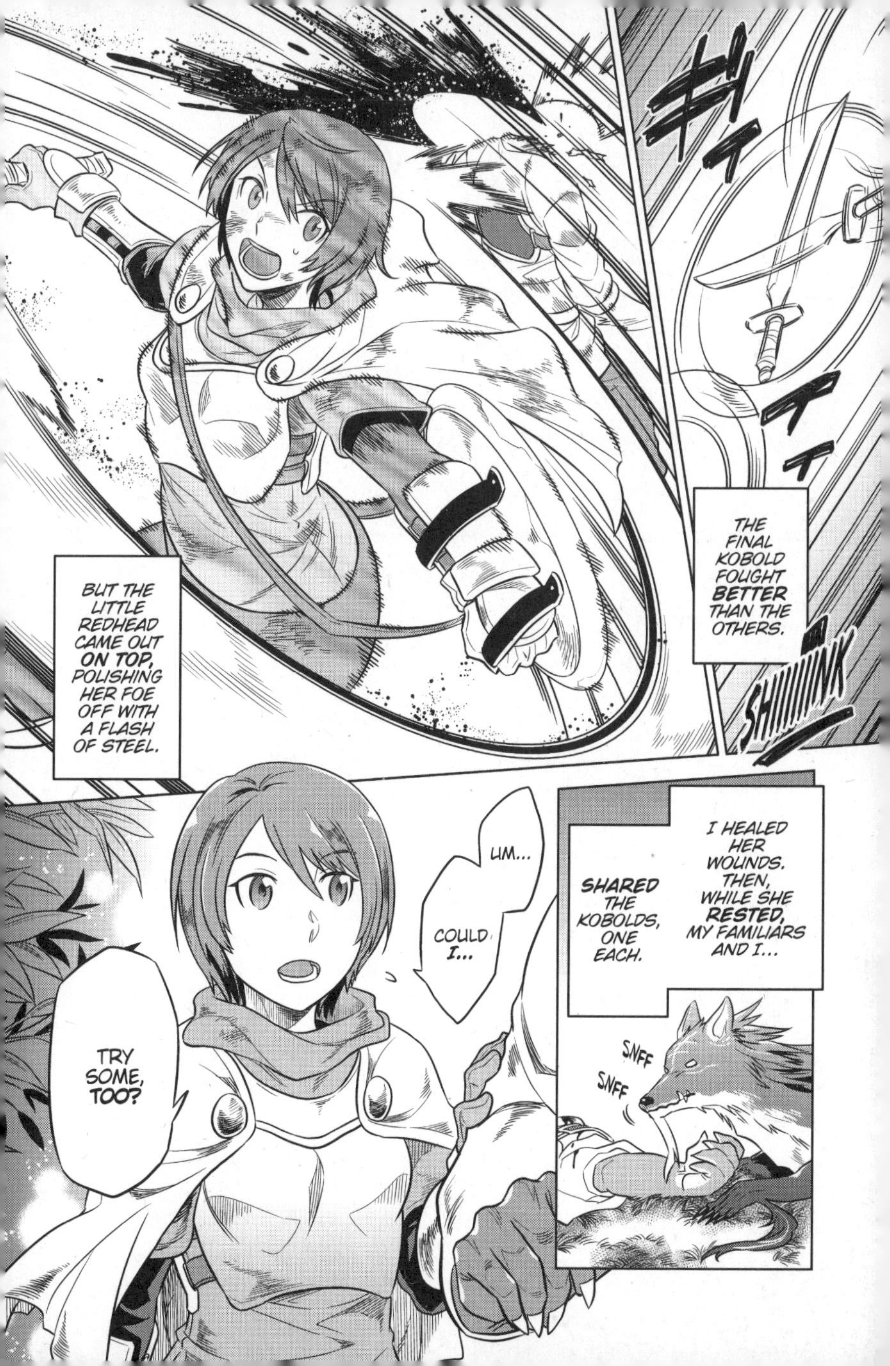
THE FINAL KOBOLD FOUGHT **BETTER** THAN THE OTHERS.
SHIIIIINK
BUT THE LITTLE REDHEAD CAME OUT **ON TOP**, POLISHING HER FOE OFF WITH A FLASH OF STEEL.
I HEALED HER WOUNDS. THEN, WHILE SHE **RESTED**, MY FAMILIARS AND I...
SHARED THE KOBOLDS, ONE EACH.
SNFF
SNFF
UM...
COULD **I**...
TRY SOME, **TOO**?

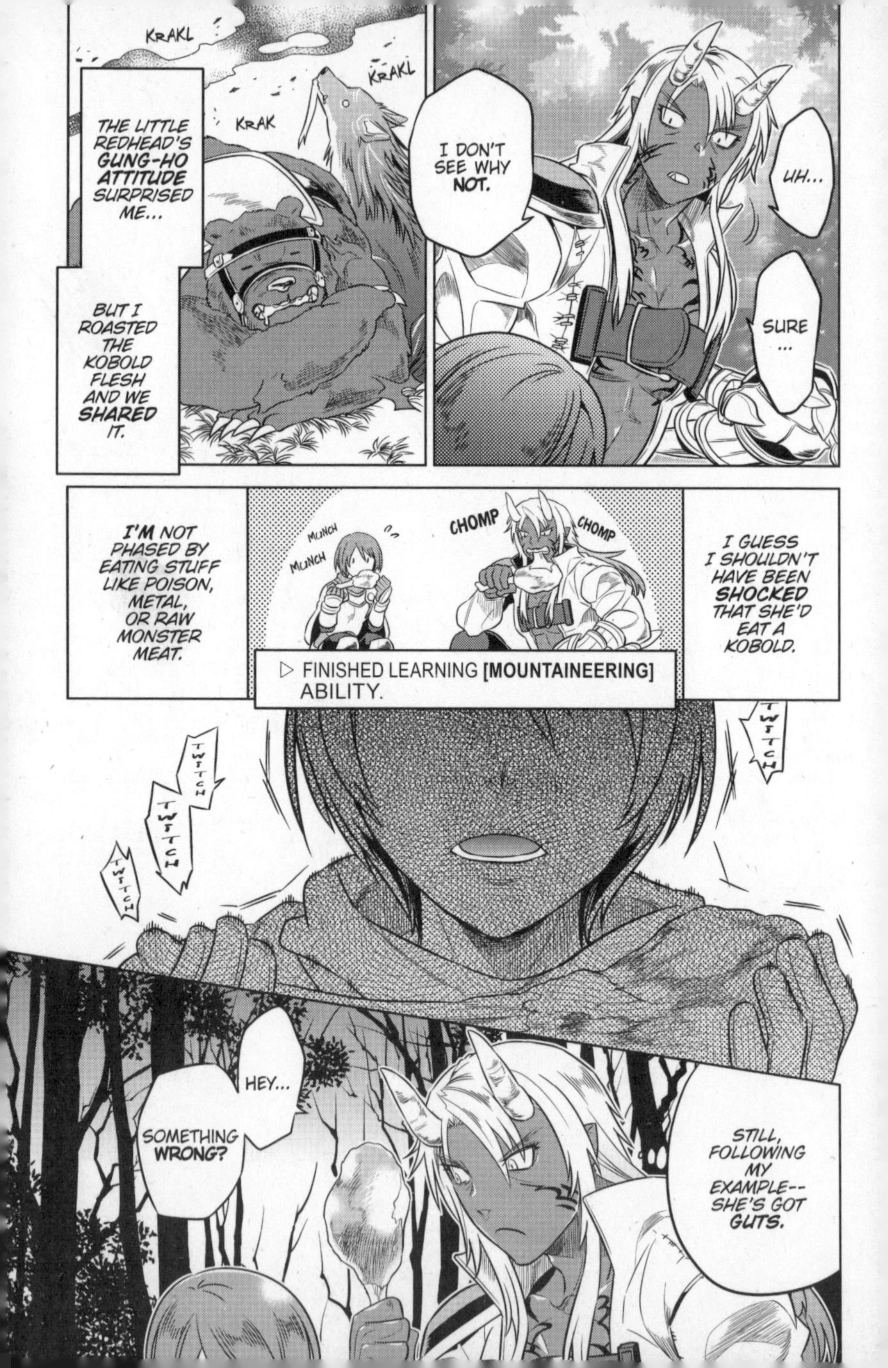

UH...
I DON'T SEE WHY NOT.
SURE...
KRAKL
KRAKL
KRAK
THE LITTLE REDHEAD'S GUNG-HO ATTITUDE SURPRISED ME...
BUT I ROASTED THE KOBOLD FLESH AND WE SHARED IT.
I GUESS I SHOULDN'T HAVE BEEN SHOCKED THAT SHE'D EAT A KOBOLD.
CHOMP
CHOMP
MUNCH
MUNCH
▷ FINISHED LEARNING [MOUNTAINEERING] ABILITY.
I'M NOT PHASED BY EATING STUFF LIKE POISON, METAL, OR RAW MONSTER MEAT.
TWITCH
TWITCH
TWITCH
TWITCH
STILL, FOLLOWING MY EXAMPLE-- SHE'S GOT GUTS.
HEY...
SOMETHING WRONG?

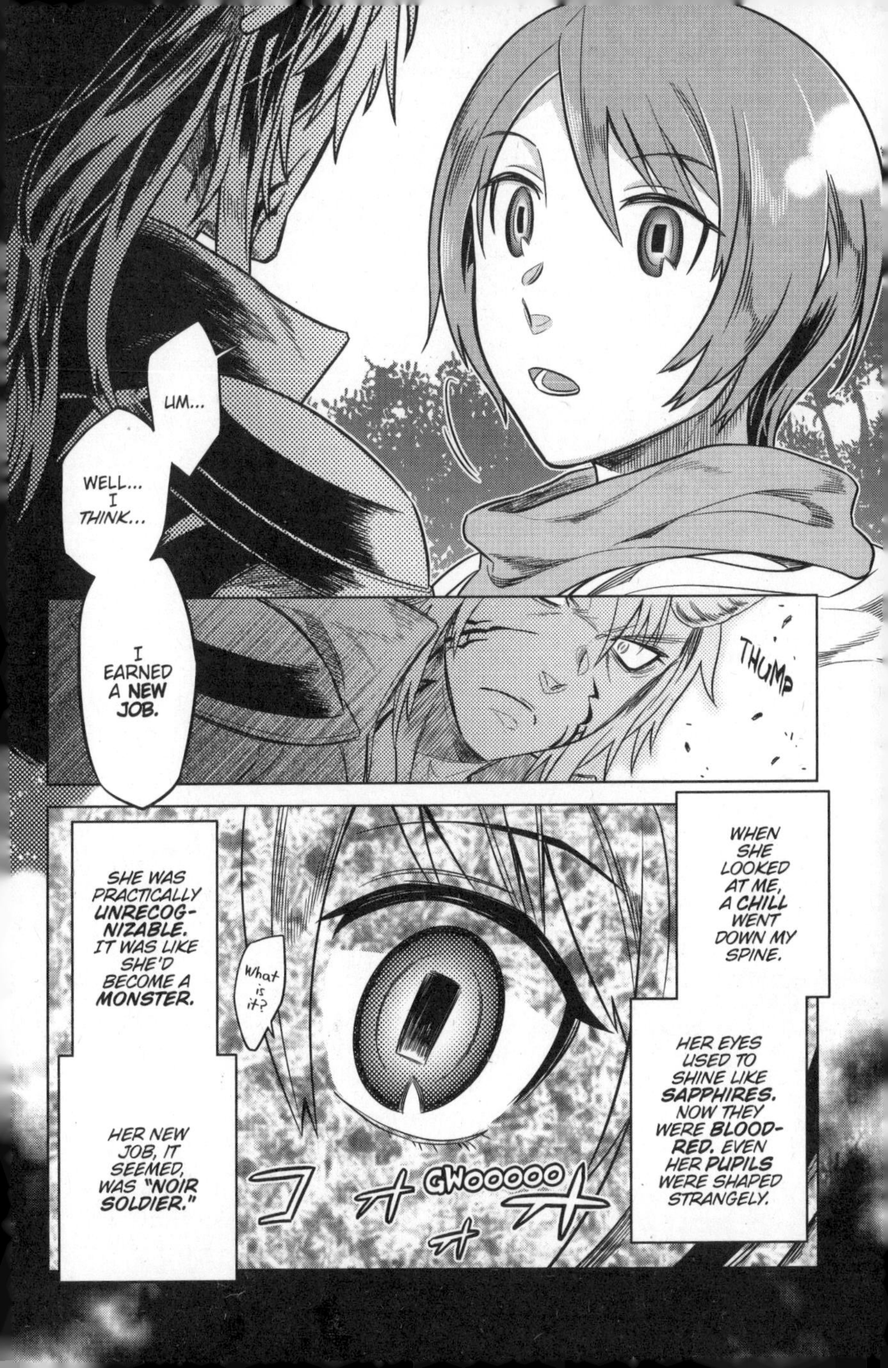
UM...
WELL... I THINK...
I EARNED A NEW JOB.
THUMP
WHEN SHE LOOKED AT ME, A CHILL WENT DOWN MY SPINE.
SHE WAS PRACTICALLY UNRECOG-NIZABLE. IT WAS LIKE SHE'D BECOME A MONSTER.
What is it?
HER EYES USED TO SHINE LIKE SAPPHIRES. NOW THEY WERE BLOOD-RED. EVEN HER PUPILS WERE SHAPED STRANGELY.
GWOOOOO
HER NEW JOB, IT SEEMED, WAS "NOIR SOLDIER."

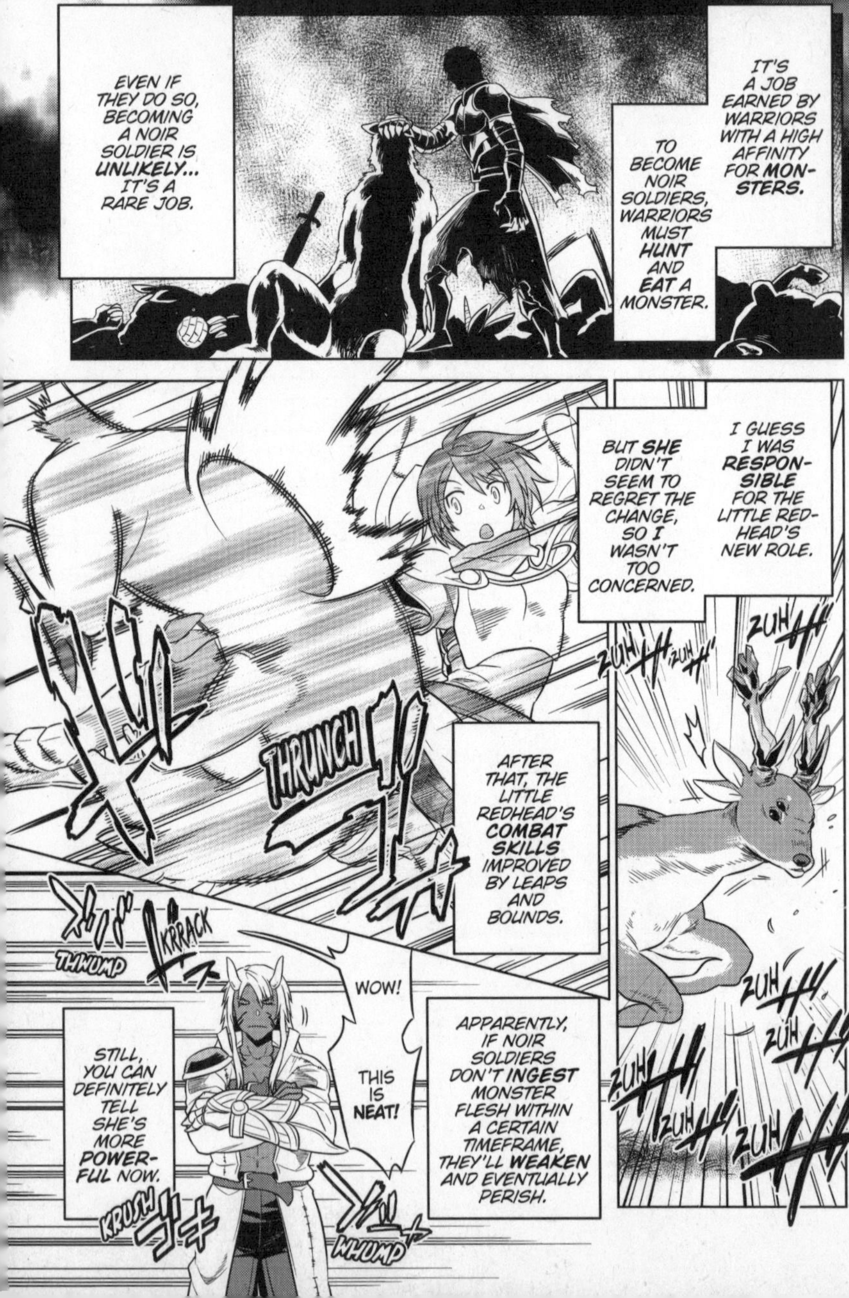

IT'S A JOB EARNED BY WARRIORS WITH A HIGH AFFINITY FOR MONSTERS.
TO BECOME NOIR SOLDIERS, WARRIORS MUST HUNT AND EAT A MONSTER.
EVEN IF THEY DO SO, BECOMING A NOIR SOLDIER IS UNLIKELY... IT'S A RARE JOB.
I GUESS I WAS RESPONSIBLE FOR THE LITTLE REDHEAD'S NEW ROLE.
BUT SHE DIDN'T SEEM TO REGRET THE CHANGE, SO I WASN'T TOO CONCERNED.
ZUH ZUH ZUH
ZUH ZUH ZUH ZUH ZUH
THRUNCH
AFTER THAT, THE LITTLE REDHEAD'S COMBAT SKILLS IMPROVED BY LEAPS AND BOUNDS.
KRRACK
THWUMP
WOW!
THIS IS NEAT!
APPARENTLY, IF NOIR SOLDIERS DON'T INGEST MONSTER FLESH WITHIN A CERTAIN TIMEFRAME, THEY'LL WEAKEN AND EVENTUALLY PERISH.
STILL, YOU CAN DEFINITELY TELL SHE'S MORE POWERFUL NOW.
WHUMP
KRUSH

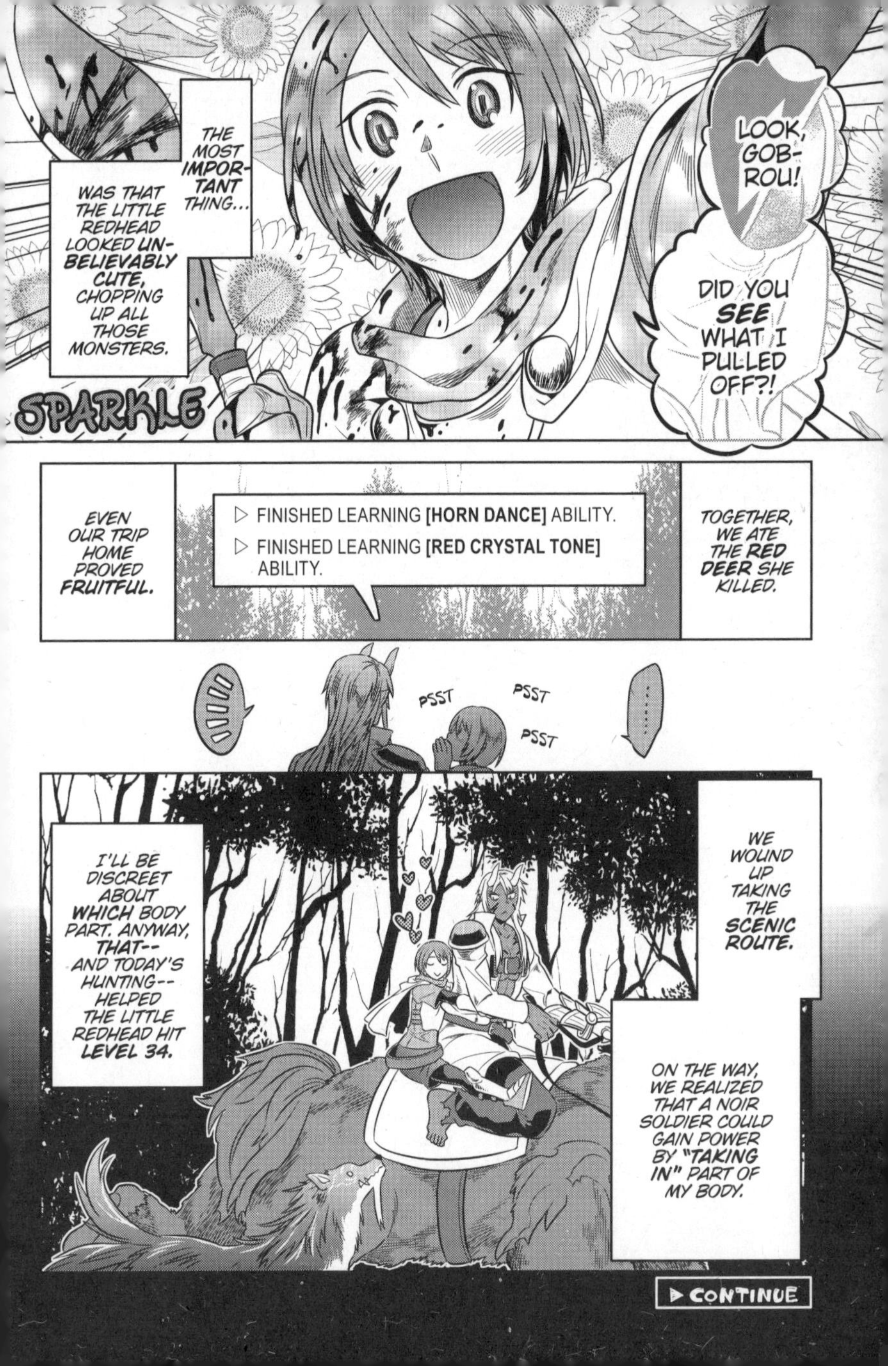
LOOK, GOB-ROU!
DID YOU SEE WHAT I PULLED OFF?!
THE MOST IMPORTANT THING...
WAS THAT THE LITTLE REDHEAD LOOKED UN-BELIEVABLY CUTE, CHOPPING UP ALL THOSE MONSTERS.
SPARKLE
TOGETHER, WE ATE THE RED DEER SHE KILLED.
▷ FINISHED LEARNING [HORN DANCE] ABILITY.
▷ FINISHED LEARNING [RED CRYSTAL TONE] ABILITY.
EVEN OUR TRIP HOME PROVED FRUITFUL.
......
PSST
PSST
PSST
!!!!
WE WOUND UP TAKING THE SCENIC ROUTE.
ON THE WAY, WE REALIZED THAT A NOIR SOLDIER COULD GAIN POWER BY "TAKING IN" PART OF MY BODY.
I'LL BE DISCREET ABOUT WHICH BODY PART. ANYWAY, THAT-- AND TODAY'S HUNTING-- HELPED THE LITTLE REDHEAD HIT LEVEL 34.
▶ CONTINUE

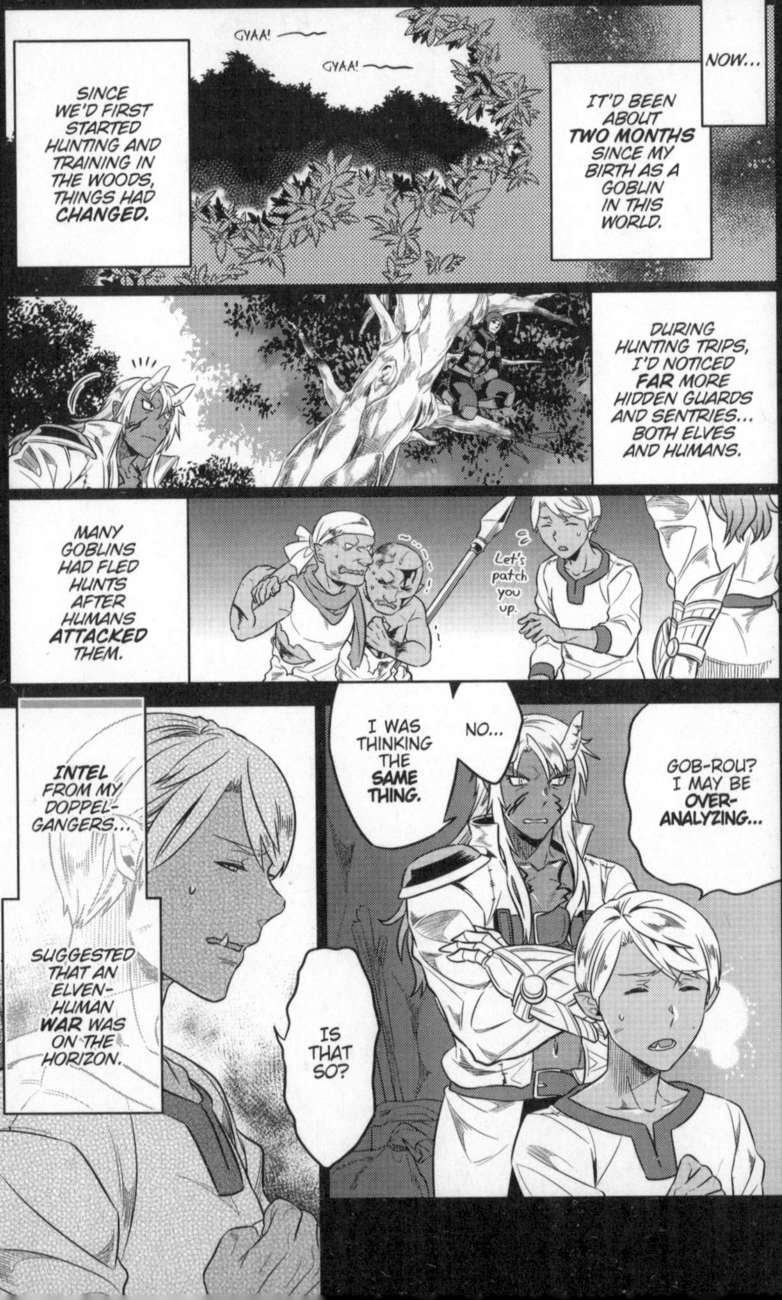
NOW...
IT'D BEEN ABOUT **TWO MONTHS** SINCE MY BIRTH AS A GOBLIN IN THIS WORLD.
GYAA!
GYAA!
SINCE WE'D FIRST STARTED HUNTING AND TRAINING IN THE WOODS, THINGS HAD **CHANGED.**
DURING HUNTING TRIPS, I'D NOTICED **FAR** MORE HIDDEN GUARDS AND SENTRIES... BOTH ELVES AND HUMANS.
Let's patch you up.
MANY GOBLINS HAD FLED HUNTS AFTER HUMANS **ATTACKED** THEM.
GOB-ROU? I MAY BE **OVER-ANALYZING...**
NO...
I WAS THINKING THE **SAME THING.**
IS THAT SO?
INTEL FROM MY DOPPEL-GANGERS...
SUGGESTED THAT AN ELVEN-HUMAN **WAR** WAS ON THE HORIZON.

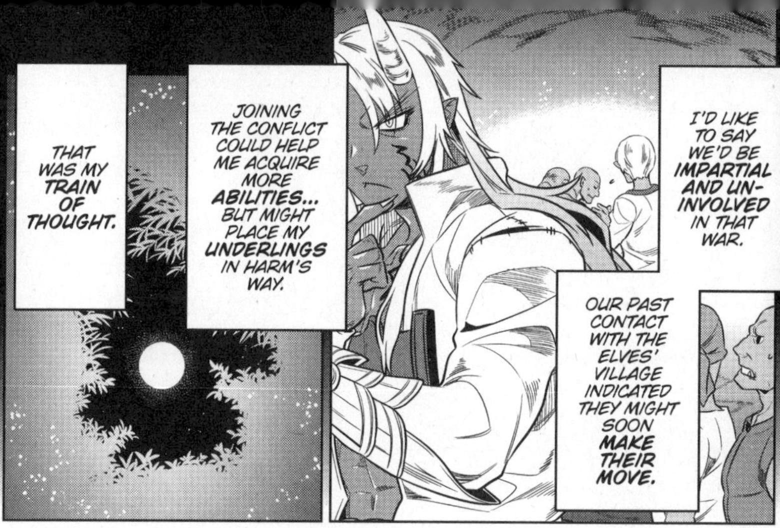
I'D LIKE TO SAY WE'D BE IMPARTIAL AND UN-INVOLVED IN THAT WAR.
OUR PAST CONTACT WITH THE ELVES' VILLAGE INDICATED THEY MIGHT SOON MAKE THEIR MOVE.
JOINING THE CONFLICT COULD HELP ME ACQUIRE MORE ABILITIES... BUT MIGHT PLACE MY UNDERLINGS IN HARM'S WAY.
THAT WAS MY TRAIN OF THOUGHT.

CHAPTER 21

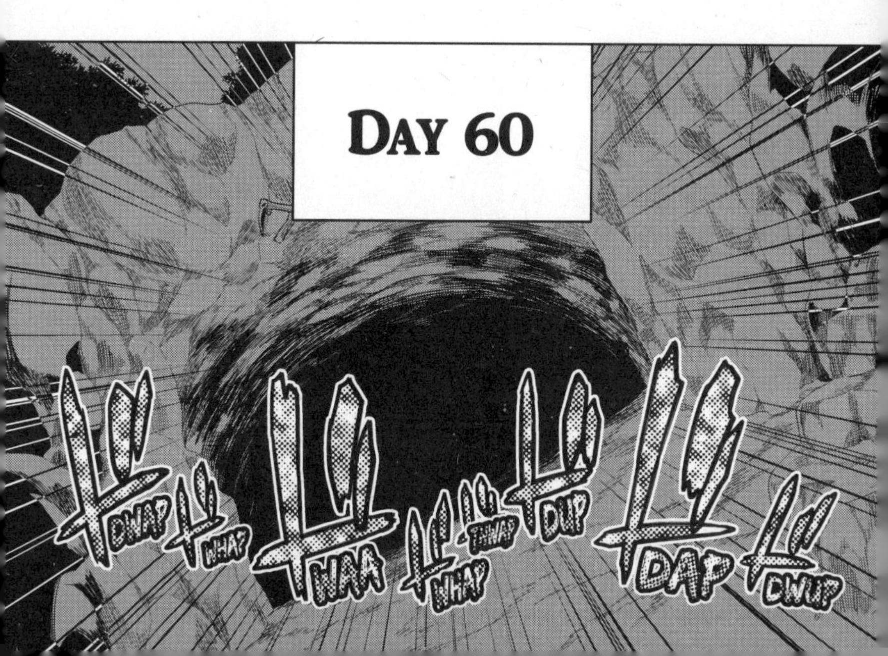
DAY 60
DWUP
DAP
DUP
THWAP
WHAP
WAA
WHAP
DWAP

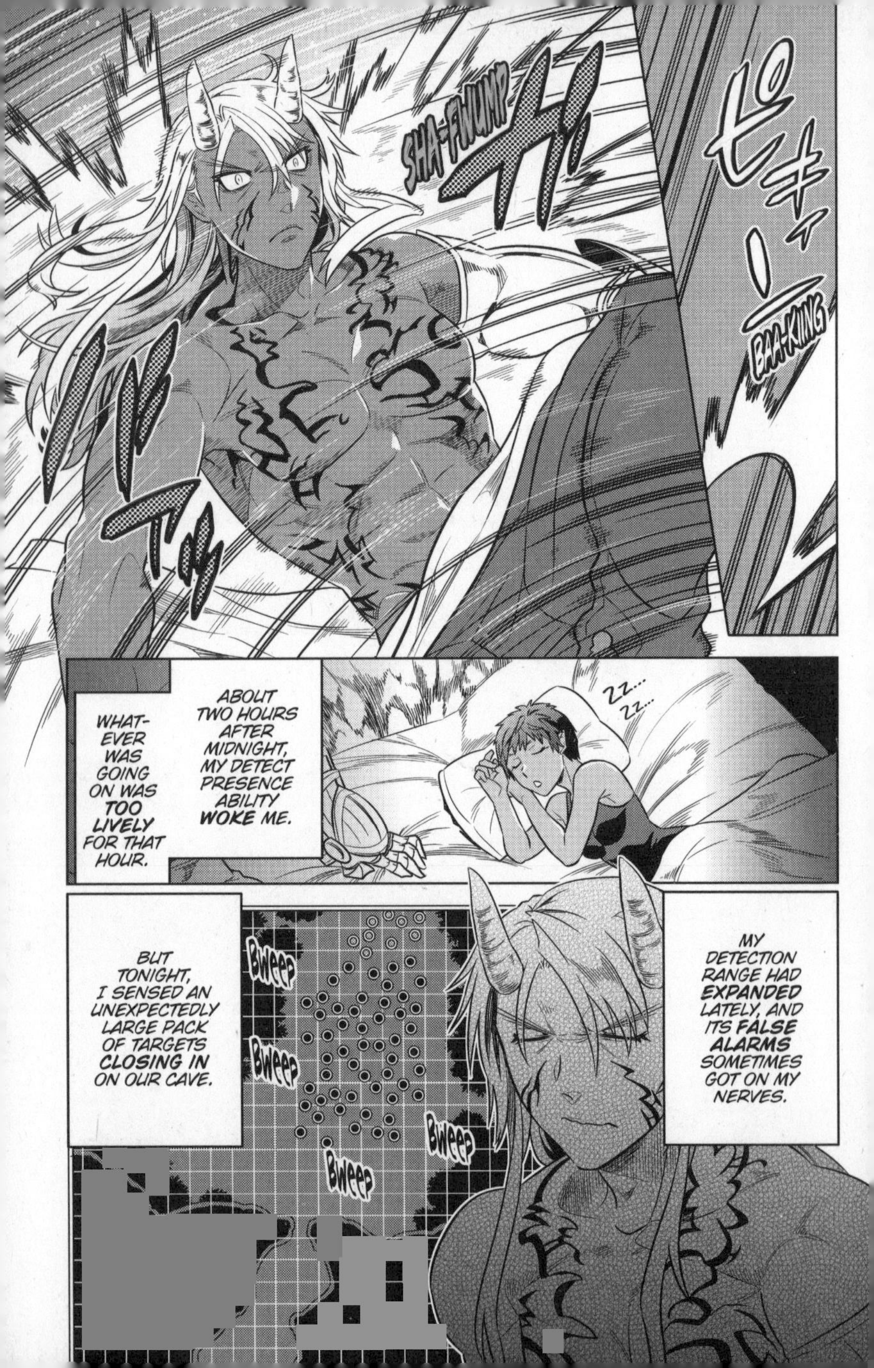
BAA-KIING
SHA-FWUMP
Zz...
Zz...
ABOUT TWO HOURS AFTER MIDNIGHT, MY DETECT PRESENCE ABILITY WOKE ME.
WHAT-EVER WAS GOING ON WAS TOO LIVELY FOR THAT HOUR.
MY DETECTION RANGE HAD EXPANDED LATELY, AND ITS FALSE ALARMS SOMETIMES GOT ON MY NERVES.
Bweep
Bweep
Bweep
Bweep
BUT TONIGHT, I SENSED AN UNEXPECTEDLY LARGE PACK OF TARGETS CLOSING IN ON OUR CAVE.

A DWINDLING PACK OF **KOBOLDS** WAS FIGHTING ITS WAY TOWARD US.

THEY WERE **UNDER ATTACK** FROM SOME RACE I DIDN'T RECOGNIZE.

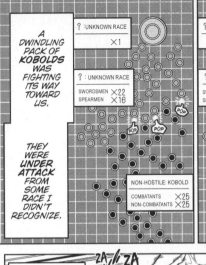

? :UNKNOWN RACE
×1

? : UNKNOWN RACE

SWORDSMEN	×22
SPEARMEN	×16

POP

POP

POP

NON-HOSTILE: KOBOLD	
COMBATANTS	×25
NON-COMBATANTS	×25

? :UNKNOWN RACE
×1

? :UNKNOWN RACE

SWORDSMEN	×22
SPEARMEN	×16

NON-HOSTILE: KOBOLD	
COMBATANTS	×28
NON-COMBATANTS	×25

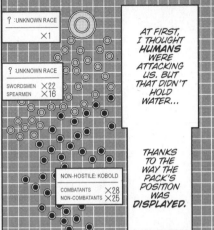

AT FIRST, I THOUGHT **HUMANS** WERE ATTACKING US. BUT THAT DIDN'T HOLD WATER...

THANKS TO THE WAY THE PACK'S POSITION WAS DISPLAYED.

WE WERE ALWAYS KILLING KOBOLDS, SO MY **PRIORITY** WAS TO FIGURE OUT THE OTHER INTRUDERS' IDENTITIES.

I IGNORED THE FIRST KOBOLD PACK, WHICH SEEMED TO BE MOSTLY **NON-COMBATANTS** AND CHECKED OUT THE ACTION AT THE CAVE MOUTH.

ZA

ZA

ZA

ZA

ZA

ZA

MUTTER

MUTTER

MURMUR

MUTTER

SO I WOKE THE OTHERS AND HAD THEM PREPARE FOR COMBAT.

I WOULD'VE PREFERRED NOT TO INTERVENE, BUT THE **INTRUDERS** DIDN'T BACK OFF...

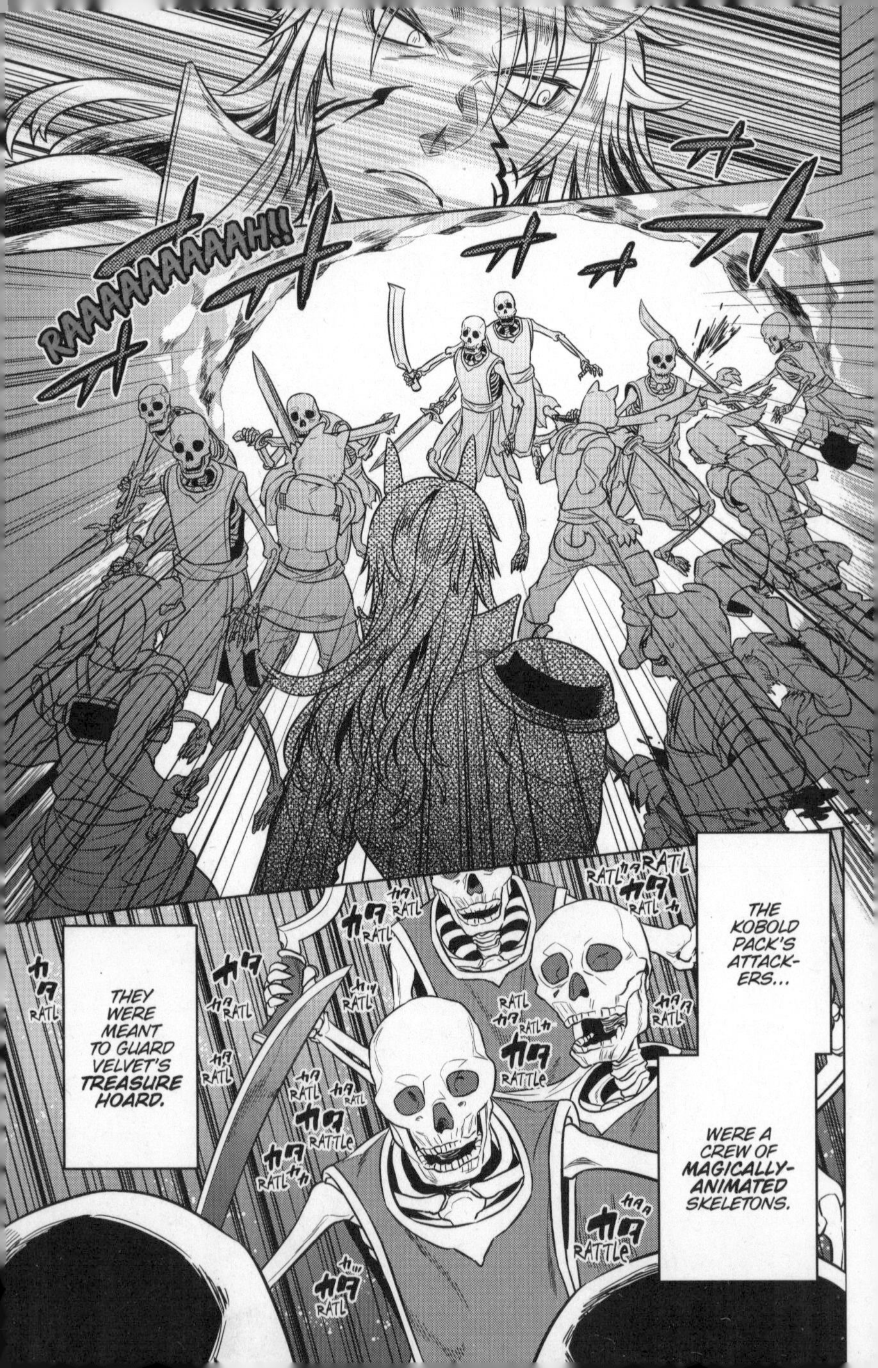

RAAAAAAAAAAH!!
THE KOBOLD PACK'S ATTACKERS...
WERE A CREW OF MAGICALLY-ANIMATED SKELETONS.
THEY WERE MEANT TO GUARD VELVET'S TREASURE HOARD.
RATL
RATTLE

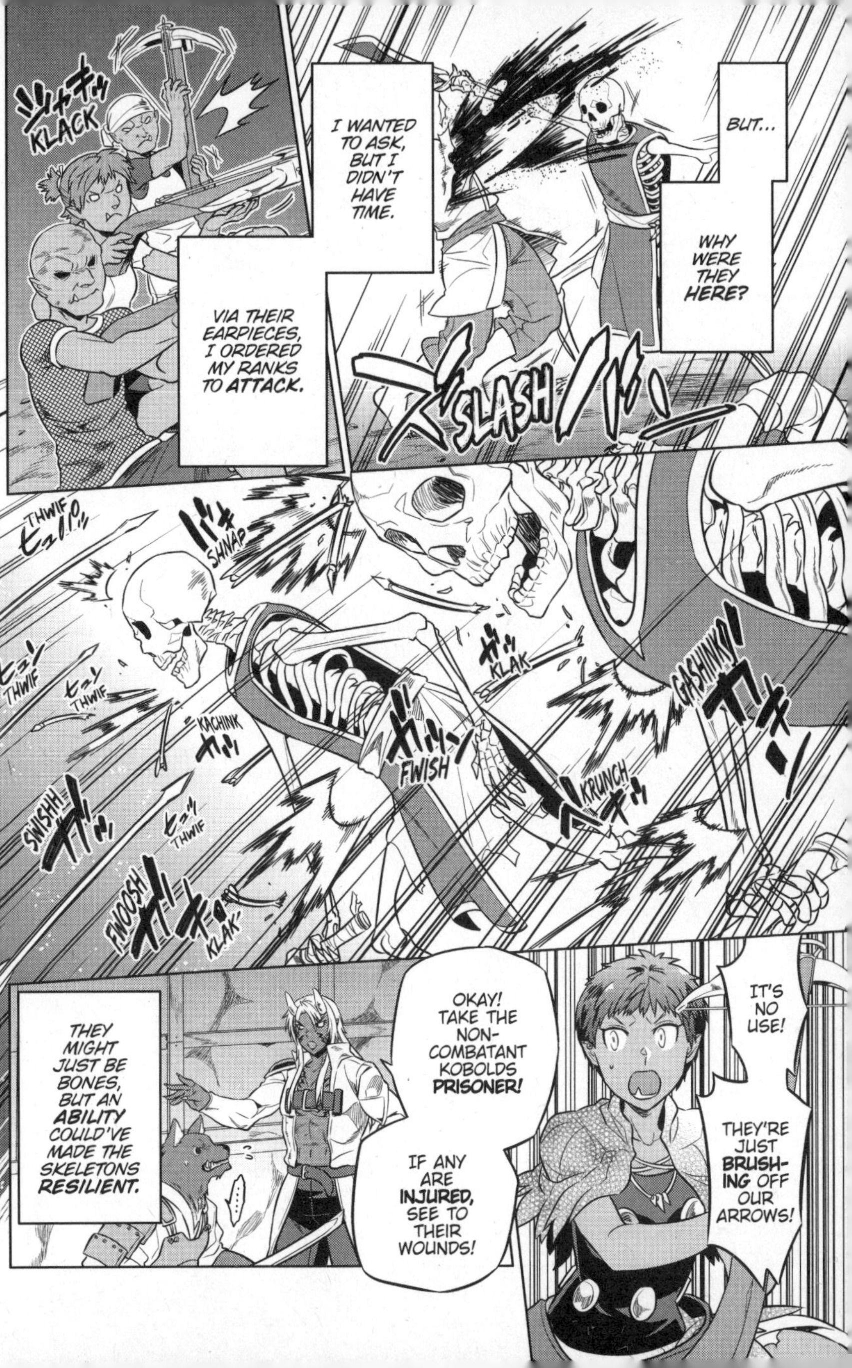

BUT...
WHY WERE THEY HERE?
I WANTED TO ASK, BUT I DIDN'T HAVE TIME.
SLASH
VIA THEIR EARPIECES, I ORDERED MY RANKS TO ATTACK.
KLACK
GASHINK
KRUNCH
KLAK
FWISH
SHNAP
THWIF
KACHINK
THWIF
THWIF
SWISHH
THWIF
FWOOSH
KLAK'
IT'S NO USE!
THEY'RE JUST BRUSHING OFF OUR ARROWS!
OKAY! TAKE THE NON-COMBATANT KOBOLDS PRISONER!
IF ANY ARE INJURED, SEE TO THEIR WOUNDS!
THEY MIGHT JUST BE BONES, BUT AN ABILITY COULD'VE MADE THE SKELETONS RESILIENT.
...

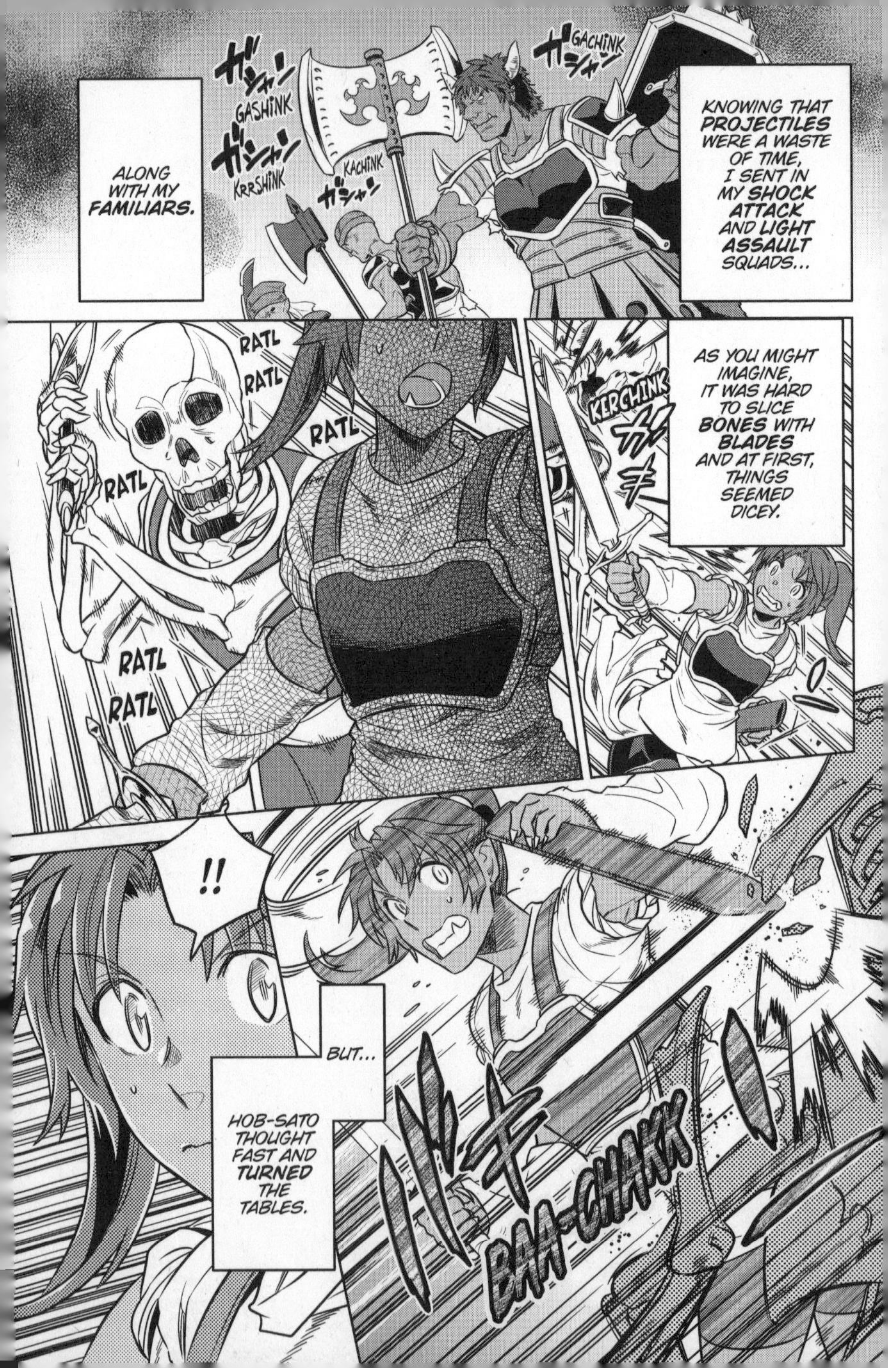

KNOWING THAT PROJECTILES WERE A WASTE OF TIME, I SENT IN MY SHOCK ATTACK AND LIGHT ASSAULT SQUADS...
GACHINK
GASHINK
KACHINK
KRRSHINK
ALONG WITH MY FAMILIARS.
AS YOU MIGHT IMAGINE, IT WAS HARD TO SLICE BONES WITH BLADES AND AT FIRST, THINGS SEEMED DICEY.
KERCHINK
RATL
RATL
RATL
RATL
RATL
RATL
!!
BUT...
HOB-SATO THOUGHT FAST AND TURNED THE TABLES.
BAA-CHAKK

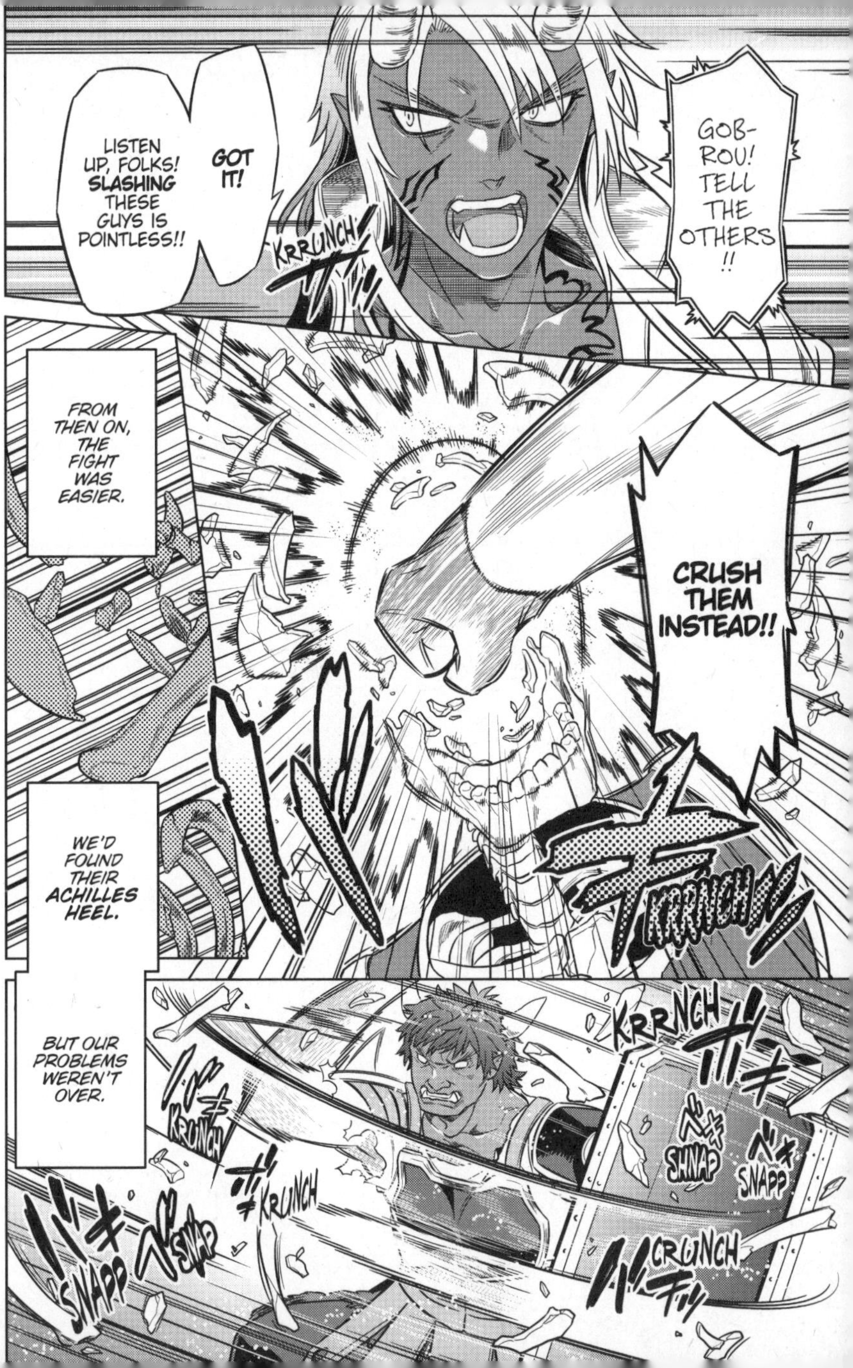
GOB-ROU! TELL THE OTHERS!!
KRRUNCH
GOT IT!
LISTEN UP, FOLKS! SLASHING THESE GUYS IS POINTLESS!!
CRUSH THEM INSTEAD!!
KRRNCH
FROM THEN ON, THE FIGHT WAS EASIER.
WE'D FOUND THEIR ACHILLES HEEL.
KRRNCH
SHNAP
SNAPP
CRUNCH
KRUNCH
KRUNCH
SNAP
SNAPP
BUT OUR PROBLEMS WEREN'T OVER.

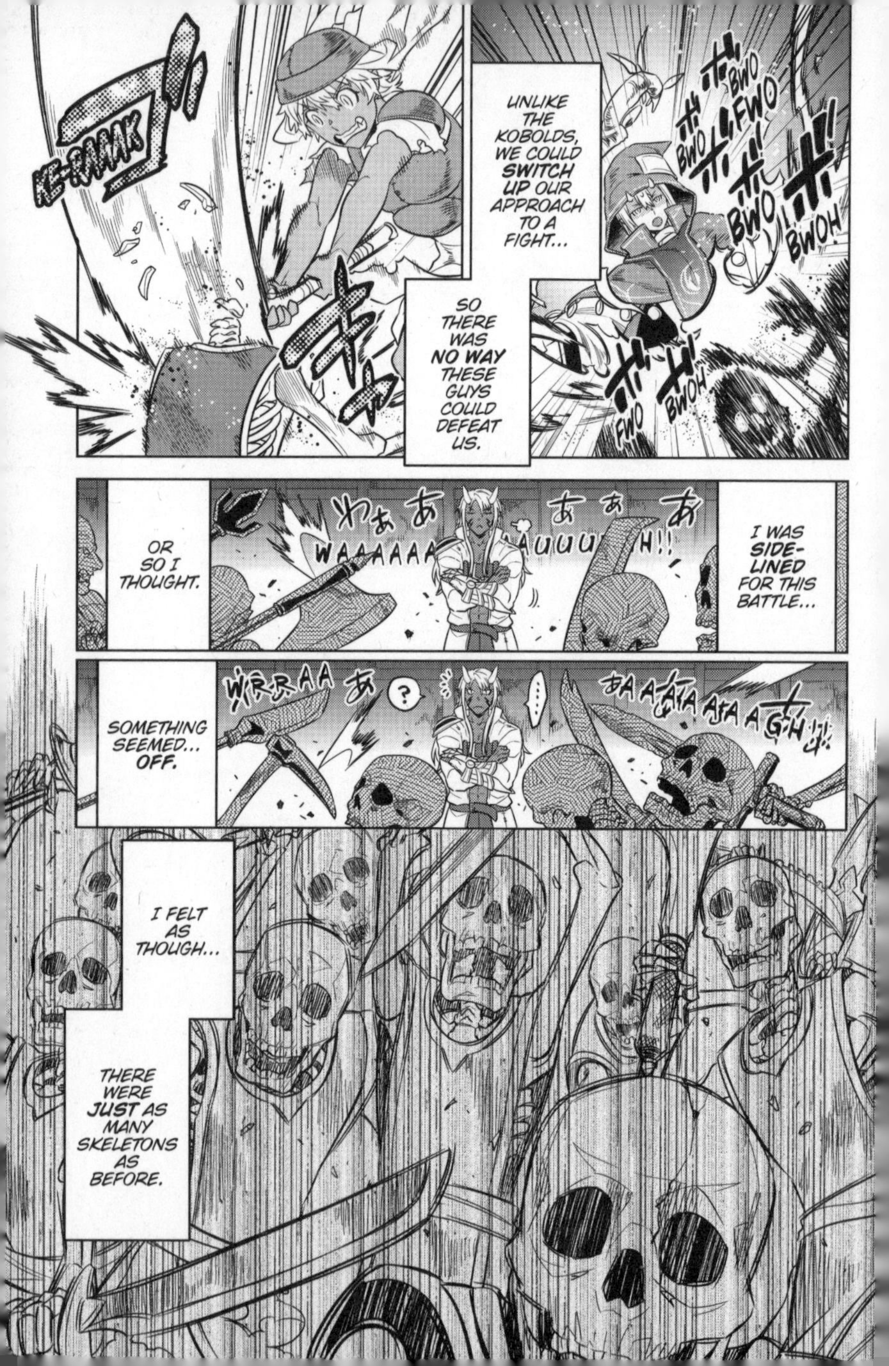
BWO FWO BWO BWO BWO BWOH
UNLIKE THE KOBOLDS, WE COULD **SWITCH UP** OUR APPROACH TO A FIGHT...
FWO BWOH
SO THERE WAS **NO WAY** THESE GUYS COULD DEFEAT US.
KE-RAAAK
I WAS **SIDE-LINED** FOR THIS BATTLE...
WAAAAAA AUUUU H!!
OR SO I THOUGHT.
AAAAAAAGH!!
...
?
WRRAA
SOMETHING SEEMED... **OFF.**
I FELT AS THOUGH...
THERE WERE **JUST** AS MANY SKELETONS AS BEFORE.

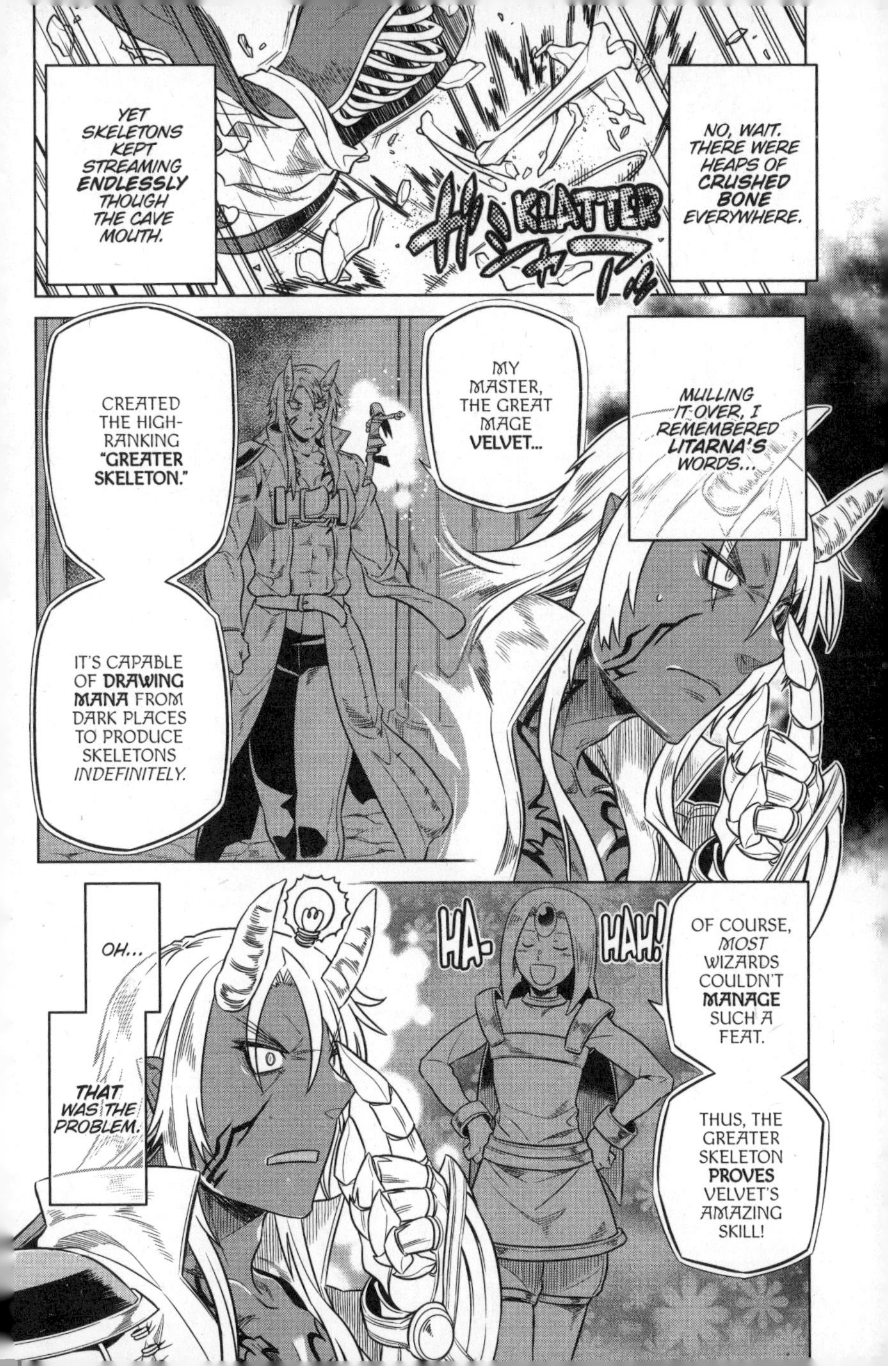

NO, WAIT. THERE WERE HEAPS OF CRUSHED BONE EVERYWHERE.
KLATTER
YET SKELETONS KEPT STREAMING ENDLESSLY THOUGH THE CAVE MOUTH.
MULLING IT OVER, I REMEMBERED LITARNA'S WORDS...
MY MASTER, THE GREAT MAGE VELVET...
CREATED THE HIGH-RANKING "GREATER SKELETON."
IT'S CAPABLE OF DRAWING MANA FROM DARK PLACES TO PRODUCE SKELETONS INDEFINITELY.
OF COURSE, MOST WIZARDS COULDN'T MANAGE SUCH A FEAT.
THUS, THE GREATER SKELETON PROVES VELVET'S AMAZING SKILL!
HA- HAH!
OH...
THAT WAS THE PROBLEM.

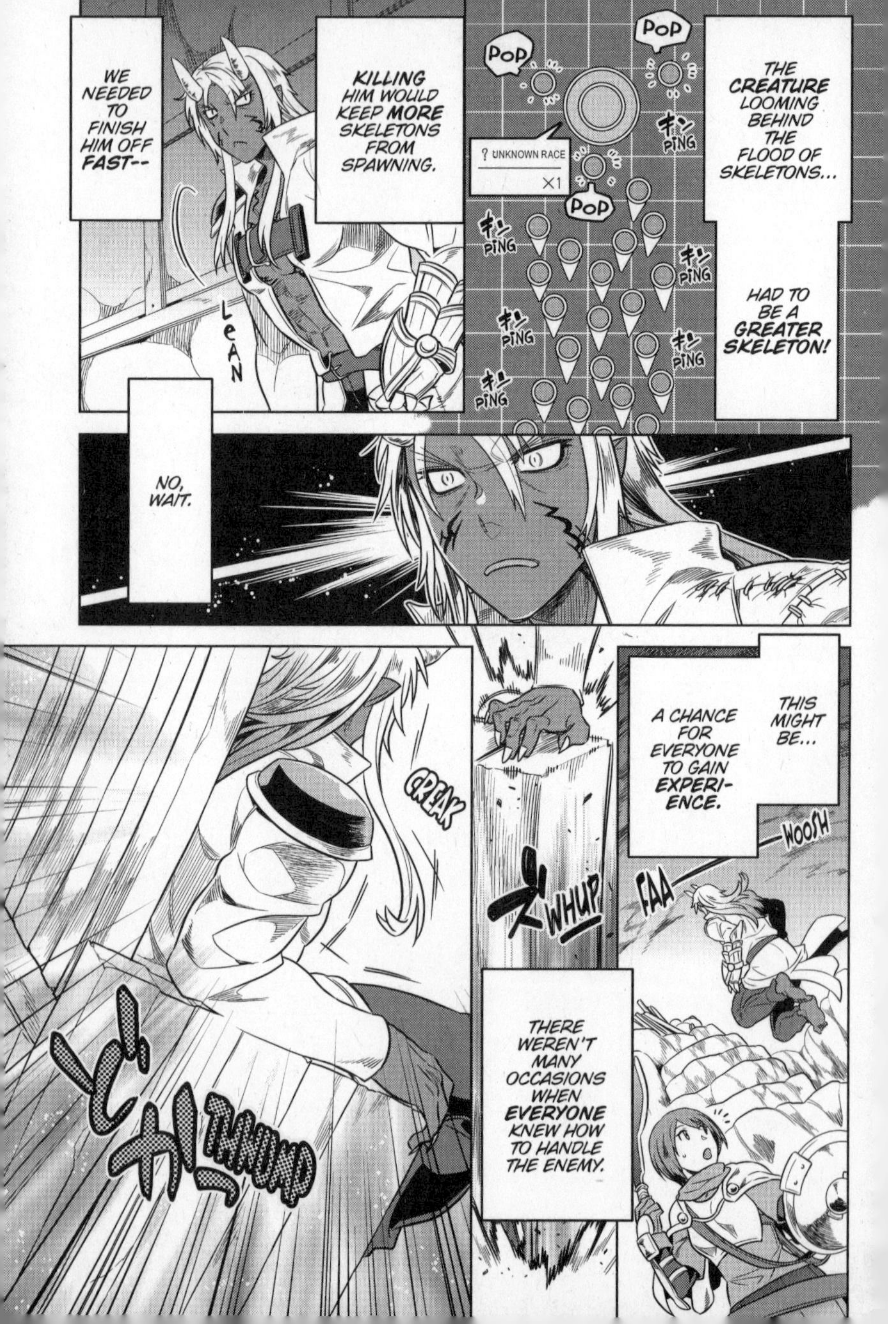
THE CREATURE LOOMING BEHIND THE FLOOD OF SKELETONS...
HAD TO BE A GREATER SKELETON!
POP
POP
? UNKNOWN RACE ×1
POP
PING
PING
PING
PING
PING
PING
KILLING HIM WOULD KEEP MORE SKELETONS FROM SPAWNING.
WE NEEDED TO FINISH HIM OFF FAST--
LEAN
NO, WAIT.
THIS MIGHT BE...
A CHANCE FOR EVERYONE TO GAIN EXPERI-ENCE.
WOOSH
FAA
THERE WEREN'T MANY OCCASIONS WHEN EVERYONE KNEW HOW TO HANDLE THE ENEMY.
CREAK
WHUP
THUMP

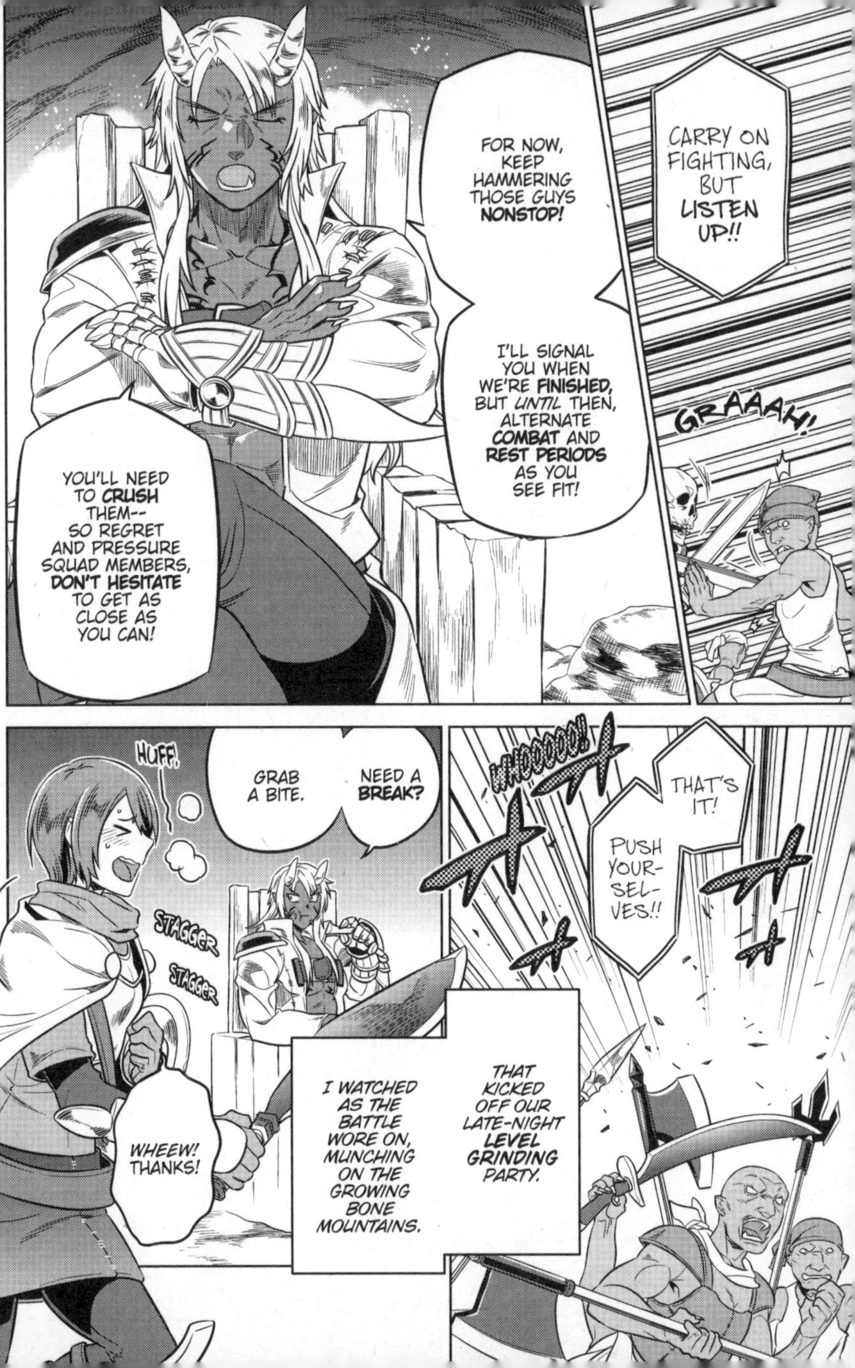
CARRY ON FIGHTING, BUT **LISTEN UP!!**
GRAAAAH!
FOR NOW, KEEP HAMMERING THOSE GUYS **NONSTOP!**
I'LL SIGNAL YOU WHEN WE'RE **FINISHED,** BUT *UNTIL* THEN, ALTERNATE **COMBAT** AND **REST PERIODS** AS YOU SEE FIT!
YOU'LL NEED TO **CRUSH** THEM-- SO REGRET AND PRESSURE SQUAD MEMBERS, **DON'T HESITATE** TO GET AS CLOSE AS YOU CAN!
WHOOOOOO!!
THAT'S IT!
PUSH YOURSELVES!!
THAT KICKED OFF OUR LATE-NIGHT ***LEVEL GRINDING*** *PARTY.*
NEED A **BREAK?**
GRAB A BITE.
HUFF!
STAGGER
STAGGER
WHEEW! THANKS!
I WATCHED AS THE BATTLE WORE ON, MUNCHING ON THE GROWING BONE MOUNTAINS.

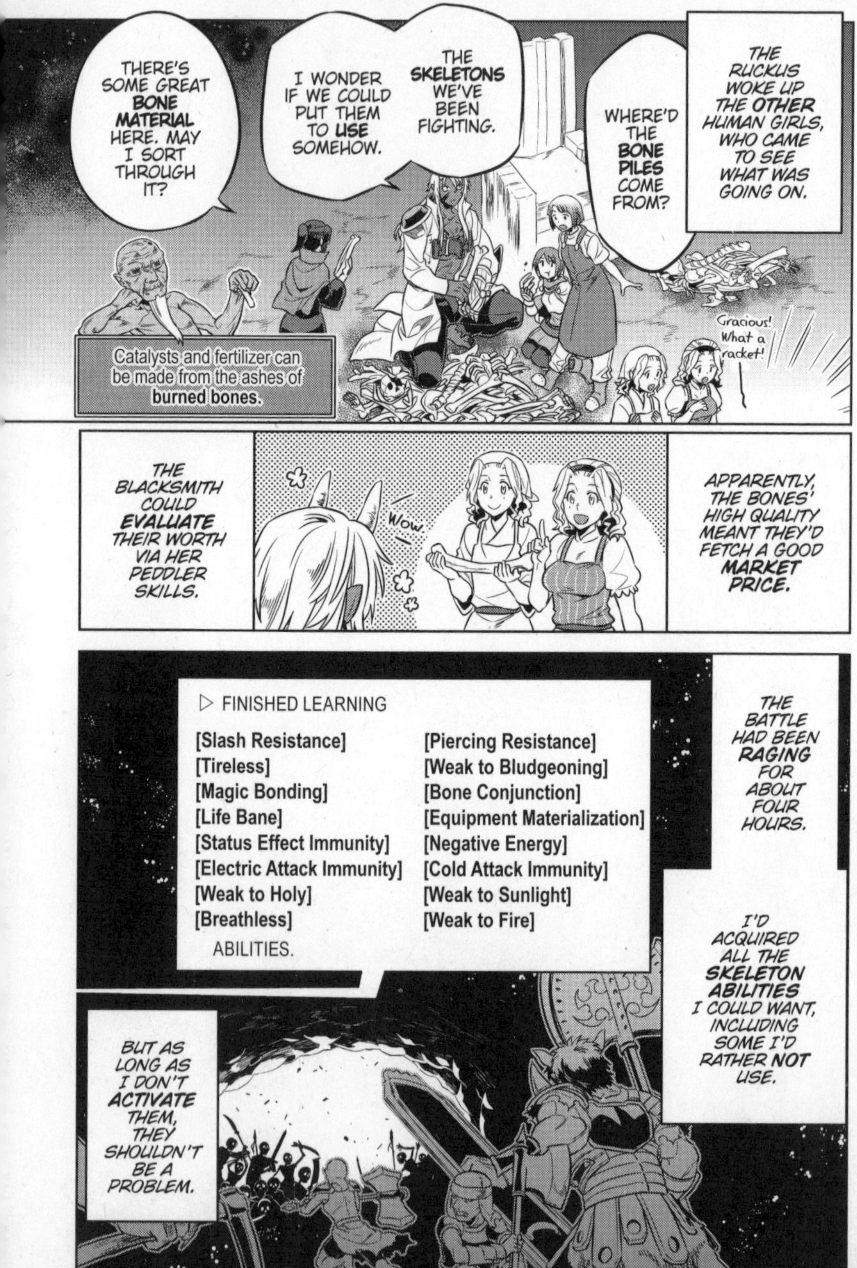
THE RUCKUS WOKE UP THE OTHER HUMAN GIRLS, WHO CAME TO SEE WHAT WAS GOING ON.
WHERE'D THE BONE PILES COME FROM?
THE SKELETONS WE'VE BEEN FIGHTING.
I WONDER IF WE COULD PUT THEM TO USE SOMEHOW.
THERE'S SOME GREAT BONE MATERIAL HERE. MAY I SORT THROUGH IT?
Gracious! What a racket!
Catalysts and fertilizer can be made from the ashes of burned bones.
APPARENTLY, THE BONES' HIGH QUALITY MEANT THEY'D FETCH A GOOD MARKET PRICE.
Wow.
THE BLACKSMITH COULD EVALUATE THEIR WORTH VIA HER PEDDLER SKILLS.
THE BATTLE HAD BEEN RAGING FOR ABOUT FOUR HOURS.
▷ FINISHED LEARNING
[Slash Resistance] [Piercing Resistance]
[Tireless] [Weak to Bludgeoning]
[Magic Bonding] [Bone Conjunction]
[Life Bane] [Equipment Materialization]
[Status Effect Immunity] [Negative Energy]
[Electric Attack Immunity] [Cold Attack Immunity]
[Weak to Holy] [Weak to Sunlight]
[Breathless] [Weak to Fire]
ABILITIES.
I'D ACQUIRED ALL THE SKELETON ABILITIES I COULD WANT, INCLUDING SOME I'D RATHER NOT USE.
BUT AS LONG AS I DON'T ACTIVATE THEM, THEY SHOULDN'T BE A PROBLEM.

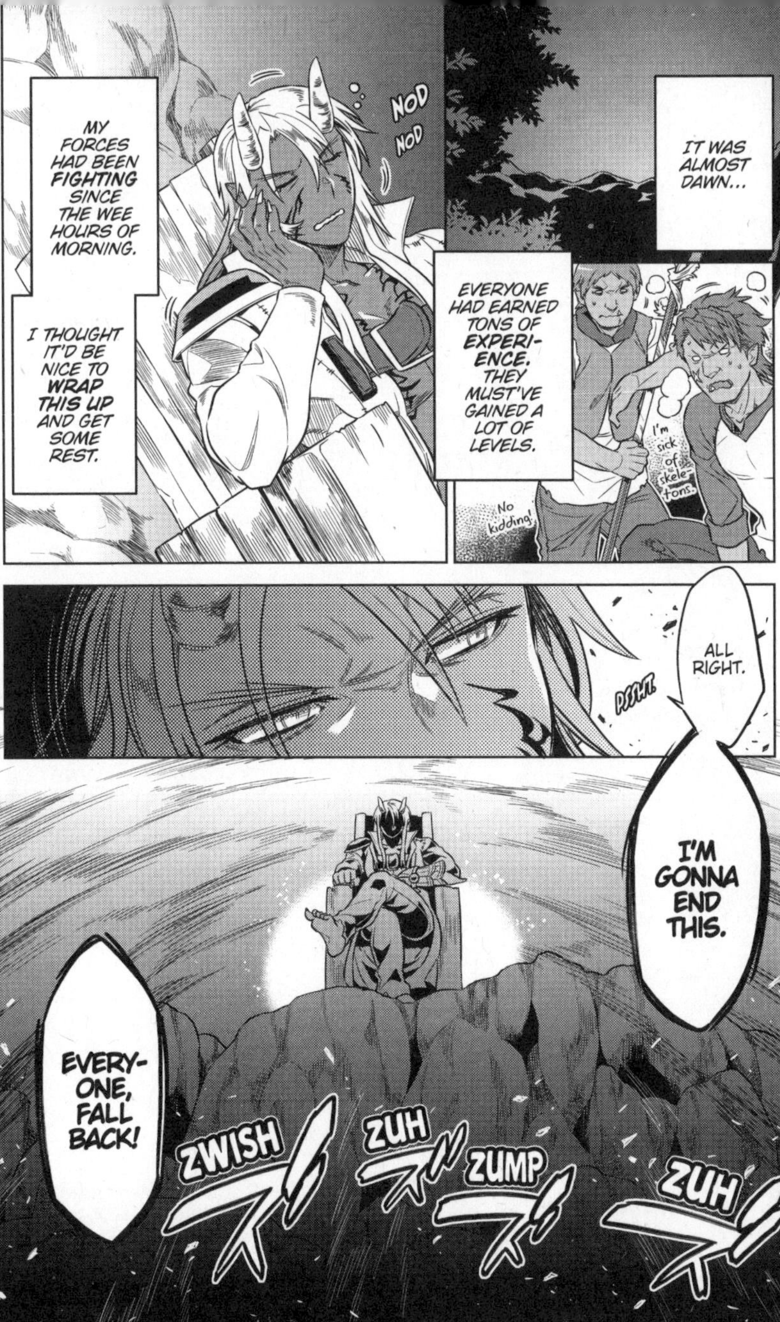
IT WAS ALMOST DAWN...
EVERYONE HAD EARNED TONS OF EXPERIENCE. THEY MUST'VE GAINED A LOT OF LEVELS.
I'm sick of skele-tons.
No kidding!
NOD NOD
MY FORCES HAD BEEN FIGHTING SINCE THE WEE HOURS OF MORNING.
I THOUGHT IT'D BE NICE TO WRAP THIS UP AND GET SOME REST.
ALL RIGHT.
PSSHT.
I'M GONNA END THIS.
EVERY-ONE, FALL BACK!
ZUH
ZUMP
ZUH
ZWISH

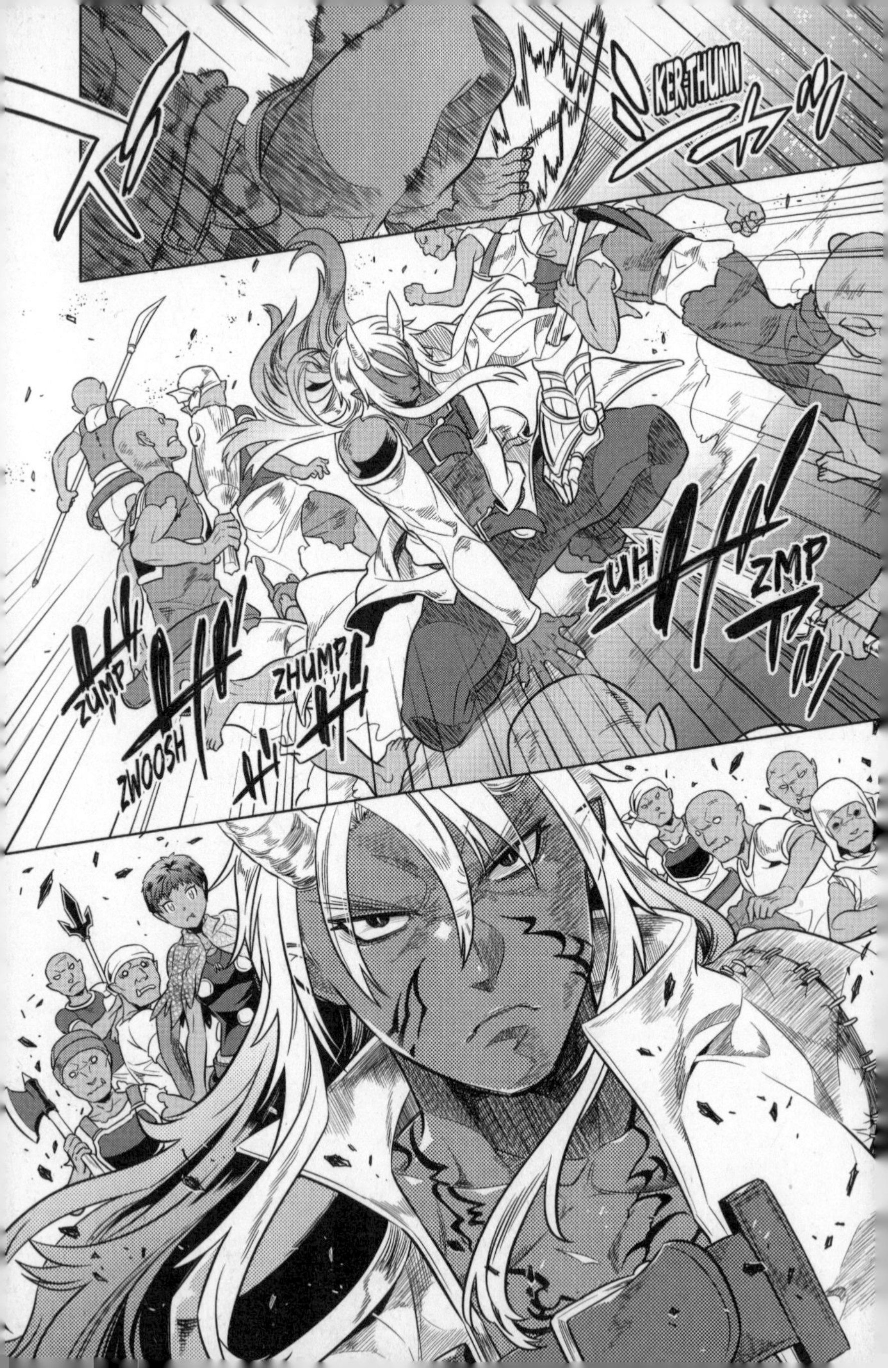
KER-THUNN
ZUH
ZMP
ZHUMP
ZWOOSH
ZUMP

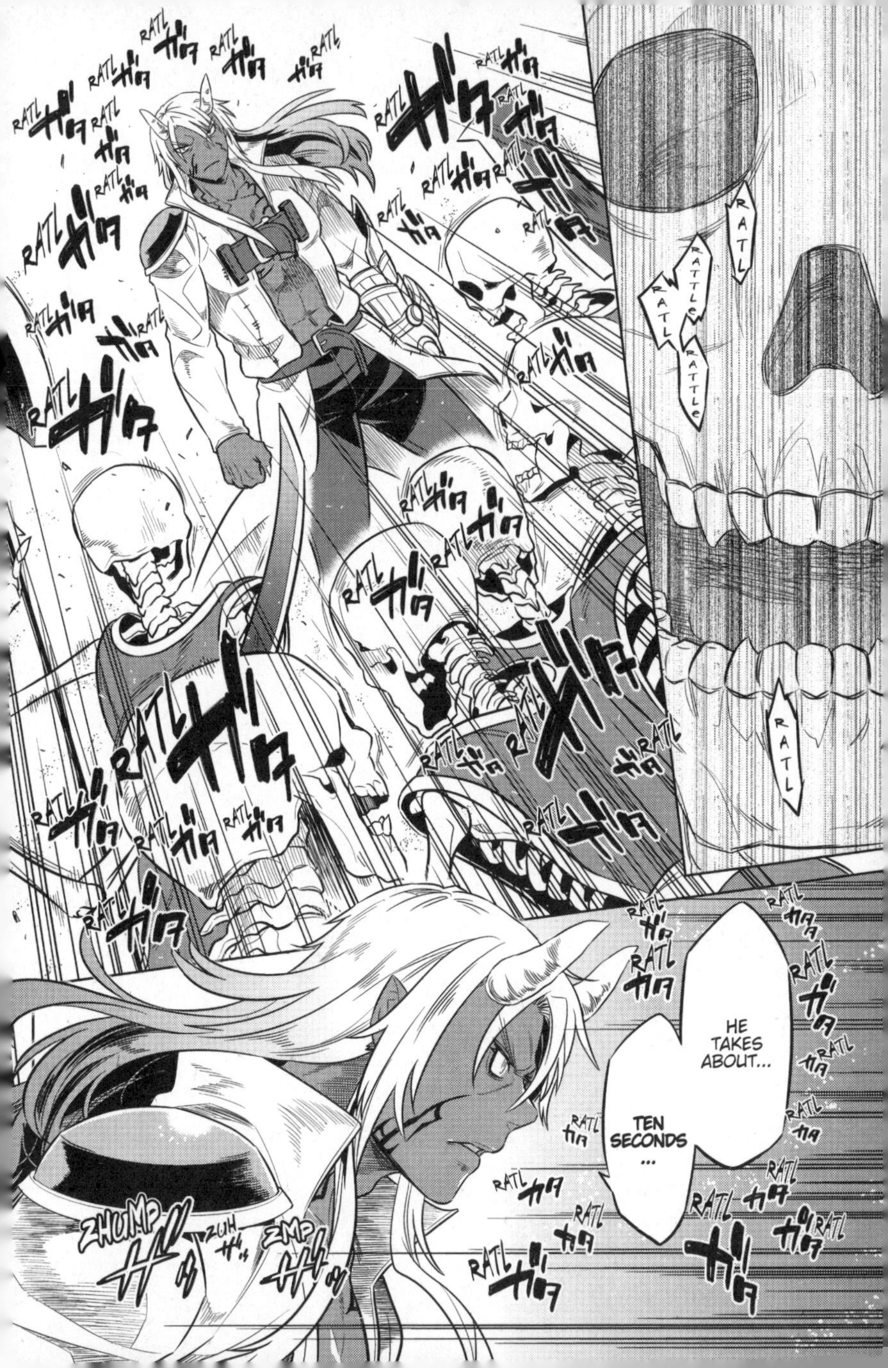

RATL
RATTLE
RATTLE
RATL
RATL
RATL RATL RATL RATL RATL
RATL RATL RATL RATL RATL
HE TAKES ABOUT...
TEN SECONDS...
RATL RATL RATL RATL RATL
ZHUMP
ZUH
ZMP

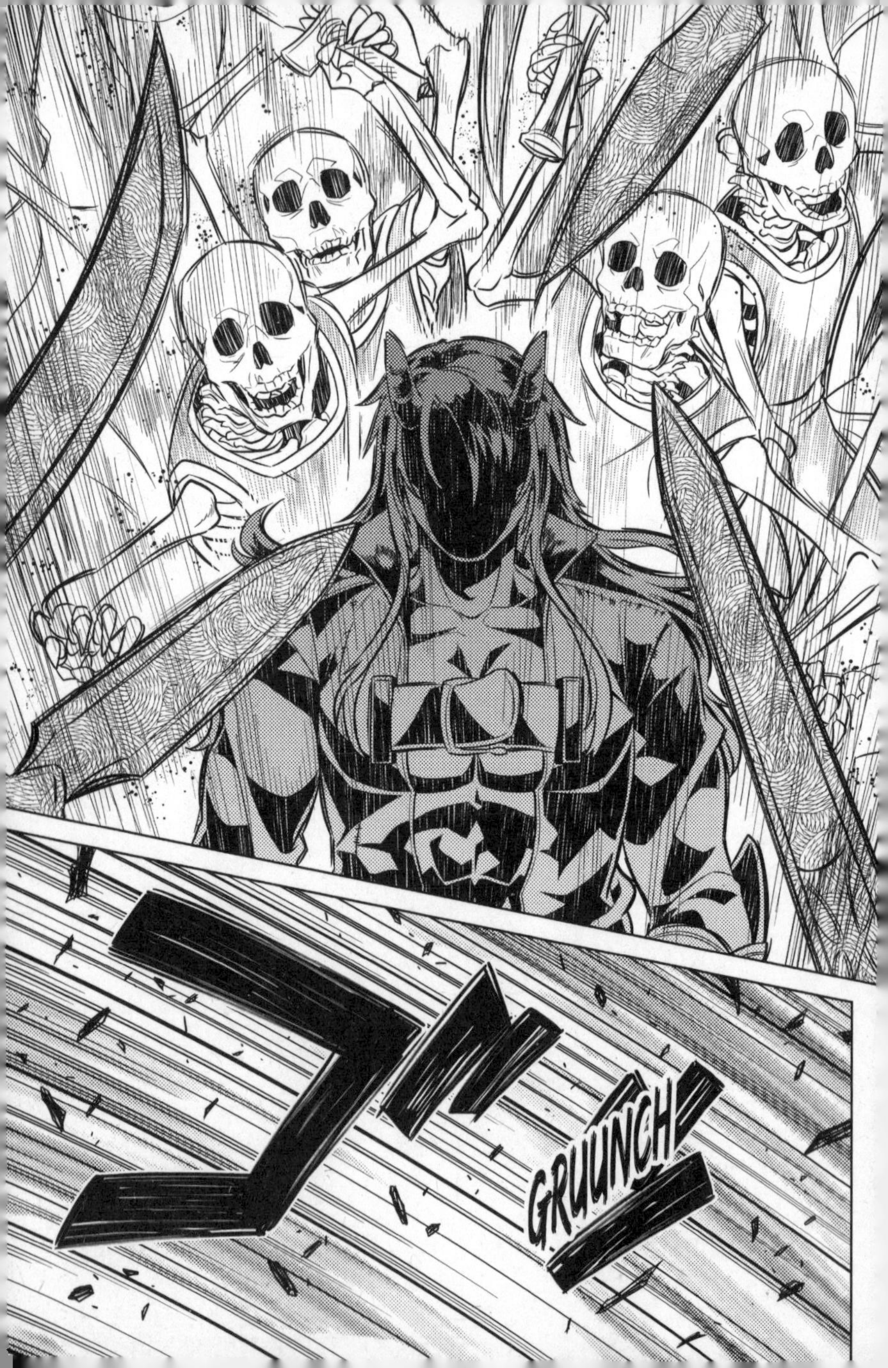
GRUUNCH

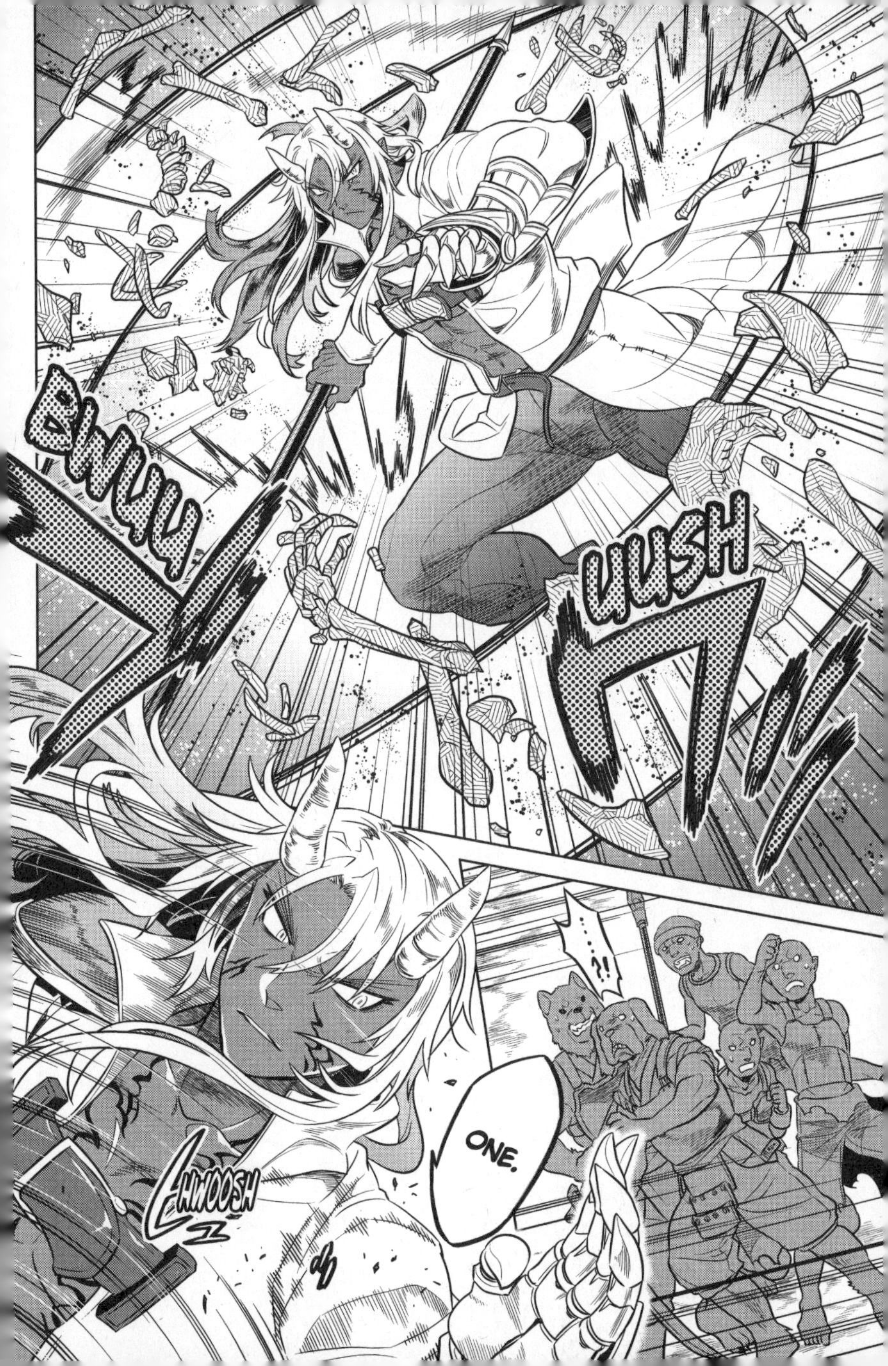
BWUUU
UUSH
......?!
ONE.
CHWOOSH

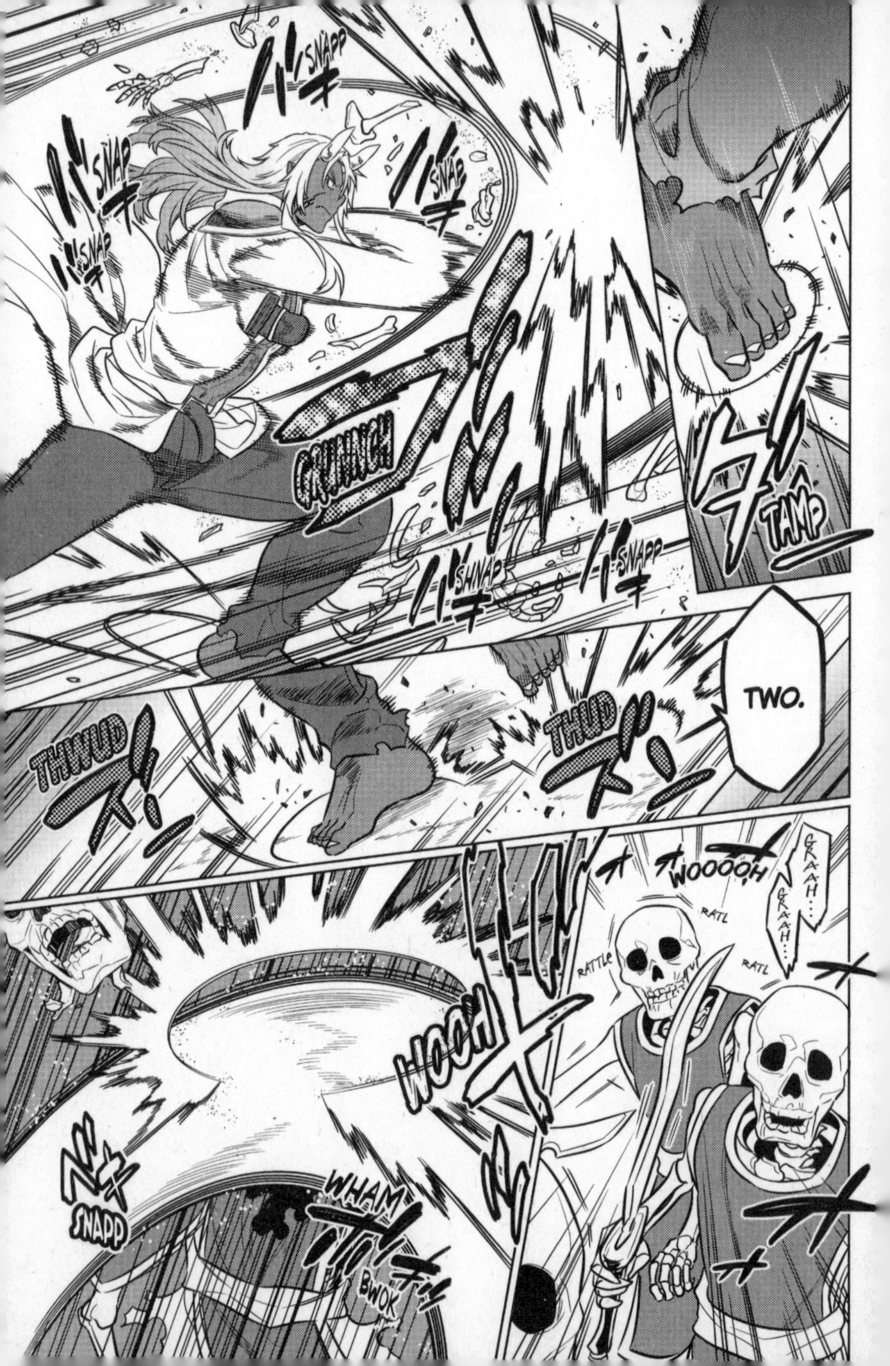
TAMP
SNAPP
SNAP
SNAP
SNAP
CRUNNCH
SNAPP
SHNAP
TWO.
THUD
THWUD
WOOOOH
GRAAH
GRAAH...
RATL
RATL
RATTLE
WOOH
WHAM
BWOK
SNAPP

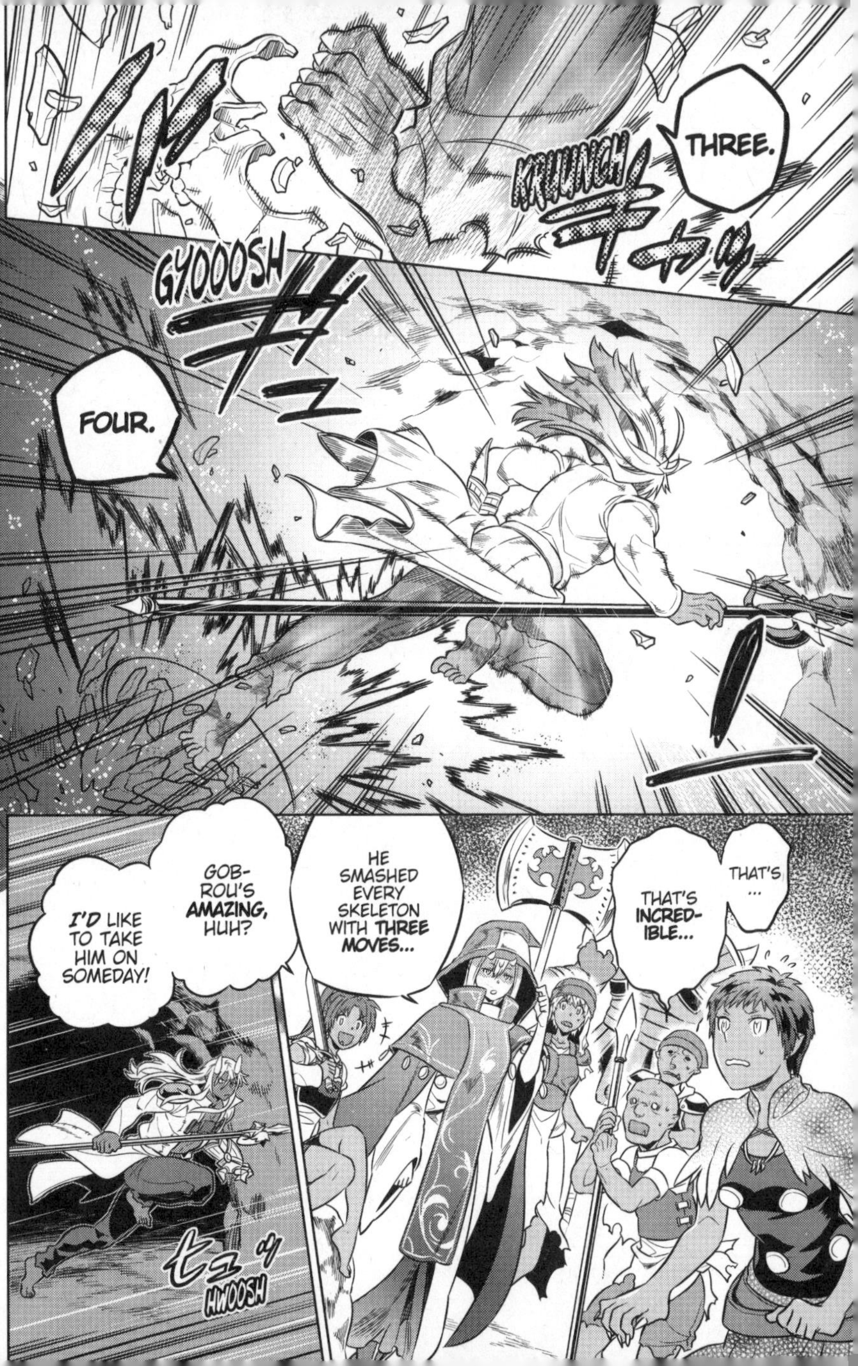
THREE.
KRUUNCH
GYOOOSH
FOUR.
THAT'S ...
THAT'S INCREDIBLE...
HE SMASHED EVERY SKELETON WITH THREE MOVES...
GOB-ROU'S AMAZING, HUH?
I'D LIKE TO TAKE HIM ON SOMEDAY!
HWOOSH

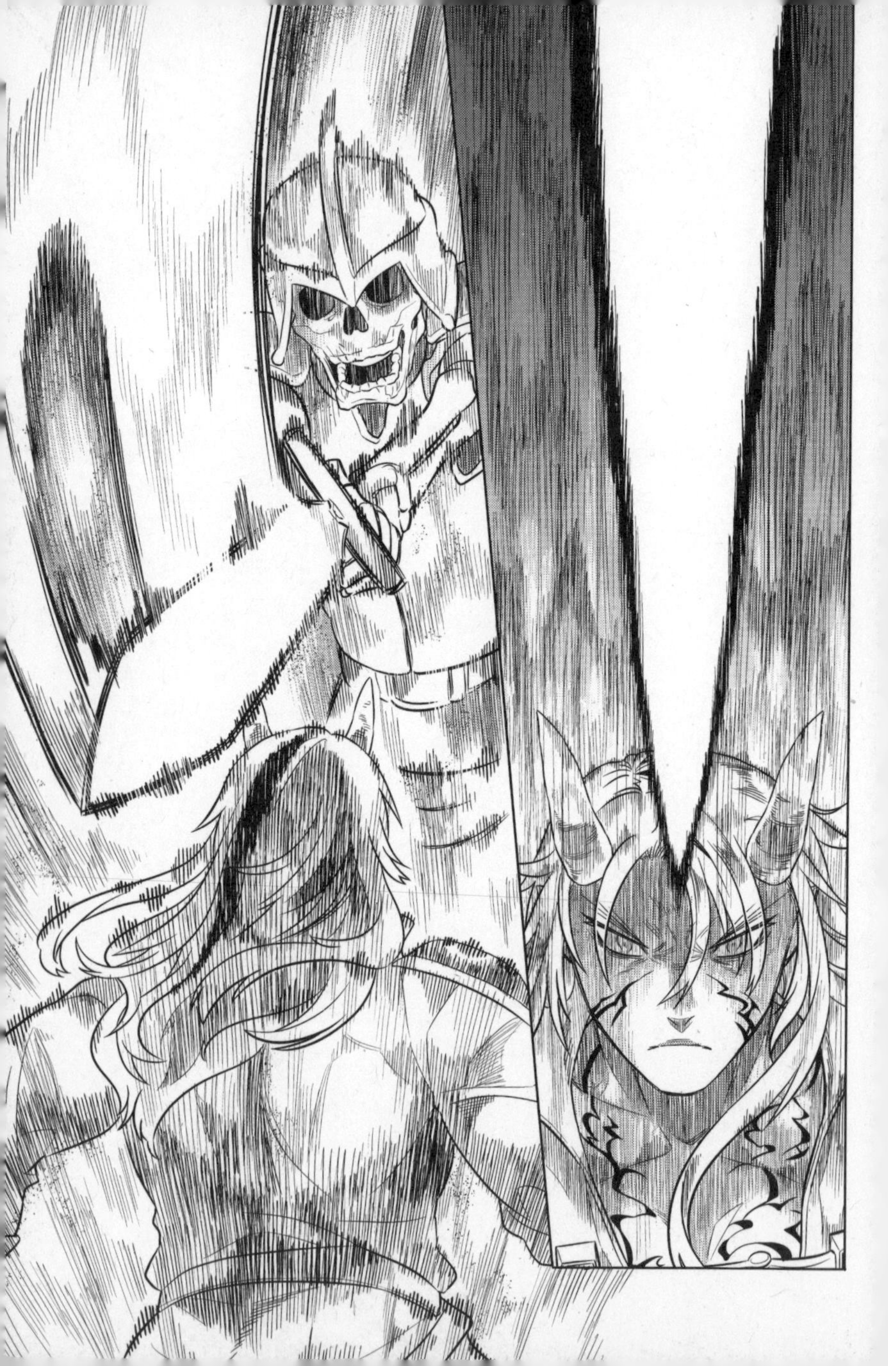

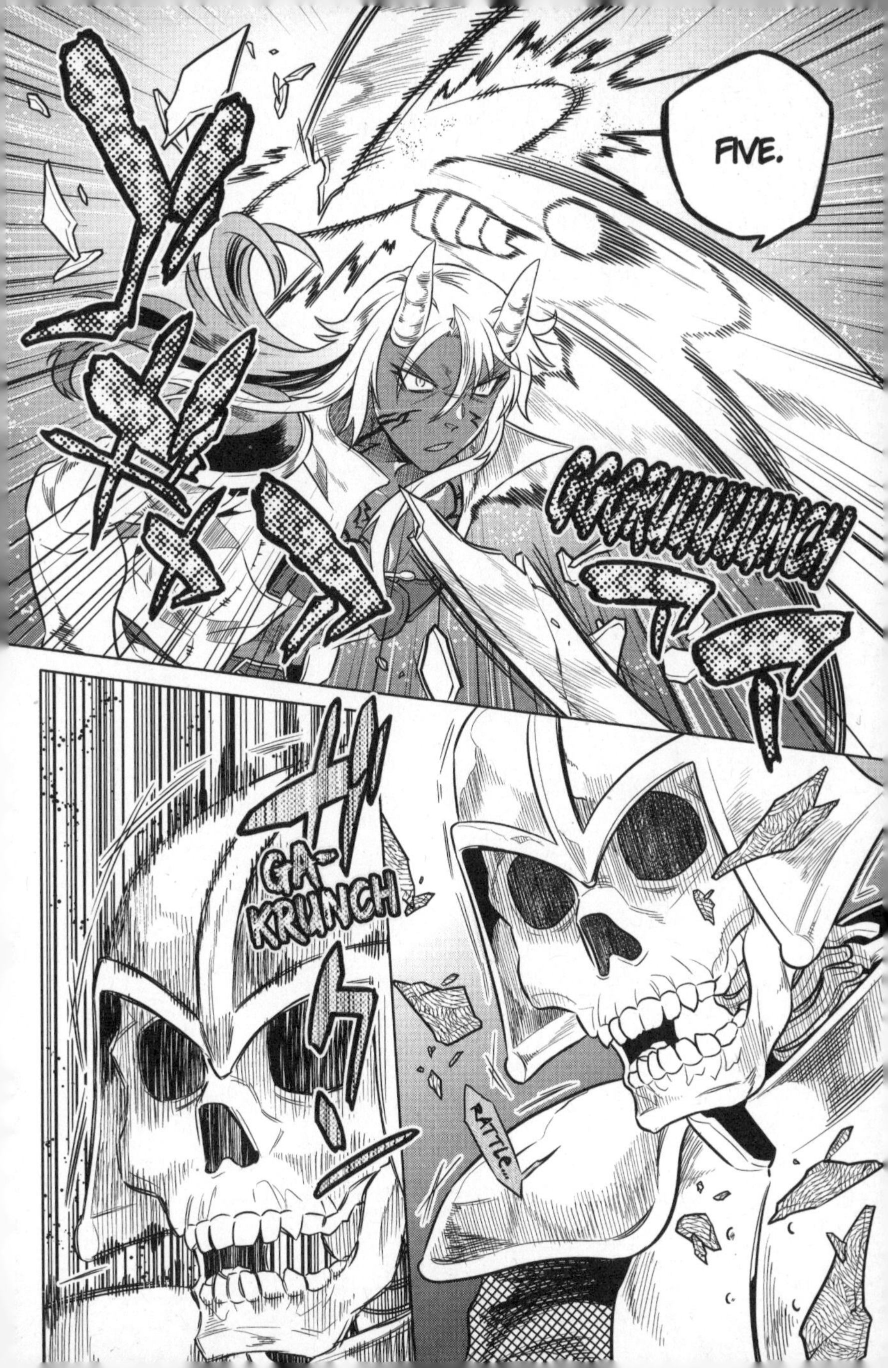
FIVE.
GGGRUNNNUNCH
GA-KRUNCH
RATTLE...

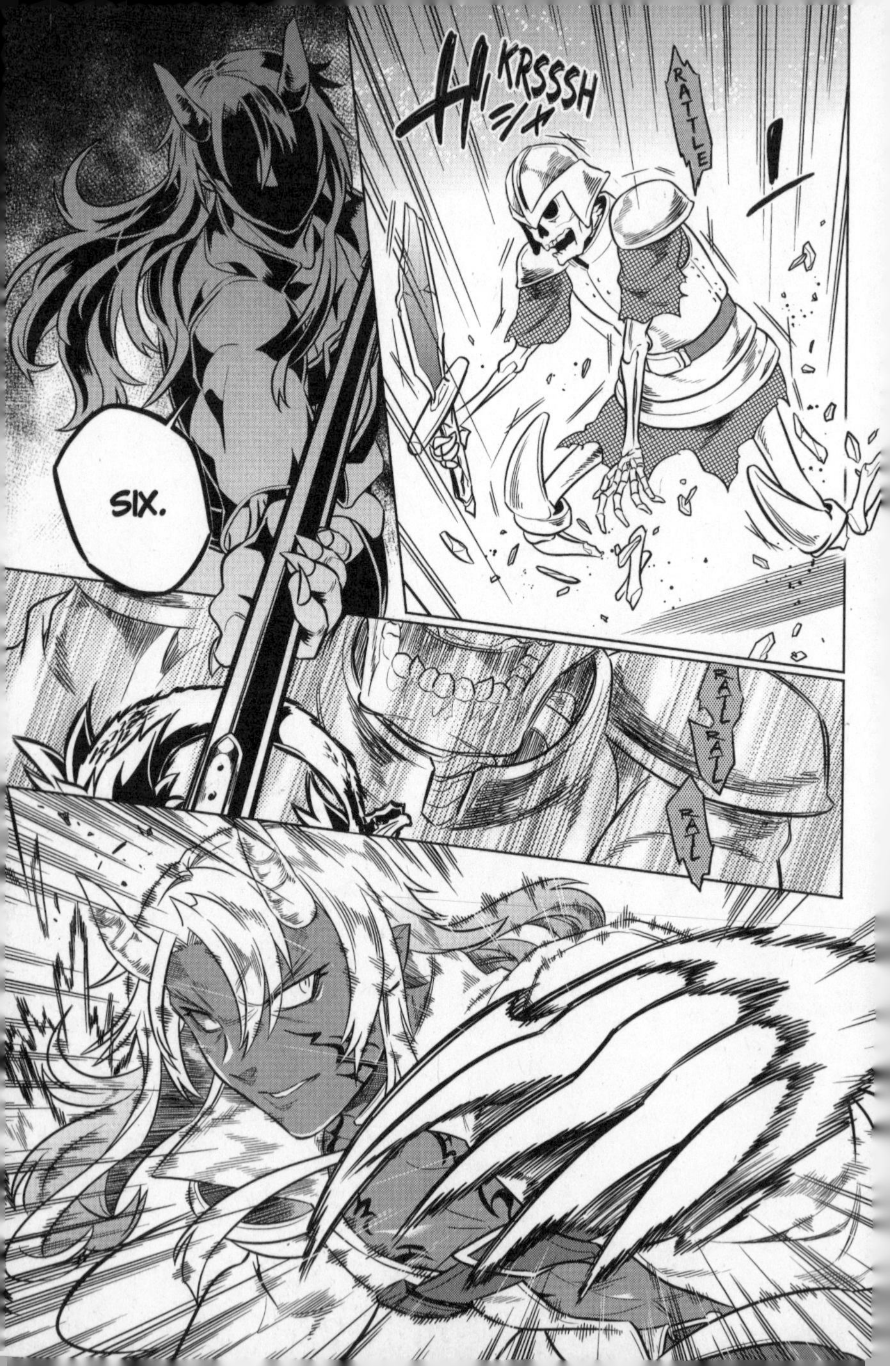
KRSSSH
RATTLE
!
SIX.
FALL FALL
FALL

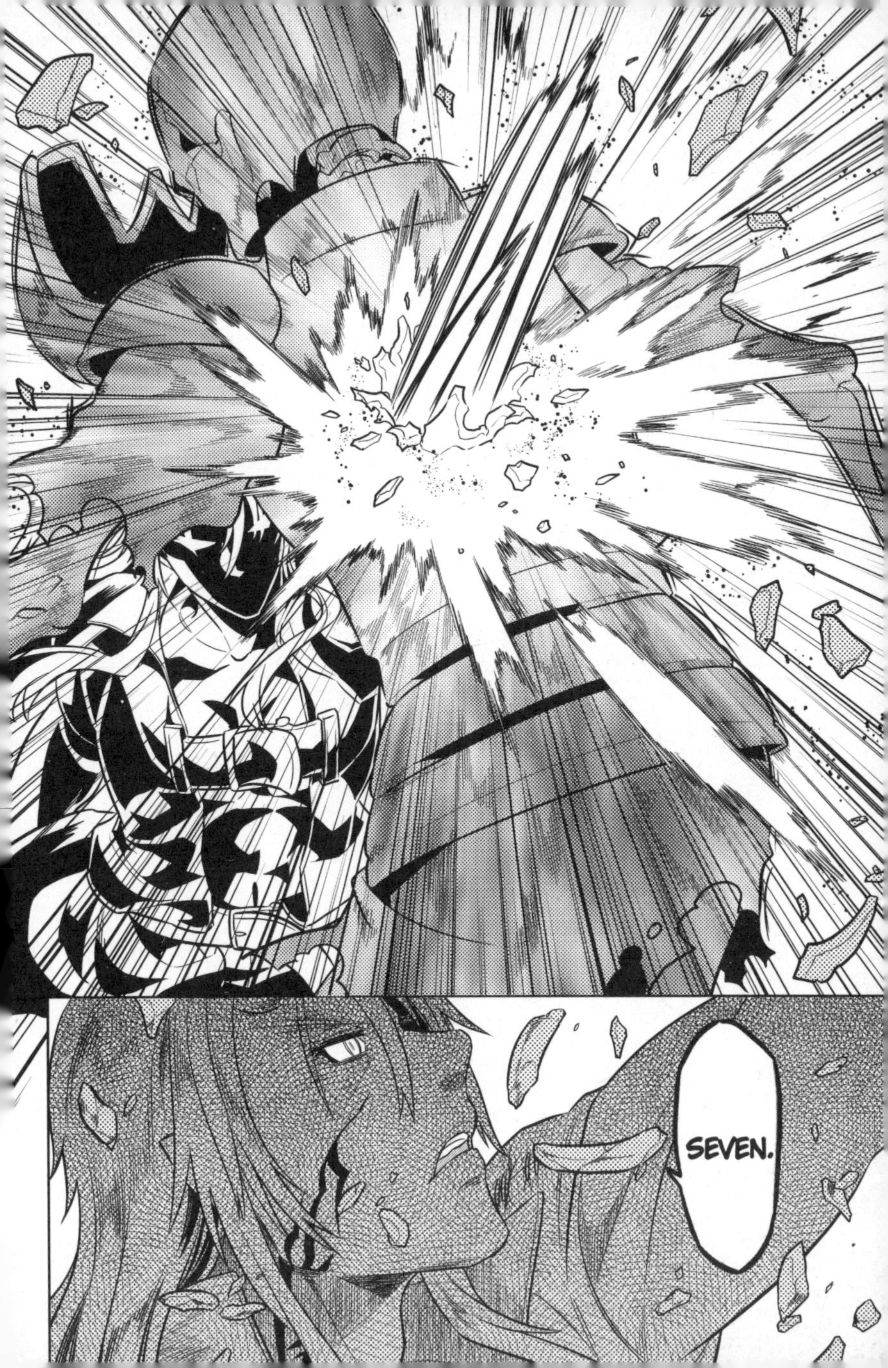
SEVEN.

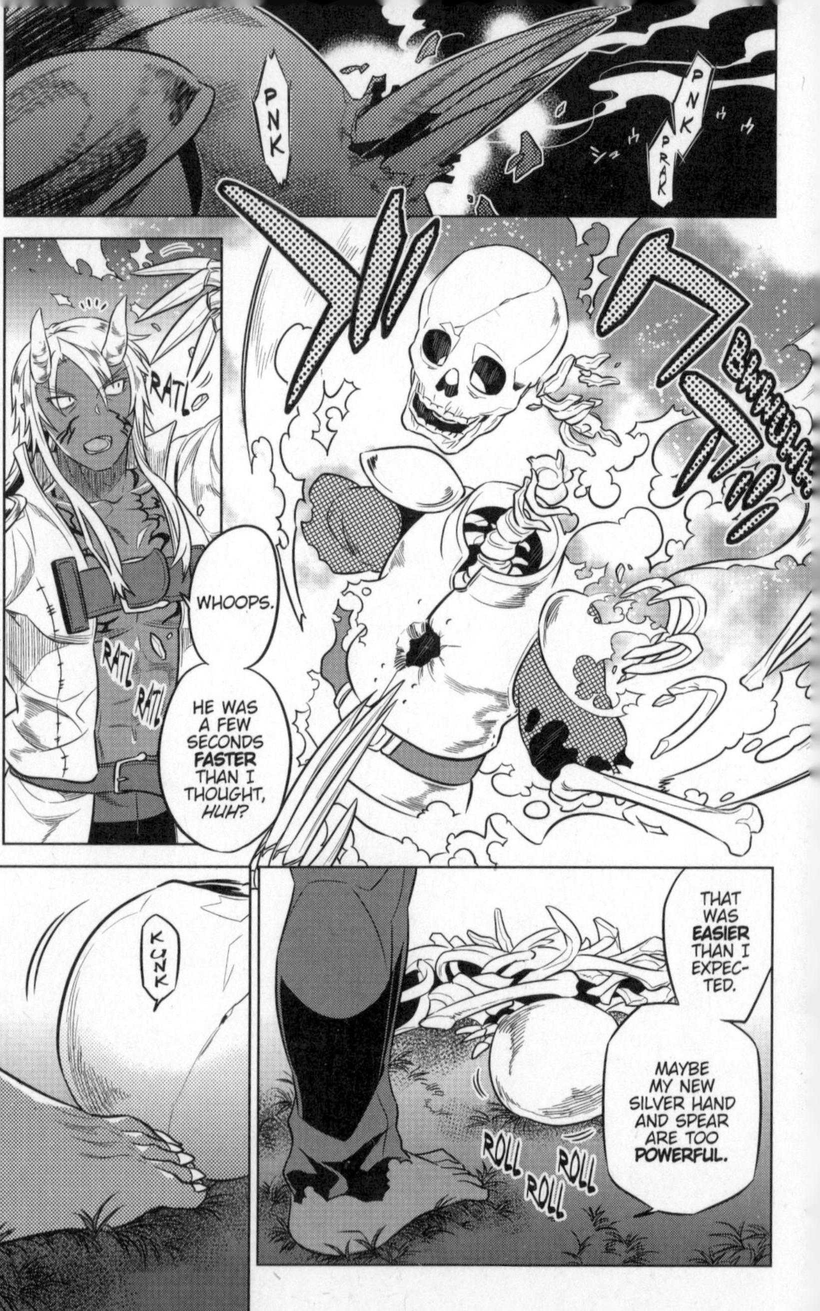
PNK
PNK
PRAK
PNK
WHOOPS.
HE WAS A FEW SECONDS **FASTER** THAN I THOUGHT, *HUH?*
RATL
RATL
RATL
THAT WAS **EASIER** THAN I EXPEC-TED.
MAYBE MY NEW SILVER HAND AND SPEAR ARE TOO **POWERFUL.**
ROLL
ROLL
ROLL
KUNK

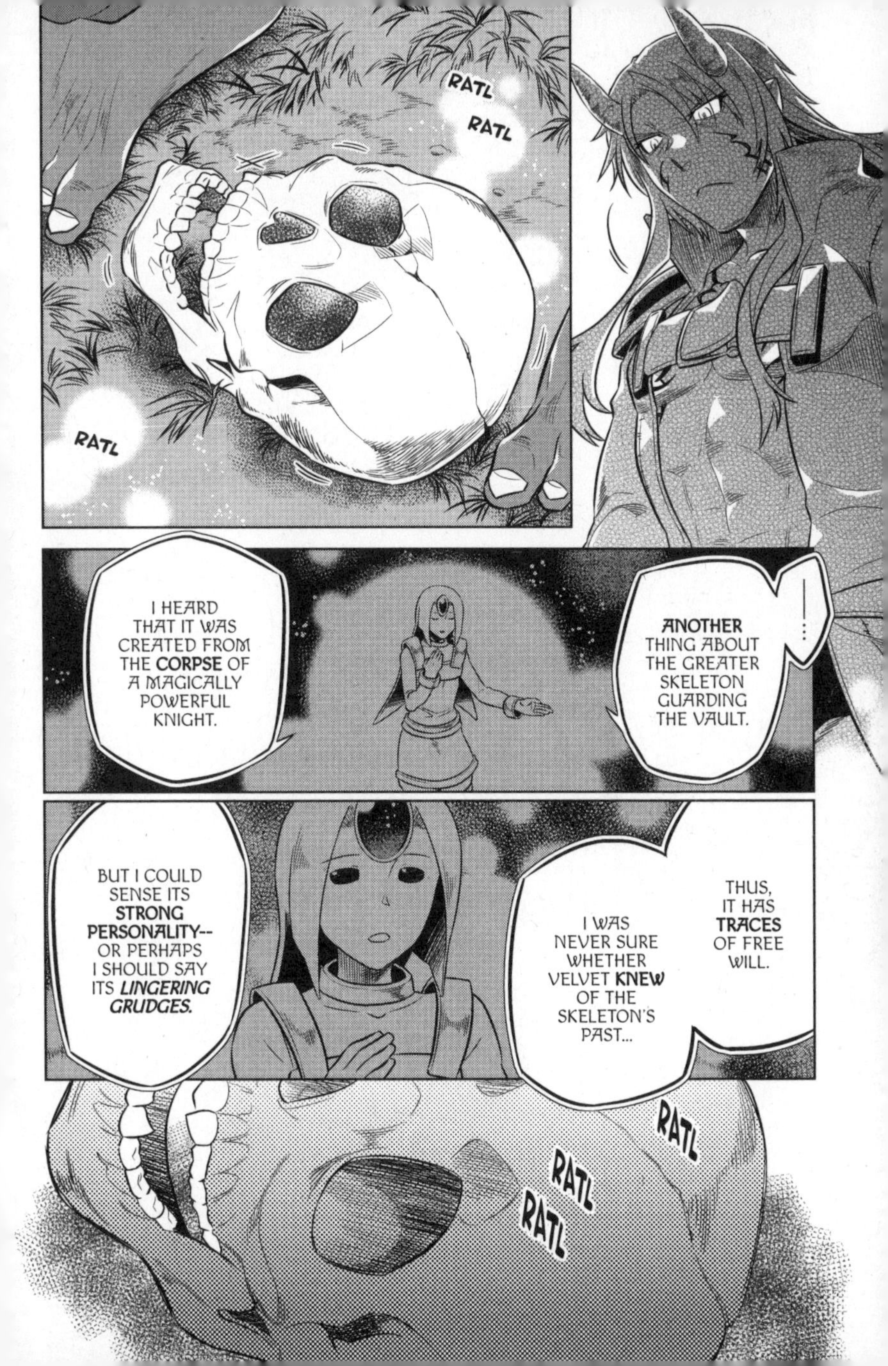
RATL
RATL
RATL
—....
ANOTHER THING ABOUT THE GREATER SKELETON GUARDING THE VAULT.
I HEARD THAT IT WAS CREATED FROM THE CORPSE OF A MAGICALLY POWERFUL KNIGHT.
THUS, IT HAS TRACES OF FREE WILL.
I WAS NEVER SURE WHETHER VELVET KNEW OF THE SKELETON'S PAST...
BUT I COULD SENSE ITS STRONG PERSONALITY-- OR PERHAPS I SHOULD SAY ITS LINGERING GRUDGES.
RATL
RATL
RATL

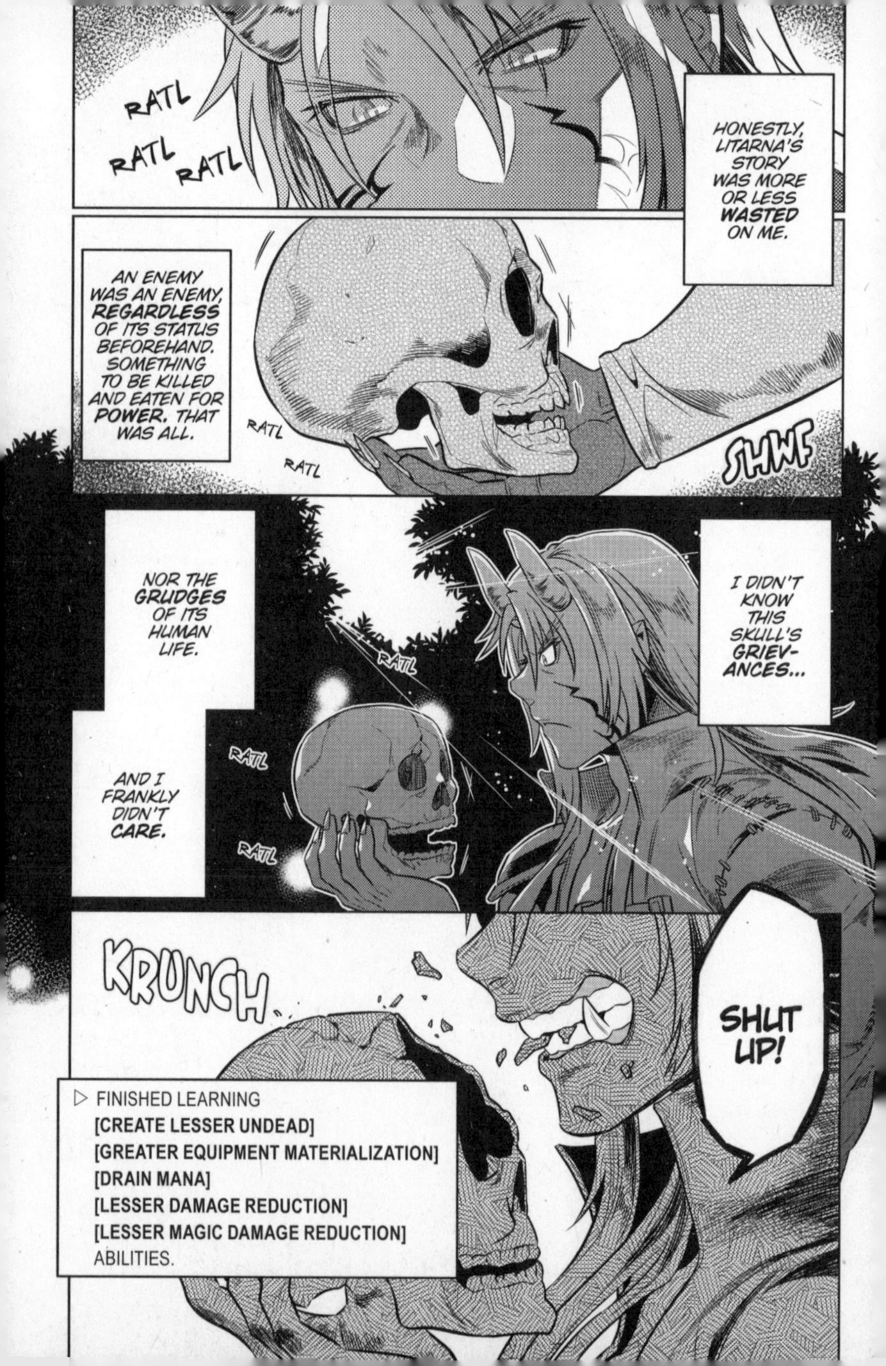
HONESTLY, LITARNA'S STORY WAS MORE OR LESS WASTED ON ME.
RATL
RATL
RATL
SHWF
AN ENEMY WAS AN ENEMY, REGARDLESS OF ITS STATUS BEFOREHAND. SOMETHING TO BE KILLED AND EATEN FOR POWER. THAT WAS ALL.
RATL
RATL
I DIDN'T KNOW THIS SKULL'S GRIEV-ANCES...
RATL
NOR THE GRUDGES OF ITS HUMAN LIFE.
AND I FRANKLY DIDN'T CARE.
RATL
RATL
SHUT UP!
KRUNCH
▷ FINISHED LEARNING
[CREATE LESSER UNDEAD]
[GREATER EQUIPMENT MATERIALIZATION]
[DRAIN MANA]
[LESSER DAMAGE REDUCTION]
[LESSER MAGIC DAMAGE REDUCTION]
ABILITIES.

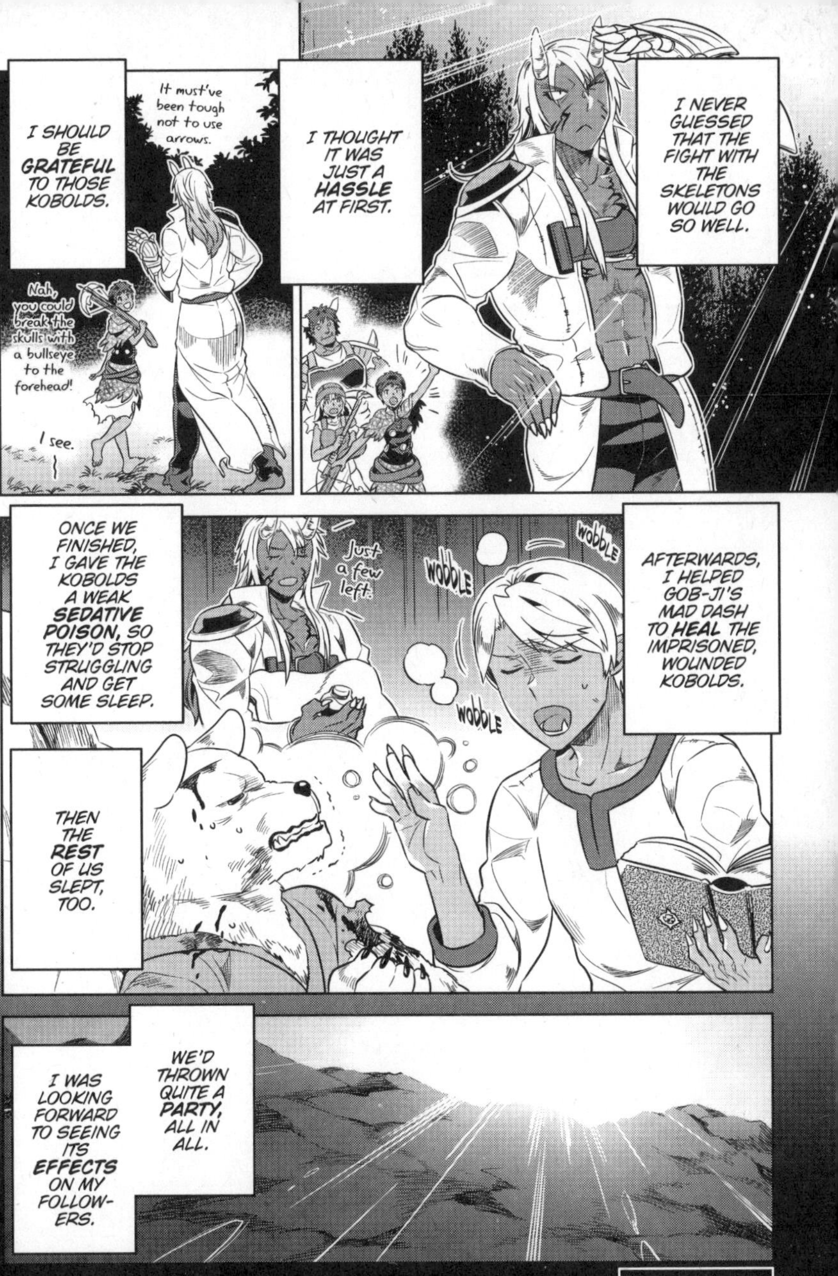
I NEVER GUESSED THAT THE FIGHT WITH THE SKELETONS WOULD GO SO WELL.
I THOUGHT IT WAS JUST A **HASSLE** AT FIRST.
It must've been tough not to use arrows.
I SHOULD BE **GRATEFUL** TO THOSE KOBOLDS.
Nah, you could break the skulls with a bullseye to the forehead!
I see.
AFTERWARDS, I HELPED GOB-JI'S MAD DASH TO **HEAL** THE IMPRISONED, WOUNDED KOBOLDS.
WOBBLE
WOBBLE
WOBBLE
Just a few left.
ONCE WE FINISHED, I GAVE THE KOBOLDS A WEAK **SEDATIVE POISON,** SO THEY'D STOP STRUGGLING AND GET SOME SLEEP.
THEN THE **REST** OF US SLEPT, TOO.
WE'D THROWN QUITE A **PARTY,** ALL IN ALL.
I WAS LOOKING FORWARD TO SEEING ITS **EFFECTS** ON MY FOLLOWERS.
▶ CONTINUE

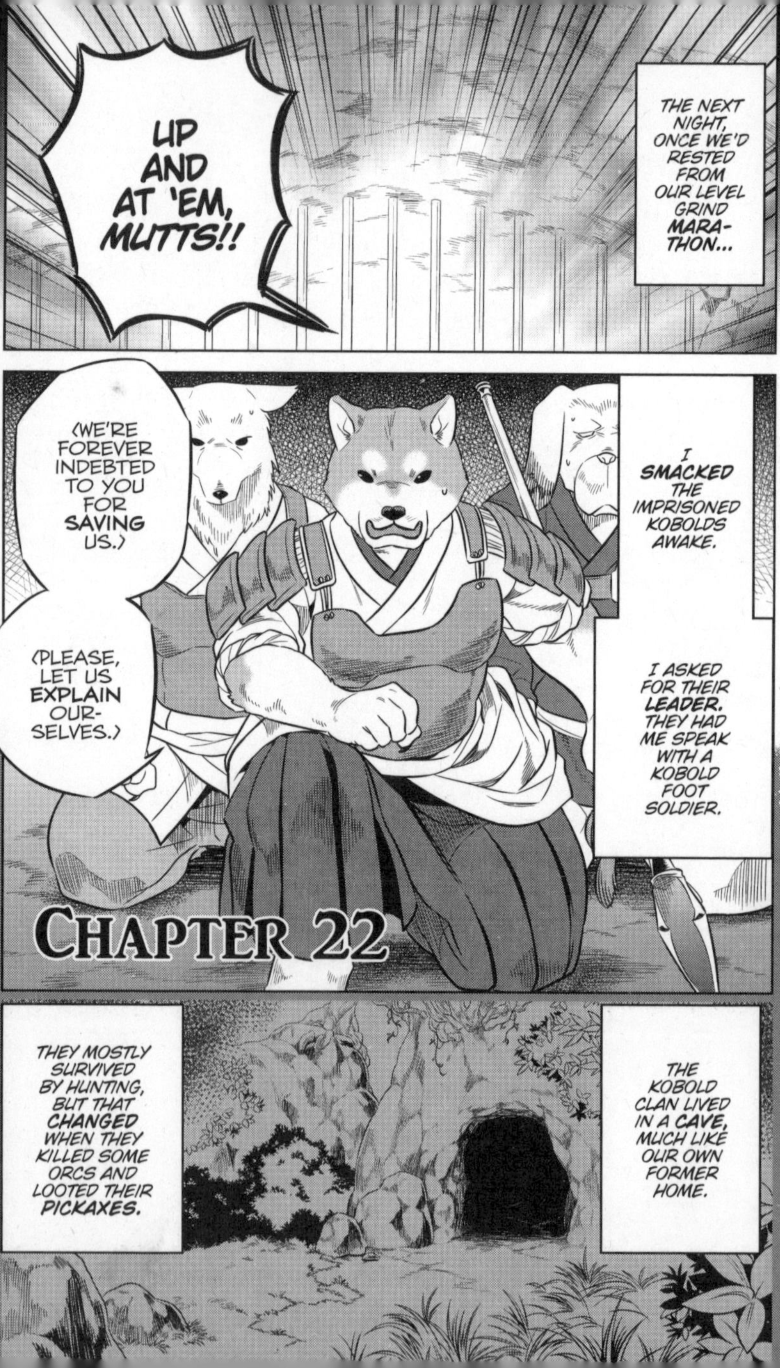
THE NEXT NIGHT, ONCE WE'D RESTED FROM OUR LEVEL GRIND MARA-THON...
UP AND AT 'EM, MUTTS!!
I SMACKED THE IMPRISONED KOBOLDS AWAKE.
I ASKED FOR THEIR LEADER. THEY HAD ME SPEAK WITH A KOBOLD FOOT SOLDIER.
‹WE'RE FOREVER INDEBTED TO YOU FOR SAVING US.›
‹PLEASE, LET US EXPLAIN OUR-SELVES.›
CHAPTER 22
THE KOBOLD CLAN LIVED IN A CAVE, MUCH LIKE OUR OWN FORMER HOME.
THEY MOSTLY SURVIVED BY HUNTING, BUT THAT CHANGED WHEN THEY KILLED SOME ORCS AND LOOTED THEIR PICKAXES.

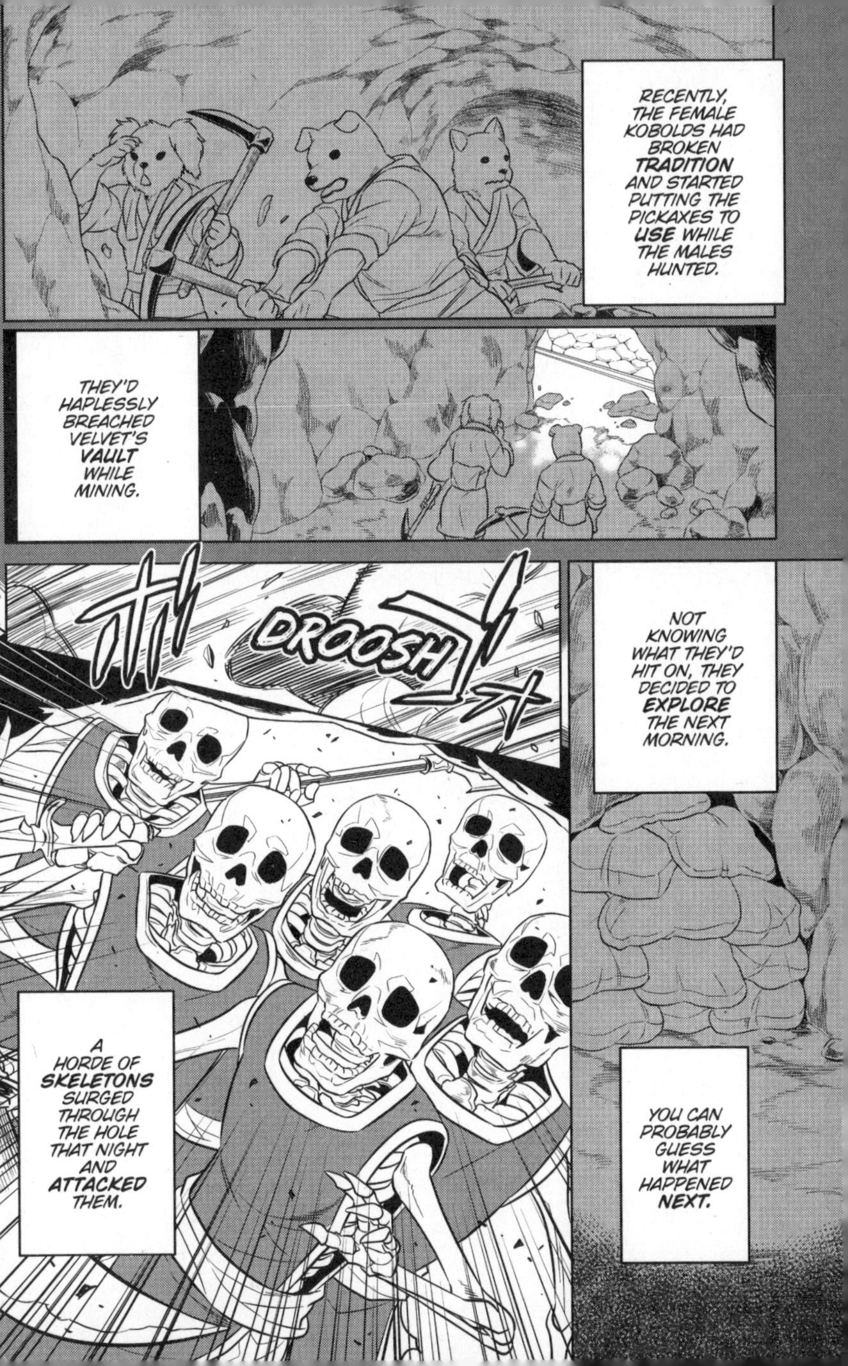
RECENTLY, THE FEMALE KOBOLDS HAD BROKEN **TRADITION** AND STARTED PUTTING THE PICKAXES TO **USE** WHILE THE MALES HUNTED.
THEY'D HAPLESSLY BREACHED VELVET'S **VAULT** WHILE MINING.
NOT KNOWING WHAT THEY'D HIT ON, THEY DECIDED TO **EXPLORE** THE NEXT MORNING.
YOU CAN PROBABLY GUESS WHAT HAPPENED **NEXT.**
DROOSH
A HORDE OF **SKELETONS** SURGED THROUGH THE HOLE THAT NIGHT AND **ATTACKED** THEM.

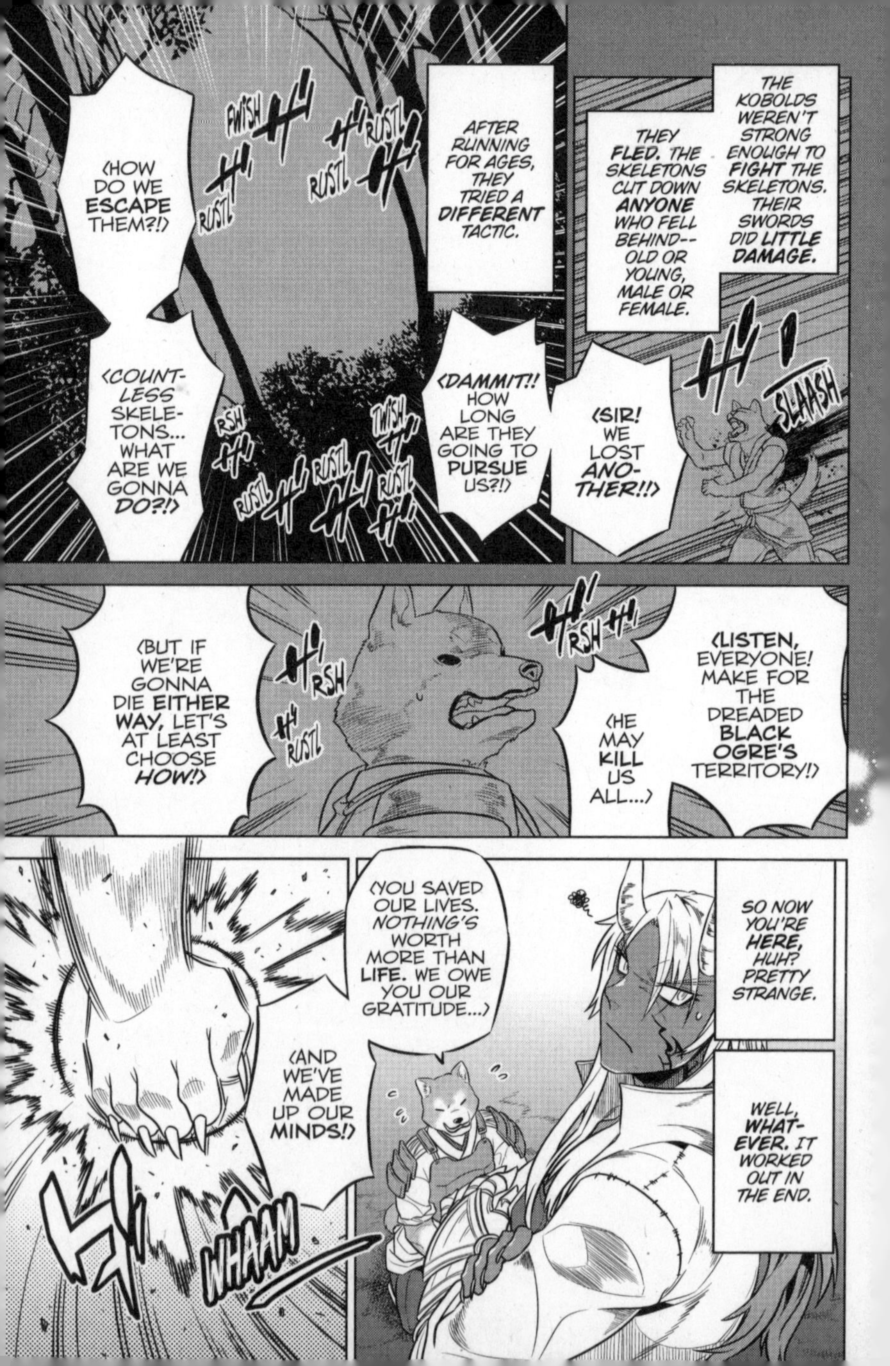
THE KOBOLDS WEREN'T STRONG ENOUGH TO FIGHT THE SKELETONS. THEIR SWORDS DID LITTLE DAMAGE.
THEY FLED. THE SKELETONS CUT DOWN ANYONE WHO FELL BEHIND--OLD OR YOUNG, MALE OR FEMALE.
SLAASH
‹SIR! WE LOST ANOTHER!!›
AFTER RUNNING FOR AGES, THEY TRIED A DIFFERENT TACTIC.
RUSTL
FWISH
RUSTL
RUSTL
‹DAMMIT!! HOW LONG ARE THEY GOING TO PURSUE US?!›
‹HOW DO WE ESCAPE THEM?!›
TWISH
RUSTL
RUSTL
RSH
RUSTL
‹COUNTLESS SKELETONS... WHAT ARE WE GONNA DO?!›
‹LISTEN, EVERYONE! MAKE FOR THE DREADED BLACK OGRE'S TERRITORY!›
‹HE MAY KILL US ALL...›
RSH
RSH
RUSTL
‹BUT IF WE'RE GONNA DIE EITHER WAY, LET'S AT LEAST CHOOSE HOW!›
SO NOW YOU'RE HERE, HUH? PRETTY STRANGE.
WELL, WHATEVER. IT WORKED OUT IN THE END.
‹YOU SAVED OUR LIVES. NOTHING'S WORTH MORE THAN LIFE. WE OWE YOU OUR GRATITUDE...›
‹AND WE'VE MADE UP OUR MINDS!›
WHAAM

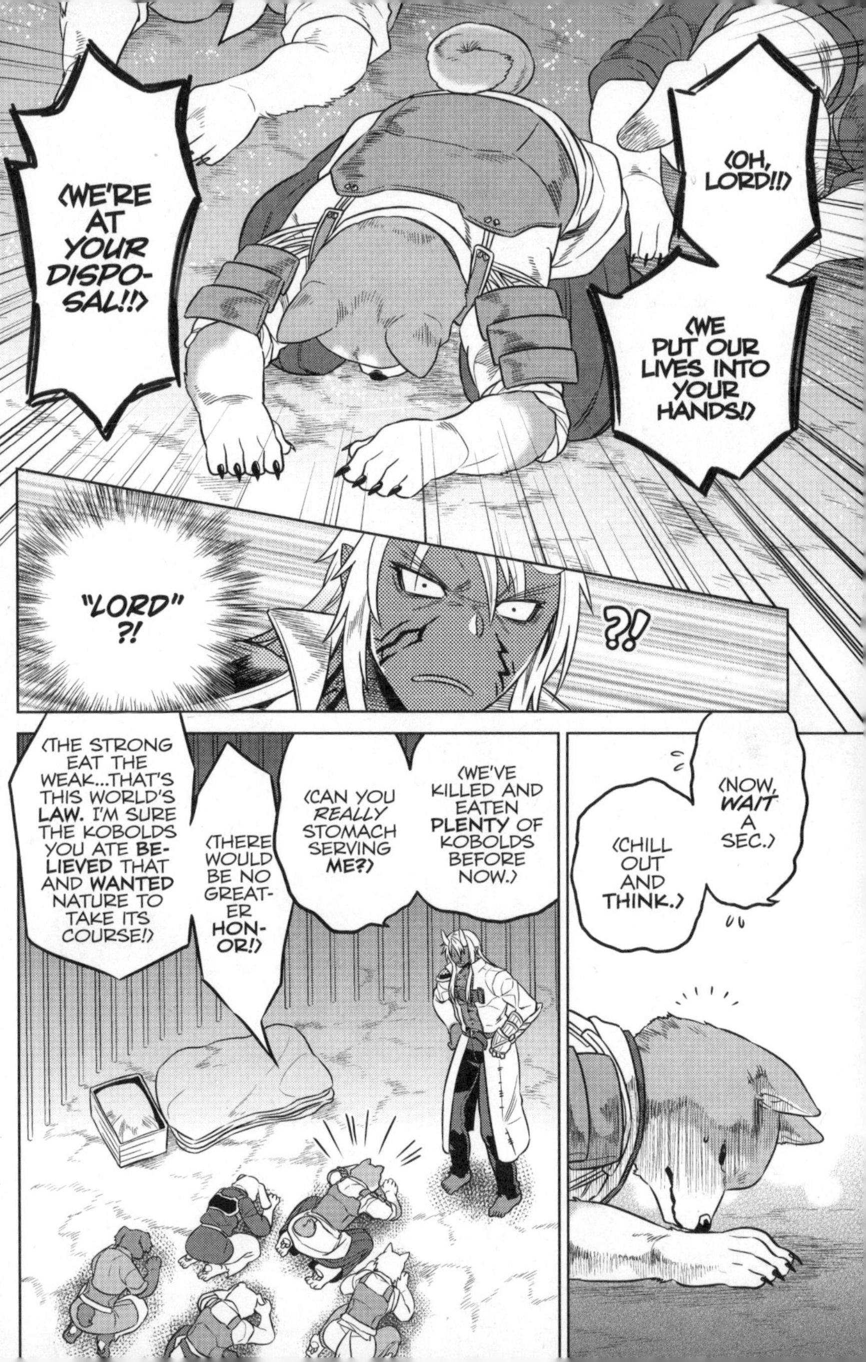
‹OH, LORD!!›
‹WE PUT OUR LIVES INTO YOUR HANDS!›
‹WE'RE AT YOUR DISPOSAL!!›
"LORD" ?!
?!
‹NOW, WAIT A SEC.›
‹CHILL OUT AND THINK.›
‹WE'VE KILLED AND EATEN PLENTY OF KOBOLDS BEFORE NOW.›
‹CAN YOU REALLY STOMACH SERVING ME?›
‹THERE WOULD BE NO GREATER HONOR!›
‹THE STRONG EAT THE WEAK...THAT'S THIS WORLD'S LAW. I'M SURE THE KOBOLDS YOU ATE BELIEVED THAT AND WANTED NATURE TO TAKE ITS COURSE!›

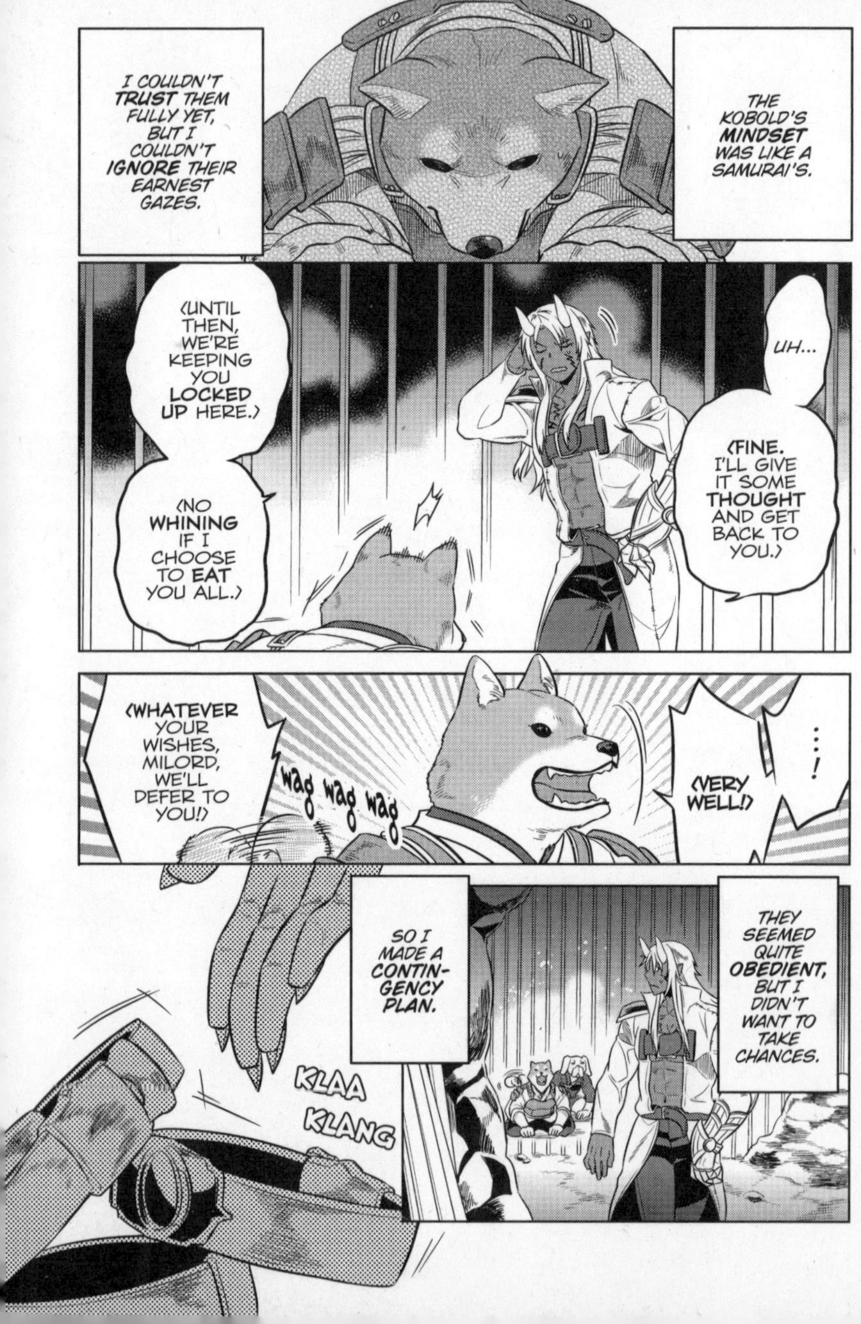
THE KOBOLD'S MINDSET WAS LIKE A SAMURAI'S.
I COULDN'T TRUST THEM FULLY YET, BUT I COULDN'T IGNORE THEIR EARNEST GAZES.
UH...
‹FINE. I'LL GIVE IT SOME THOUGHT AND GET BACK TO YOU.›
‹UNTIL THEN, WE'RE KEEPING YOU LOCKED UP HERE.›
‹NO WHINING IF I CHOOSE TO EAT YOU ALL.›
...!
‹VERY WELL!›
‹WHATEVER YOUR WISHES, MILORD, WE'LL DEFER TO YOU!›
wag wag wag
THEY SEEMED QUITE OBEDIENT, BUT I DIDN'T WANT TO TAKE CHANCES.
SO I MADE A CONTIN-GENCY PLAN.
KLAA KLANG

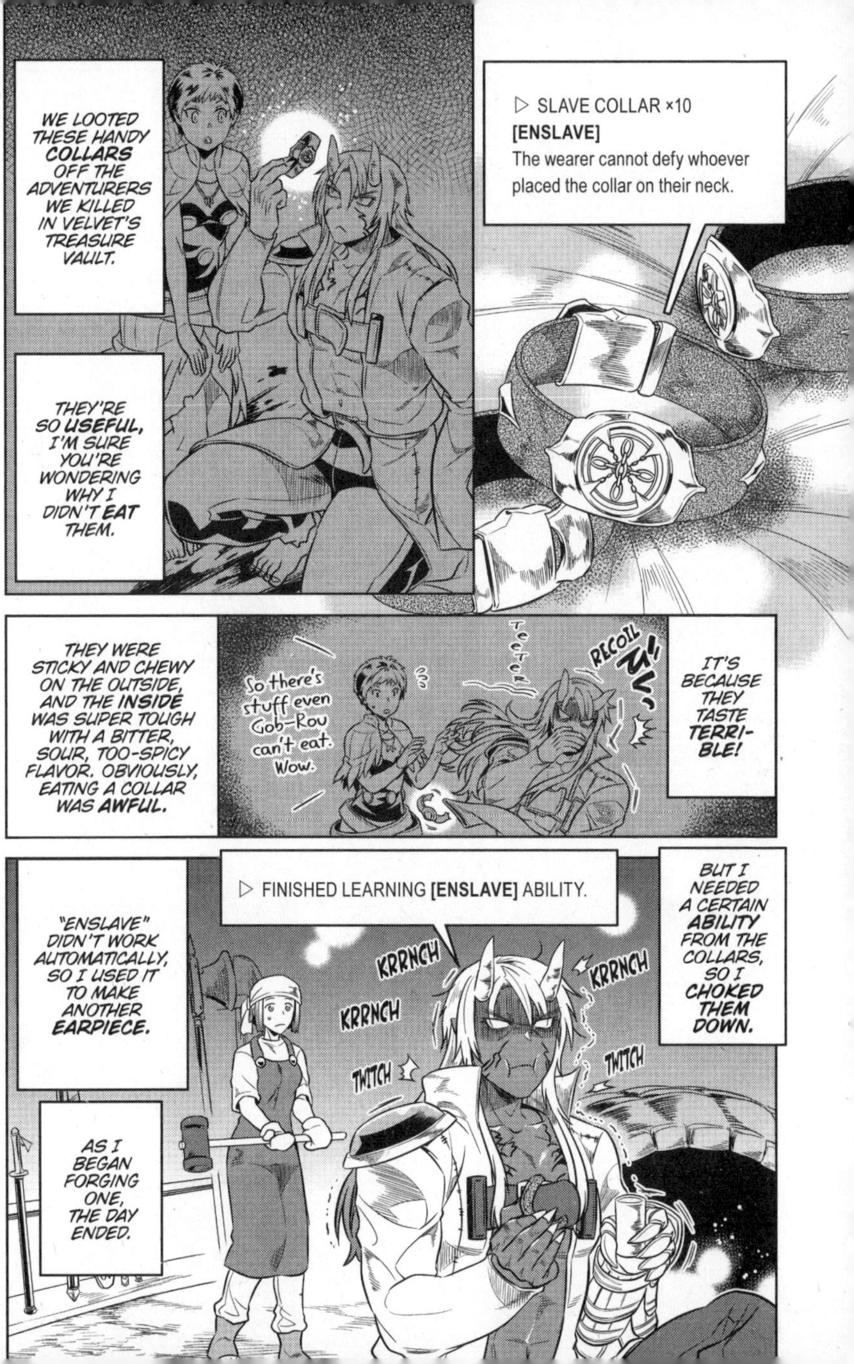
▷ SLAVE COLLAR ×10
[ENSLAVE]
The wearer cannot defy whoever placed the collar on their neck.
WE LOOTED THESE HANDY COLLARS OFF THE ADVENTURERS WE KILLED IN VELVET'S TREASURE VAULT.
THEY'RE SO USEFUL, I'M SURE YOU'RE WONDERING WHY I DIDN'T EAT THEM.
IT'S BECAUSE THEY TASTE TERRI-BLE!
RECOIL
TEETER
So there's stuff even Gob-Rou can't eat. Wow.
THEY WERE STICKY AND CHEWY ON THE OUTSIDE, AND THE INSIDE WAS SUPER TOUGH WITH A BITTER, SOUR, TOO-SPICY FLAVOR. OBVIOUSLY, EATING A COLLAR WAS AWFUL.
BUT I NEEDED A CERTAIN ABILITY FROM THE COLLARS, SO I CHOKED THEM DOWN.
▷ FINISHED LEARNING [ENSLAVE] ABILITY.
KRRNCH
KRRNCH
KRRNCH
TWITCH
TWITCH
"ENSLAVE" DIDN'T WORK AUTOMATICALLY, SO I USED IT TO MAKE ANOTHER EARPIECE.
AS I BEGAN FORGING ONE, THE DAY ENDED.

DAY 61

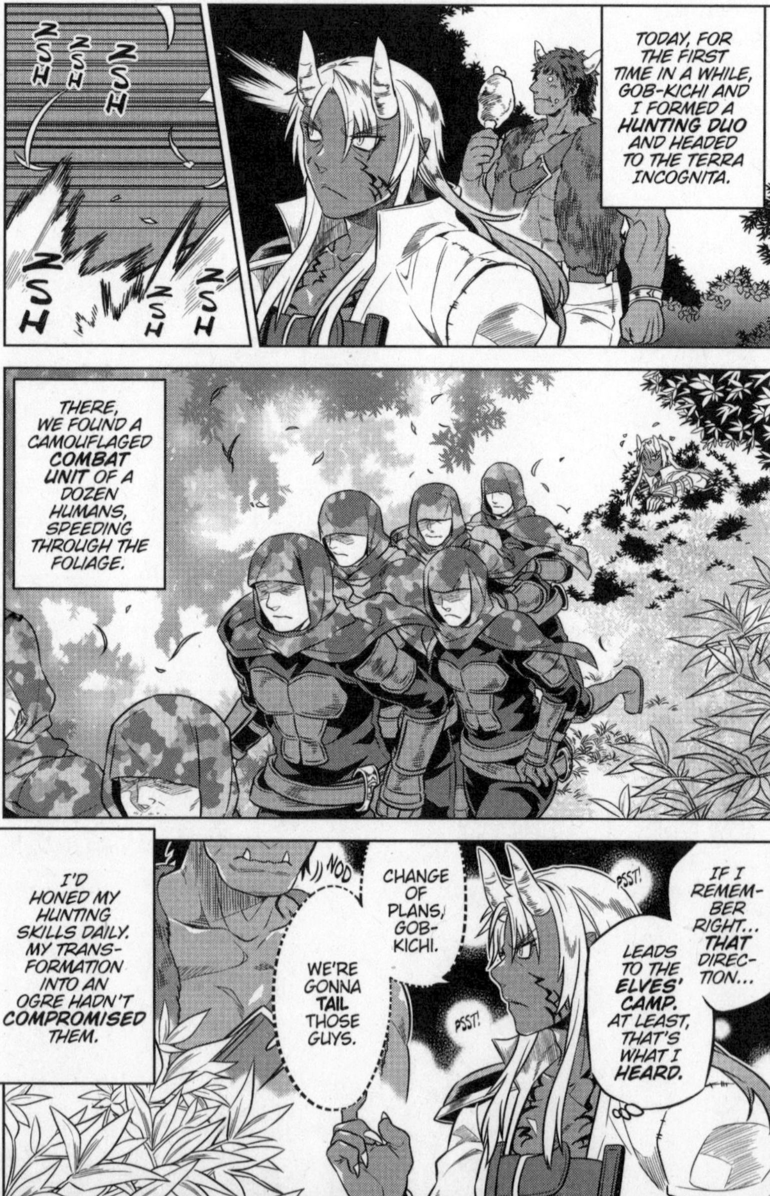
TODAY, FOR THE FIRST TIME IN A WHILE, GOB-KICHI AND I FORMED A **HUNTING DUO** AND HEADED TO THE TERRA INCOGNITA.
ZSH ZSH ZSH
ZSH ZSH ZSH
THERE, WE FOUND A CAMOUFLAGED **COMBAT UNIT** OF A DOZEN HUMANS, SPEEDING THROUGH THE FOLIAGE.
IF I REMEMBER RIGHT... **THAT** DIRECTION...
PSST!
LEADS TO THE **ELVES' CAMP.** AT LEAST, THAT'S WHAT I **HEARD.**
PSST!
CHANGE OF PLANS, GOB-KICHI.
WE'RE GONNA **TAIL** THOSE GUYS.
NOD
I'D HONED MY HUNTING SKILLS DAILY. MY TRANS-FORMATION INTO AN OGRE HADN'T **COMPROMISED** THEM.

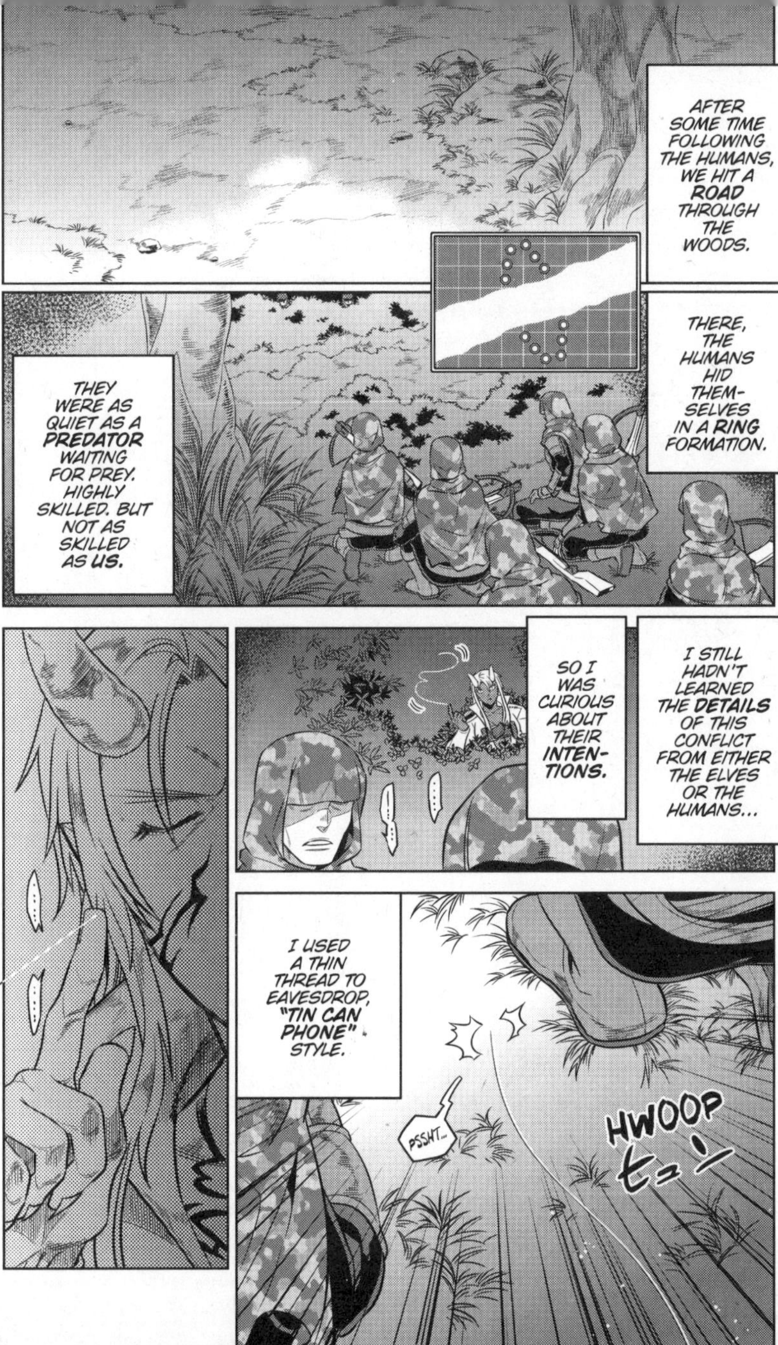
AFTER SOME TIME FOLLOWING THE HUMANS, WE HIT A ROAD THROUGH THE WOODS.
THERE, THE HUMANS HID THEM-SELVES IN A RING FORMATION.
THEY WERE AS QUIET AS A PREDATOR WAITING FOR PREY. HIGHLY SKILLED. BUT NOT AS SKILLED AS US.
I STILL HADN'T LEARNED THE DETAILS OF THIS CONFLICT FROM EITHER THE ELVES OR THE HUMANS...
SO I WAS CURIOUS ABOUT THEIR INTEN-TIONS.
!.....
.....
I USED A THIN THREAD TO EAVESDROP, "TIN CAN PHONE" STYLE.
HWOOP
PSSHT...
.....
.....

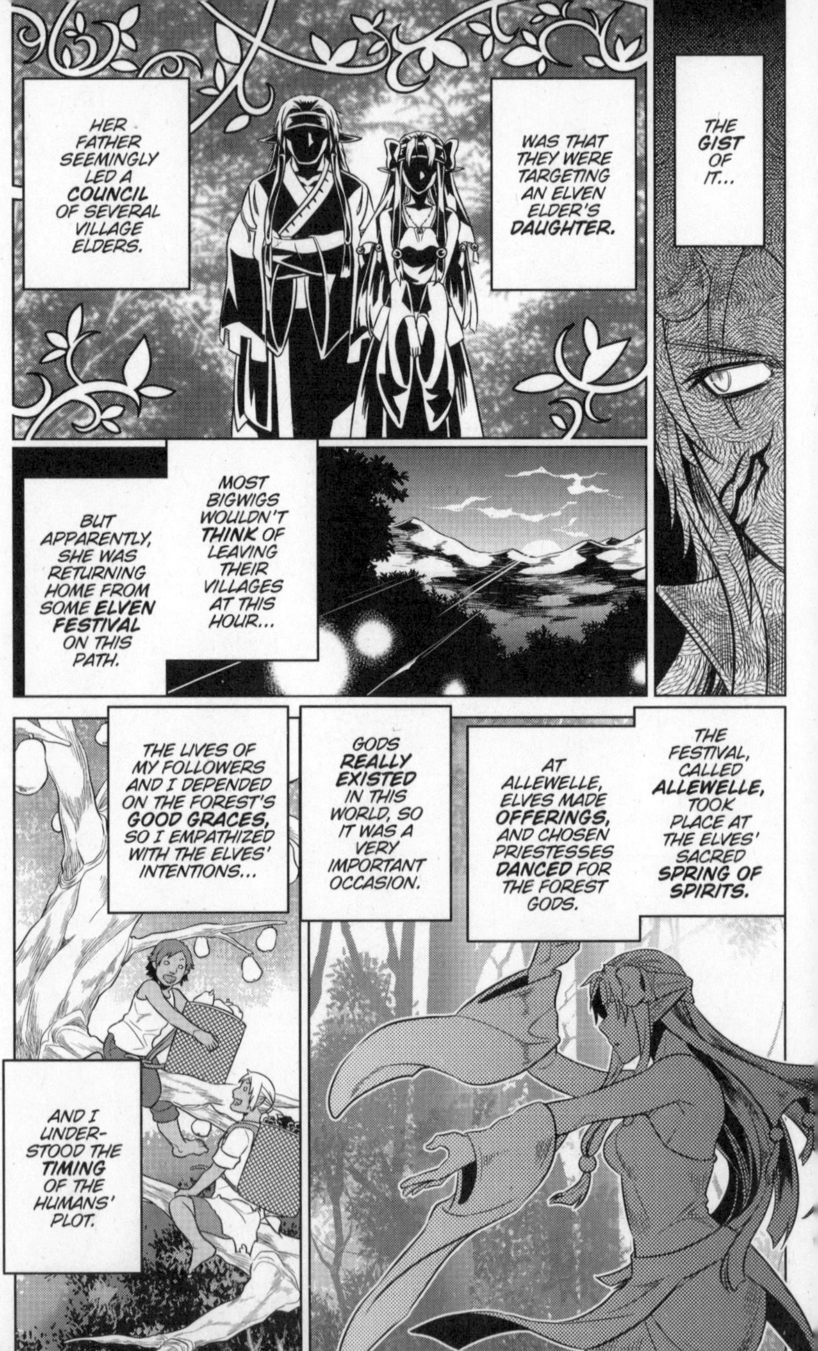
THE GIST OF IT...
WAS THAT THEY WERE TARGETING AN ELVEN ELDER'S DAUGHTER.
HER FATHER SEEMINGLY LED A COUNCIL OF SEVERAL VILLAGE ELDERS.
MOST BIGWIGS WOULDN'T THINK OF LEAVING THEIR VILLAGES AT THIS HOUR...
BUT APPARENTLY, SHE WAS RETURNING HOME FROM SOME ELVEN FESTIVAL ON THIS PATH.
THE FESTIVAL, CALLED ALLEWELLE, TOOK PLACE AT THE ELVES' SACRED SPRING OF SPIRITS.
AT ALLEWELLE, ELVES MADE OFFERINGS, AND CHOSEN PRIESTESSES DANCED FOR THE FOREST GODS.
GODS REALLY EXISTED IN THIS WORLD, SO IT WAS A VERY IMPORTANT OCCASION.
THE LIVES OF MY FOLLOWERS AND I DEPENDED ON THE FOREST'S GOOD GRACES, SO I EMPATHIZED WITH THE ELVES' INTENTIONS...
AND I UNDER-STOOD THE TIMING OF THE HUMANS' PLOT.

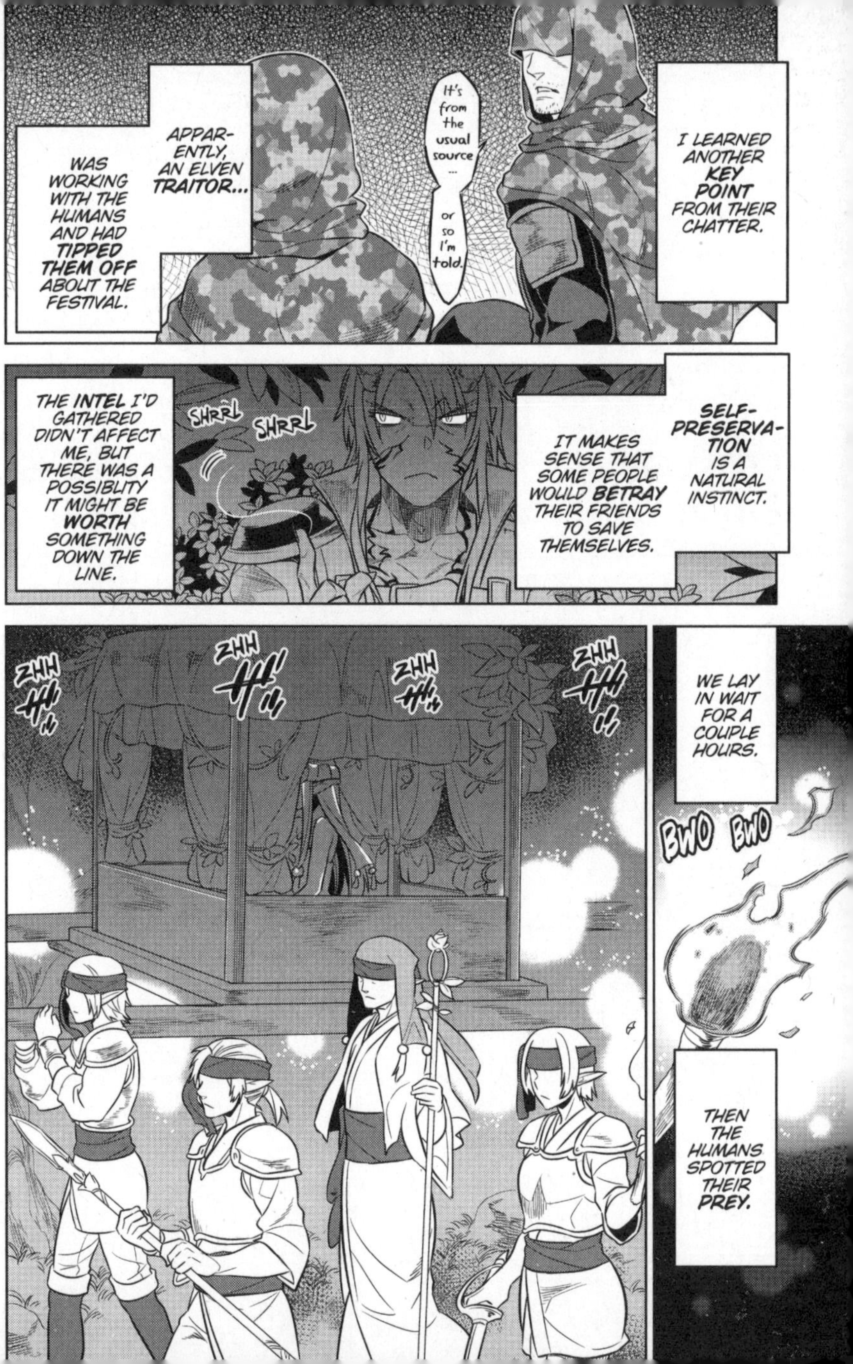
I LEARNED ANOTHER KEY POINT FROM THEIR CHATTER.
It's from the usual source... or so I'm told.
APPARENTLY, AN ELVEN TRAITOR...
WAS WORKING WITH THE HUMANS AND HAD TIPPED THEM OFF ABOUT THE FESTIVAL.
SELF-PRESERVATION IS A NATURAL INSTINCT.
IT MAKES SENSE THAT SOME PEOPLE WOULD BETRAY THEIR FRIENDS TO SAVE THEMSELVES.
SHRRL
SHRRL
THE INTEL I'D GATHERED DIDN'T AFFECT ME, BUT THERE WAS A POSSIBLITY IT MIGHT BE WORTH SOMETHING DOWN THE LINE.
WE LAY IN WAIT FOR A COUPLE HOURS.
BWO BWO
THEN THE HUMANS SPOTTED THEIR PREY.
ZHH
ZHH
ZHH
ZHH

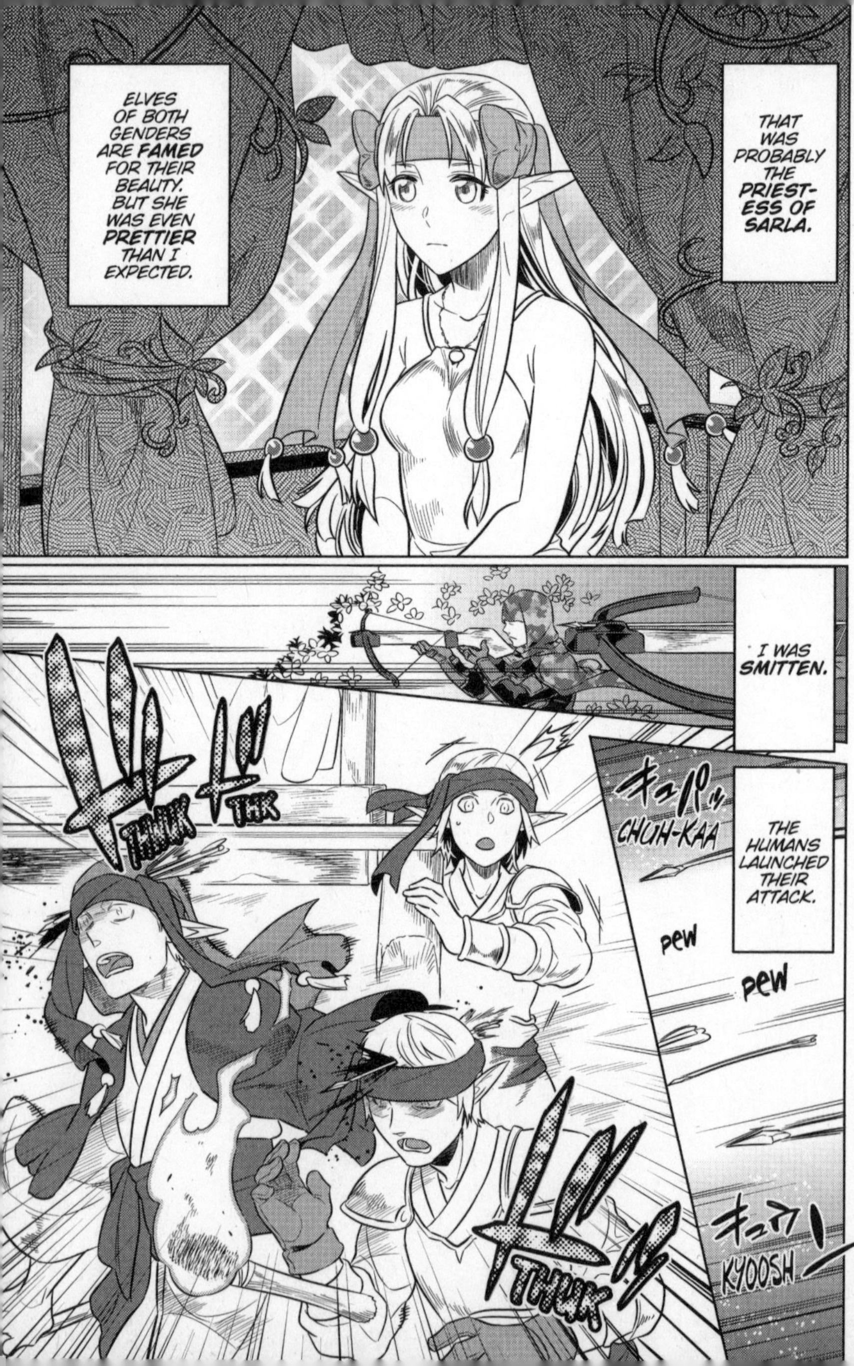
THAT WAS PROBABLY THE PRIESTESS OF SARLA.
ELVES OF BOTH GENDERS ARE FAMED FOR THEIR BEAUTY. BUT SHE WAS EVEN PRETTIER THAN I EXPECTED.
I WAS SMITTEN.
THE HUMANS LAUNCHED THEIR ATTACK.
CHUH-KAA
THK
THUNK
pew
pew
KYOOSH
THUNK

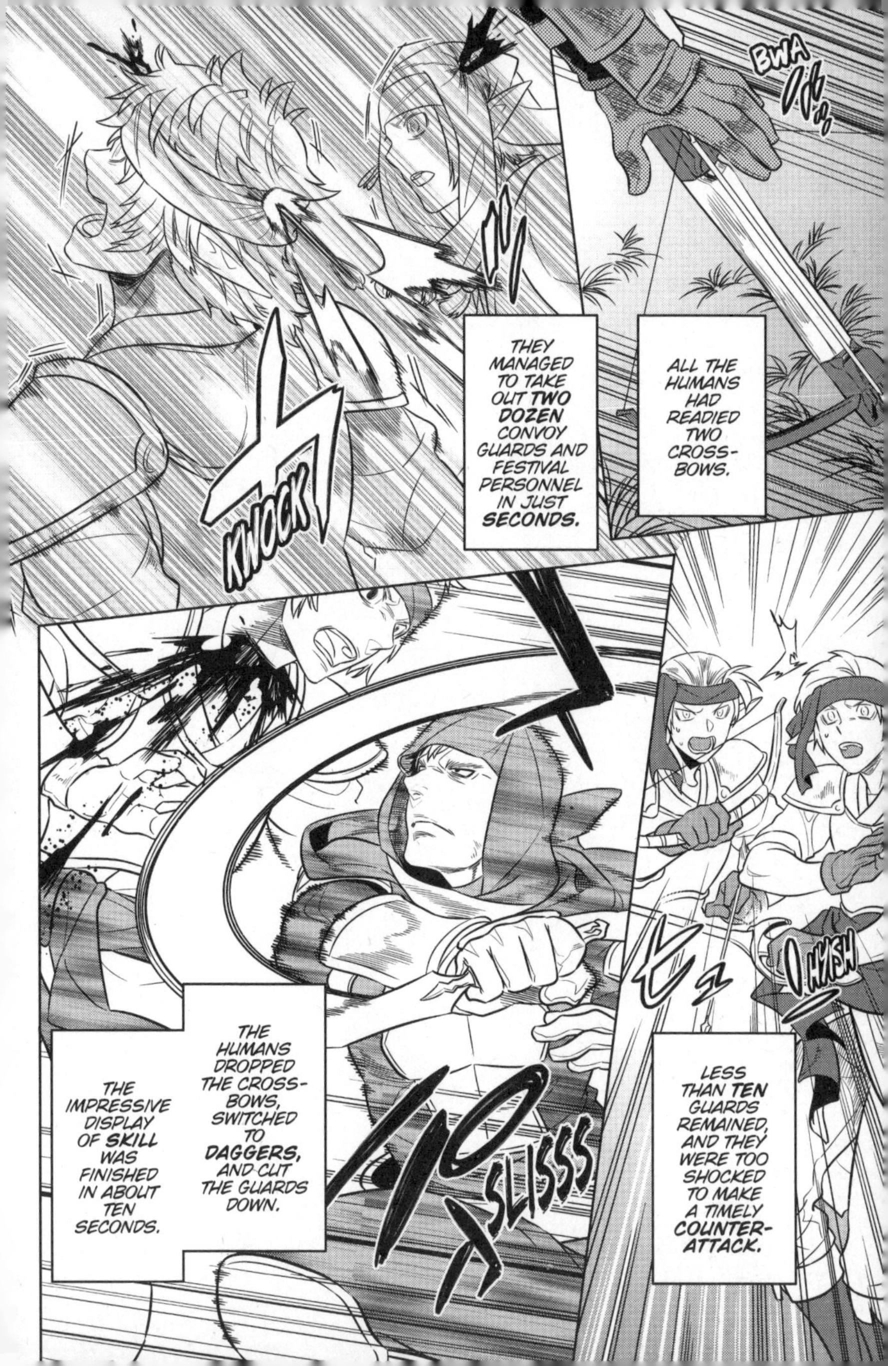
BWA
ALL THE HUMANS HAD READIED TWO CROSS-BOWS.
KWOCK
THEY MANAGED TO TAKE OUT **TWO DOZEN** CONVOY GUARDS AND FESTIVAL PERSONNEL IN JUST **SECONDS.**
HYISH
LESS THAN **TEN** GUARDS REMAINED, AND THEY WERE TOO SHOCKED TO MAKE A TIMELY **COUNTER-ATTACK.**
SLISSS
THE HUMANS DROPPED THE CROSS-BOWS, SWITCHED TO **DAGGERS,** AND CUT THE GUARDS DOWN.
THE IMPRESSIVE DISPLAY OF **SKILL** WAS FINISHED IN ABOUT TEN SECONDS.

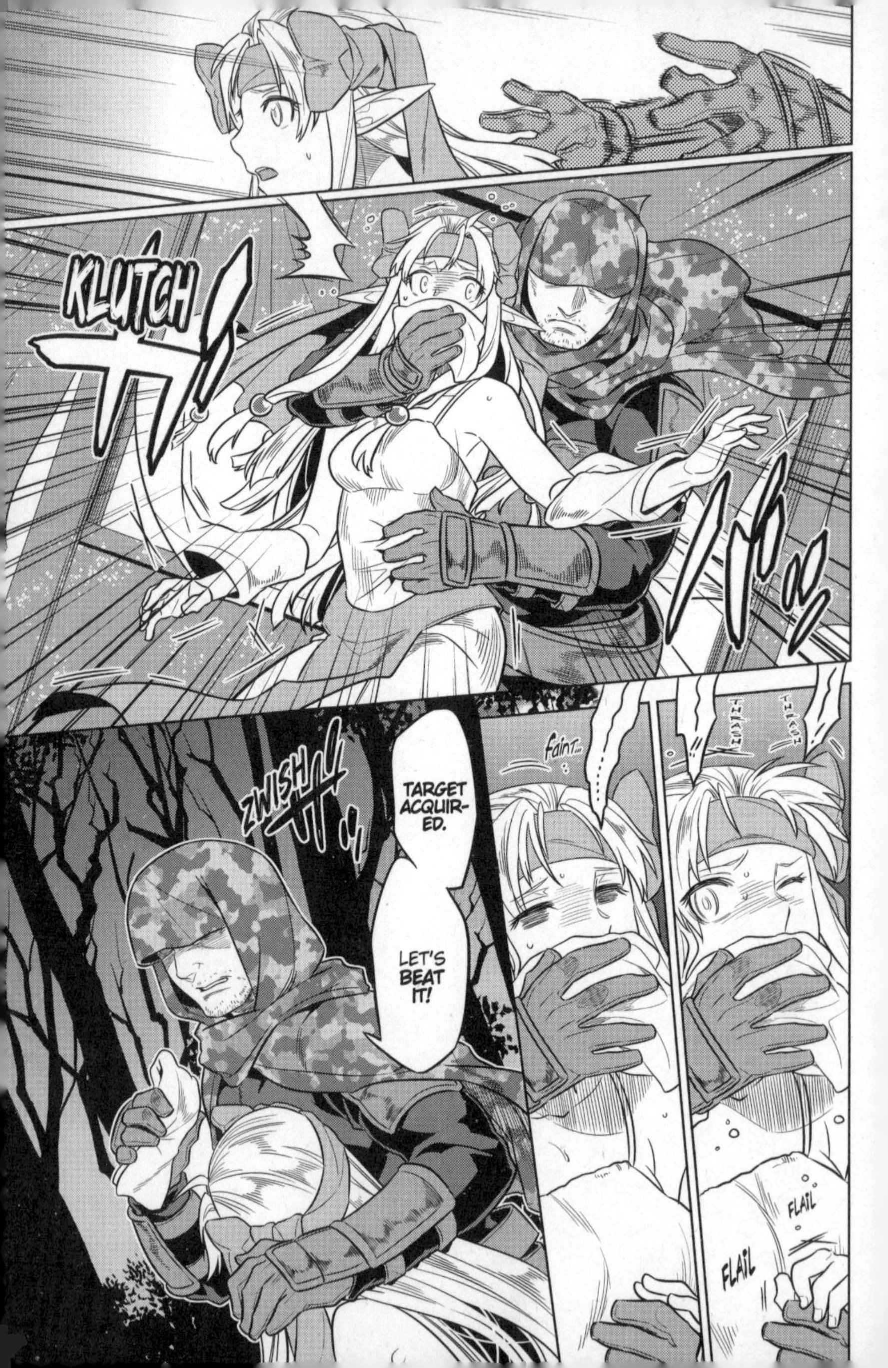
KLUTCH
THRASH
THRASH
FLAIL
faint...
FLAIL
TARGET ACQUIR-ED.
LET'S BEAT IT!
ZWISH

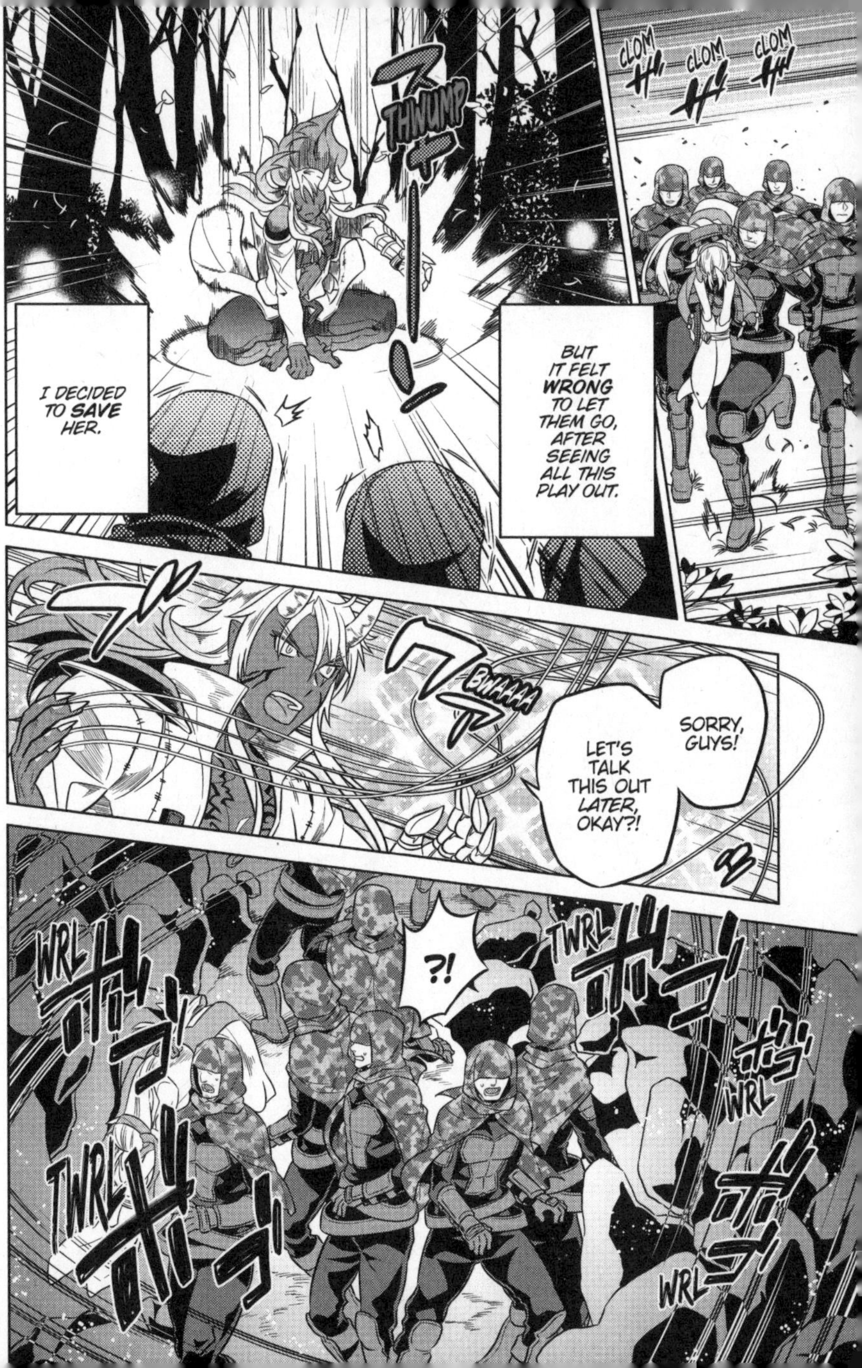
CLOM
CLOM
CLOM
THWUMP
BUT IT FELT WRONG TO LET THEM GO, AFTER SEEING ALL THIS PLAY OUT.
I DECIDED TO SAVE HER.
BWAAAA
SORRY, GUYS!
LET'S TALK THIS OUT LATER, OKAY?!
TWRL
WRL
WRL
?!
WRL
TWRL

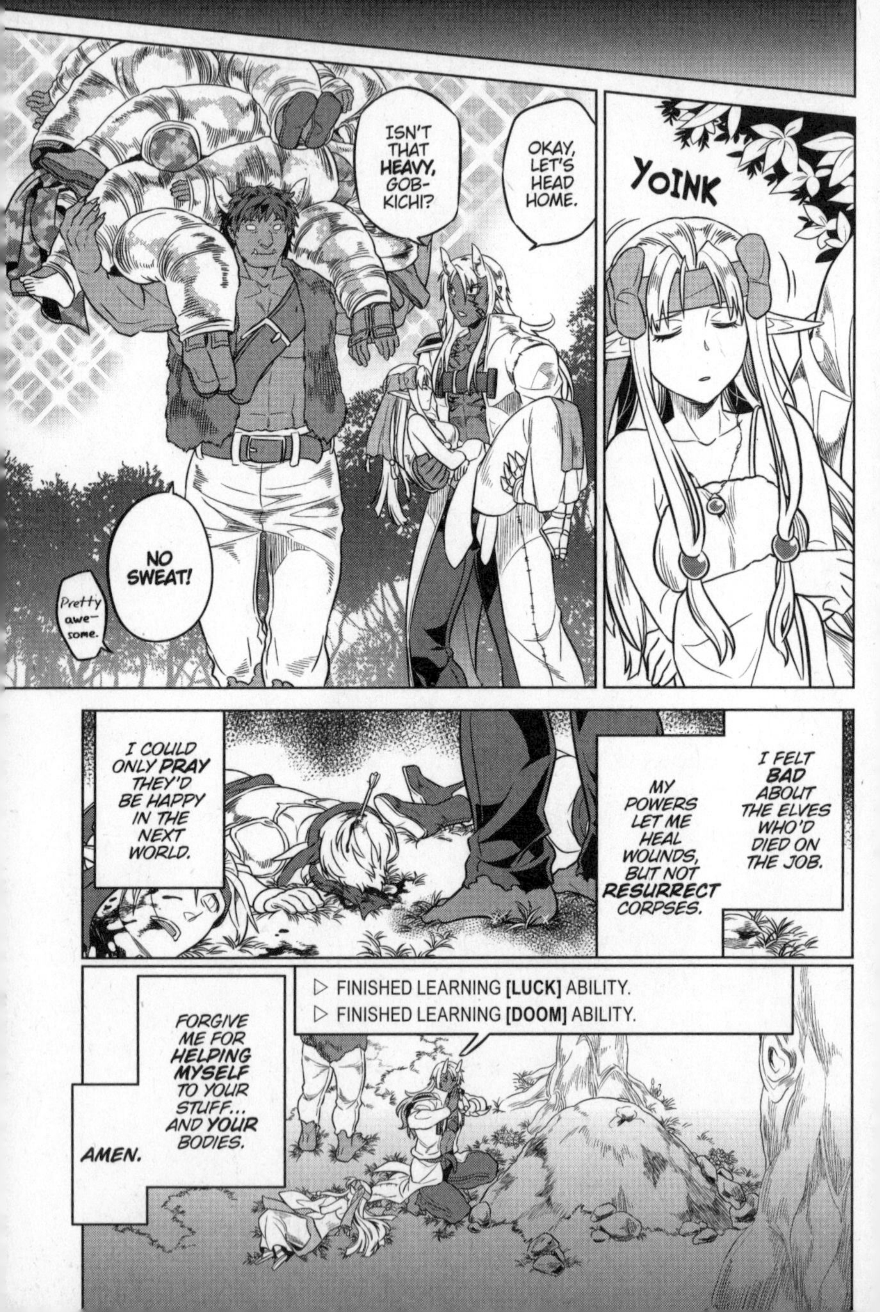
YOINK
OKAY, LET'S HEAD HOME.
ISN'T THAT HEAVY, GOB-KICHI?
NO SWEAT!
Pretty awe-some.
I FELT BAD ABOUT THE ELVES WHO'D DIED ON THE JOB.
MY POWERS LET ME HEAL WOUNDS, BUT NOT RESURRECT CORPSES.
I COULD ONLY PRAY THEY'D BE HAPPY IN THE NEXT WORLD.
▷ FINISHED LEARNING [LUCK] ABILITY.
▷ FINISHED LEARNING [DOOM] ABILITY.
FORGIVE ME FOR HELPING MYSELF TO YOUR STUFF... AND YOUR BODIES.
AMEN.

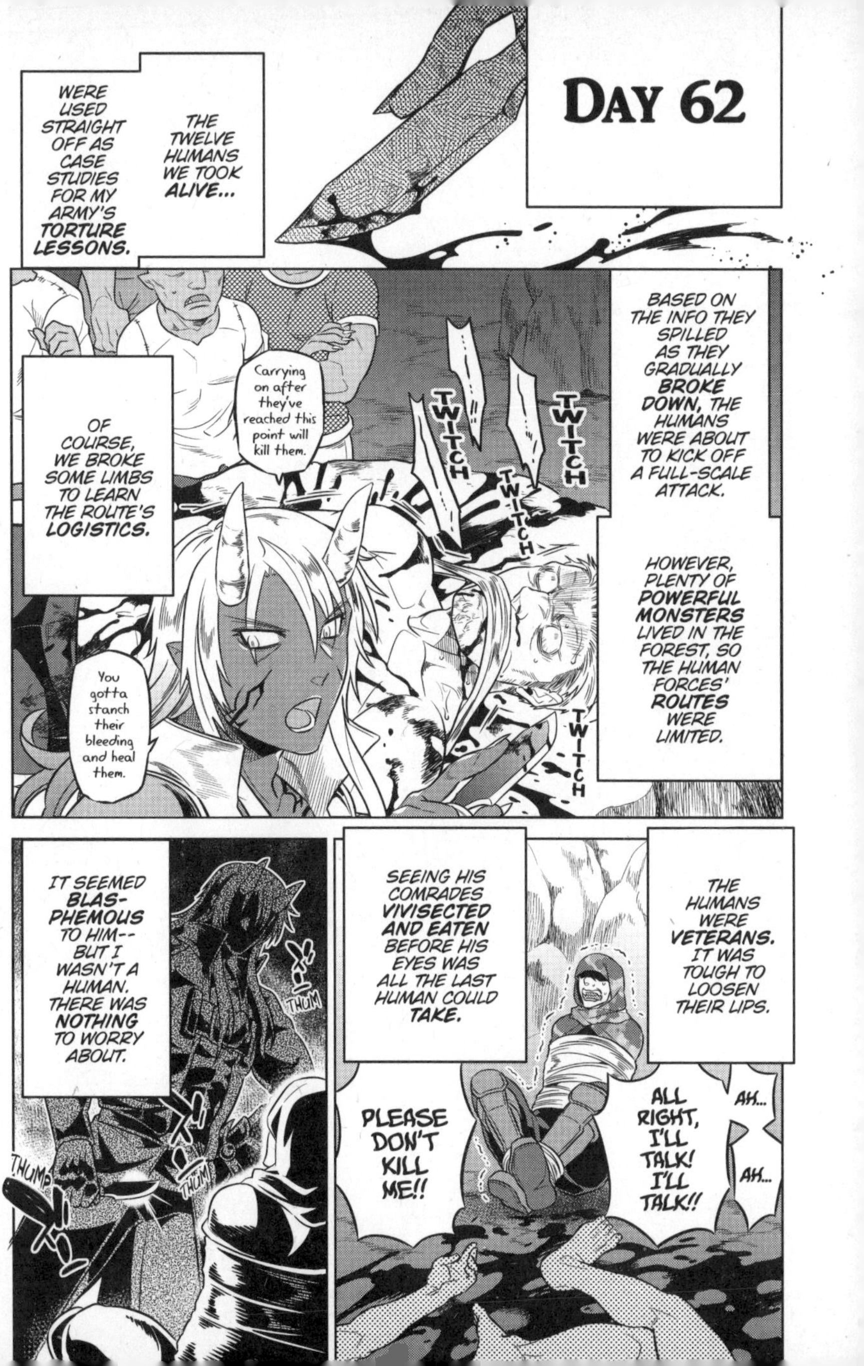
DAY 62
THE TWELVE HUMANS WE TOOK ALIVE...
WERE USED STRAIGHT OFF AS CASE STUDIES FOR MY ARMY'S TORTURE LESSONS.
BASED ON THE INFO THEY SPILLED AS THEY GRADUALLY BROKE DOWN, THE HUMANS WERE ABOUT TO KICK OFF A FULL-SCALE ATTACK.
HOWEVER, PLENTY OF POWERFUL MONSTERS LIVED IN THE FOREST, SO THE HUMAN FORCES' ROUTES WERE LIMITED.
TWITCH
TWITCH
TWITCH
TWITCH
Carrying on after they've reached this point will kill them.
OF COURSE, WE BROKE SOME LIMBS TO LEARN THE ROUTE'S LOGISTICS.
You gotta stanch their bleeding and heal them.
THE HUMANS WERE VETERANS. IT WAS TOUGH TO LOOSEN THEIR LIPS.
SEEING HIS COMRADES VIVISECTED AND EATEN BEFORE HIS EYES WAS ALL THE LAST HUMAN COULD TAKE.
AH...
AH...
ALL RIGHT, I'LL TALK! I'LL TALK!!
PLEASE DON'T KILL ME!!
IT SEEMED BLAS-PHEMOUS TO HIM-- BUT I WASN'T A HUMAN. THERE WAS NOTHING TO WORRY ABOUT.
THUM
THUM
THUMP

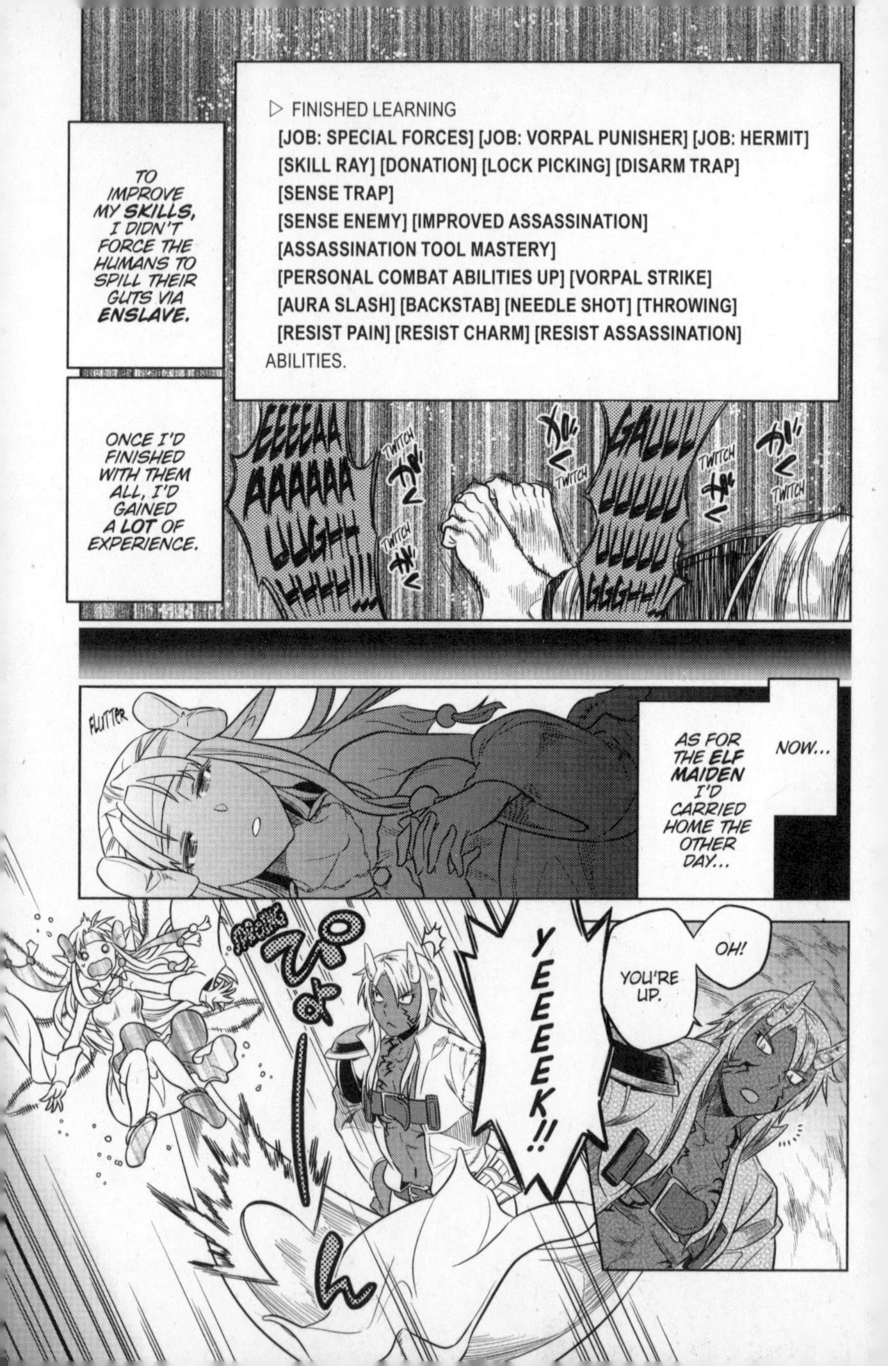

▷ FINISHED LEARNING
[JOB: SPECIAL FORCES] [JOB: VORPAL PUNISHER] [JOB: HERMIT]
[SKILL RAY] [DONATION] [LOCK PICKING] [DISARM TRAP]
[SENSE TRAP]
[SENSE ENEMY] [IMPROVED ASSASSINATION]
[ASSASSINATION TOOL MASTERY]
[PERSONAL COMBAT ABILITIES UP] [VORPAL STRIKE]
[AURA SLASH] [BACKSTAB] [NEEDLE SHOT] [THROWING]
[RESIST PAIN] [RESIST CHARM] [RESIST ASSASSINATION]
ABILITIES.
TO IMPROVE MY SKILLS, I DIDN'T FORCE THE HUMANS TO SPILL THEIR GUTS VIA ENSLAVE.
ONCE I'D FINISHED WITH THEM ALL, I'D GAINED A LOT OF EXPERIENCE.
TWITCH
TWITCH
TWITCH
TWITCH
GAUUUUUUUUUUGGGH!!
TWITCH
EEEEAAAAAAAAUUGH!!!
NOW...
AS FOR THE ELF MAIDEN I'D CARRIED HOME THE OTHER DAY...
FLUTTER
OH!
YOU'RE UP.
YEEEEEK!!

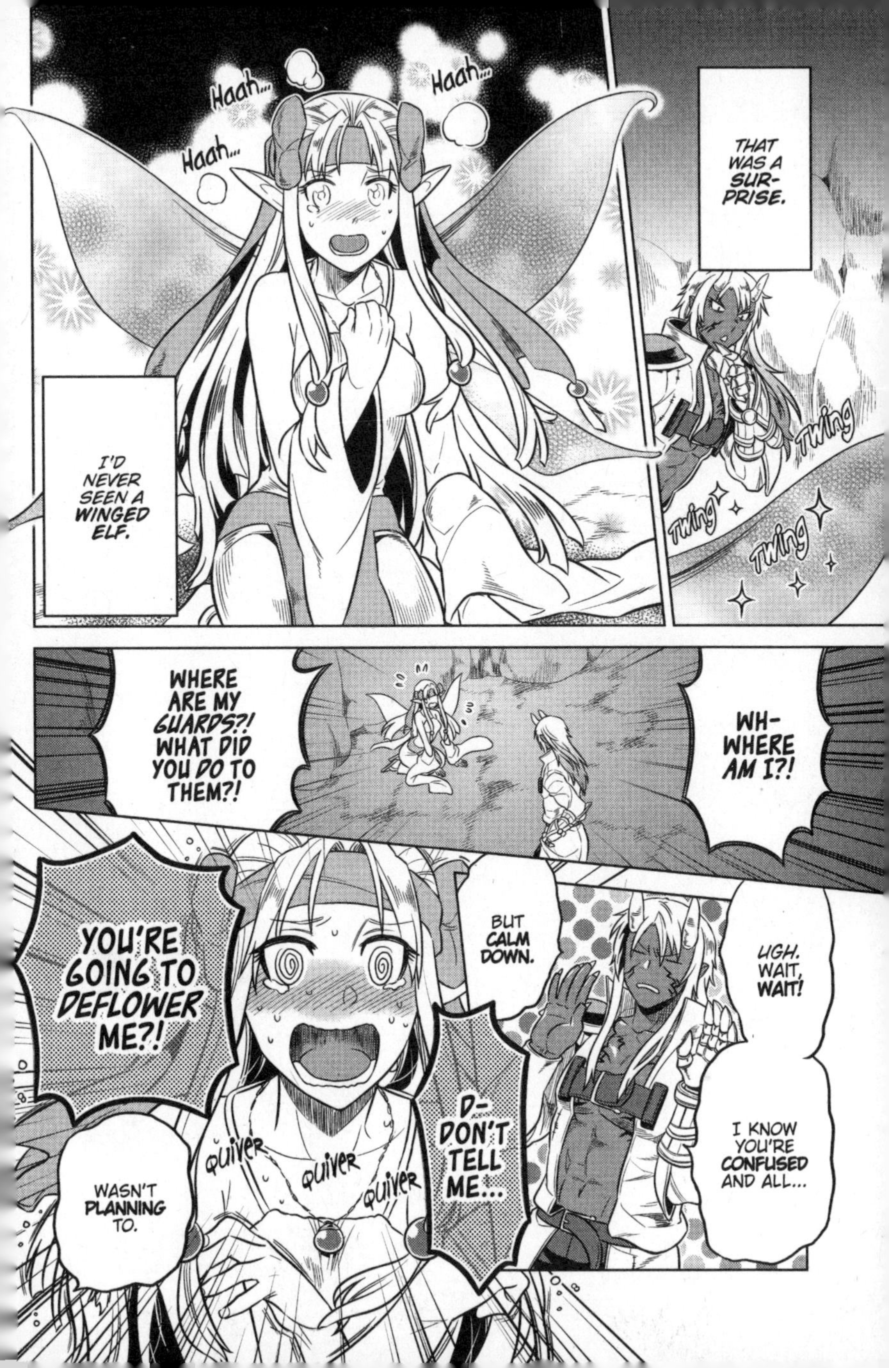

THAT WAS A SUR-PRISE.
Twing
Twing
Twing
Haah...
Haah...
Haah...
I'D NEVER SEEN A WINGED ELF.
WH-WHERE AM I?!
WHERE ARE MY GUARDS?! WHAT DID YOU DO TO THEM?!
UGH. WAIT, WAIT!
BUT CALM DOWN.
I KNOW YOU'RE CONFUSED AND ALL...
D-DON'T TELL ME...
YOU'RE GOING TO DEFLOWER ME?!
quiver
quiver
quiver
WASN'T PLANNING TO.

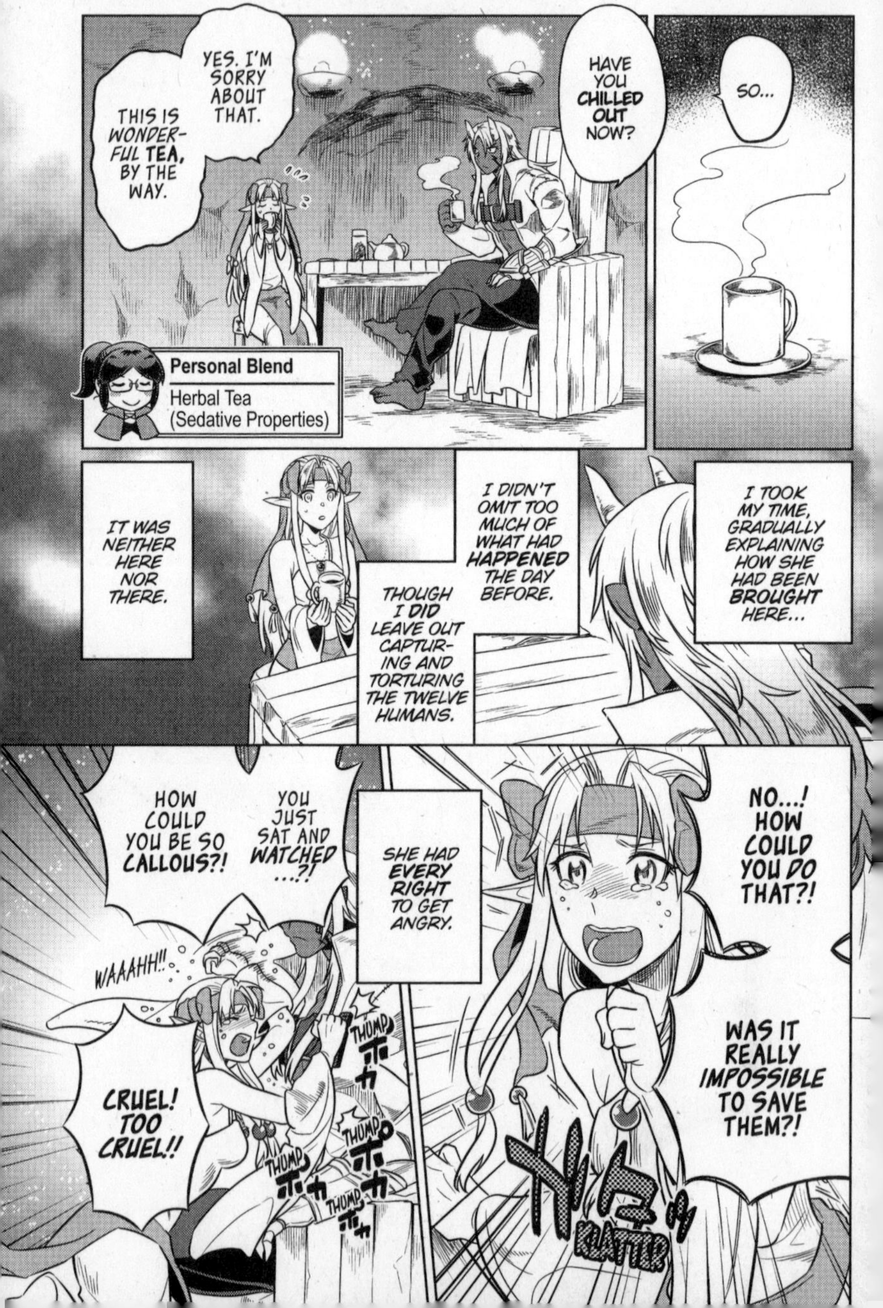
SO...
HAVE YOU CHILLED OUT NOW?
YES. I'M SORRY ABOUT THAT.
THIS IS WONDERFUL TEA, BY THE WAY.
Personal Blend
Herbal Tea (Sedative Properties)
I TOOK MY TIME, GRADUALLY EXPLAINING HOW SHE HAD BEEN BROUGHT HERE...
I DIDN'T OMIT TOO MUCH OF WHAT HAD HAPPENED THE DAY BEFORE.
THOUGH I DID LEAVE OUT CAPTURING AND TORTURING THE TWELVE HUMANS.
IT WAS NEITHER HERE NOR THERE.
NO...! HOW COULD YOU DO THAT?!
WAS IT REALLY IMPOSSIBLE TO SAVE THEM?!
KLATTER
SHE HAD EVERY RIGHT TO GET ANGRY.
YOU JUST SAT AND WATCHED...?!
HOW COULD YOU BE SO CALLOUS?!
WAAAHH!!
THUMP
THUMP
THUMP
THUMP
CRUEL! TOO CRUEL!!

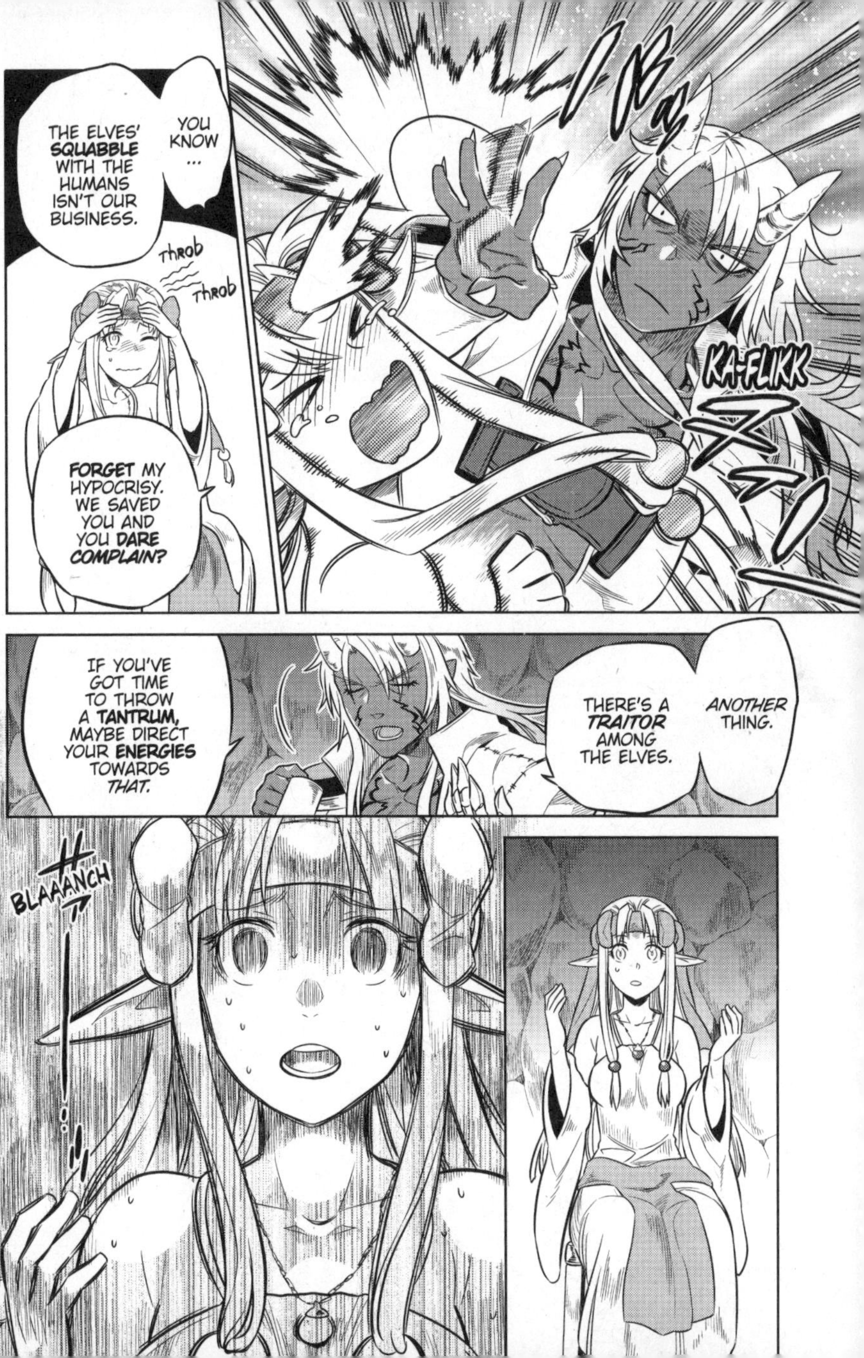
KA-FLIKK
YOU KNOW ...
THE ELVES' SQUABBLE WITH THE HUMANS ISN'T OUR BUSINESS.
Throb
Throb
FORGET MY HYPOCRISY. WE SAVED YOU AND YOU DARE COMPLAIN?
ANOTHER THING.
THERE'S A TRAITOR AMONG THE ELVES.
IF YOU'VE GOT TIME TO THROW A TANTRUM, MAYBE DIRECT YOUR ENERGIES TOWARDS THAT.
BLAAANCH

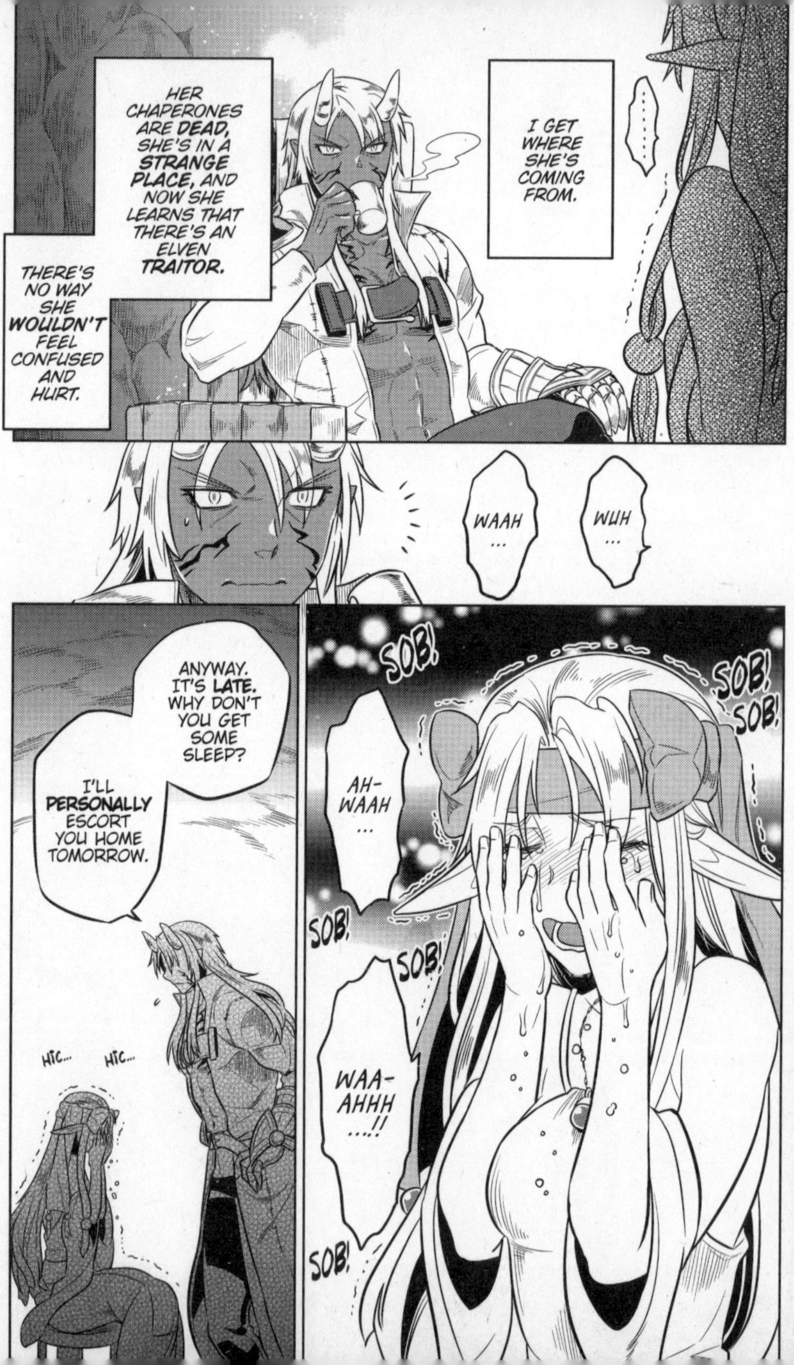
......
I GET WHERE SHE'S COMING FROM.
HER CHAPERONES ARE **DEAD**, SHE'S IN A **STRANGE PLACE**, AND NOW SHE LEARNS THAT THERE'S AN ELVEN **TRAITOR**.
THERE'S NO WAY SHE **WOULDN'T** FEEL CONFUSED AND HURT.
WUH ...
WAAH ...
SOB! SOB!
SOB!
AH-WAAH ...
SOB!
SOB!
WAA-AHHH .....!!
SOB!
ANYWAY. IT'S **LATE**. WHY DON'T YOU GET SOME SLEEP?
I'LL **PERSONALLY** ESCORT YOU HOME TOMORROW.
HIC... HIC...

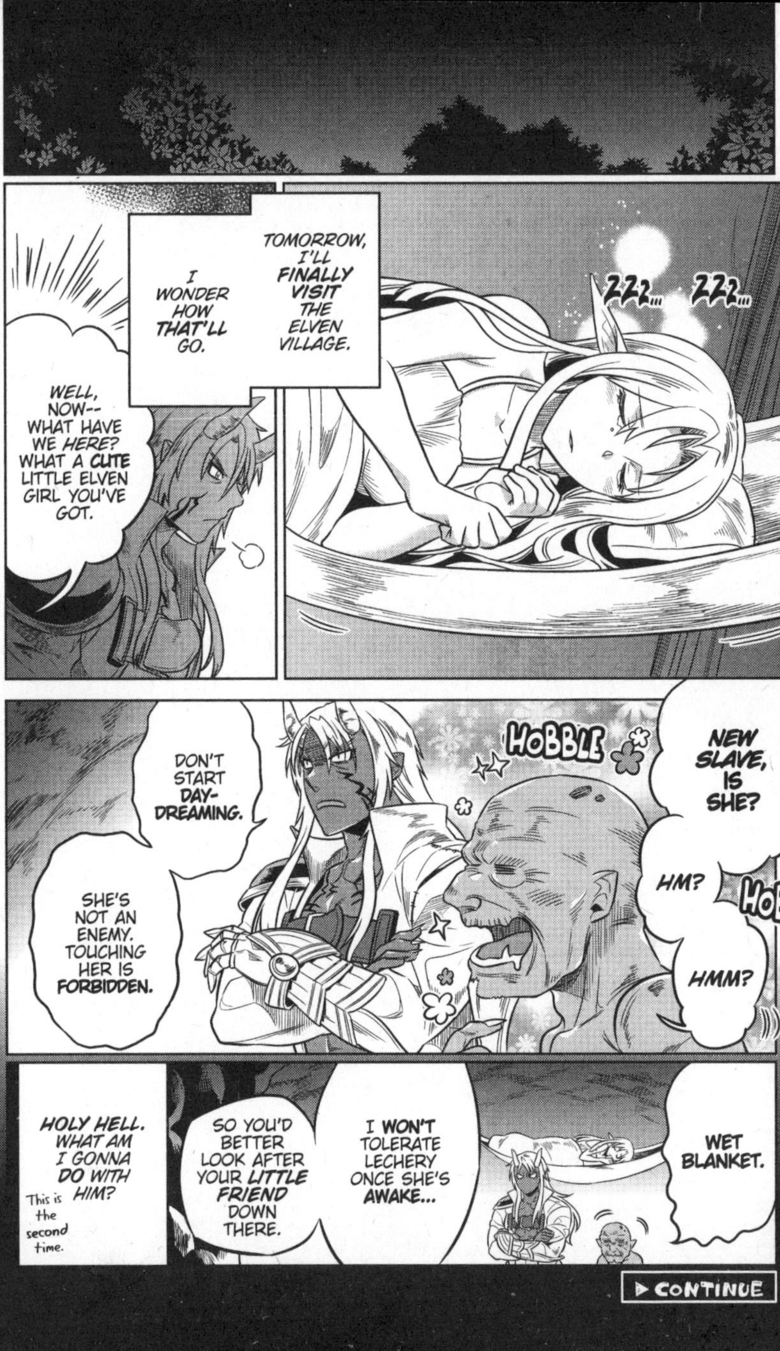
ZZZ... ZZZ...
TOMORROW, I'LL FINALLY VISIT THE ELVEN VILLAGE.
I WONDER HOW THAT'LL GO.
WELL, NOW-- WHAT HAVE WE HERE? WHAT A CUTE LITTLE ELVEN GIRL YOU'VE GOT.
NEW SLAVE, IS SHE?
HOBBLE
HM?
HOBBLE
HMM?
DON'T START DAY-DREAMING.
SHE'S NOT AN ENEMY. TOUCHING HER IS FORBIDDEN.
WET BLANKET.
I WON'T TOLERATE LECHERY ONCE SHE'S AWAKE...
SO YOU'D BETTER LOOK AFTER YOUR LITTLE FRIEND DOWN THERE.
HOLY HELL. WHAT AM I GONNA DO WITH HIM?
This is the second time.
CONTINUE

Day 63

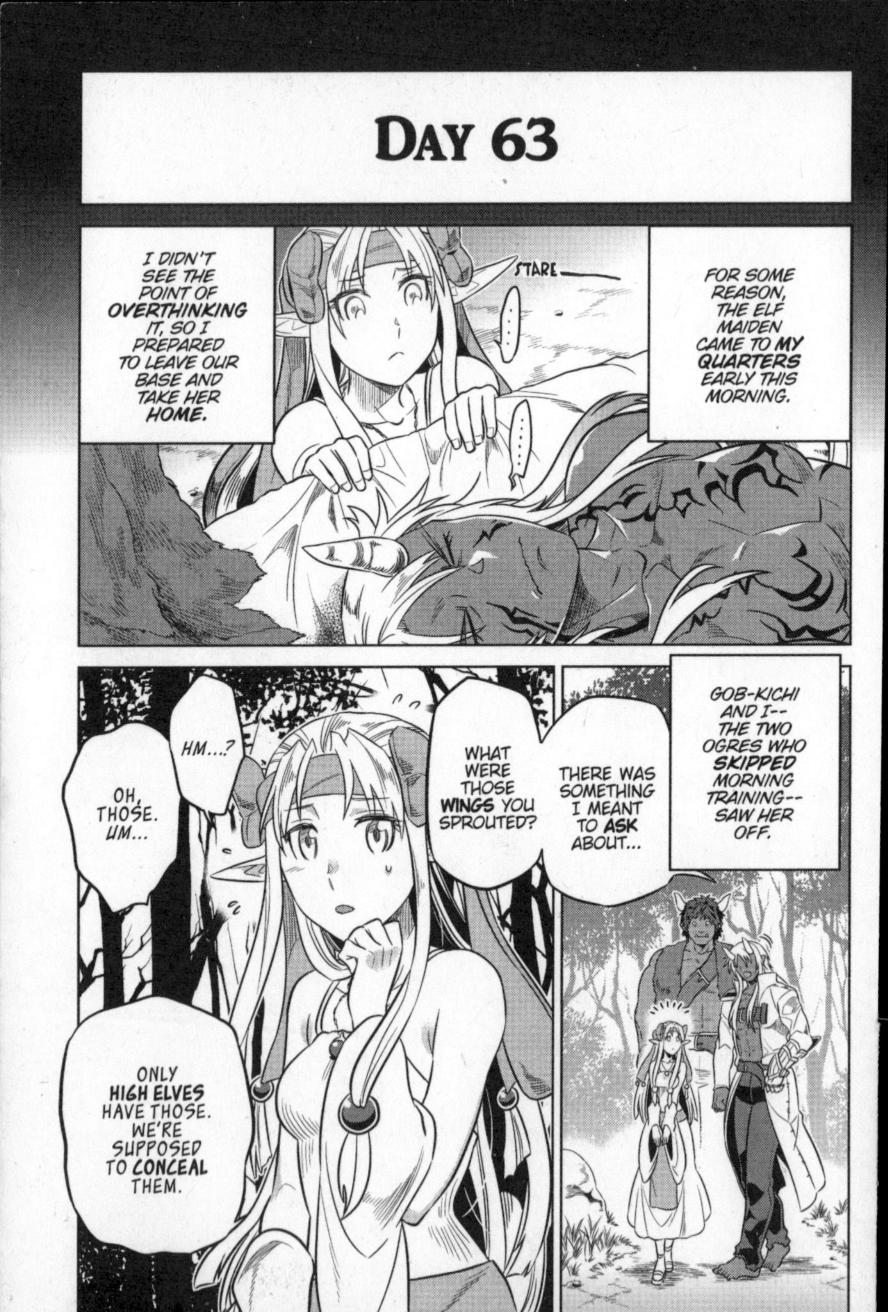
FOR SOME REASON, THE ELF MAIDEN CAME TO MY QUARTERS EARLY THIS MORNING.
STARE
...
...
I DIDN'T SEE THE POINT OF OVERTHINKING IT, SO I PREPARED TO LEAVE OUR BASE AND TAKE HER HOME.
GOB-KICHI AND I-- THE TWO OGRES WHO SKIPPED MORNING TRAINING-- SAW HER OFF.
THERE WAS SOMETHING I MEANT TO ASK ABOUT...
WHAT WERE THOSE WINGS YOU SPROUTED?
HM...?
OH, THOSE. UM...
ONLY HIGH ELVES HAVE THOSE. WE'RE SUPPOSED TO CONCEAL THEM.

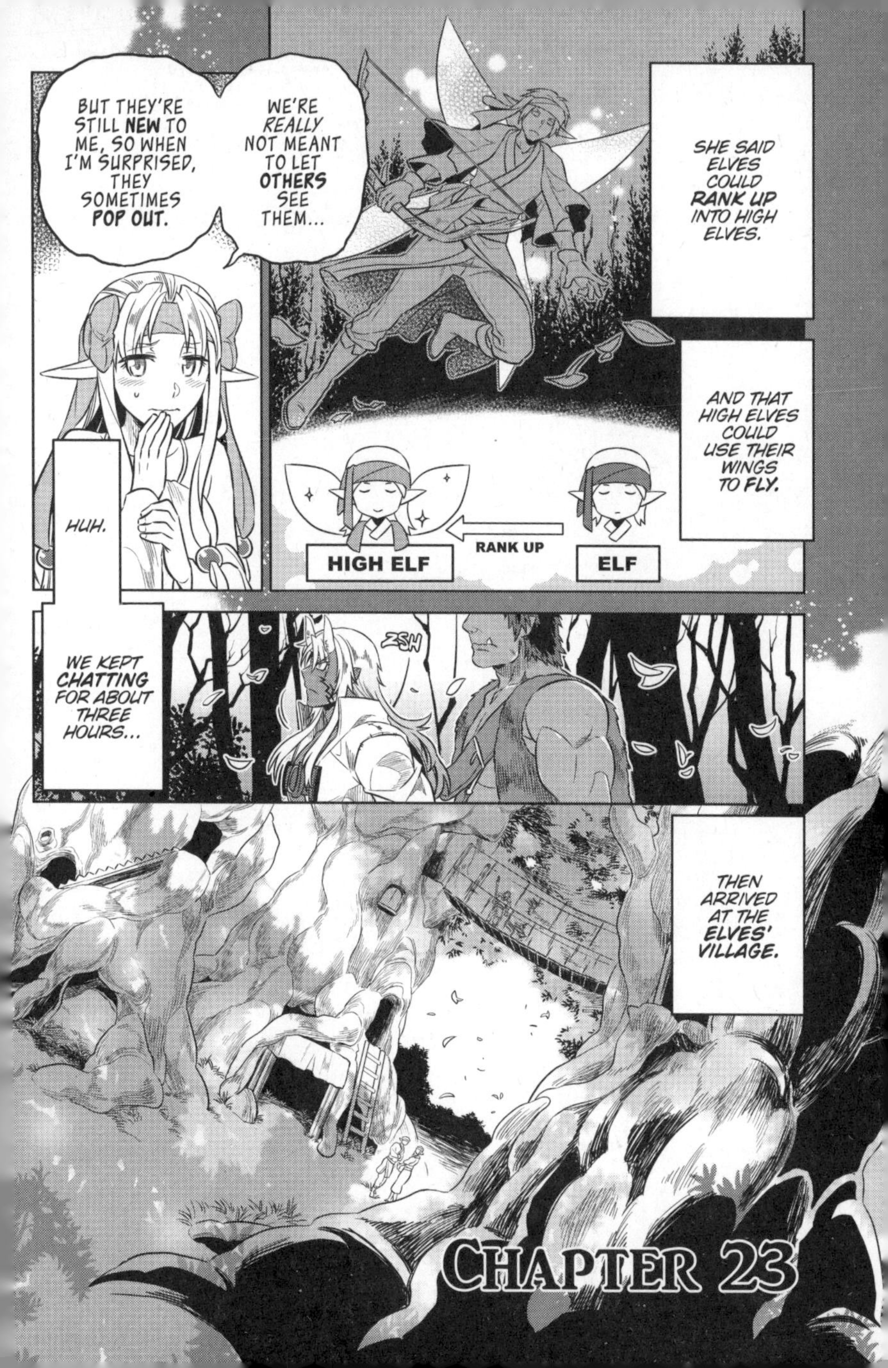
SHE SAID ELVES COULD RANK UP INTO HIGH ELVES.
AND THAT HIGH ELVES COULD USE THEIR WINGS TO FLY.
ELF
RANK UP
HIGH ELF
WE'RE REALLY NOT MEANT TO LET OTHERS SEE THEM...
BUT THEY'RE STILL NEW TO ME, SO WHEN I'M SURPRISED, THEY SOMETIMES POP OUT.
HUH.
ZSH
WE KEPT CHATTING FOR ABOUT THREE HOURS...
THEN ARRIVED AT THE ELVES' VILLAGE.
CHAPTER 23

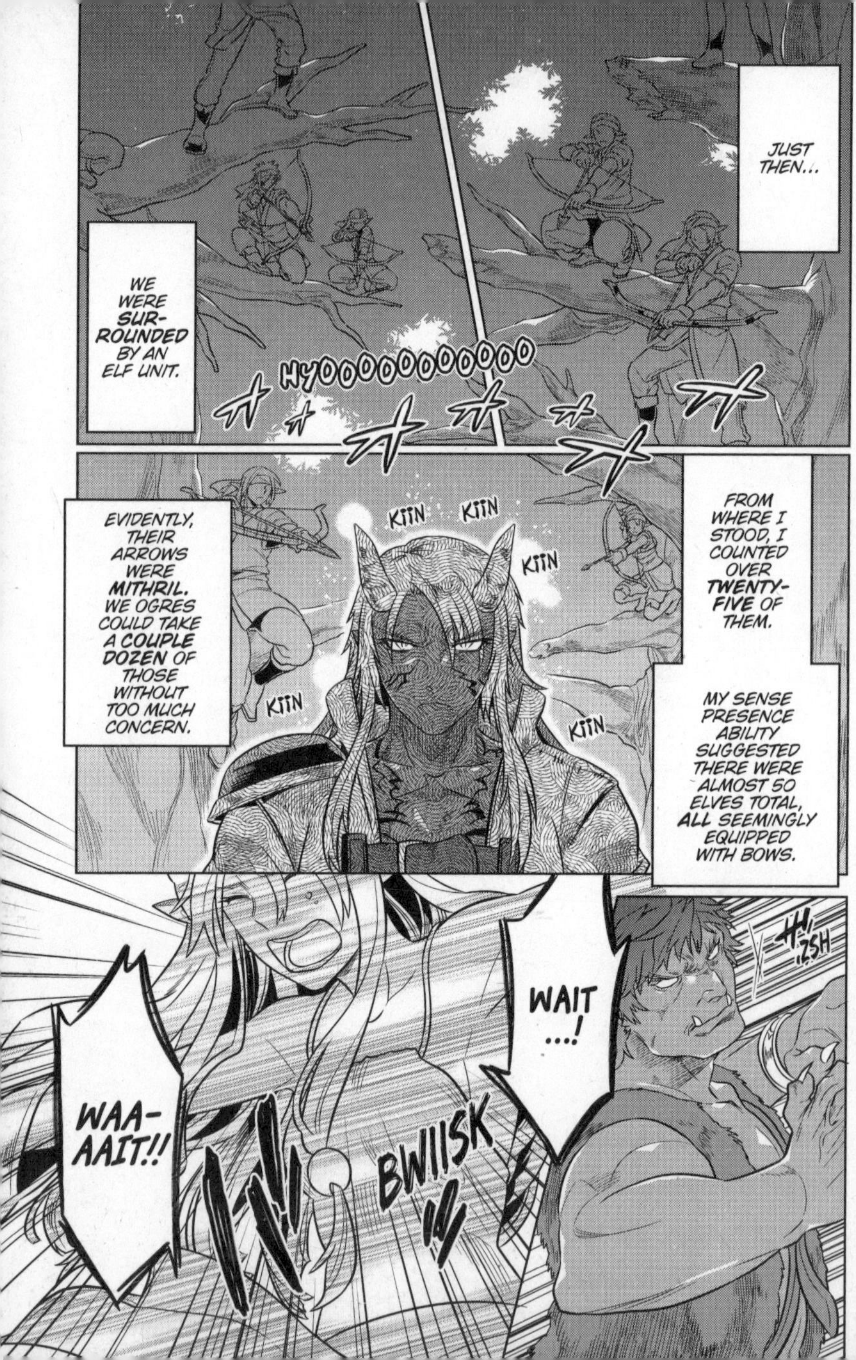
JUST THEN...
WE WERE SURROUNDED BY AN ELF UNIT.
HYOOOOOOOOOOO
FROM WHERE I STOOD, I COUNTED OVER TWENTY-FIVE OF THEM.
MY SENSE PRESENCE ABILITY SUGGESTED THERE WERE ALMOST 50 ELVES TOTAL, ALL SEEMINGLY EQUIPPED WITH BOWS.
KIIN KIIN
KIIN
KIIN
KIIN
EVIDENTLY, THEIR ARROWS WERE MITHRIL. WE OGRES COULD TAKE A COUPLE DOZEN OF THOSE WITHOUT TOO MUCH CONCERN.
ZSH
WAIT ...!
WAA-AAIT!!
BWIISK

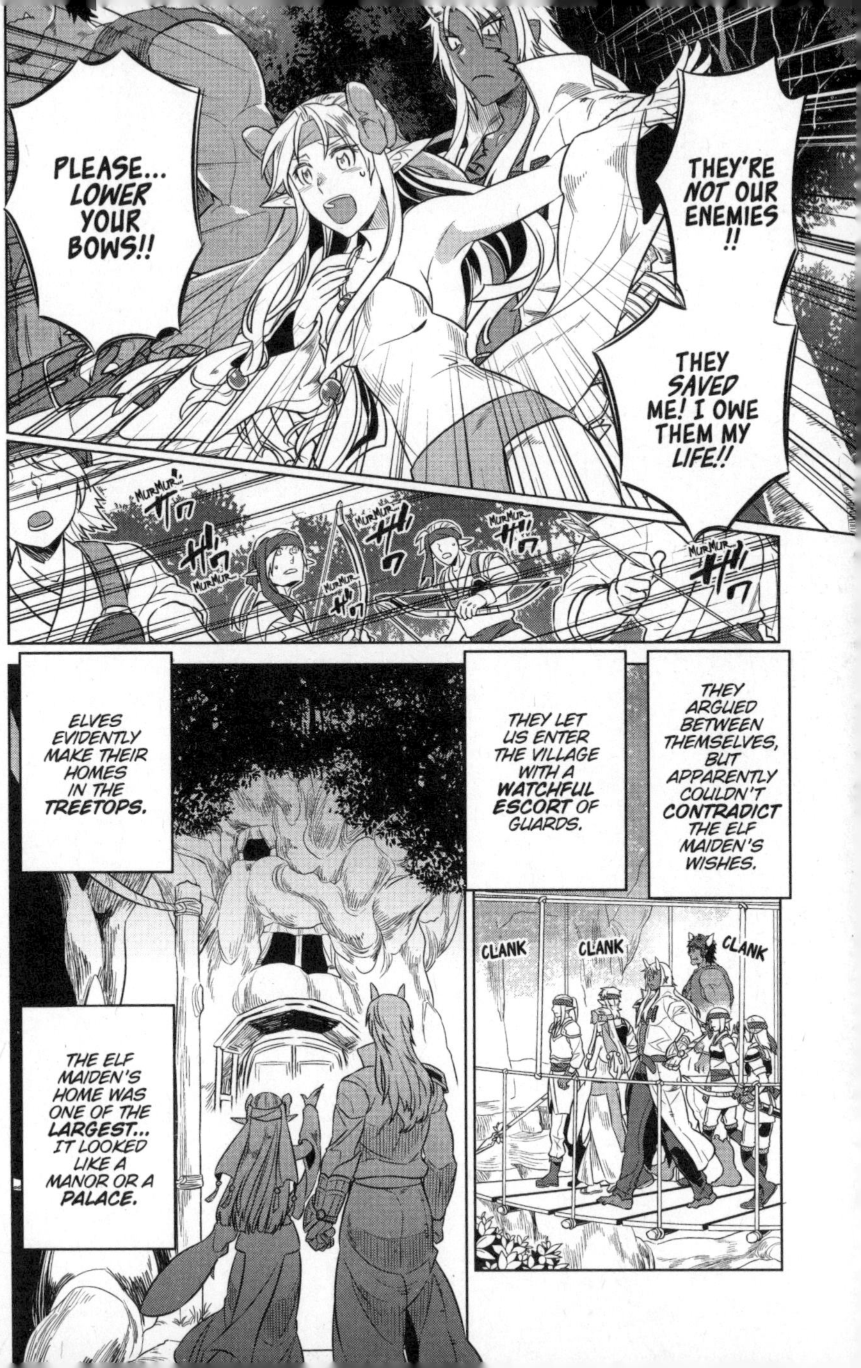

THEY'RE NOT OUR ENEMIES!!
THEY SAVED ME! I OWE THEM MY LIFE!!
PLEASE... LOWER YOUR BOWS!!
MURMUR... ザワ
MURMUR... ザワ
MURMUR... ザワ
MURMUR... ザワ
MURMUR... ザワ
THEY ARGUED BETWEEN THEMSELVES, BUT APPARENTLY COULDN'T CONTRADICT THE ELF MAIDEN'S WISHES.
THEY LET US ENTER THE VILLAGE WITH A WATCHFUL ESCORT OF GUARDS.
CLANK
CLANK
CLANK
ELVES EVIDENTLY MAKE THEIR HOMES IN THE TREETOPS.
THE ELF MAIDEN'S HOME WAS ONE OF THE LARGEST... IT LOOKED LIKE A MANOR OR A PALACE.

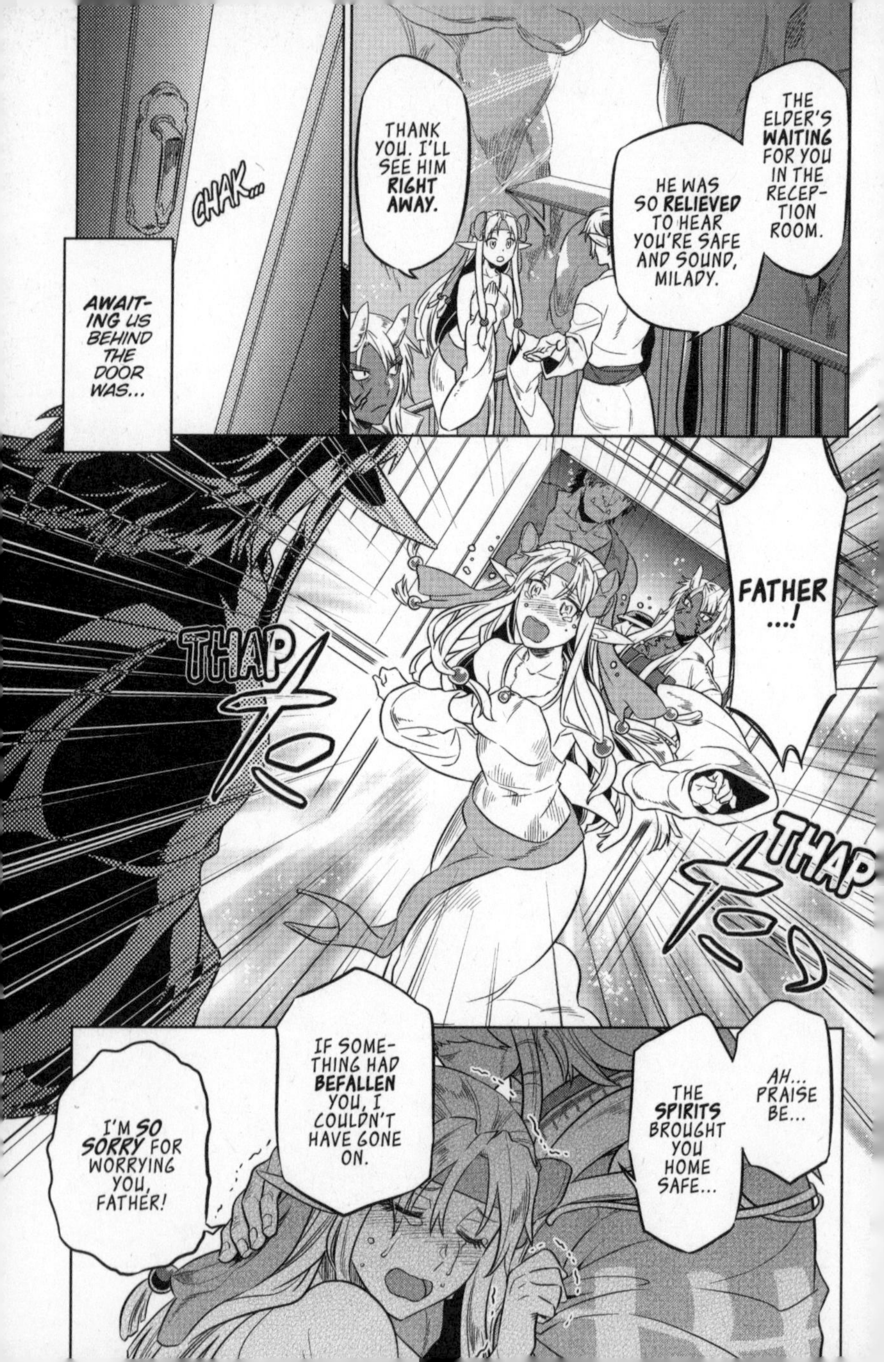
THE ELDER'S WAITING FOR YOU IN THE RECEPTION ROOM.
HE WAS SO RELIEVED TO HEAR YOU'RE SAFE AND SOUND, MILADY.
THANK YOU. I'LL SEE HIM RIGHT AWAY.
CHAK...
AWAITING US BEHIND THE DOOR WAS...
FATHER ...!
THAP
THAP
AH... PRAISE BE...
THE SPIRITS BROUGHT YOU HOME SAFE...
IF SOMETHING HAD BEFALLEN YOU, I COULDN'T HAVE GONE ON.
I'M SO SORRY FOR WORRYING YOU, FATHER!

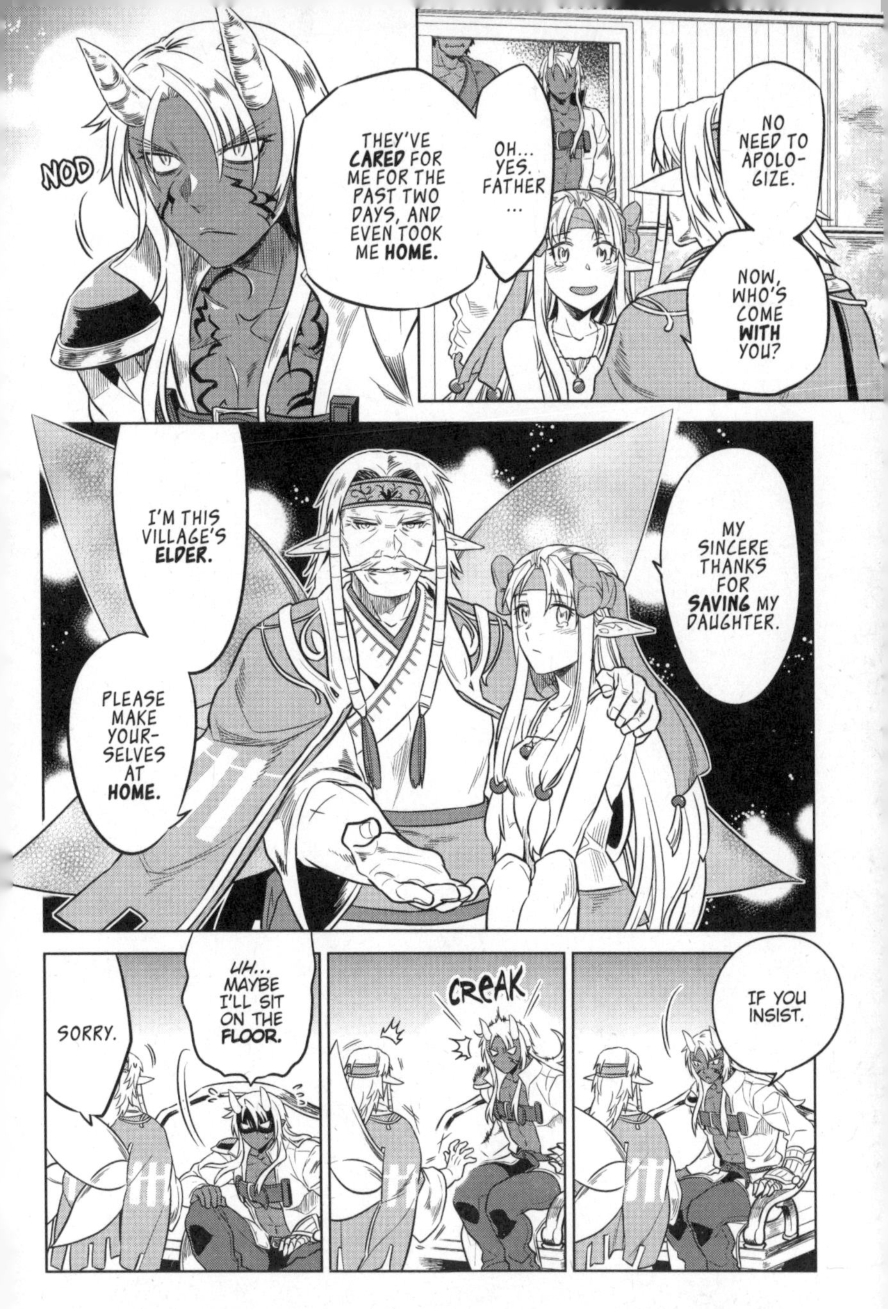
NO NEED TO APOLOGIZE.
NOW, WHO'S COME WITH YOU?
OH... YES. FATHER...
THEY'VE CARED FOR ME FOR THE PAST TWO DAYS, AND EVEN TOOK ME HOME.
NOD
MY SINCERE THANKS FOR SAVING MY DAUGHTER.
I'M THIS VILLAGE'S ELDER.
PLEASE MAKE YOURSELVES AT HOME.
IF YOU INSIST.
CREAK
UH... MAYBE I'LL SIT ON THE FLOOR.
SORRY.

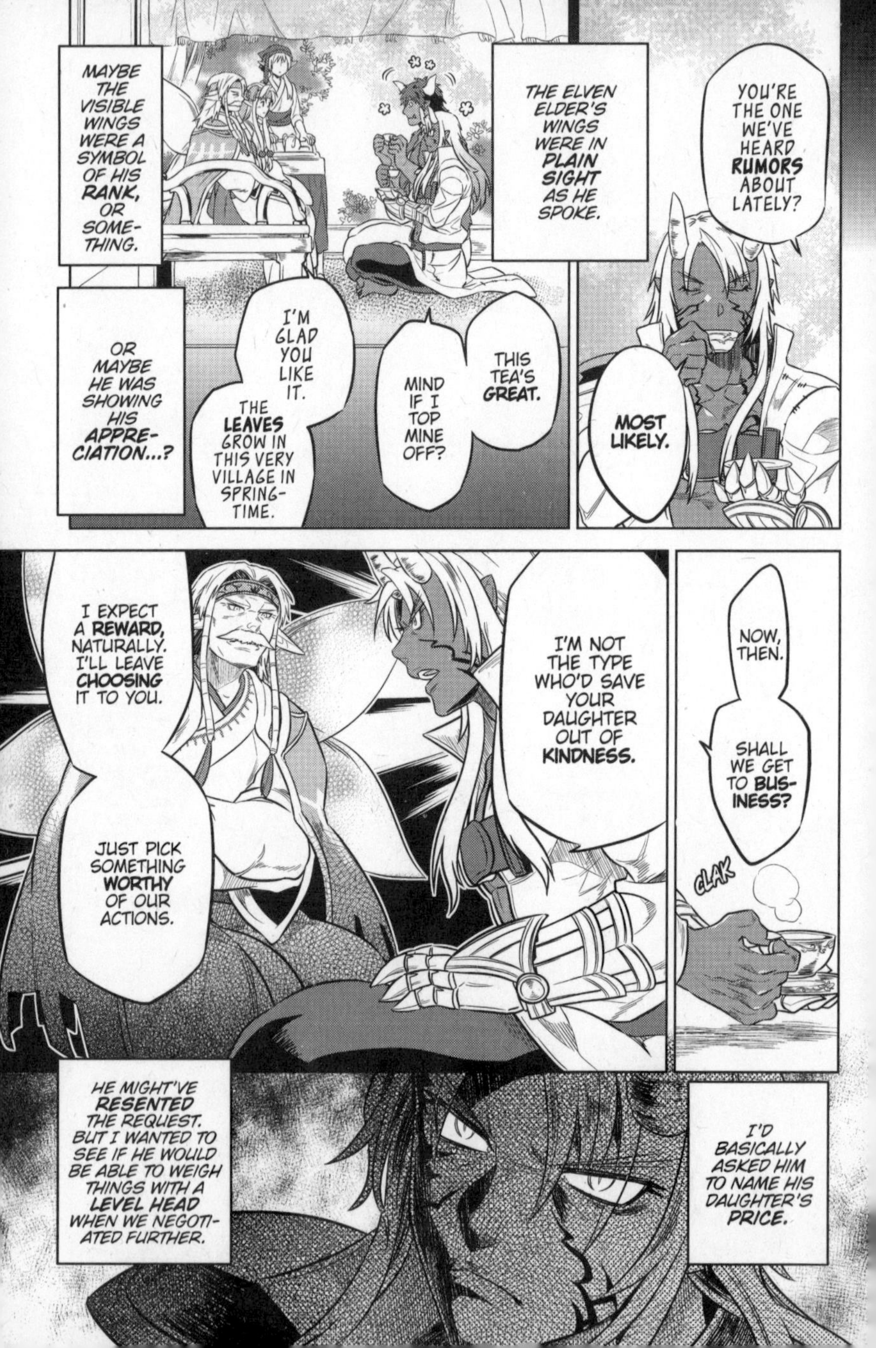
YOU'RE THE ONE WE'VE HEARD RUMORS ABOUT LATELY?
MOST LIKELY.
THE ELVEN ELDER'S WINGS WERE IN PLAIN SIGHT AS HE SPOKE.
MAYBE THE VISIBLE WINGS WERE A SYMBOL OF HIS RANK, OR SOME-THING.
THIS TEA'S GREAT.
MIND IF I TOP MINE OFF?
I'M GLAD YOU LIKE IT.
THE LEAVES GROW IN THIS VERY VILLAGE IN SPRING-TIME.
OR MAYBE HE WAS SHOWING HIS APPRE-CIATION...?
NOW, THEN.
SHALL WE GET TO BUS-INESS?
CLAK
I'M NOT THE TYPE WHO'D SAVE YOUR DAUGHTER OUT OF KINDNESS.
I EXPECT A REWARD, NATURALLY. I'LL LEAVE CHOOSING IT TO YOU.
JUST PICK SOMETHING WORTHY OF OUR ACTIONS.
I'D BASICALLY ASKED HIM TO NAME HIS DAUGHTER'S PRICE.
HE MIGHT'VE RESENTED THE REQUEST. BUT I WANTED TO SEE IF HE WOULD BE ABLE TO WEIGH THINGS WITH A LEVEL HEAD WHEN WE NEGOTI-ATED FURTHER.

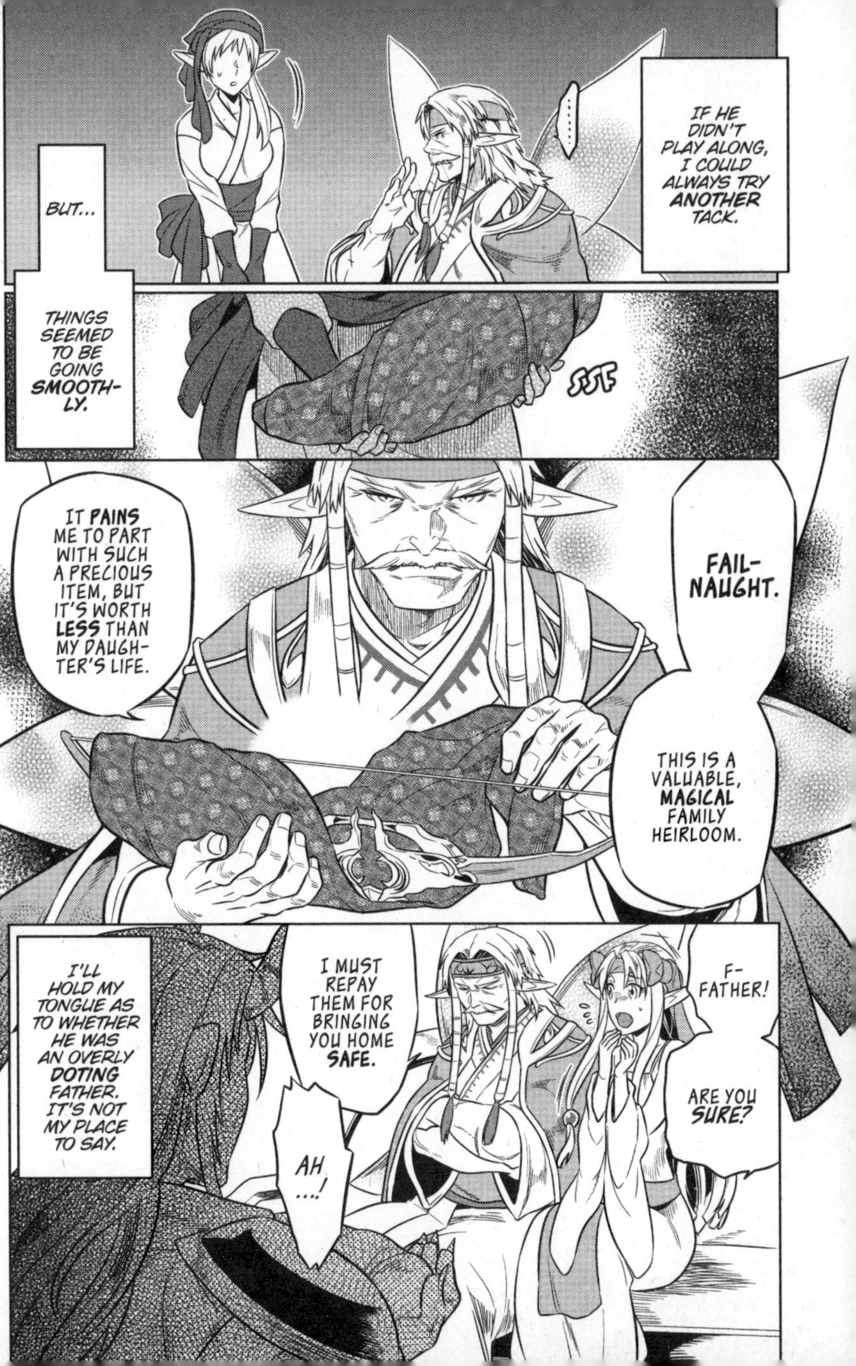
IF HE DIDN'T PLAY ALONG, I COULD ALWAYS TRY ANOTHER TACK.
...
BUT...
SSF
THINGS SEEMED TO BE GOING SMOOTH-LY.
FAIL-NAUGHT.
THIS IS A VALUABLE, MAGICAL FAMILY HEIRLOOM.
IT PAINS ME TO PART WITH SUCH A PRECIOUS ITEM, BUT IT'S WORTH LESS THAN MY DAUGH-TER'S LIFE.
F-FATHER!
ARE YOU SURE?
I MUST REPAY THEM FOR BRINGING YOU HOME SAFE.
AH ...!
I'LL HOLD MY TONGUE AS TO WHETHER HE WAS AN OVERLY DOTING FATHER. IT'S NOT MY PLACE TO SAY.

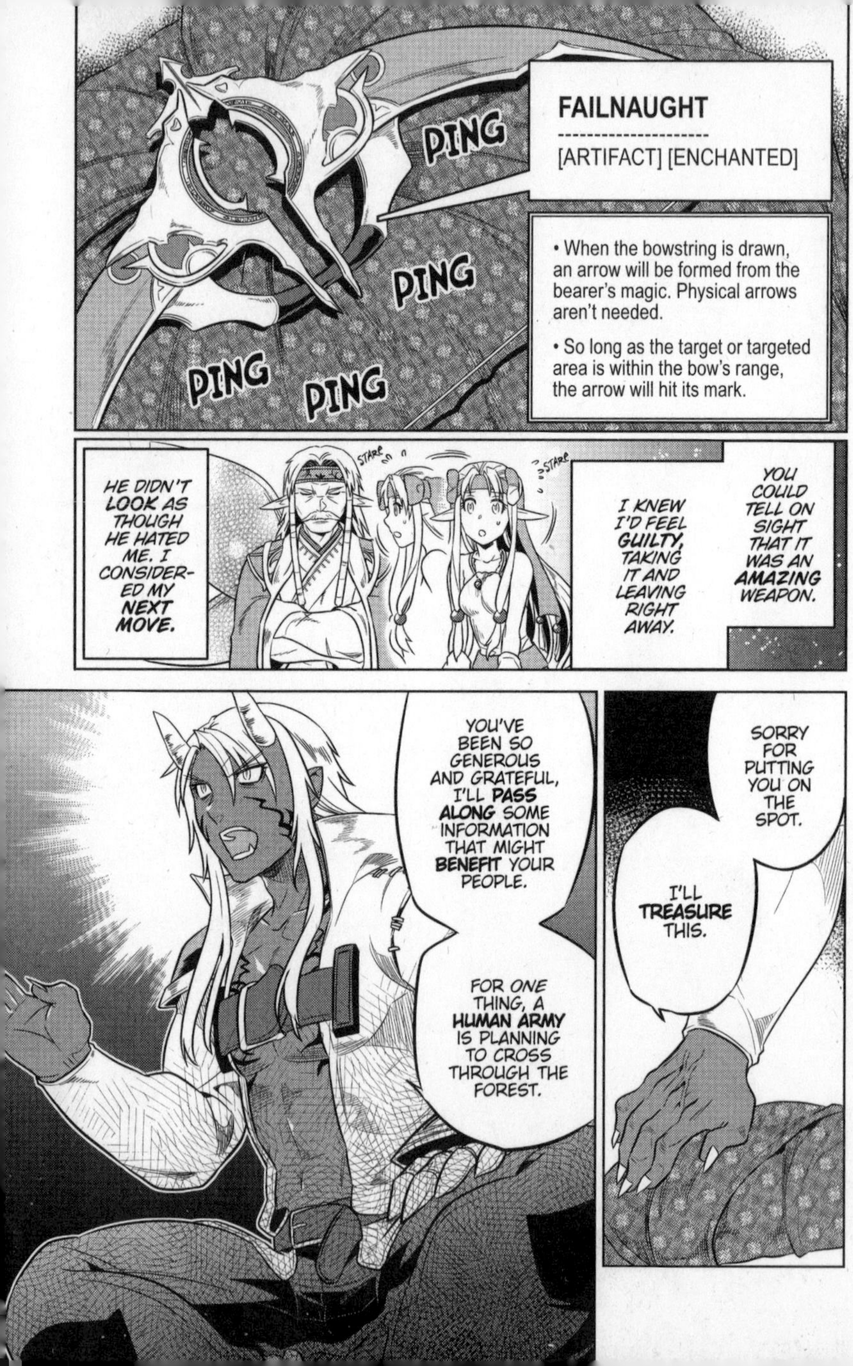
FAILNAUGHT
[ARTIFACT] [ENCHANTED]
• When the bowstring is drawn, an arrow will be formed from the bearer's magic. Physical arrows aren't needed.
• So long as the target or targeted area is within the bow's range, the arrow will hit its mark.
PING
PING
PING
PING
YOU COULD TELL ON SIGHT THAT IT WAS AN **AMAZING** WEAPON.
I KNEW I'D FEEL **GUILTY,** TAKING IT AND LEAVING RIGHT AWAY.
STARE
STARE
HE DIDN'T **LOOK** AS THOUGH HE HATED ME. I CONSIDERED MY **NEXT MOVE.**
SORRY FOR PUTTING YOU ON THE SPOT.
I'LL **TREASURE** THIS.
YOU'VE BEEN SO GENEROUS AND GRATEFUL, I'LL **PASS ALONG** SOME INFORMATION THAT MIGHT **BENEFIT** YOUR PEOPLE.
FOR ONE THING, A **HUMAN ARMY** IS PLANNING TO CROSS THROUGH THE FOREST.

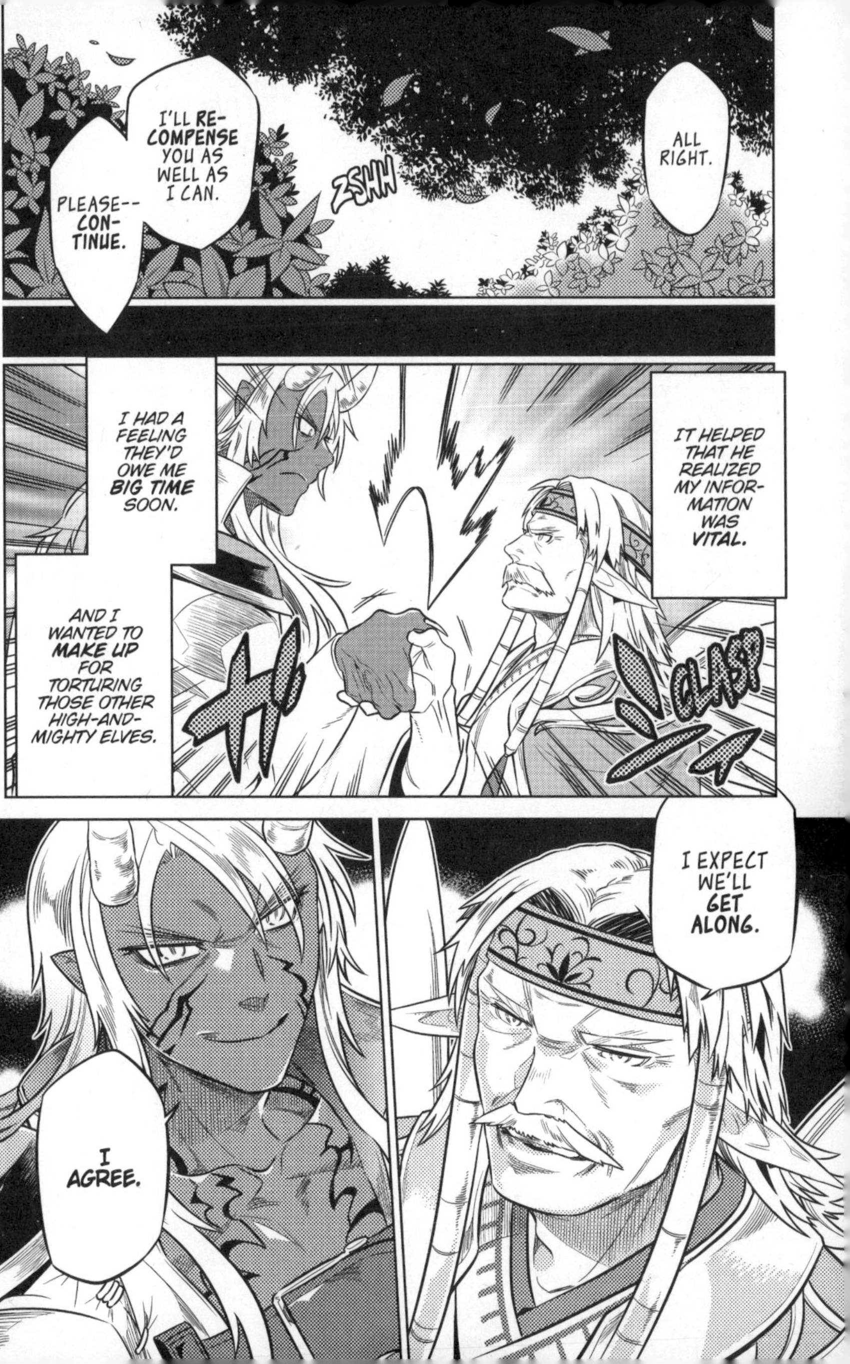
ALL RIGHT.
ZSHH
I'LL RE-COMPENSE YOU AS WELL AS I CAN.
PLEASE-- CON-TINUE.
IT HELPED THAT HE REALIZED MY INFOR-MATION WAS VITAL.
CLASP
I HAD A FEELING THEY'D OWE ME BIG TIME SOON.
AND I WANTED TO MAKE UP FOR TORTURING THOSE OTHER HIGH-AND-MIGHTY ELVES.
I EXPECT WE'LL GET ALONG.
I AGREE.

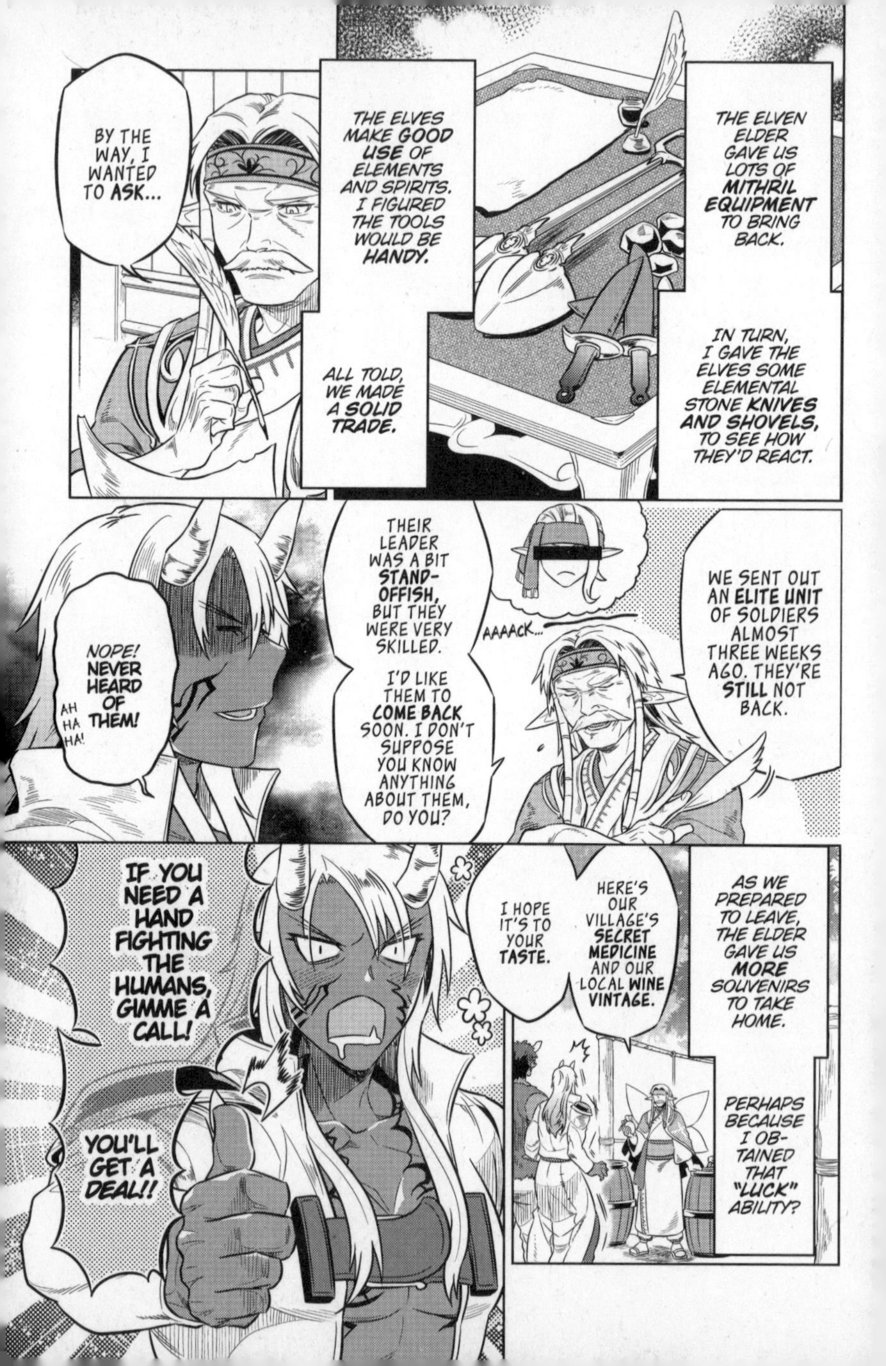
THE ELVEN ELDER GAVE US LOTS OF MITHRIL EQUIPMENT TO BRING BACK.
IN TURN, I GAVE THE ELVES SOME ELEMENTAL STONE KNIVES AND SHOVELS, TO SEE HOW THEY'D REACT.
THE ELVES MAKE GOOD USE OF ELEMENTS AND SPIRITS. I FIGURED THE TOOLS WOULD BE HANDY.
ALL TOLD, WE MADE A SOLID TRADE.
BY THE WAY, I WANTED TO ASK...
WE SENT OUT AN ELITE UNIT OF SOLDIERS ALMOST THREE WEEKS AGO. THEY'RE STILL NOT BACK.
AAAACK...
THEIR LEADER WAS A BIT STAND-OFFISH, BUT THEY WERE VERY SKILLED.
I'D LIKE THEM TO COME BACK SOON. I DON'T SUPPOSE YOU KNOW ANYTHING ABOUT THEM, DO YOU?
NOPE! NEVER HEARD OF THEM!
AH HA HA!
AS WE PREPARED TO LEAVE, THE ELDER GAVE US MORE SOUVENIRS TO TAKE HOME.
PERHAPS BECAUSE I OBTAINED THAT "LUCK" ABILITY?
HERE'S OUR VILLAGE'S SECRET MEDICINE AND OUR LOCAL WINE VINTAGE.
I HOPE IT'S TO YOUR TASTE.
IF YOU NEED A HAND FIGHTING THE HUMANS, GIMME A CALL!
YOU'LL GET A DEAL!!

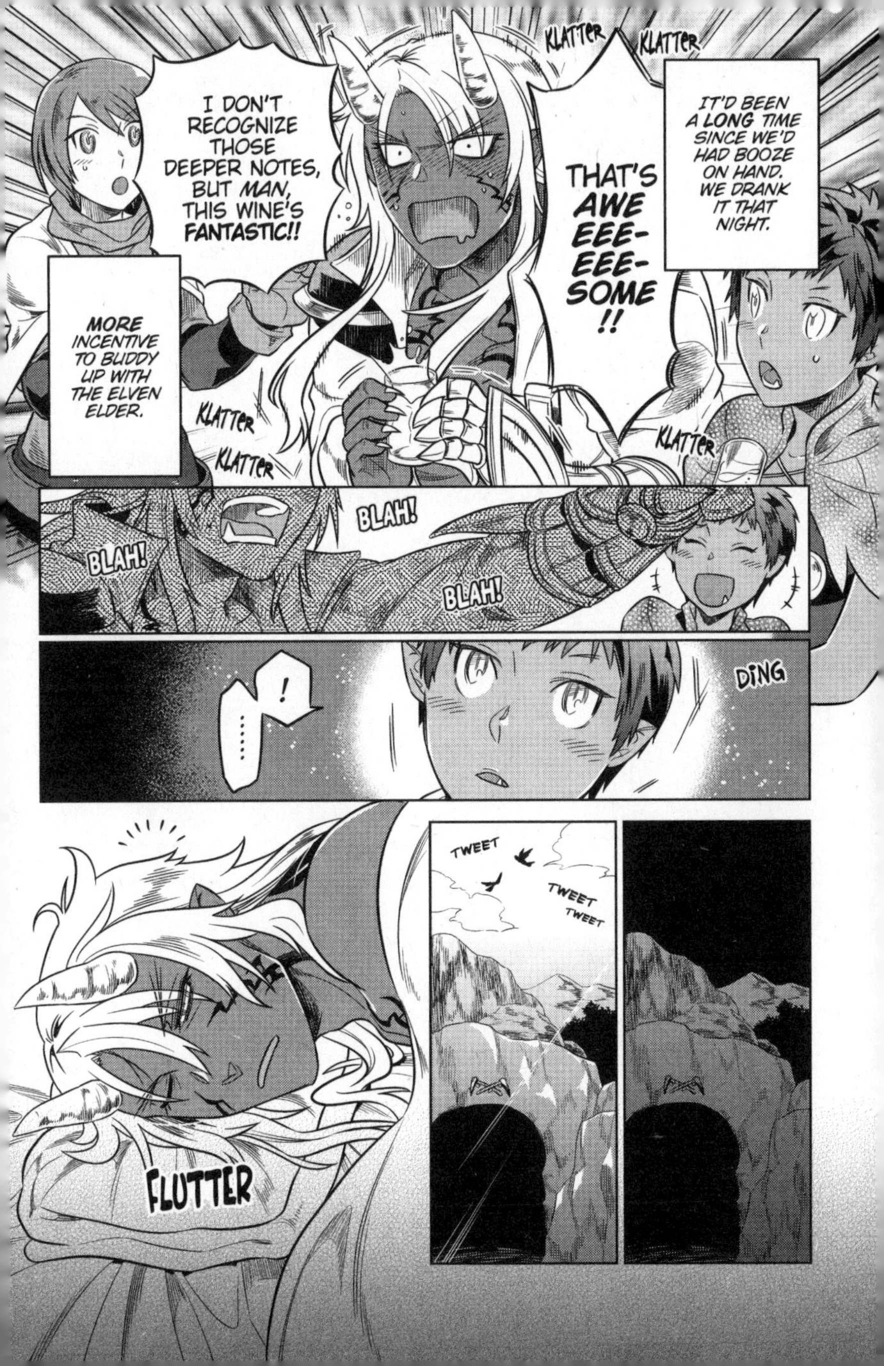
KLATTER
KLATTER
IT'D BEEN A LONG TIME SINCE WE'D HAD BOOZE ON HAND. WE DRANK IT THAT NIGHT.
THAT'S AWEEEE-EEE-SOME!!
I DON'T RECOGNIZE THOSE DEEPER NOTES, BUT MAN, THIS WINE'S FANTASTIC!!
KLATTER
MORE INCENTIVE TO BUDDY UP WITH THE ELVEN ELDER.
KLATTER
KLATTER
BLAH!
BLAH!
BLAH!
DING
!
......
TWEET
TWEET
TWEET
FLUTTER

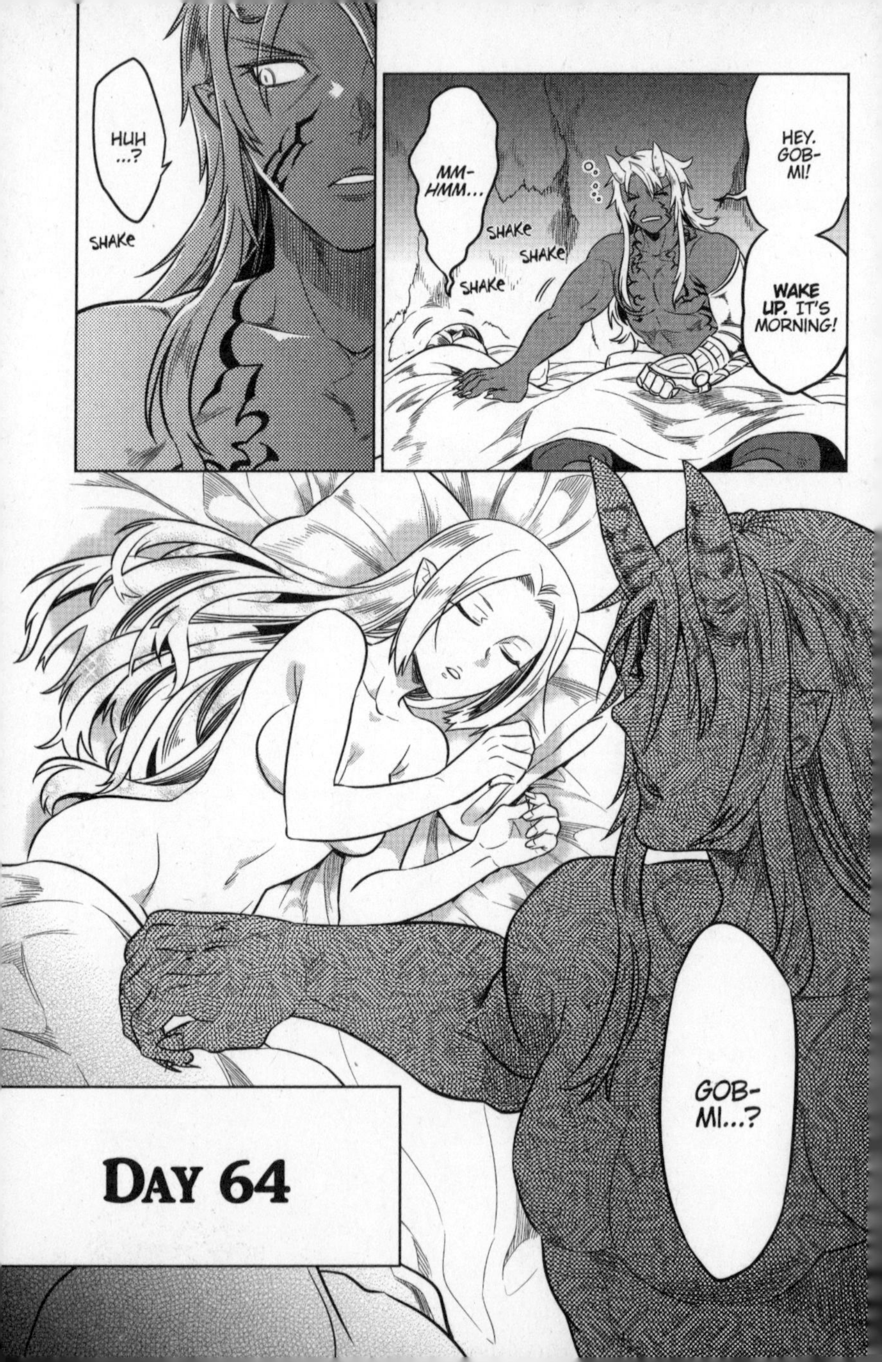
HEY. GOB-MI!
WAKE UP. IT'S MORNING!
MM-HMM...
SHAKE
SHAKE
SHAKE
HUH ...?
SHAKE
GOB-MI...?
DAY 64

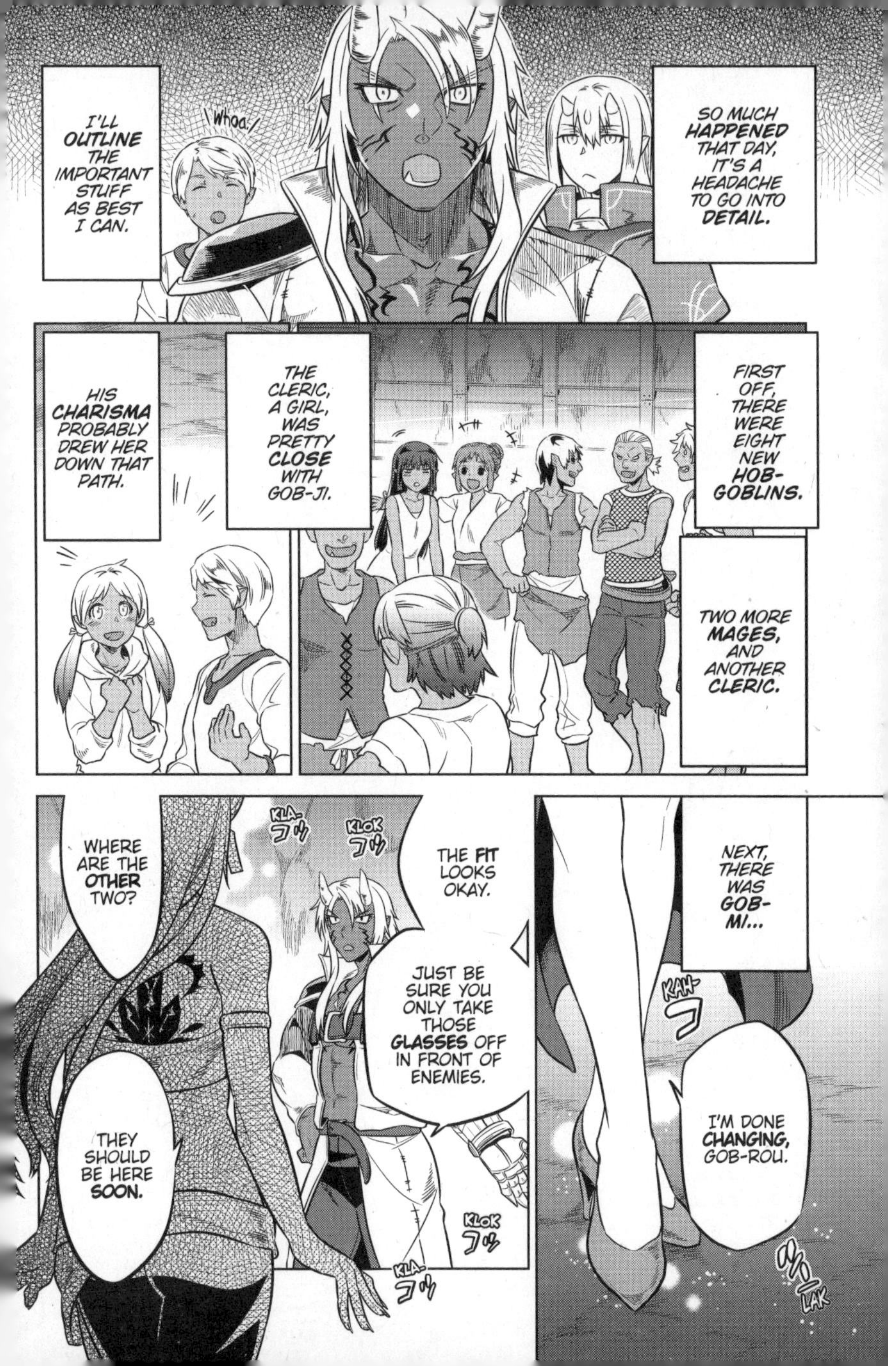
SO MUCH HAPPENED THAT DAY, IT'S A HEADACHE TO GO INTO DETAIL.
I'LL OUTLINE THE IMPORTANT STUFF AS BEST I CAN.
Whoa!
FIRST OFF, THERE WERE EIGHT NEW HOB-GOBLINS.
TWO MORE MAGES, AND ANOTHER CLERIC.
THE CLERIC, A GIRL, WAS PRETTY CLOSE WITH GOB-JI.
HIS CHARISMA PROBABLY DREW HER DOWN THAT PATH.
NEXT, THERE WAS GOB-MI...
KAH-
I'M DONE CHANGING, GOB-ROU.
LAK
KLOK
KLA-
THE FIT LOOKS OKAY.
WHERE ARE THE OTHER TWO?
JUST BE SURE YOU ONLY TAKE THOSE GLASSES OFF IN FRONT OF ENEMIES.
THEY SHOULD BE HERE SOON.
KLOK
KLA-

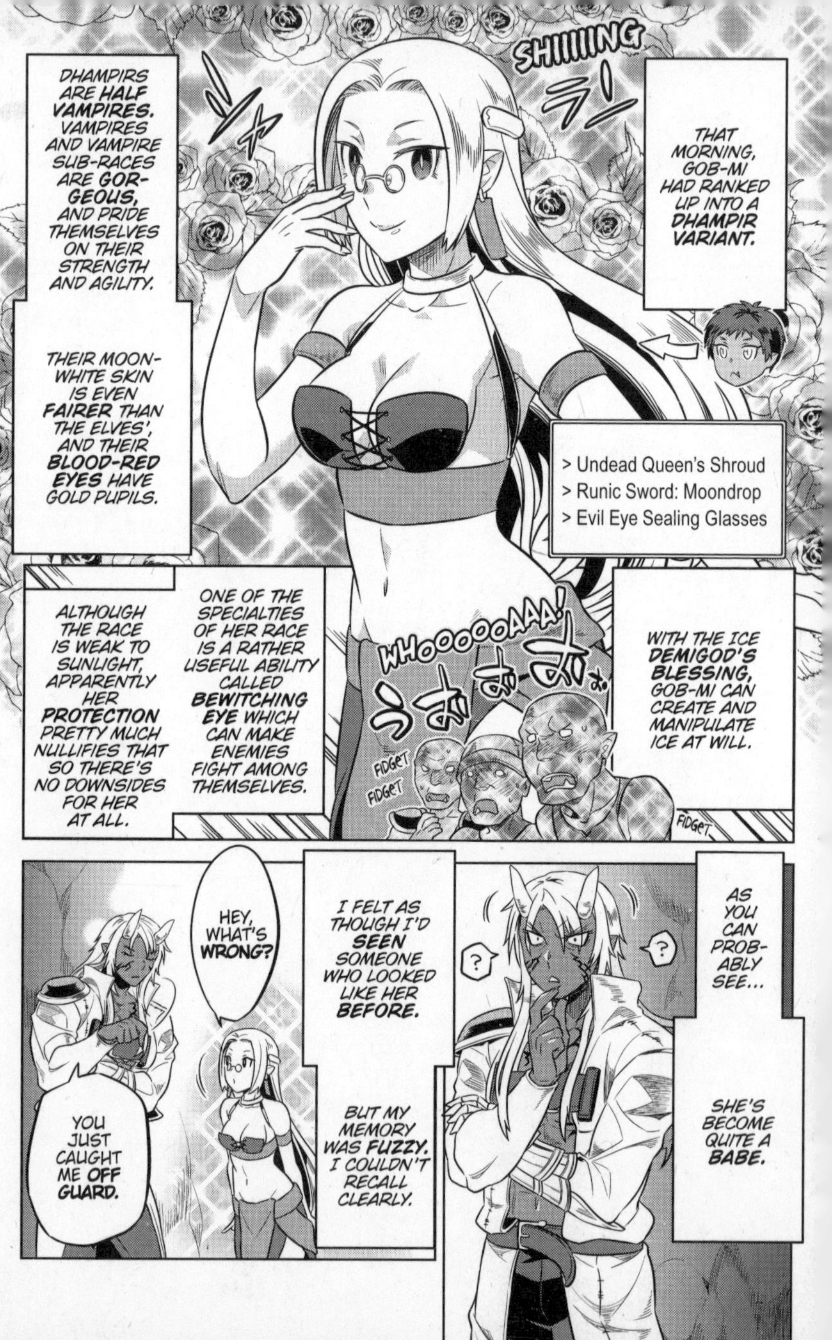

SHIIIIIING
THAT MORNING, GOB-MI HAD RANKED UP INTO A **DHAMPIR VARIANT.**
> Undead Queen's Shroud
> Runic Sword: Moondrop
> Evil Eye Sealing Glasses
DHAMPIRS ARE **HALF VAMPIRES.** VAMPIRES AND VAMPIRE SUB-RACES ARE **GORGEOUS,** AND PRIDE THEMSELVES ON THEIR STRENGTH AND AGILITY.
THEIR MOON-WHITE SKIN IS EVEN **FAIRER** THAN THE ELVES', AND THEIR **BLOOD-RED EYES** HAVE GOLD PUPILS.
WITH THE ICE **DEMIGOD'S BLESSING,** GOB-MI CAN CREATE AND MANIPULATE ICE AT WILL.
WHOOOOOAAA!
FIDGET
FIDGET
FIDGET
ONE OF THE SPECIALTIES OF HER RACE IS A RATHER USEFUL ABILITY CALLED **BEWITCHING EYE** WHICH CAN MAKE ENEMIES FIGHT AMONG THEMSELVES.
ALTHOUGH THE RACE IS WEAK TO SUNLIGHT, APPARENTLY HER **PROTECTION** PRETTY MUCH NULLIFIES THAT SO THERE'S NO DOWNSIDES FOR HER AT ALL.
AS YOU CAN PROBABLY SEE...
SHE'S BECOME QUITE A **BABE.**
?
?
I FELT AS THOUGH I'D **SEEN** SOMEONE WHO LOOKED LIKE HER **BEFORE.**
BUT MY MEMORY WAS **FUZZY.** I COULDN'T RECALL CLEARLY.
HEY, WHAT'S **WRONG?**
YOU JUST CAUGHT ME **OFF GUARD.**

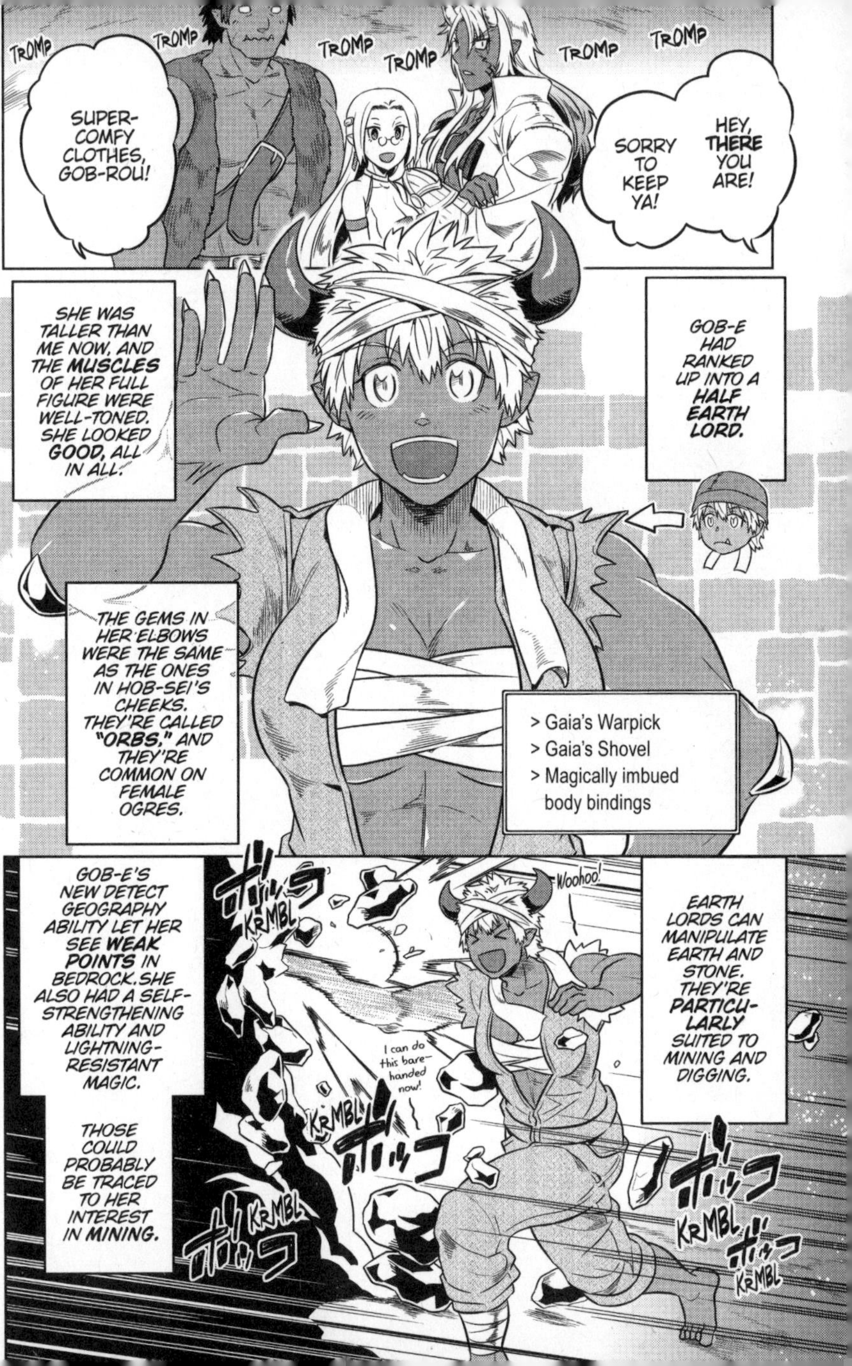
TROMP TROMP TROMP TROMP TROMP TROMP
HEY, THERE YOU ARE!
SORRY TO KEEP YA!
SUPER-COMFY CLOTHES, GOB-ROU!
GOB-E HAD RANKED UP INTO A HALF EARTH LORD.
SHE WAS TALLER THAN ME NOW, AND THE MUSCLES OF HER FULL FIGURE WERE WELL-TONED. SHE LOOKED GOOD, ALL IN ALL.
THE GEMS IN HER ELBOWS WERE THE SAME AS THE ONES IN HOB-SEI'S CHEEKS. THEY'RE CALLED "ORBS," AND THEY'RE COMMON ON FEMALE OGRES.
> Gaia's Warpick
> Gaia's Shovel
> Magically imbued body bindings
EARTH LORDS CAN MANIPULATE EARTH AND STONE. THEY'RE PARTICU-LARLY SUITED TO MINING AND DIGGING.
Woohoo!
I can do this bare-handed now!
GOB-E'S NEW DETECT GEOGRAPHY ABILITY LET HER SEE WEAK POINTS IN BEDROCK. SHE ALSO HAD A SELF-STRENGTHENING ABILITY AND LIGHTNING-RESISTANT MAGIC.
THOSE COULD PROBABLY BE TRACED TO HER INTEREST IN MINING.
KRMBL KRMBL KRMBL KRMBL KRMBL

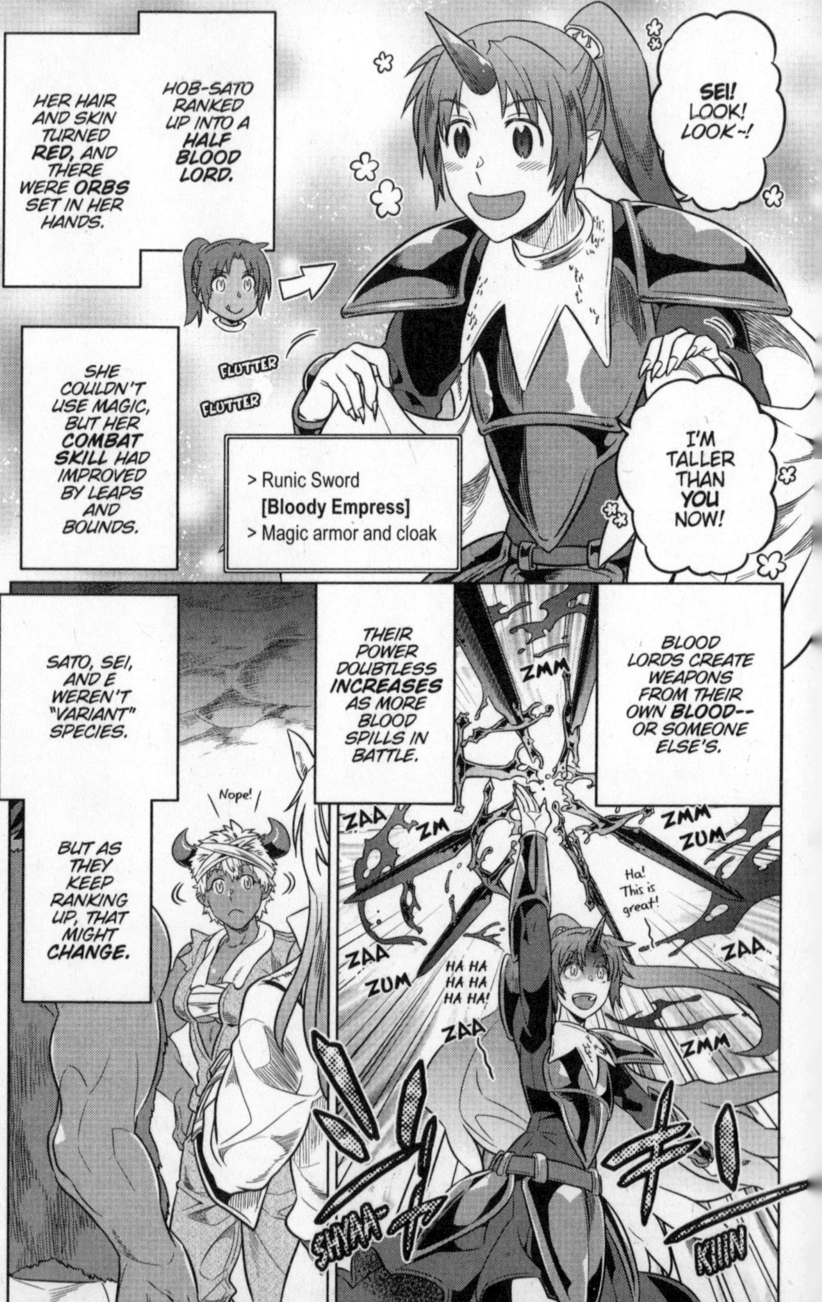
SEI! LOOK! LOOK~!
HOB-SATO RANKED UP INTO A HALF BLOOD LORD.
HER HAIR AND SKIN TURNED RED, AND THERE WERE ORBS SET IN HER HANDS.
I'M TALLER THAN YOU NOW!
FLUTTER
FLUTTER
> Runic Sword
[Bloody Empress]
> Magic armor and cloak
SHE COULDN'T USE MAGIC, BUT HER COMBAT SKILL HAD IMPROVED BY LEAPS AND BOUNDS.
BLOOD LORDS CREATE WEAPONS FROM THEIR OWN BLOOD--OR SOMEONE ELSE'S.
THEIR POWER DOUBTLESS INCREASES AS MORE BLOOD SPILLS IN BATTLE.
ZMM
ZMM
ZUM
ZAA
Ha! This is great!
ZAA
ZM
ZAA
ZUM
HA HA HA HA HA HA!
ZAA
ZMM
SHYAA-
KIIIN
SATO, SEI, AND E WEREN'T "VARIANT" SPECIES.
Nope!
BUT AS THEY KEEP RANKING UP, THAT MIGHT CHANGE.

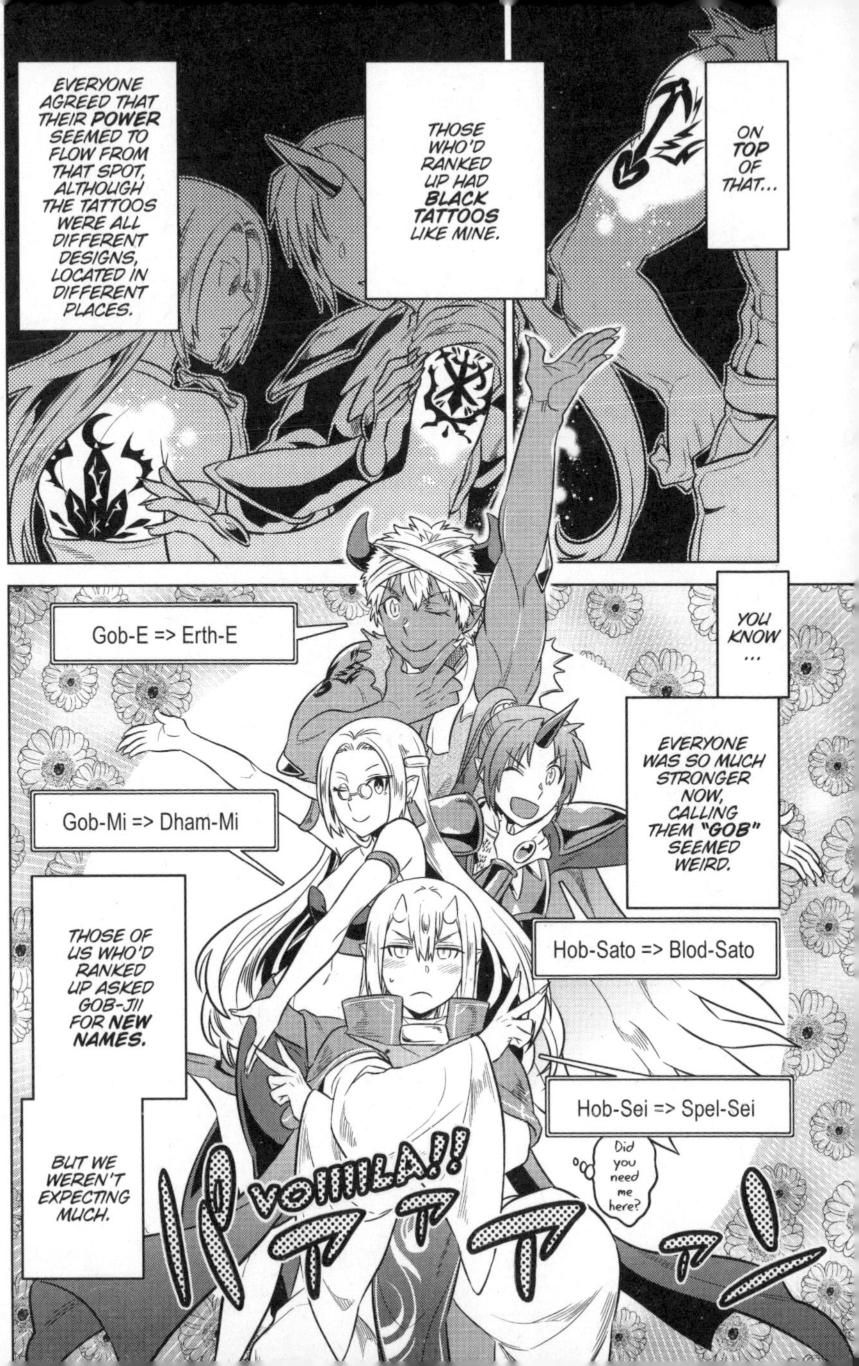
ON TOP OF THAT...
THOSE WHO'D RANKED UP HAD BLACK TATTOOS LIKE MINE.
EVERYONE AGREED THAT THEIR POWER SEEMED TO FLOW FROM THAT SPOT, ALTHOUGH THE TATTOOS WERE ALL DIFFERENT DESIGNS, LOCATED IN DIFFERENT PLACES.
YOU KNOW...
Gob-E => Erth-E
EVERYONE WAS SO MUCH STRONGER NOW, CALLING THEM "GOB" SEEMED WEIRD.
Gob-Mi => Dham-Mi
THOSE OF US WHO'D RANKED UP ASKED GOB-JII FOR NEW NAMES.
Hob-Sato => Blod-Sato
Hob-Sei => Spel-Sei
Did you need me here?
BUT WE WEREN'T EXPECTING MUCH.
VOIIIILA!!

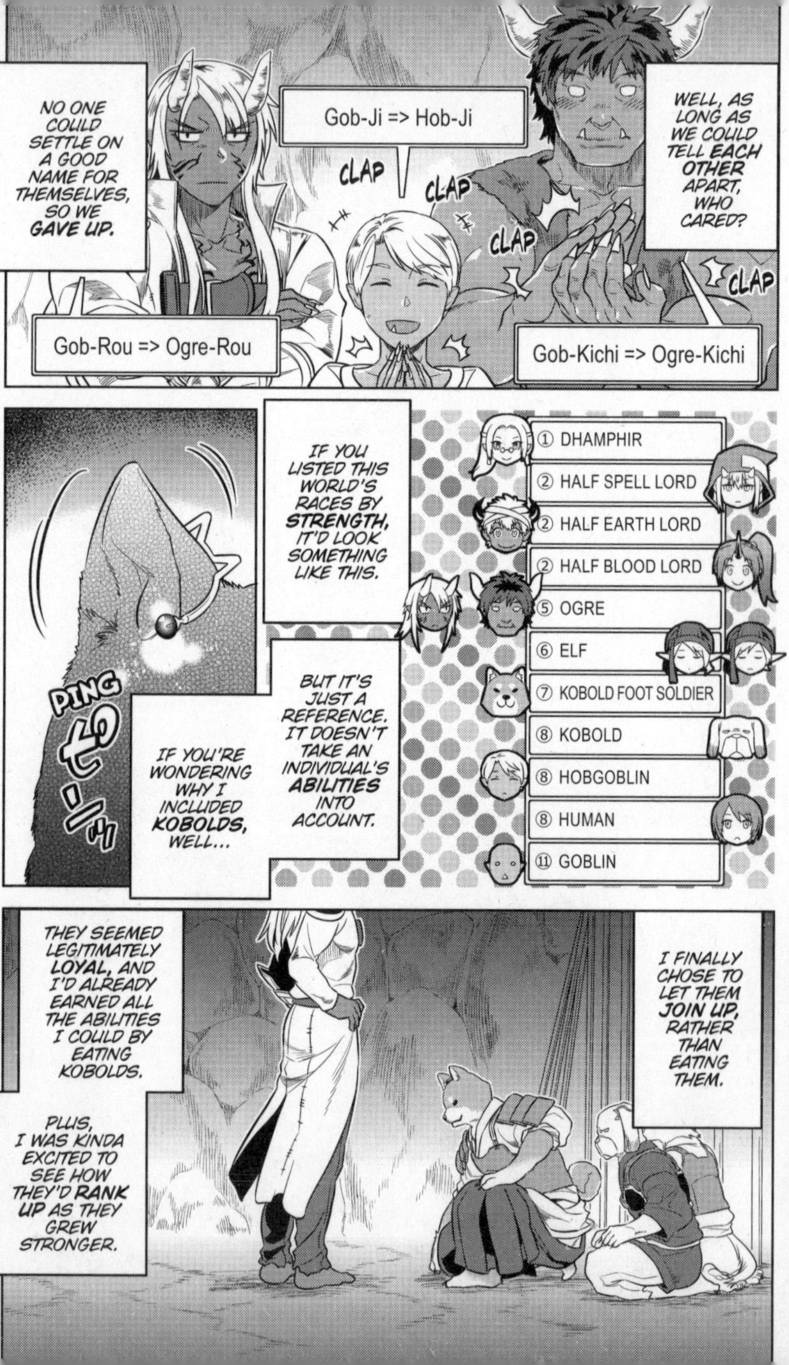
NO ONE COULD SETTLE ON A GOOD NAME FOR THEMSELVES, SO WE GAVE UP.
Gob-Rou => Ogre-Rou
Gob-Ji => Hob-Ji
CLAP
CLAP
CLAP
CLAP
WELL, AS LONG AS WE COULD TELL EACH OTHER APART, WHO CARED?
Gob-Kichi => Ogre-Kichi
PING
IF YOU LISTED THIS WORLD'S RACES BY STRENGTH, IT'D LOOK SOMETHING LIKE THIS.
① DHAMPHIR
② HALF SPELL LORD
② HALF EARTH LORD
② HALF BLOOD LORD
⑤ OGRE
⑥ ELF
⑦ KOBOLD FOOT SOLDIER
⑧ KOBOLD
⑧ HOBGOBLIN
⑧ HUMAN
⑪ GOBLIN
BUT IT'S JUST A REFERENCE. IT DOESN'T TAKE AN INDIVIDUAL'S ABILITIES INTO ACCOUNT.
IF YOU'RE WONDERING WHY I INCLUDED KOBOLDS, WELL...
THEY SEEMED LEGITIMATELY LOYAL, AND I'D ALREADY EARNED ALL THE ABILITIES I COULD BY EATING KOBOLDS.
PLUS, I WAS KINDA EXCITED TO SEE HOW THEY'D RANK UP AS THEY GREW STRONGER.
I FINALLY CHOSE TO LET THEM JOIN UP, RATHER THAN EATING THEM.

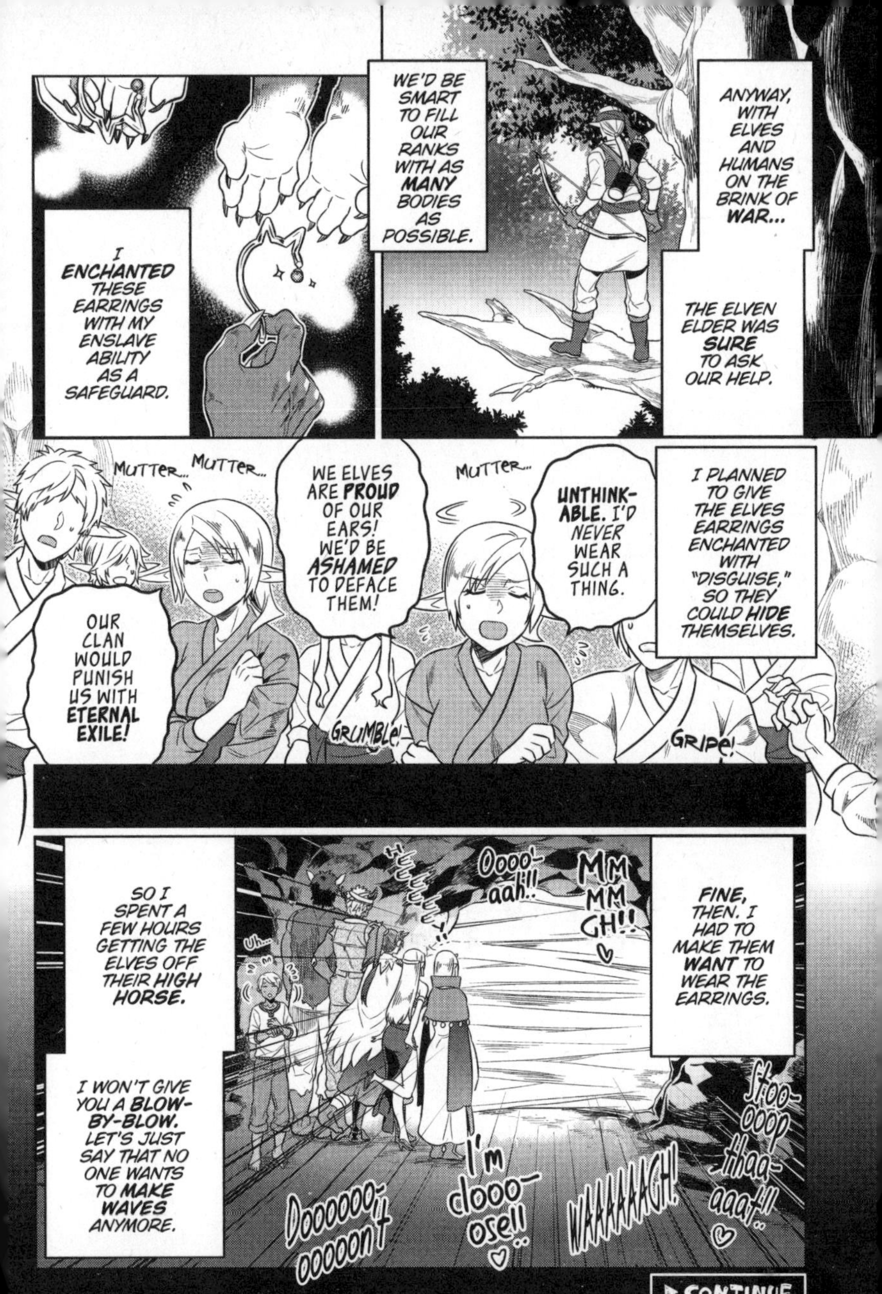
ANYWAY, WITH ELVES AND HUMANS ON THE BRINK OF WAR...
THE ELVEN ELDER WAS SURE TO ASK OUR HELP.
WE'D BE SMART TO FILL OUR RANKS WITH AS MANY BODIES AS POSSIBLE.
I ENCHANTED THESE EARRINGS WITH MY ENSLAVE ABILITY AS A SAFEGUARD.
I PLANNED TO GIVE THE ELVES EARRINGS ENCHANTED WITH "DISGUISE," SO THEY COULD HIDE THEMSELVES.
UNTHINKABLE. I'D NEVER WEAR SUCH A THING.
MUTTER...
WE ELVES ARE PROUD OF OUR EARS! WE'D BE ASHAMED TO DEFACE THEM!
MUTTER...
MUTTER...
OUR CLAN WOULD PUNISH US WITH ETERNAL EXILE!
GRIPE!
GRUMBLE!
FINE, THEN. I HAD TO MAKE THEM WANT TO WEAR THE EARRINGS.
Stoo-ooop thaa-aaat!!
MM MM GH!!
Oooo-aah!!
WAAAAAAGH!
I'm clooo-ose!!
Uh...
Doooooo-oooooon't
SO I SPENT A FEW HOURS GETTING THE ELVES OFF THEIR HIGH HORSE.
I WON'T GIVE YOU A BLOW-BY-BLOW. LET'S JUST SAY THAT NO ONE WANTS TO MAKE WAVES ANYMORE.
CONTINUE

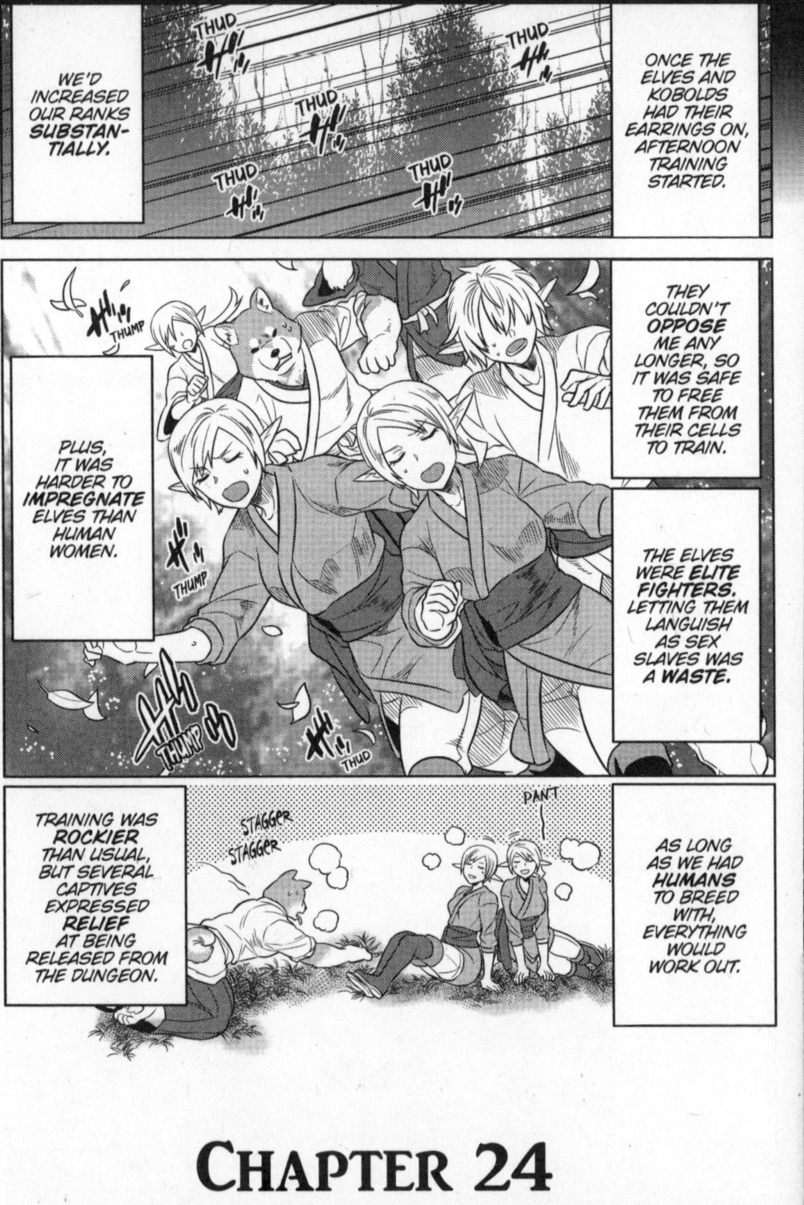
ONCE THE ELVES AND KOBOLDS HAD THEIR EARRINGS ON, AFTERNOON TRAINING STARTED.
THUD
THUD
THUD
THUD
THUD
WE'D INCREASED OUR RANKS SUBSTANTIALLY.
THEY COULDN'T OPPOSE ME ANY LONGER, SO IT WAS SAFE TO FREE THEM FROM THEIR CELLS TO TRAIN.
THE ELVES WERE ELITE FIGHTERS. LETTING THEM LANGUISH AS SEX SLAVES WAS A WASTE.
THUMP
PLUS, IT WAS HARDER TO IMPREGNATE ELVES THAN HUMAN WOMEN.
THUMP
THUMP
THUD
AS LONG AS WE HAD HUMANS TO BREED WITH, EVERYTHING WOULD WORK OUT.
PANT
STAGGER
STAGGER
TRAINING WAS ROCKIER THAN USUAL, BUT SEVERAL CAPTIVES EXPRESSED RELIEF AT BEING RELEASED FROM THE DUNGEON.

CHAPTER 24

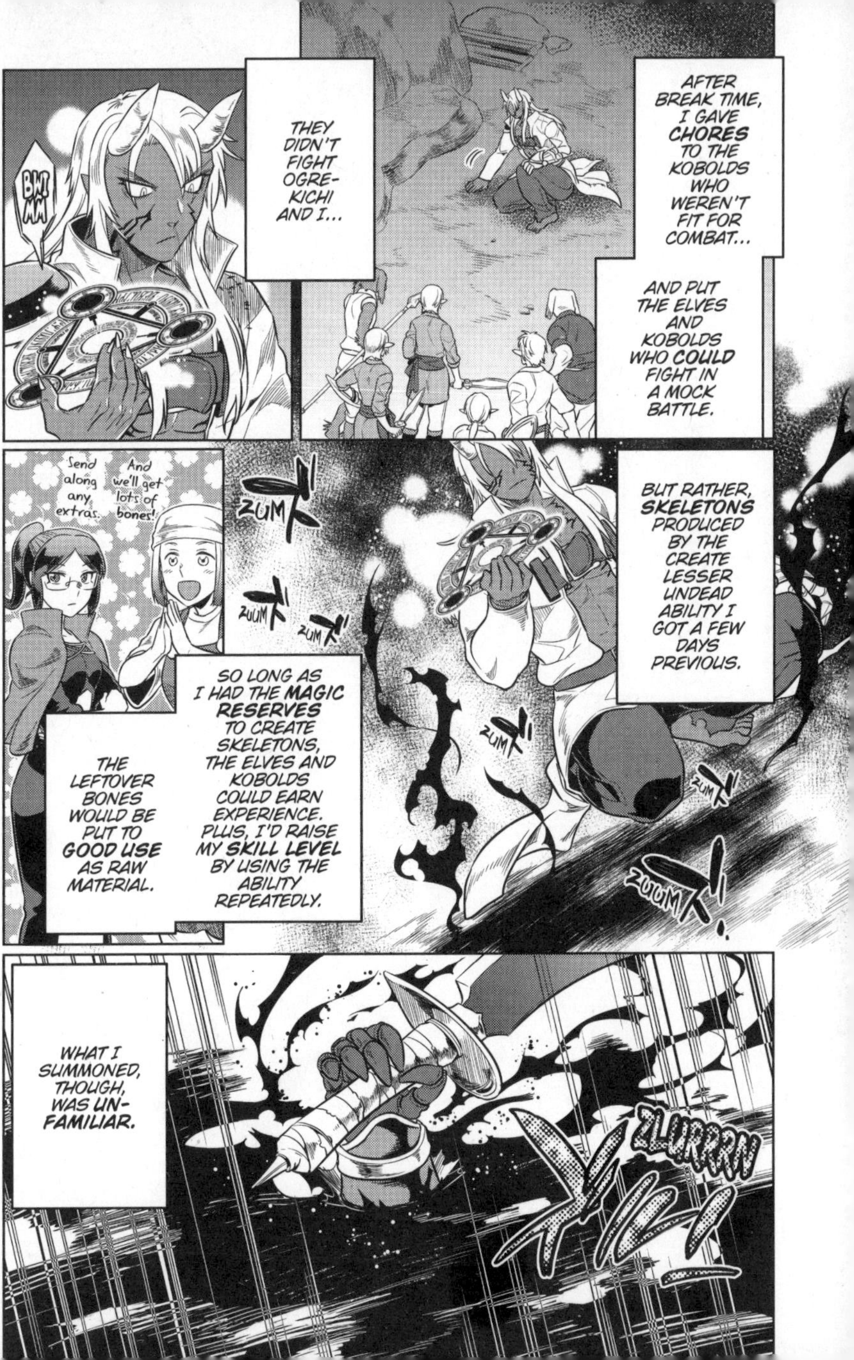
AFTER BREAK TIME, I GAVE **CHORES** TO THE KOBOLDS WHO WEREN'T FIT FOR COMBAT...
AND PUT THE ELVES AND KOBOLDS WHO **COULD** FIGHT IN A MOCK BATTLE.
THEY DIDN'T FIGHT OGRE-KICHI AND I...
BWIMM
ZUM
ZUUM
ZUM
ZUM
ZUM
ZUUM
BUT RATHER, **SKELETONS** PRODUCED BY THE CREATE LESSER UNDEAD ABILITY I GOT A FEW DAYS PREVIOUS.
Send along any extras.
And we'll get lots of bones!
SO LONG AS I HAD THE **MAGIC RESERVES** TO CREATE SKELETONS, THE ELVES AND KOBOLDS COULD EARN EXPERIENCE. PLUS, I'D RAISE MY **SKILL LEVEL** BY USING THE ABILITY REPEATEDLY.
THE LEFTOVER BONES WOULD BE PUT TO **GOOD USE** AS RAW MATERIAL.
ZLURRRN
WHAT I SUMMONED, THOUGH, WAS **UN-FAMILIAR.**

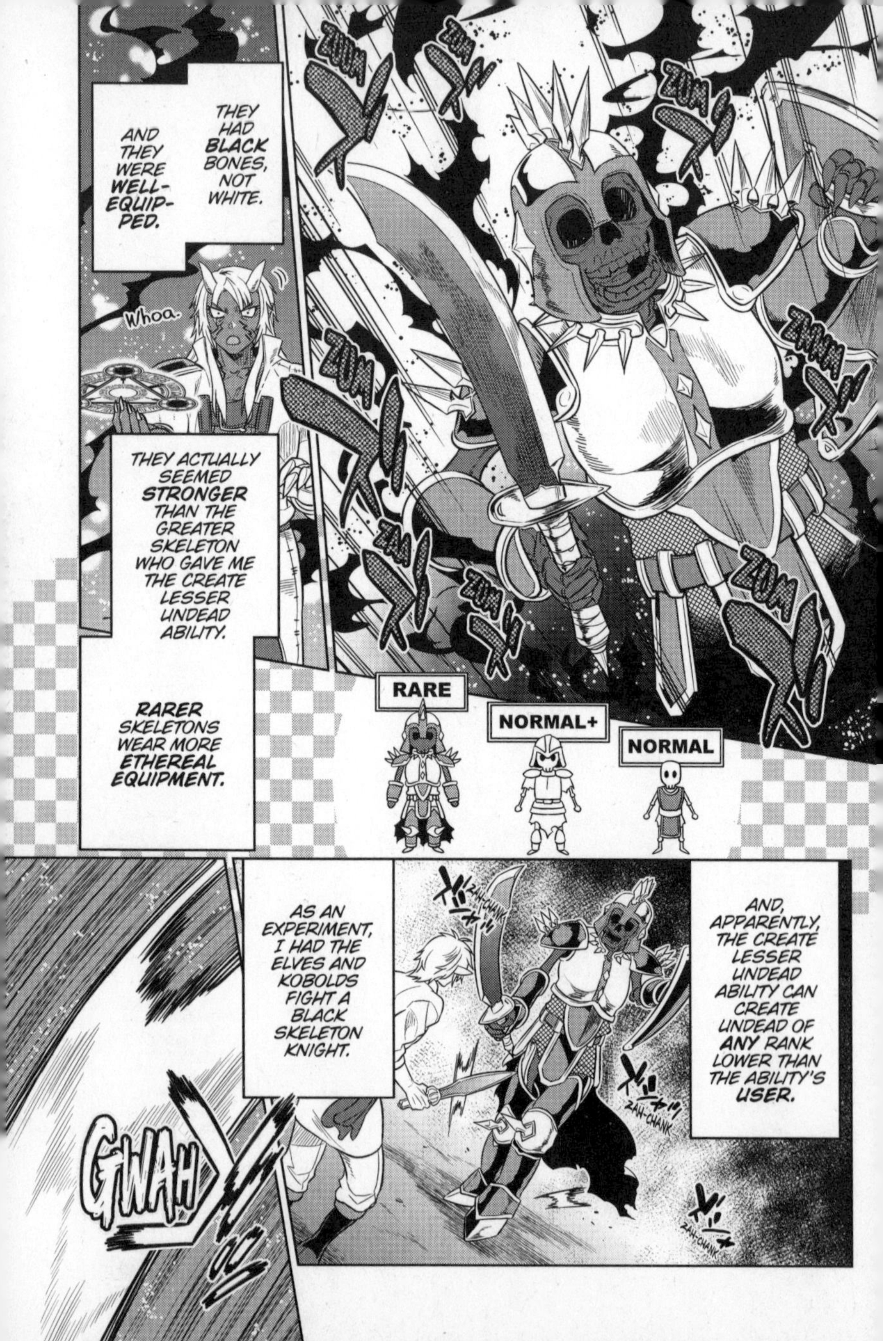
ZUM
ZUM
ZUM
ZUM
ZUM
ZUM
THEY HAD BLACK BONES, NOT WHITE.
AND THEY WERE WELL-EQUIPPED.
Whoa.
THEY ACTUALLY SEEMED STRONGER THAN THE GREATER SKELETON WHO GAVE ME THE CREATE LESSER UNDEAD ABILITY.
RARER SKELETONS WEAR MORE ETHEREAL EQUIPMENT.
RARE
NORMAL+
NORMAL
AND, APPARENTLY, THE CREATE LESSER UNDEAD ABILITY CAN CREATE UNDEAD OF ANY RANK LOWER THAN THE ABILITY'S USER.
AS AN EXPERIMENT, I HAD THE ELVES AND KOBOLDS FIGHT A BLACK SKELETON KNIGHT.
ZAH-CHANK
ZAH-CHANK
ZAH-CHANK
GWAH

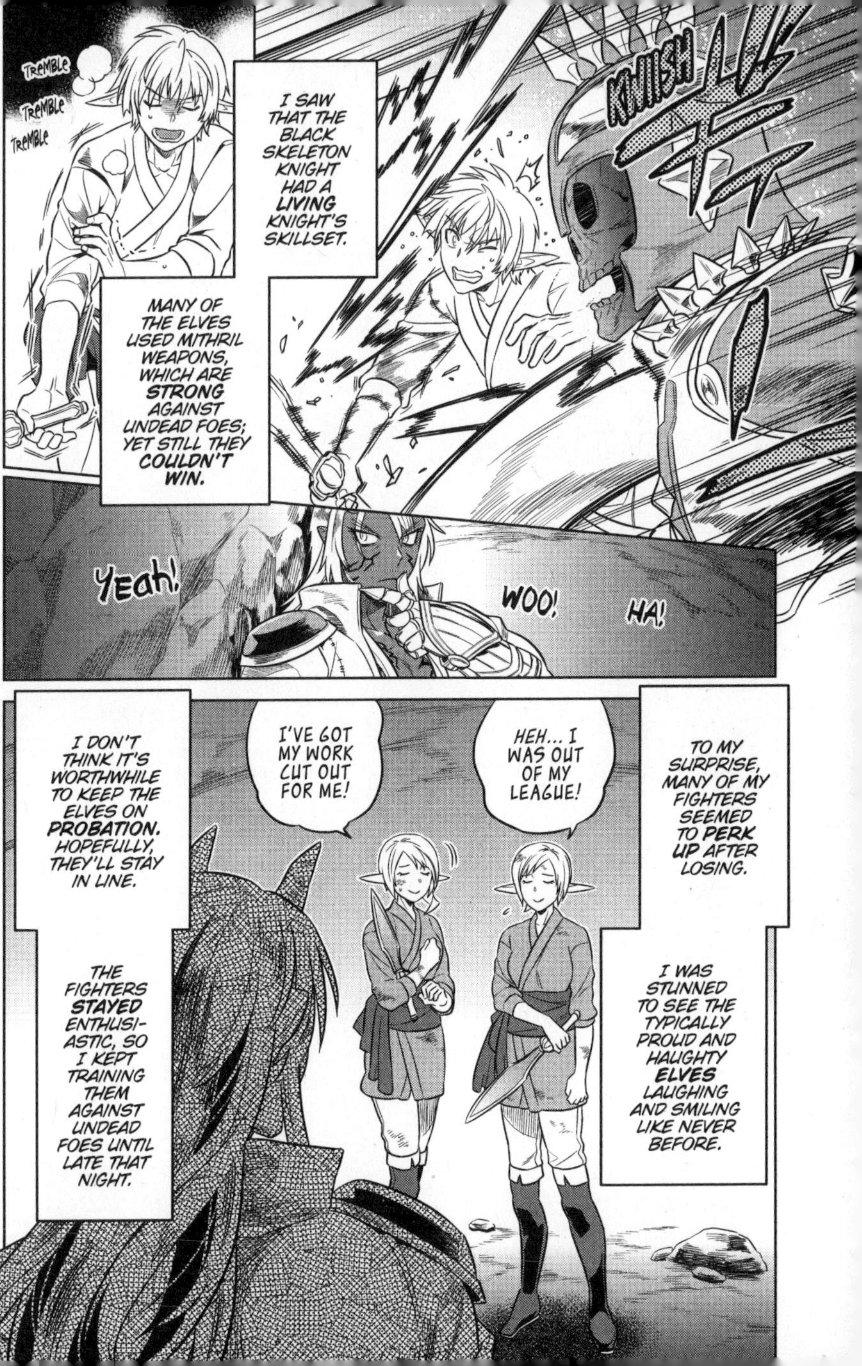
KWIISH
I SAW THAT THE BLACK SKELETON KNIGHT HAD A LIVING KNIGHT'S SKILLSET.
TREMBLE
TREMBLE
TREMBLE
MANY OF THE ELVES USED MITHRIL WEAPONS, WHICH ARE STRONG AGAINST UNDEAD FOES; YET STILL THEY COULDN'T WIN.
HA!
WOO!
Yeah!
TO MY SURPRISE, MANY OF MY FIGHTERS SEEMED TO PERK UP AFTER LOSING.
HEH... I WAS OUT OF MY LEAGUE!
I'VE GOT MY WORK CUT OUT FOR ME!
I DON'T THINK IT'S WORTHWHILE TO KEEP THE ELVES ON PROBATION. HOPEFULLY, THEY'LL STAY IN LINE.
I WAS STUNNED TO SEE THE TYPICALLY PROUD AND HAUGHTY ELVES LAUGHING AND SMILING LIKE NEVER BEFORE.
THE FIGHTERS STAYED ENTHUSI-ASTIC, SO I KEPT TRAINING THEM AGAINST UNDEAD FOES UNTIL LATE THAT NIGHT.

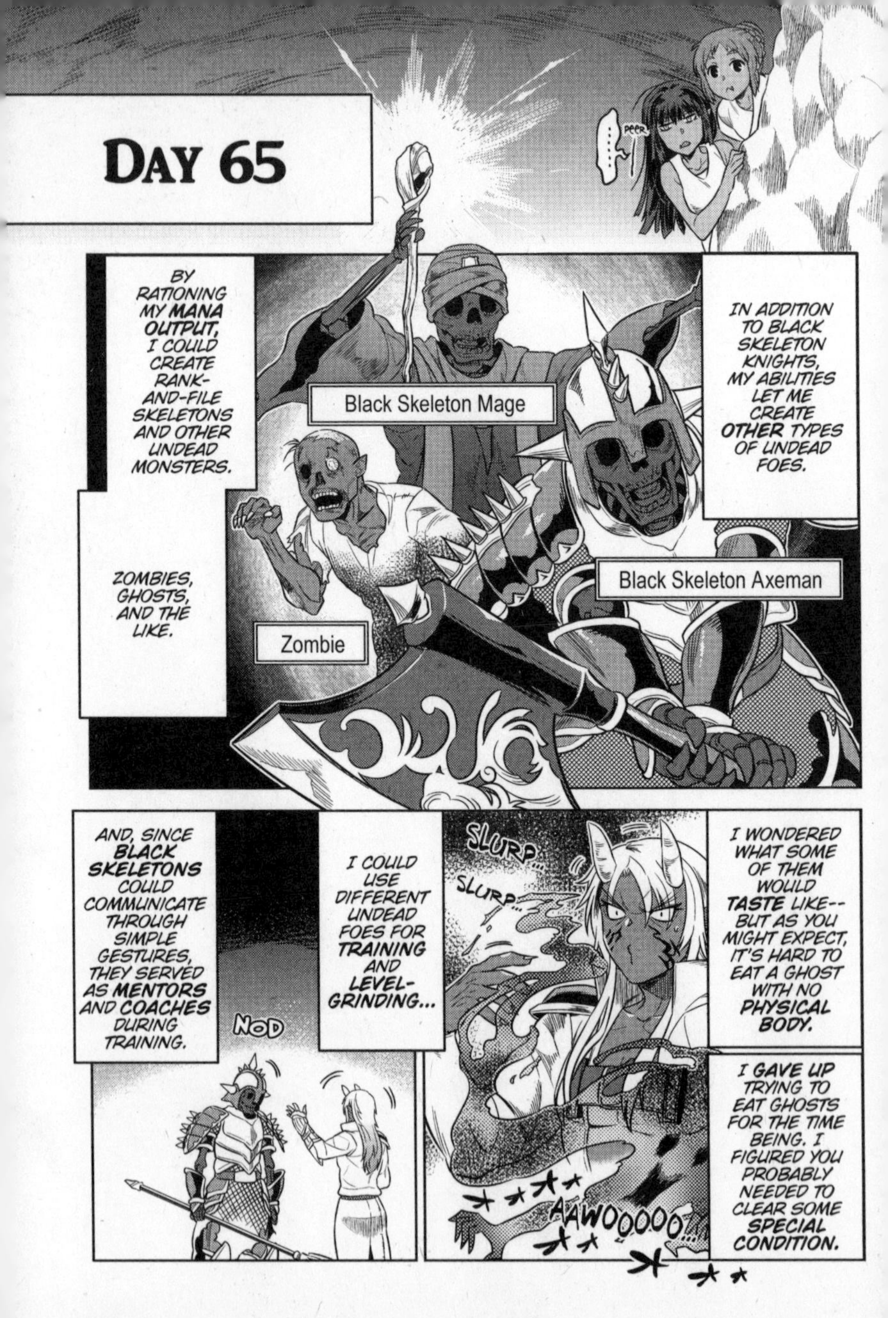
DAY 65
PEER
...
IN ADDITION TO BLACK SKELETON KNIGHTS, MY ABILITIES LET ME CREATE OTHER TYPES OF UNDEAD FOES.
Black Skeleton Mage
BY RATIONING MY MANA OUTPUT, I COULD CREATE RANK-AND-FILE SKELETONS AND OTHER UNDEAD MONSTERS.
Black Skeleton Axeman
ZOMBIES, GHOSTS, AND THE LIKE.
Zombie
I WONDERED WHAT SOME OF THEM WOULD TASTE LIKE-- BUT AS YOU MIGHT EXPECT, IT'S HARD TO EAT A GHOST WITH NO PHYSICAL BODY.
SLURP...
SLURP...
I GAVE UP TRYING TO EAT GHOSTS FOR THE TIME BEING. I FIGURED YOU PROBABLY NEEDED TO CLEAR SOME SPECIAL CONDITION.
AAWOOOOO...
I COULD USE DIFFERENT UNDEAD FOES FOR TRAINING AND LEVEL-GRINDING...
AND, SINCE BLACK SKELETONS COULD COMMUNICATE THROUGH SIMPLE GESTURES, THEY SERVED AS MENTORS AND COACHES DURING TRAINING.
NOD

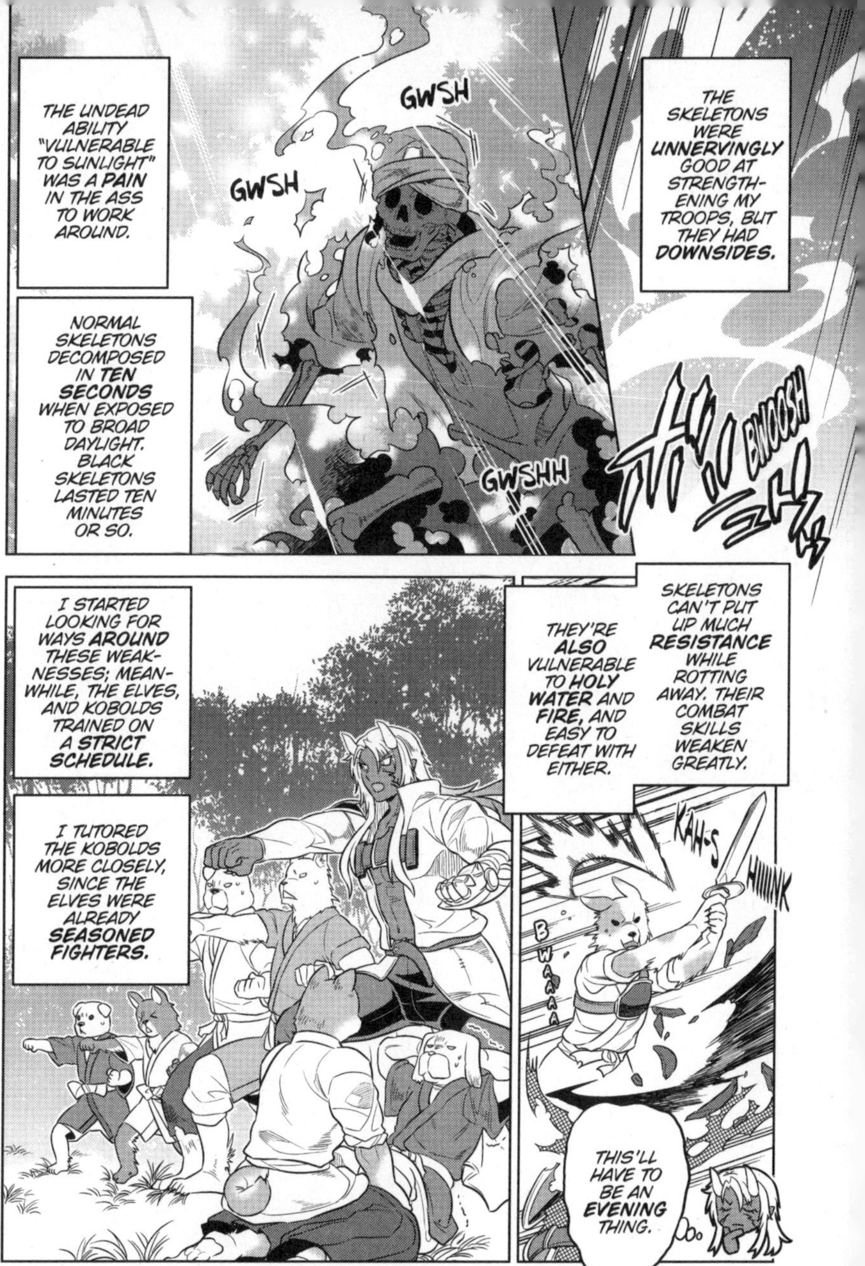
THE SKELETONS WERE UNNERVINGLY GOOD AT STRENGTHENING MY TROOPS, BUT THEY HAD DOWNSIDES.
BWOOSH
GWSH
THE UNDEAD ABILITY "VULNERABLE TO SUNLIGHT" WAS A PAIN IN THE ASS TO WORK AROUND.
GWSH
NORMAL SKELETONS DECOMPOSED IN TEN SECONDS WHEN EXPOSED TO BROAD DAYLIGHT. BLACK SKELETONS LASTED TEN MINUTES OR SO.
GWSHH
SKELETONS CAN'T PUT UP MUCH RESISTANCE WHILE ROTTING AWAY. THEIR COMBAT SKILLS WEAKEN GREATLY.
THEY'RE ALSO VULNERABLE TO HOLY WATER AND FIRE, AND EASY TO DEFEAT WITH EITHER.
KAH-S
HIIIINK
BWAAAAA
THIS'LL HAVE TO BE AN EVENING THING.
I STARTED LOOKING FOR WAYS AROUND THESE WEAKNESSES; MEANWHILE, THE ELVES, AND KOBOLDS TRAINED ON A STRICT SCHEDULE.
I TUTORED THE KOBOLDS MORE CLOSELY, SINCE THE ELVES WERE ALREADY SEASONED FIGHTERS.

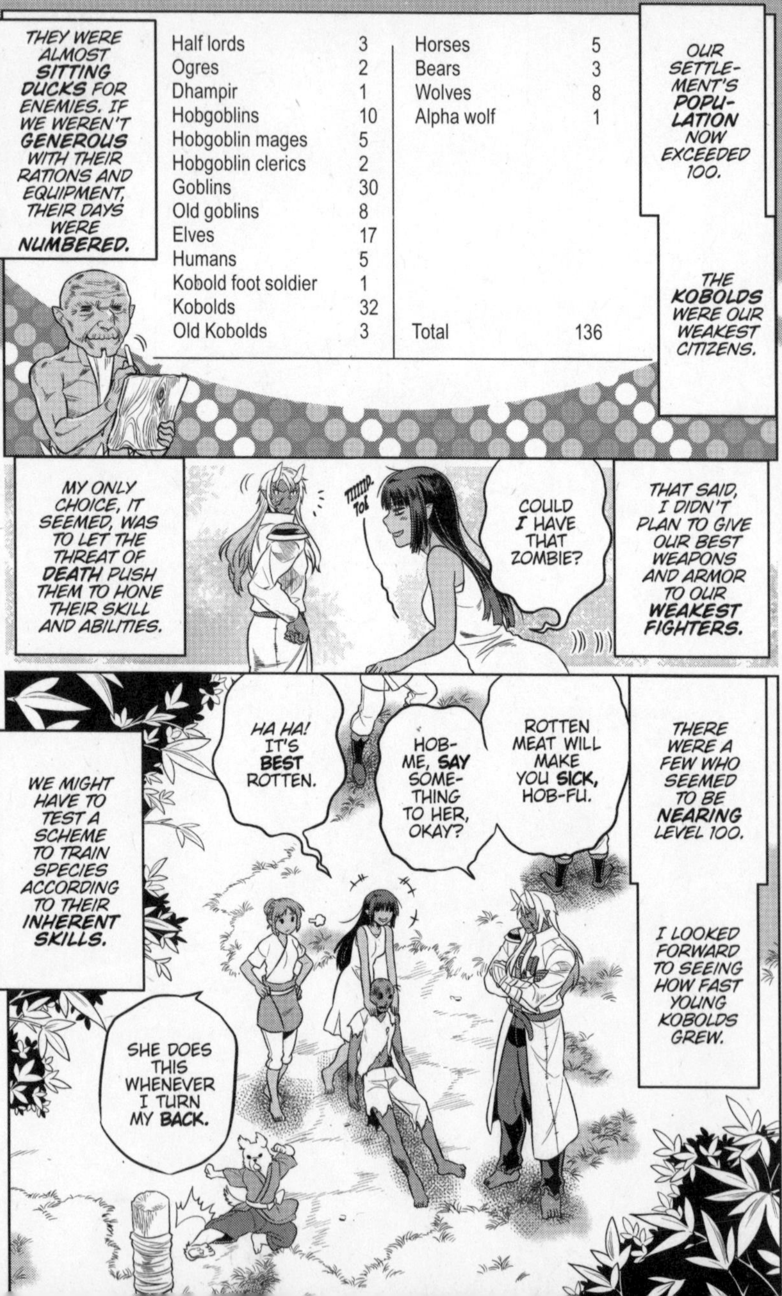

OUR SETTLEMENT'S POPULATION NOW EXCEEDED 100.

Half lords	3	Horses	5
Ogres	2	Bears	3
Dhampir	1	Wolves	8
Hobgoblins	10	Alpha wolf	1
Hobgoblin mages	5		
Hobgoblin clerics	2		
Goblins	30		
Old goblins	8		
Elves	17		
Humans	5		
Kobold foot soldier	1		
Kobolds	32		
Old Kobolds	3	Total	136

THE KOBOLDS WERE OUR WEAKEST CITIZENS.
THEY WERE ALMOST SITTING DUCKS FOR ENEMIES. IF WE WEREN'T GENEROUS WITH THEIR RATIONS AND EQUIPMENT, THEIR DAYS WERE NUMBERED.
THAT SAID, I DIDN'T PLAN TO GIVE OUR BEST WEAPONS AND ARMOR TO OUR WEAKEST FIGHTERS.
COULD I HAVE THAT ZOMBIE?
MY ONLY CHOICE, IT SEEMED, WAS TO LET THE THREAT OF DEATH PUSH THEM TO HONE THEIR SKILL AND ABILITIES.
THERE WERE A FEW WHO SEEMED TO BE NEARING LEVEL 100.
I LOOKED FORWARD TO SEEING HOW FAST YOUNG KOBOLDS GREW.
ROTTEN MEAT WILL MAKE YOU SICK, HOB-FU.
HOB-ME, SAY SOMETHING TO HER, OKAY?
HA HA! IT'S BEST ROTTEN.
WE MIGHT HAVE TO TEST A SCHEME TO TRAIN SPECIES ACCORDING TO THEIR INHERENT SKILLS.
SHE DOES THIS WHENEVER I TURN MY BACK.

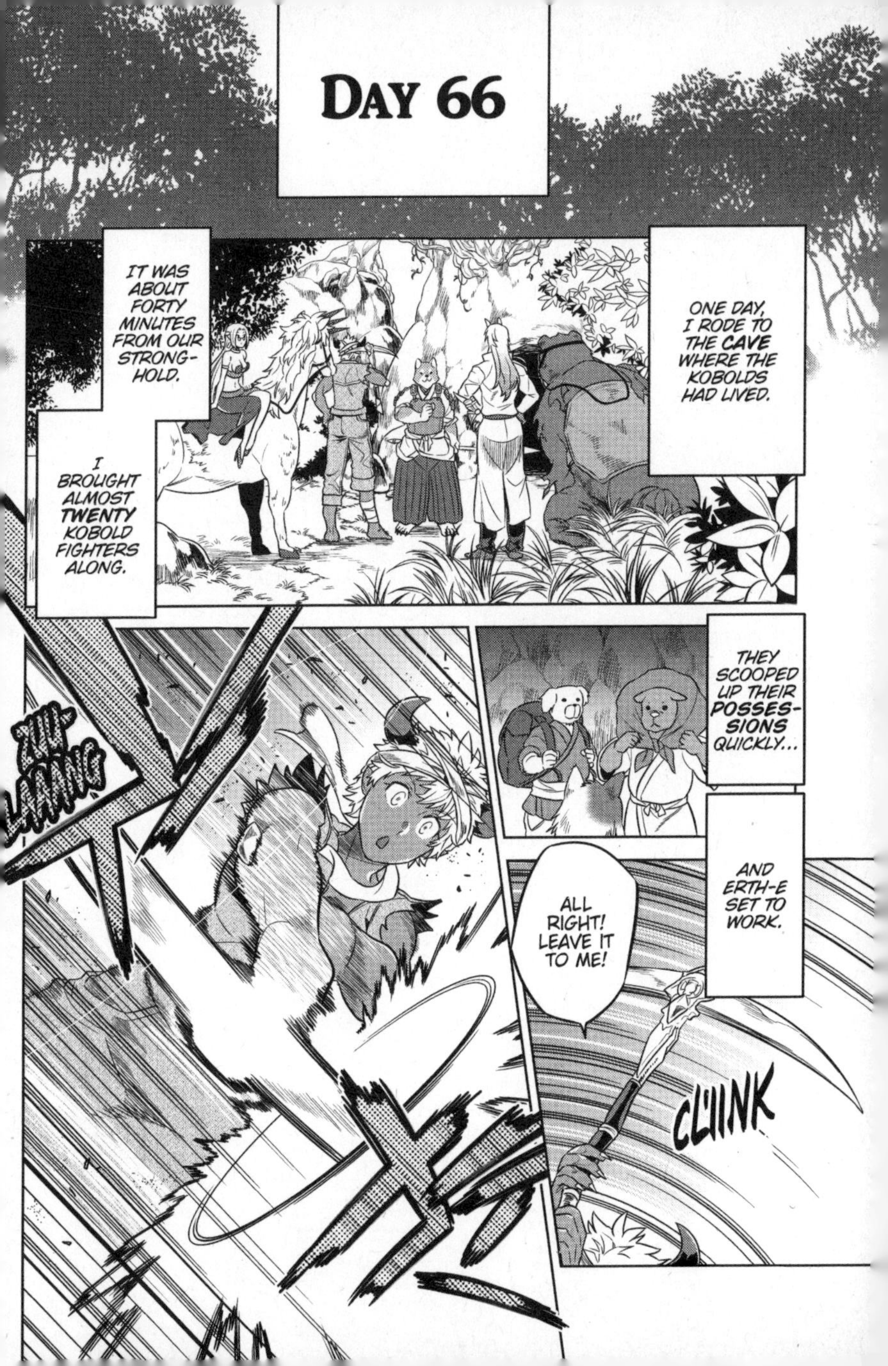
DAY 66
ONE DAY, I RODE TO THE CAVE WHERE THE KOBOLDS HAD LIVED.
IT WAS ABOUT FORTY MINUTES FROM OUR STRONGHOLD.
I BROUGHT ALMOST TWENTY KOBOLD FIGHTERS ALONG.
THEY SCOOPED UP THEIR POSSESSIONS QUICKLY...
AND ERTH-E SET TO WORK.
ALL RIGHT! LEAVE IT TO ME!
CLIINK
ZUU-LAAANG

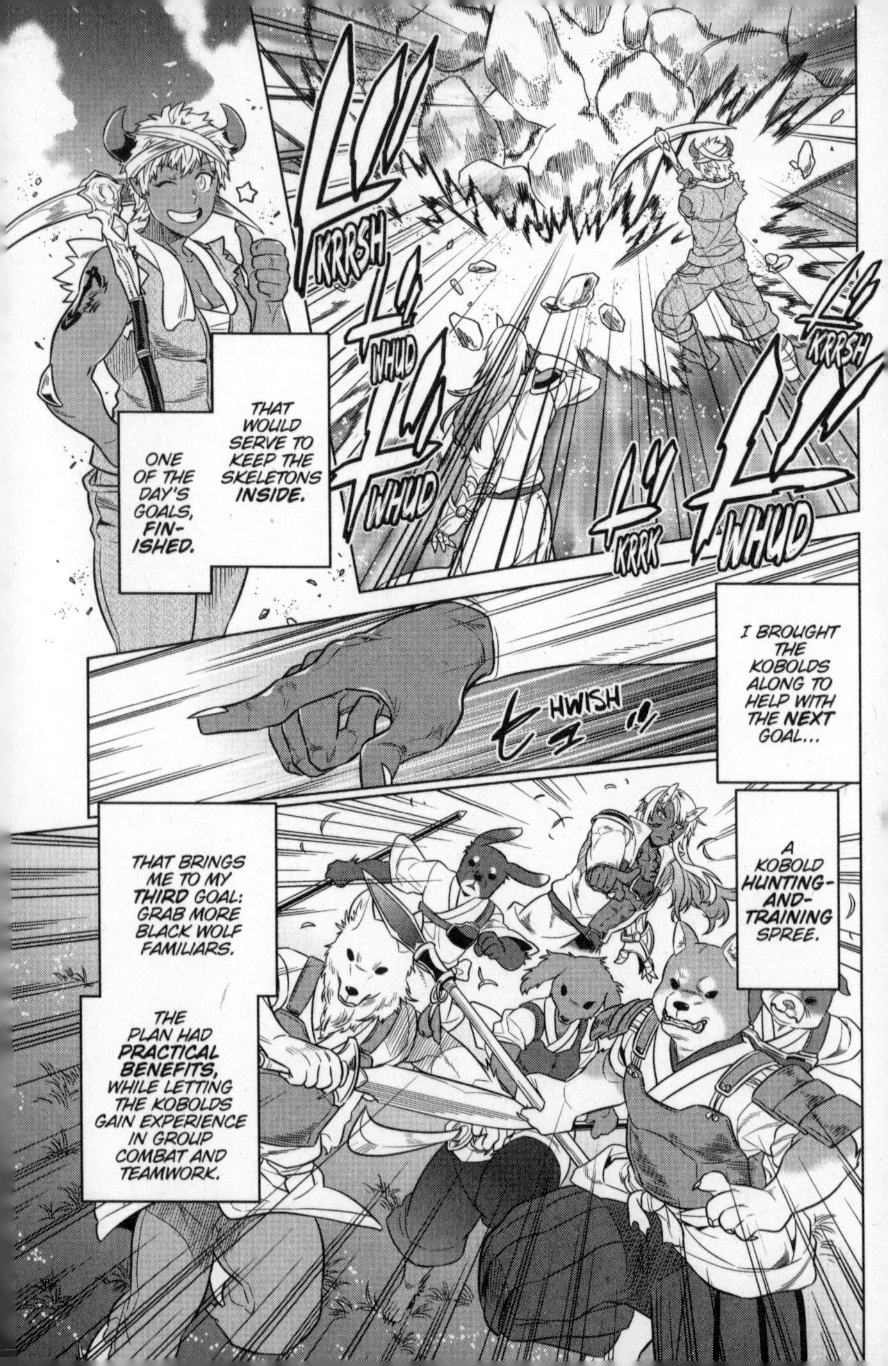
KRRSH
KRRSH
WHUD
WHUD
KRRK
WHUD
THAT WOULD SERVE TO KEEP THE SKELETONS INSIDE.
ONE OF THE DAY'S GOALS, FIN-ISHED.
I BROUGHT THE KOBOLDS ALONG TO HELP WITH THE NEXT GOAL...
HWISH
A KOBOLD HUNTING-AND-TRAINING SPREE.
THAT BRINGS ME TO MY THIRD GOAL: GRAB MORE BLACK WOLF FAMILIARS.
THE PLAN HAD PRACTICAL BENEFITS, WHILE LETTING THE KOBOLDS GAIN EXPERIENCE IN GROUP COMBAT AND TEAMWORK.

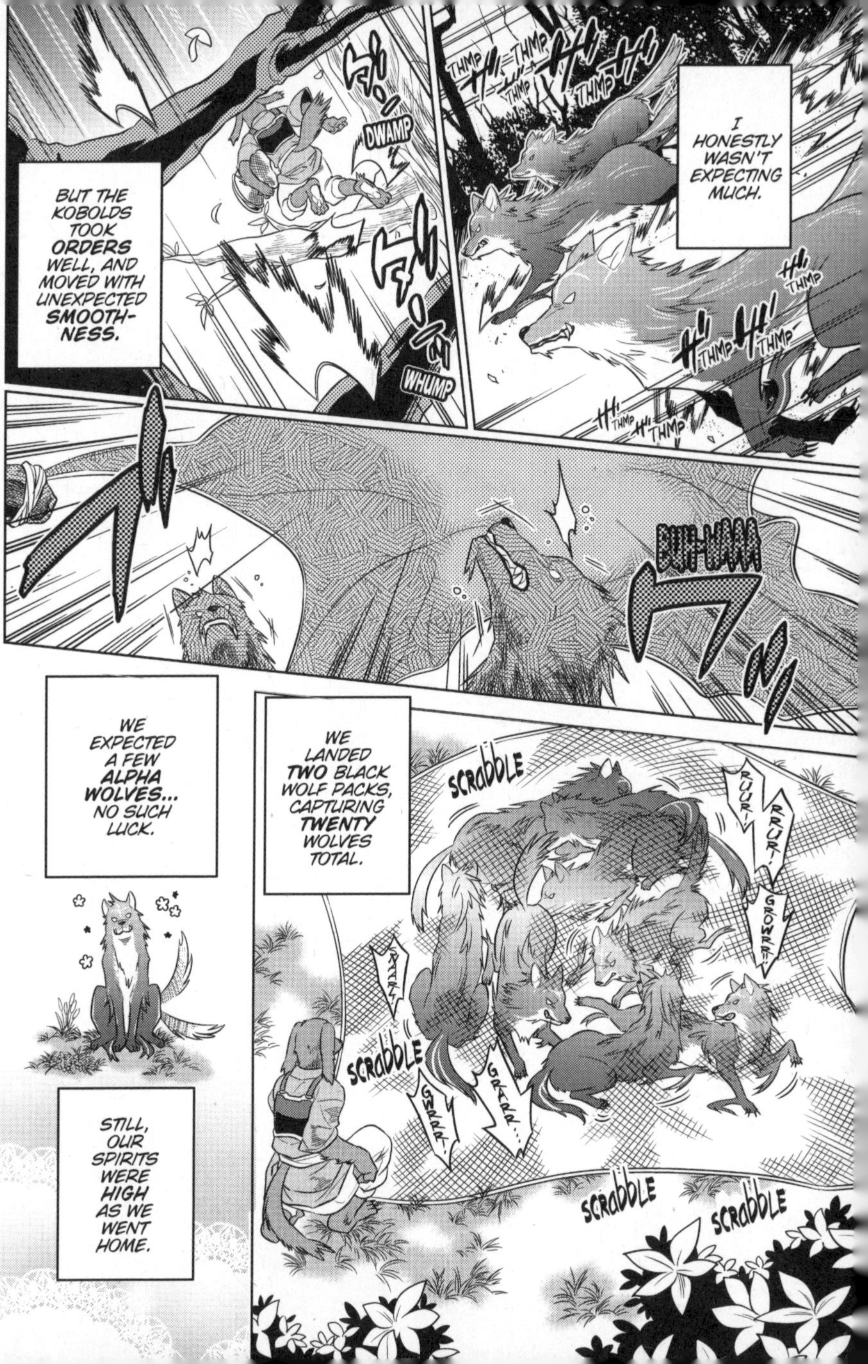
THMP
THMP
THMP
THMP
I HONESTLY WASN'T EXPECTING MUCH.
THMP
THMP
THMP
THMP
THMP
DWAMP
BUT THE KOBOLDS TOOK ORDERS WELL, AND MOVED WITH UNEXPECTED SMOOTHNESS.
WHUMP
BUH-WAA
WE LANDED TWO BLACK WOLF PACKS, CAPTURING TWENTY WOLVES TOTAL.
SCRABBLE
RRUR!
RRUR!
GROWRR!!
SCRABBLE
GRARR...
GWRRR!
SCRABBLE
SCRABBLE
WE EXPECTED A FEW ALPHA WOLVES... NO SUCH LUCK.
STILL, OUR SPIRITS WERE HIGH AS WE WENT HOME.

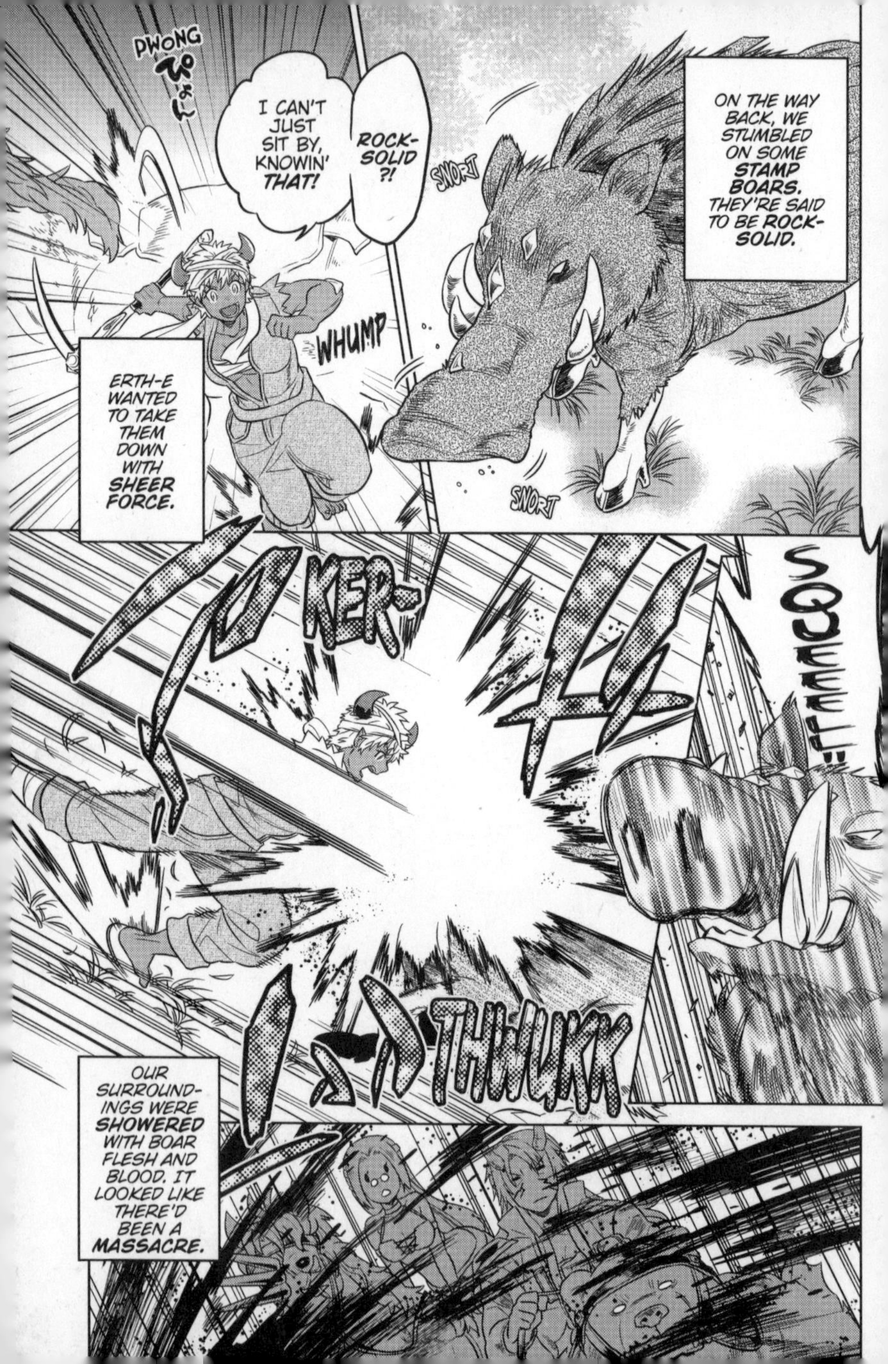

ON THE WAY BACK, WE STUMBLED ON SOME STAMP BOARS. THEY'RE SAID TO BE ROCK-SOLID.
SNORT
SNORT
WHUMP
ROCK-SOLID?!
I CAN'T JUST SIT BY, KNOWIN' THAT!
PWONG ぴょん
ERTH-E WANTED TO TAKE THEM DOWN WITH SHEER FORCE.
SQUEEEEL!!
KER-
THWUKK
OUR SURROUNDINGS WERE SHOWERED WITH BOAR FLESH AND BLOOD. IT LOOKED LIKE THERE'D BEEN A MASSACRE.

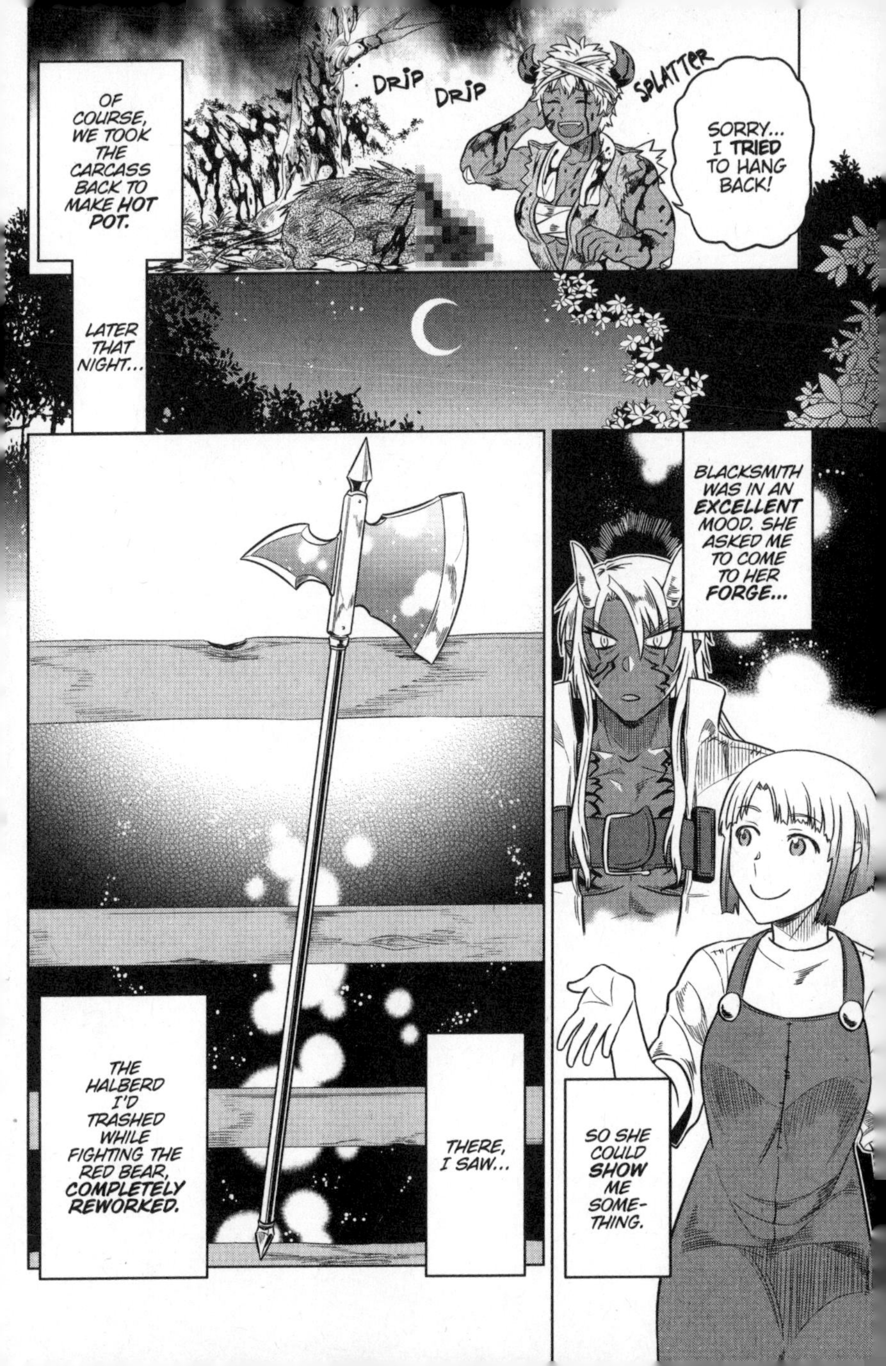
SORRY... I TRIED TO HANG BACK!
SPLATTER
DRIP
DRIP
OF COURSE, WE TOOK THE CARCASS BACK TO MAKE HOT POT.
LATER THAT NIGHT...
BLACKSMITH WAS IN AN EXCELLENT MOOD. SHE ASKED ME TO COME TO HER FORGE...
SO SHE COULD SHOW ME SOME-THING.
THERE, I SAW...
THE HALBERD I'D TRASHED WHILE FIGHTING THE RED BEAR, COMPLETELY REWORKED.

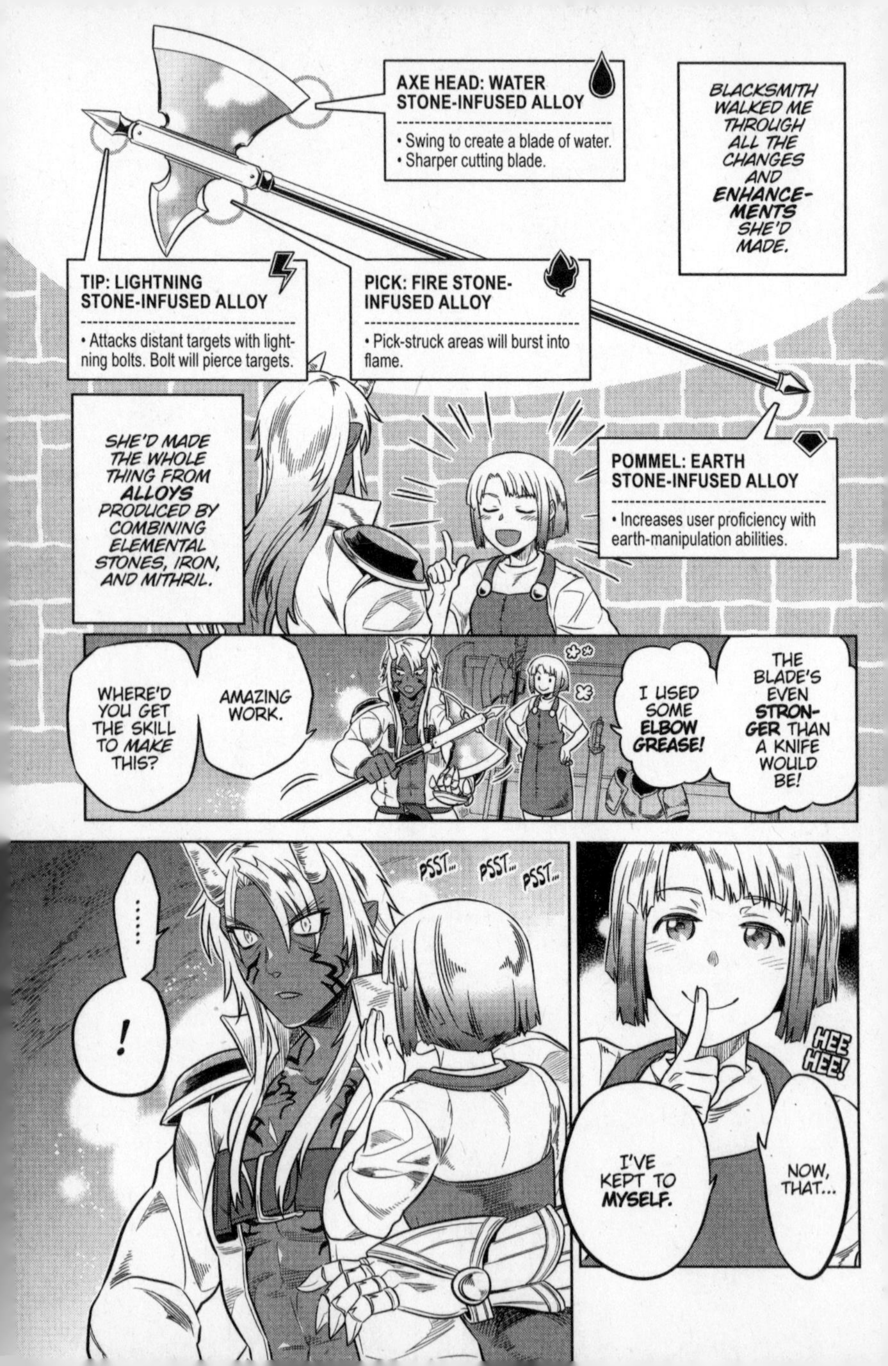

BLACKSMITH WALKED ME THROUGH ALL THE CHANGES AND ENHANCEMENTS SHE'D MADE.
AXE HEAD: WATER STONE-INFUSED ALLOY
• Swing to create a blade of water.
• Sharper cutting blade.
PICK: FIRE STONE-INFUSED ALLOY
• Pick-struck areas will burst into flame.
TIP: LIGHTNING STONE-INFUSED ALLOY
• Attacks distant targets with lightning bolts. Bolt will pierce targets.
POMMEL: EARTH STONE-INFUSED ALLOY
• Increases user proficiency with earth-manipulation abilities.
SHE'D MADE THE WHOLE THING FROM ALLOYS PRODUCED BY COMBINING ELEMENTAL STONES, IRON, AND MITHRIL.
THE BLADE'S EVEN STRONGER THAN A KNIFE WOULD BE!
I USED SOME ELBOW GREASE!
AMAZING WORK.
WHERE'D YOU GET THE SKILL TO MAKE THIS?
HEE HEE!
NOW, THAT...
I'VE KEPT TO MYSELF.
PSST... PSST... PSST...
......
!

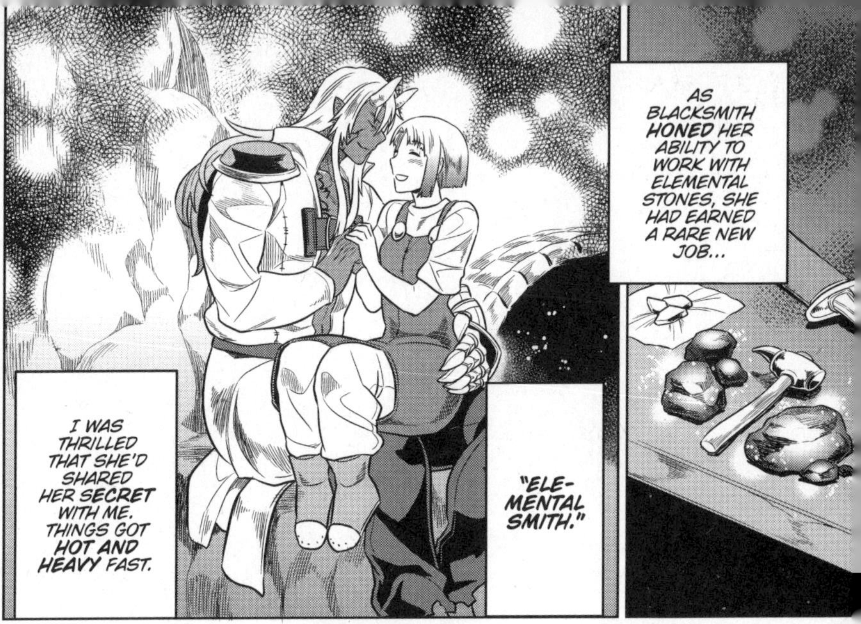
AS BLACKSMITH HONED HER ABILITY TO WORK WITH ELEMENTAL STONES, SHE HAD EARNED A RARE NEW JOB...
"ELE-MENTAL SMITH."
I WAS THRILLED THAT SHE'D SHARED HER SECRET WITH ME. THINGS GOT HOT AND HEAVY FAST.

DAY 67

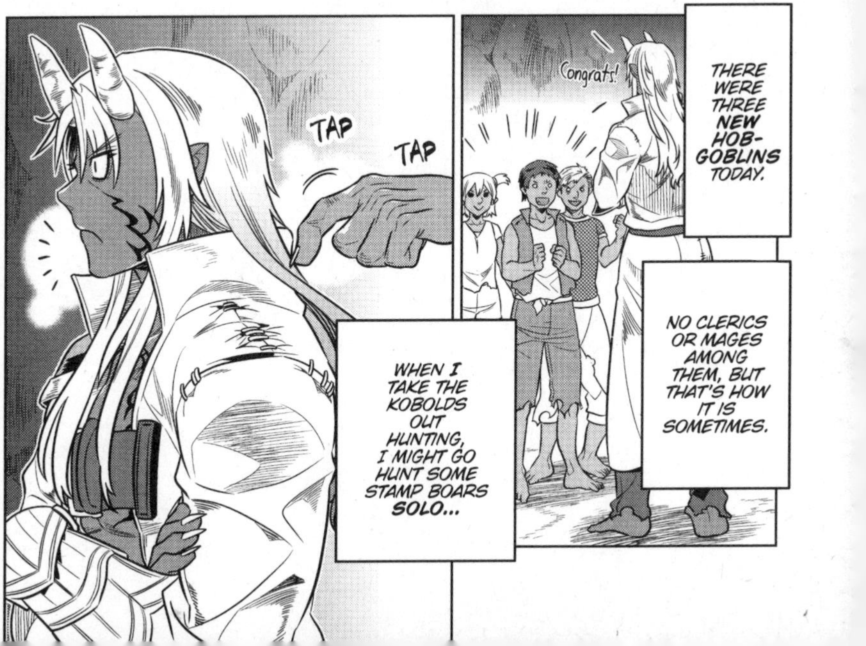
THERE WERE THREE NEW HOB-GOBLINS TODAY.
Congrats!
NO CLERICS OR MAGES AMONG THEM, BUT THAT'S HOW IT IS SOMETIMES.
TAP
TAP
WHEN I TAKE THE KOBOLDS OUT HUNTING, I MIGHT GO HUNT SOME STAMP BOARS SOLO...

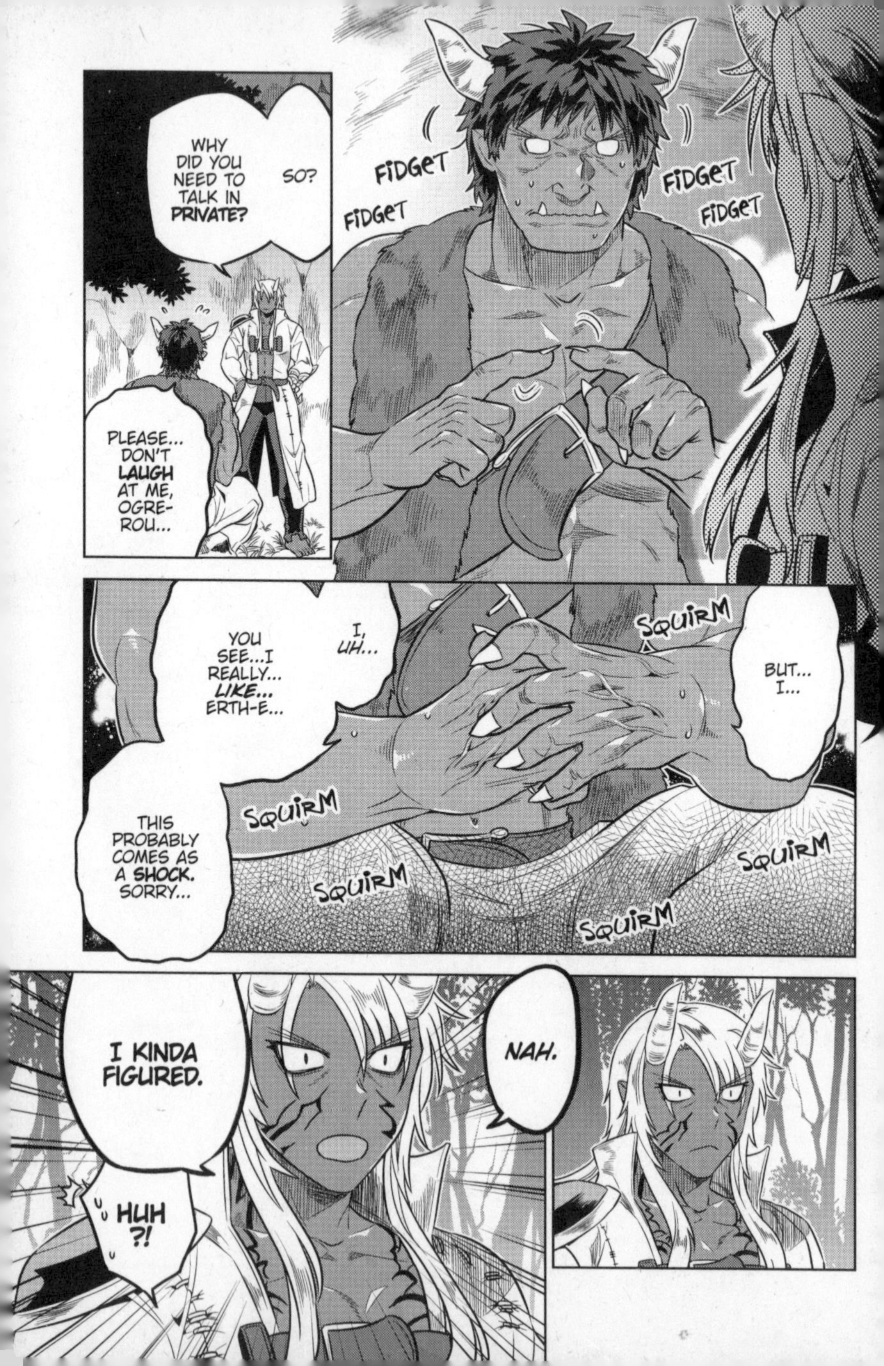
FIDGET
FIDGET
FIDGET
FIDGET
SO?
WHY DID YOU NEED TO TALK IN PRIVATE?
PLEASE... DON'T LAUGH AT ME, OGRE-ROU...
BUT... I...
SQUIRM
I, UH...
YOU SEE...I REALLY... LIKE... ERTH-E...
THIS PROBABLY COMES AS A SHOCK. SORRY...
SQUIRM
SQUIRM
SQUIRM
SQUIRM
NAH.
I KINDA FIGURED.
HUH?!

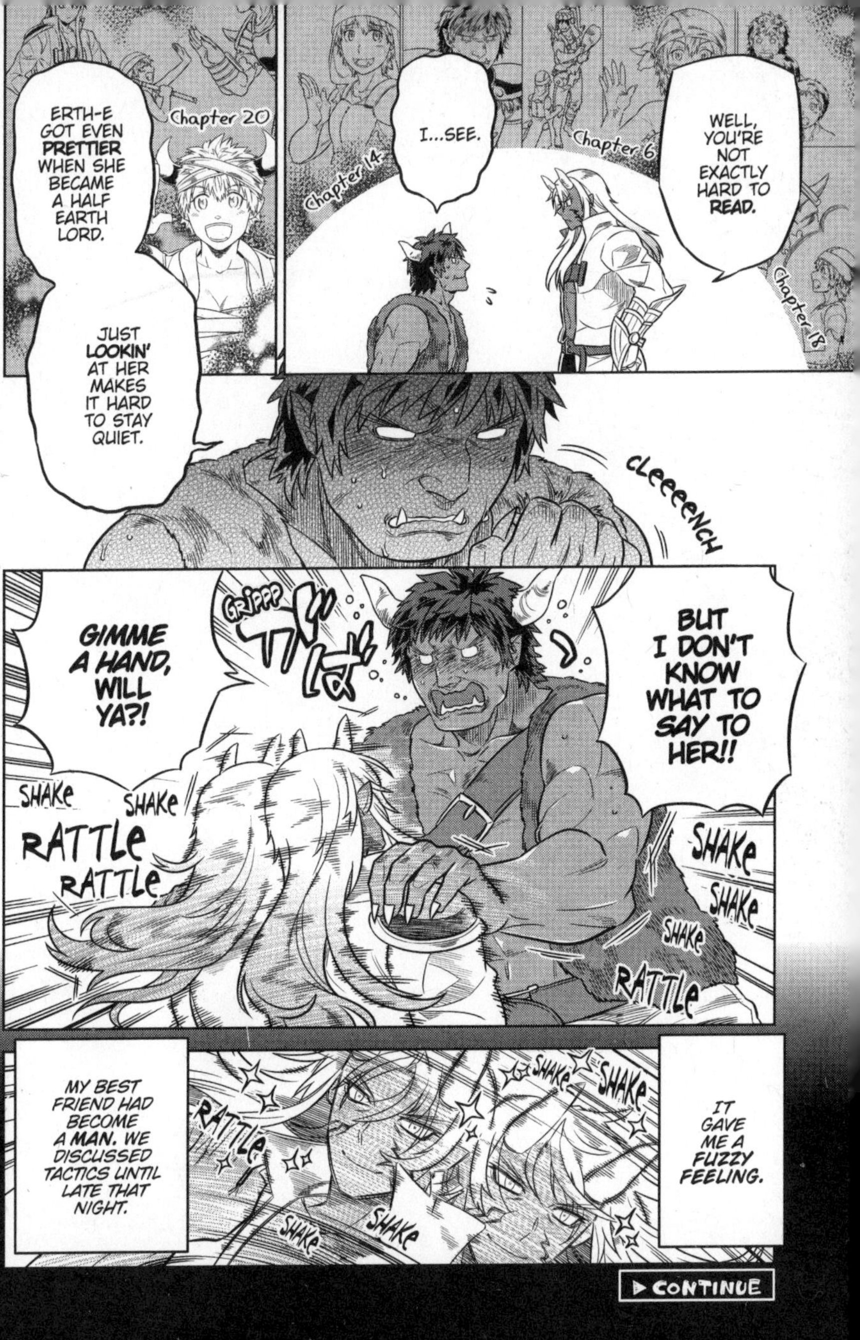

WELL, YOU'RE NOT EXACTLY HARD TO READ.
Chapter 6
Chapter 18
I...SEE.
Chapter 14
ERTH-E GOT EVEN PRETTIER WHEN SHE BECAME A HALF EARTH LORD.
Chapter 20
JUST LOOKIN' AT HER MAKES IT HARD TO STAY QUIET.
CLEEEENCH
BUT I DON'T KNOW WHAT TO SAY TO HER!!
GIMME A HAND, WILL YA?!
GRIPPP
SHAKE SHAKE SHAKE RATTLE
SHAKE SHAKE RATTLE RATTLE
IT GAVE ME A FUZZY FEELING.
SHAKE SHAKE
RATTLE
SHAKE SHAKE
MY BEST FRIEND HAD BECOME A MAN. WE DISCUSSED TACTICS UNTIL LATE THAT NIGHT.
▷ CONTINUE

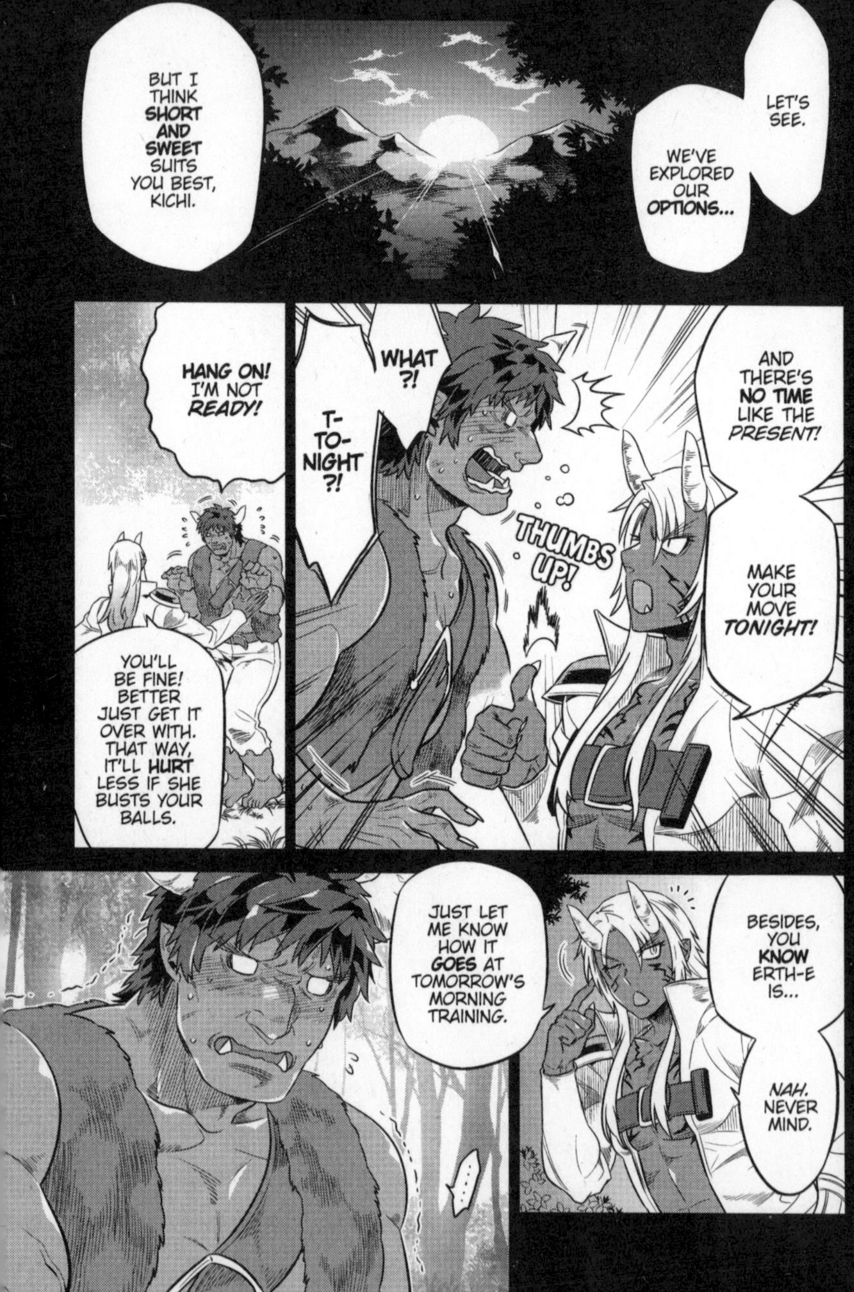
LET'S SEE.
WE'VE EXPLORED OUR OPTIONS...
BUT I THINK SHORT AND SWEET SUITS YOU BEST, KICHI.
AND THERE'S NO TIME LIKE THE PRESENT!
MAKE YOUR MOVE TONIGHT!
THUMBS UP!
WHAT?!
T-TO-NIGHT?!
HANG ON! I'M NOT READY!
YOU'LL BE FINE! BETTER JUST GET IT OVER WITH. THAT WAY, IT'LL HURT LESS IF SHE BUSTS YOUR BALLS.
BESIDES, YOU KNOW ERTH-E IS...
NAH. NEVER MIND.
JUST LET ME KNOW HOW IT GOES AT TOMORROW'S MORNING TRAINING.
...

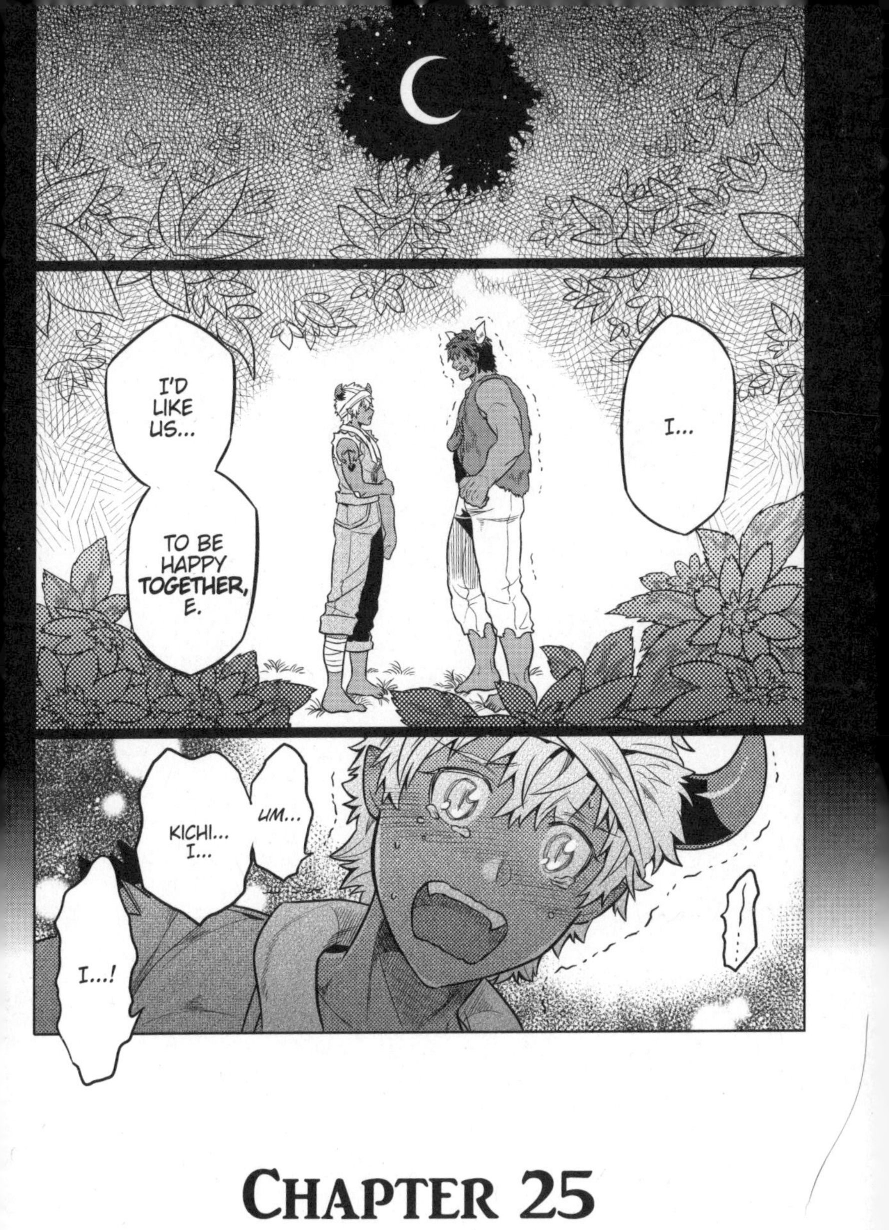
I...
I'D LIKE US...
TO BE HAPPY TOGETHER, E.
UM...
KICHI... I...
I...!

CHAPTER 25

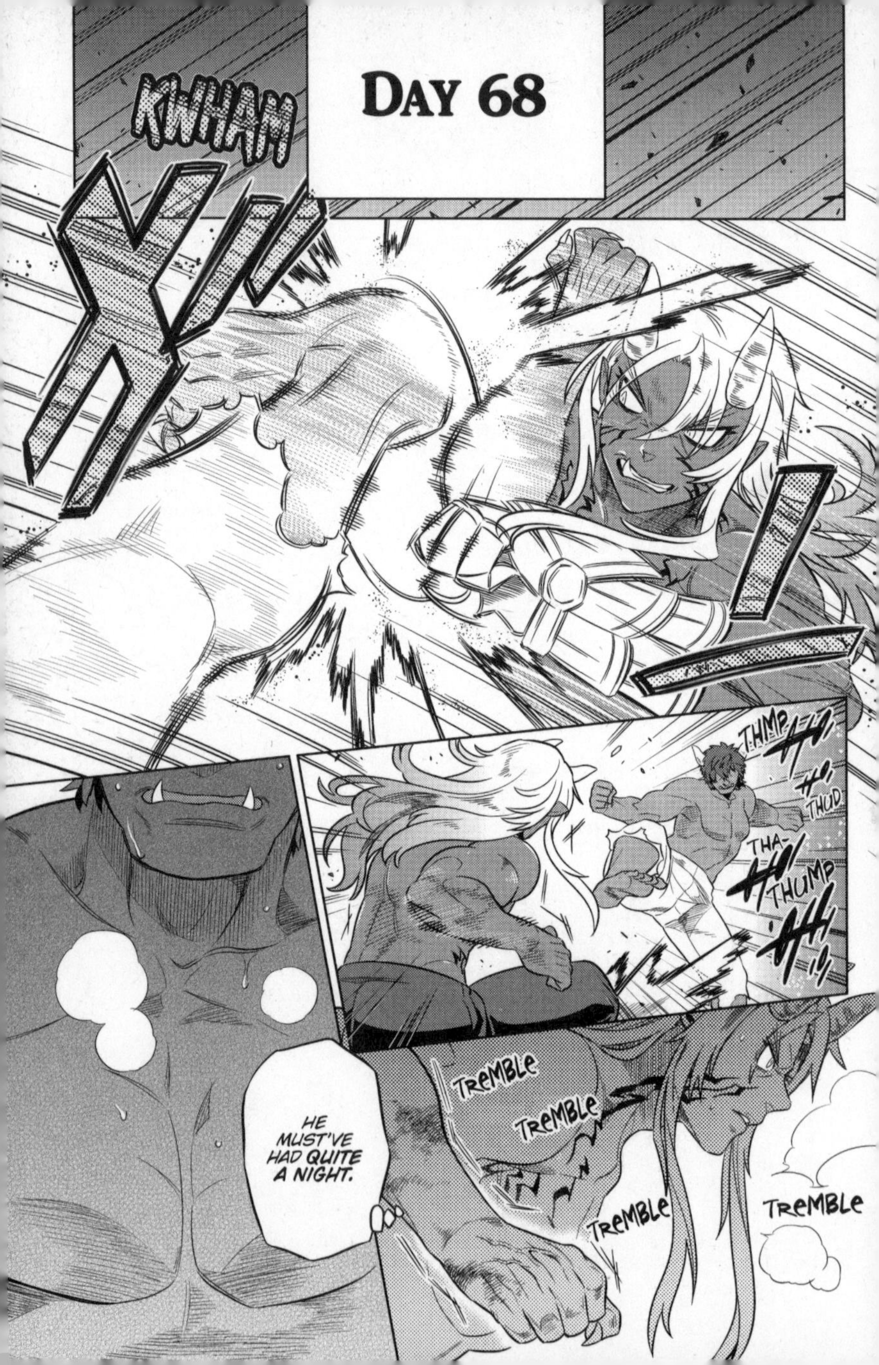
DAY 68
KWHAM
THMP
THUD
THA-THUMP
TREMBLE
TREMBLE
TREMBLE
TREMBLE
HE MUST'VE HAD QUITE A NIGHT.

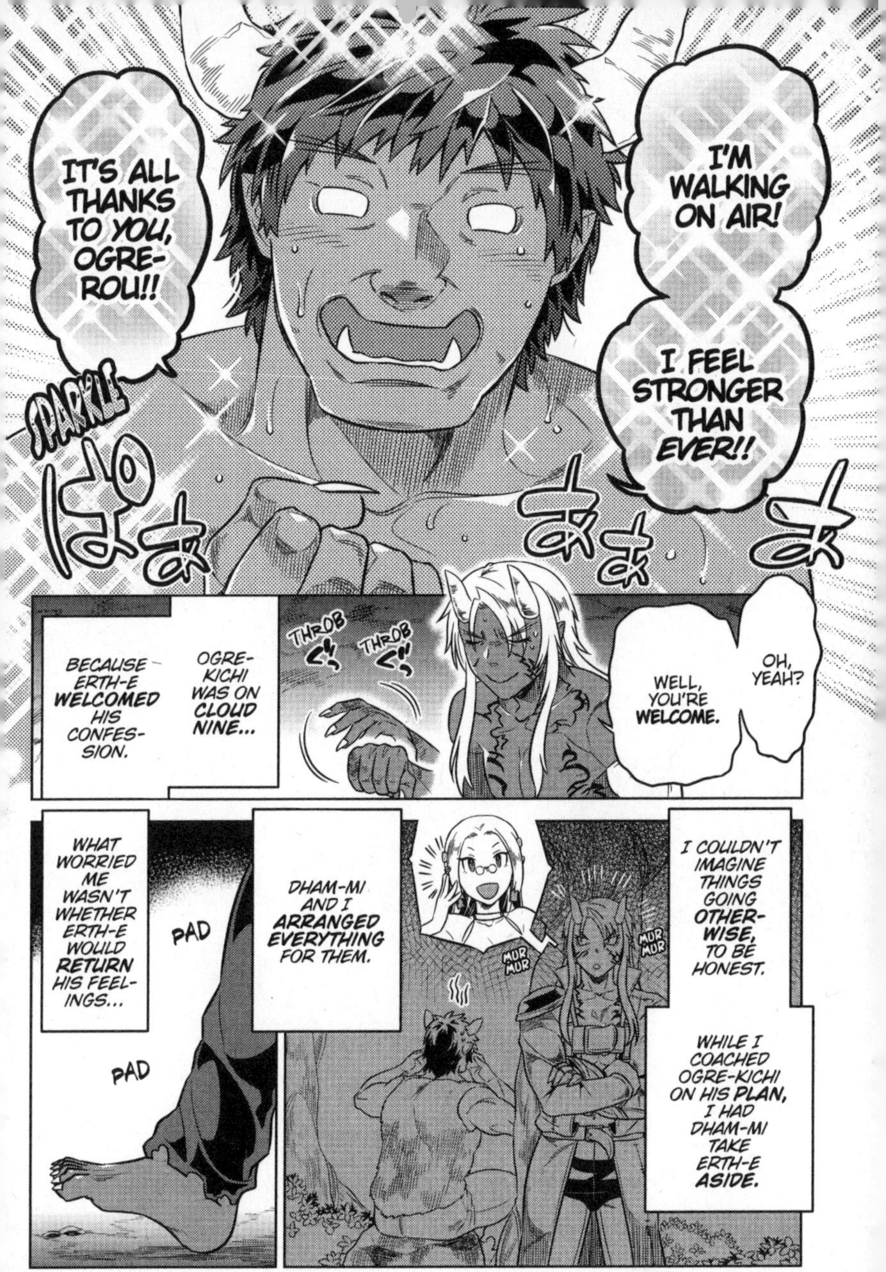
I'M WALKING ON AIR!
I FEEL STRONGER THAN EVER!!
IT'S ALL THANKS TO YOU, OGRE-ROU!!
SPARKLE
OH, YEAH?
WELL, YOU'RE WELCOME.
THROB
THROB
OGRE-KICHI WAS ON CLOUD NINE...
BECAUSE ERTH-E WELCOMED HIS CONFESSION.
I COULDN'T IMAGINE THINGS GOING OTHERWISE, TO BE HONEST.
WHILE I COACHED OGRE-KICHI ON HIS PLAN, I HAD DHAM-MI TAKE ERTH-E ASIDE.
MUR MUR
MUR MUR
DHAM-MI AND I ARRANGED EVERYTHING FOR THEM.
WHAT WORRIED ME WASN'T WHETHER ERTH-E WOULD RETURN HIS FEELINGS...
PAD
PAD

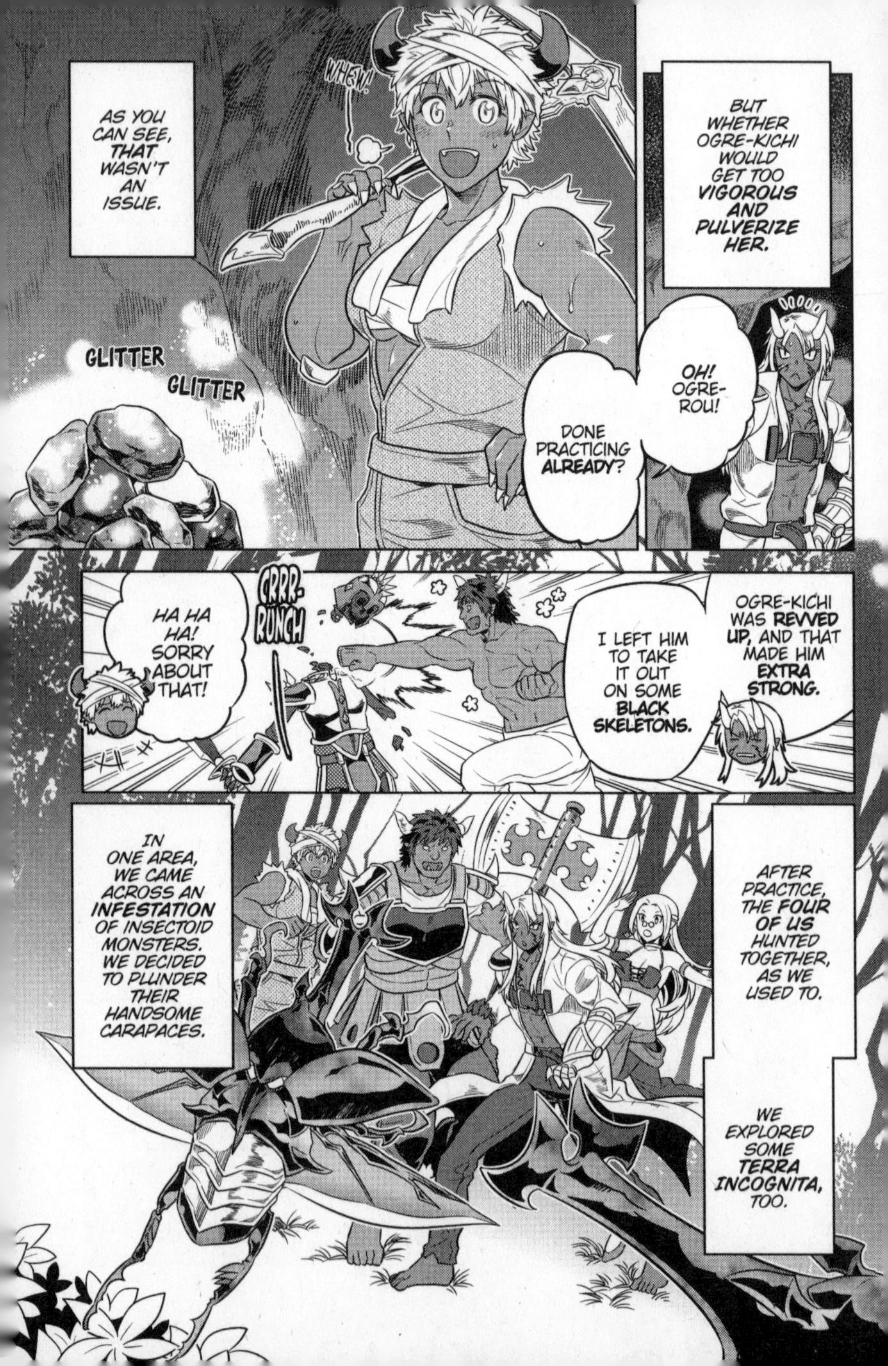
BUT WHETHER OGRE-KICHI WOULD GET TOO VIGOROUS AND PULVERIZE HER.
OH! OGRE-ROU!
DONE PRACTICING ALREADY?
AS YOU CAN SEE, THAT WASN'T AN ISSUE.
WHEW!
GLITTER
GLITTER
OGRE-KICHI WAS REVVED UP, AND THAT MADE HIM EXTRA STRONG.
I LEFT HIM TO TAKE IT OUT ON SOME BLACK SKELETONS.
CRRR-RUNCH
HA HA HA! SORRY ABOUT THAT!
AFTER PRACTICE, THE FOUR OF US HUNTED TOGETHER, AS WE USED TO.
WE EXPLORED SOME TERRA INCOGNITA, TOO.
IN ONE AREA, WE CAME ACROSS AN INFESTATION OF INSECTOID MONSTERS. WE DECIDED TO PLUNDER THEIR HANDSOME CARAPACES.

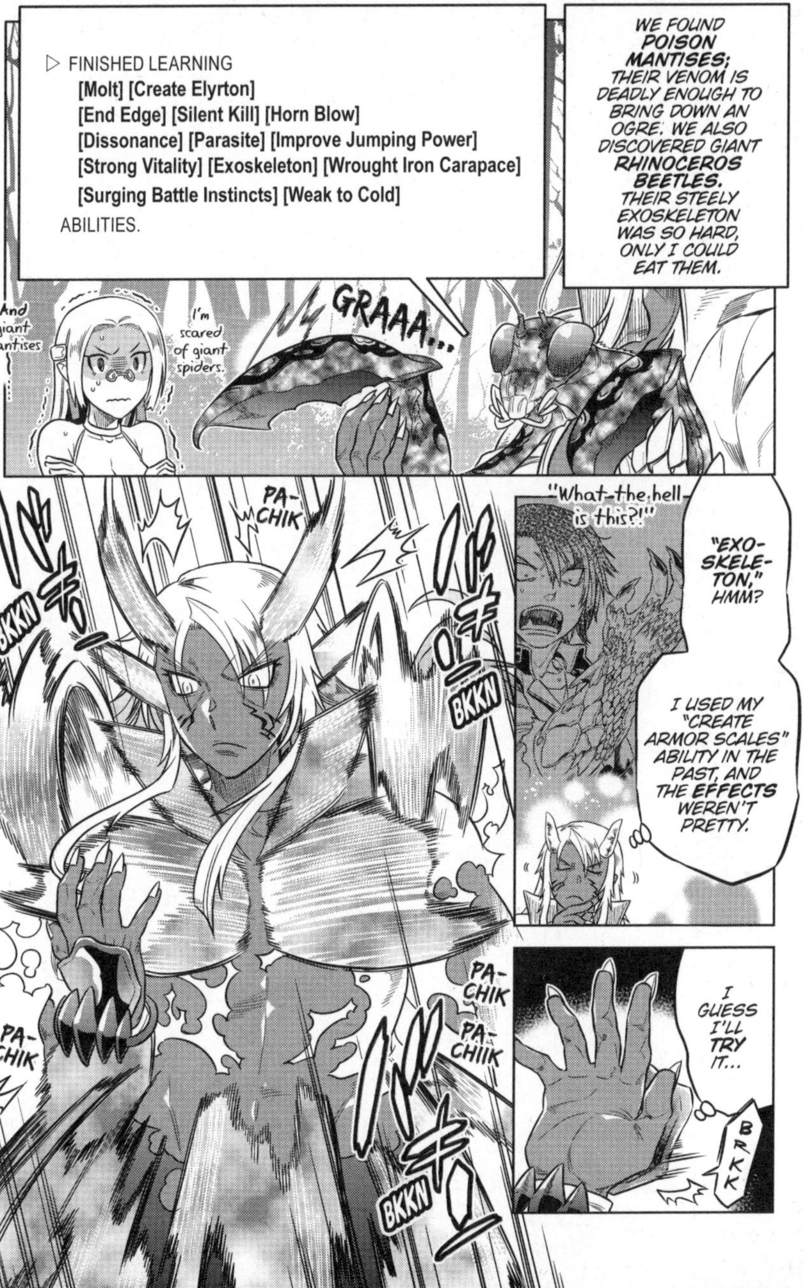

WE FOUND **POISON MANTISES;** THEIR VENOM IS DEADLY ENOUGH TO BRING DOWN AN OGRE. WE ALSO DISCOVERED GIANT **RHINOCEROS BEETLES.** THEIR STEELY EXOSKELETON WAS SO HARD, ONLY I COULD EAT THEM.
▷ FINISHED LEARNING
[Molt] [Create Elyrton]
[End Edge] [Silent Kill] [Horn Blow]
[Dissonance] [Parasite] [Improve Jumping Power]
[Strong Vitality] [Exoskeleton] [Wrought Iron Carapace]
[Surging Battle Instincts] [Weak to Cold]
ABILITIES.
GRAAAA...
I'm scared of giant spiders.
And giant mantises
"EXO-SKELE-TON," HMM?
"What the hell is this?!"
I USED MY "CREATE ARMOR SCALES" ABILITY IN THE PAST, AND THE **EFFECTS** WEREN'T PRETTY.
I GUESS I'LL **TRY** IT...
BRKK
PA-CHIK
BKKN
BKKN
PA-CHIK
PA-CHIIK
BKKN
PA-CHIK

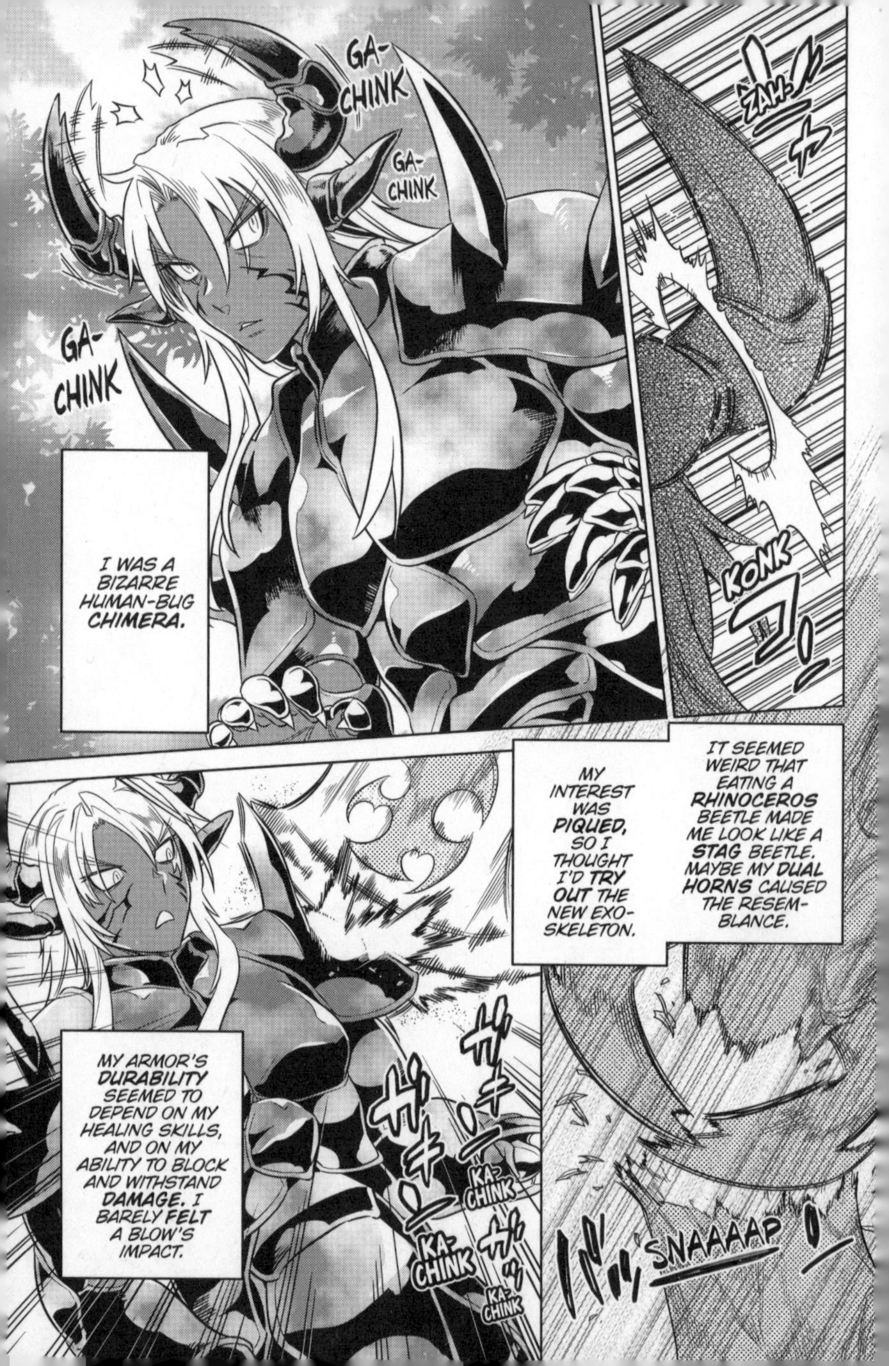
ZAH
KONK
GA-CHINK
GA-CHINK
GA-CHINK
I WAS A BIZARRE HUMAN-BUG CHIMERA.
IT SEEMED WEIRD THAT EATING A RHINOCEROS BEETLE MADE ME LOOK LIKE A STAG BEETLE. MAYBE MY DUAL HORNS CAUSED THE RESEMBLANCE.
MY INTEREST WAS PIQUED, SO I THOUGHT I'D TRY OUT THE NEW EXOSKELETON.
SNAAAAP
MY ARMOR'S DURABILITY SEEMED TO DEPEND ON MY HEALING SKILLS, AND ON MY ABILITY TO BLOCK AND WITHSTAND DAMAGE. I BARELY FELT A BLOW'S IMPACT.
KA-CHINK
KA-CHINK
KA-CHINK

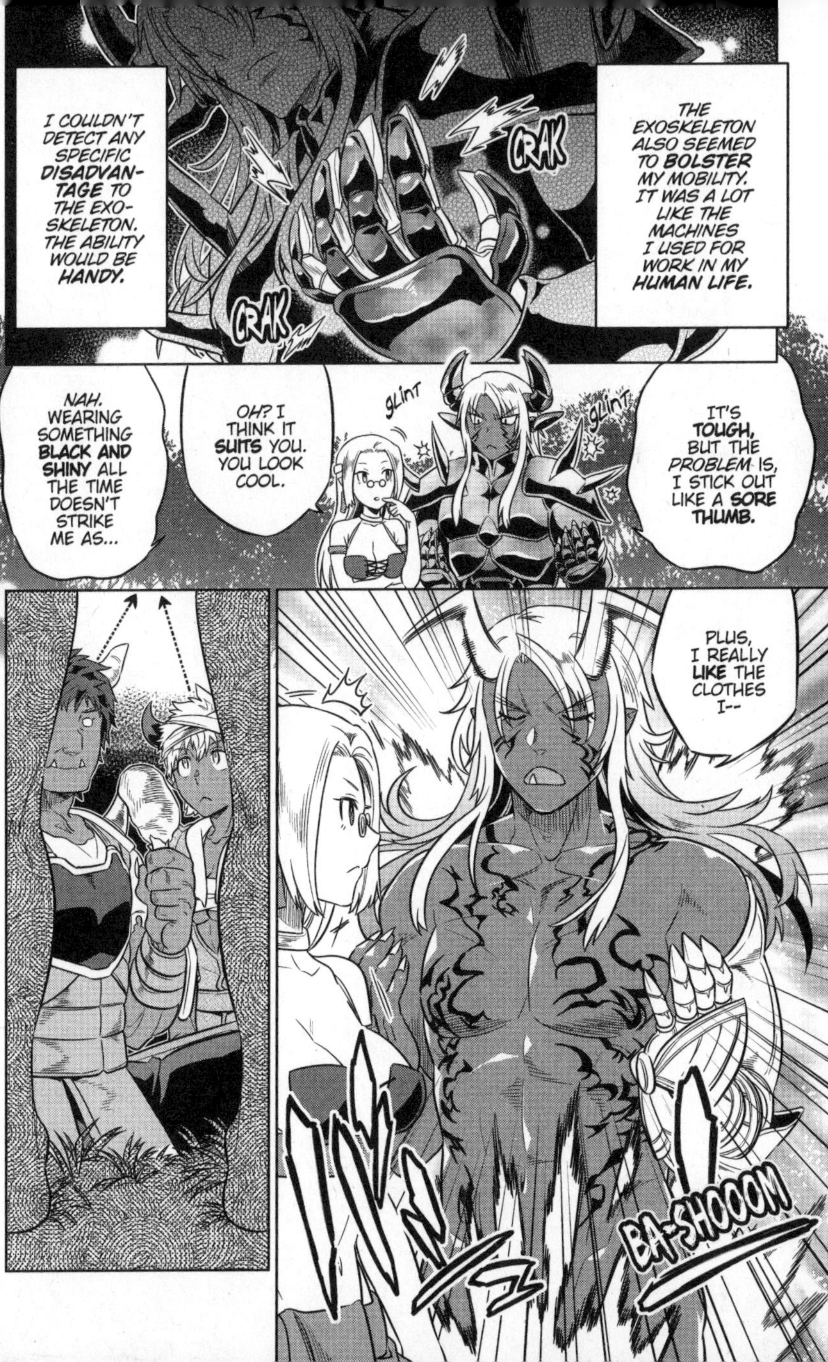
THE EXOSKELETON ALSO SEEMED TO BOLSTER MY MOBILITY. IT WAS A LOT LIKE THE MACHINES I USED FOR WORK IN MY HUMAN LIFE.
CRAK
I COULDN'T DETECT ANY SPECIFIC DISADVANTAGE TO THE EXOSKELETON. THE ABILITY WOULD BE HANDY.
CRAK
IT'S TOUGH, BUT THE PROBLEM IS, I STICK OUT LIKE A SORE THUMB.
GLINT
GLINT
OH? I THINK IT SUITS YOU. YOU LOOK COOL.
NAH. WEARING SOMETHING BLACK AND SHINY ALL THE TIME DOESN'T STRIKE ME AS...
PLUS, I REALLY LIKE THE CLOTHES I--
BA-SHOOOM

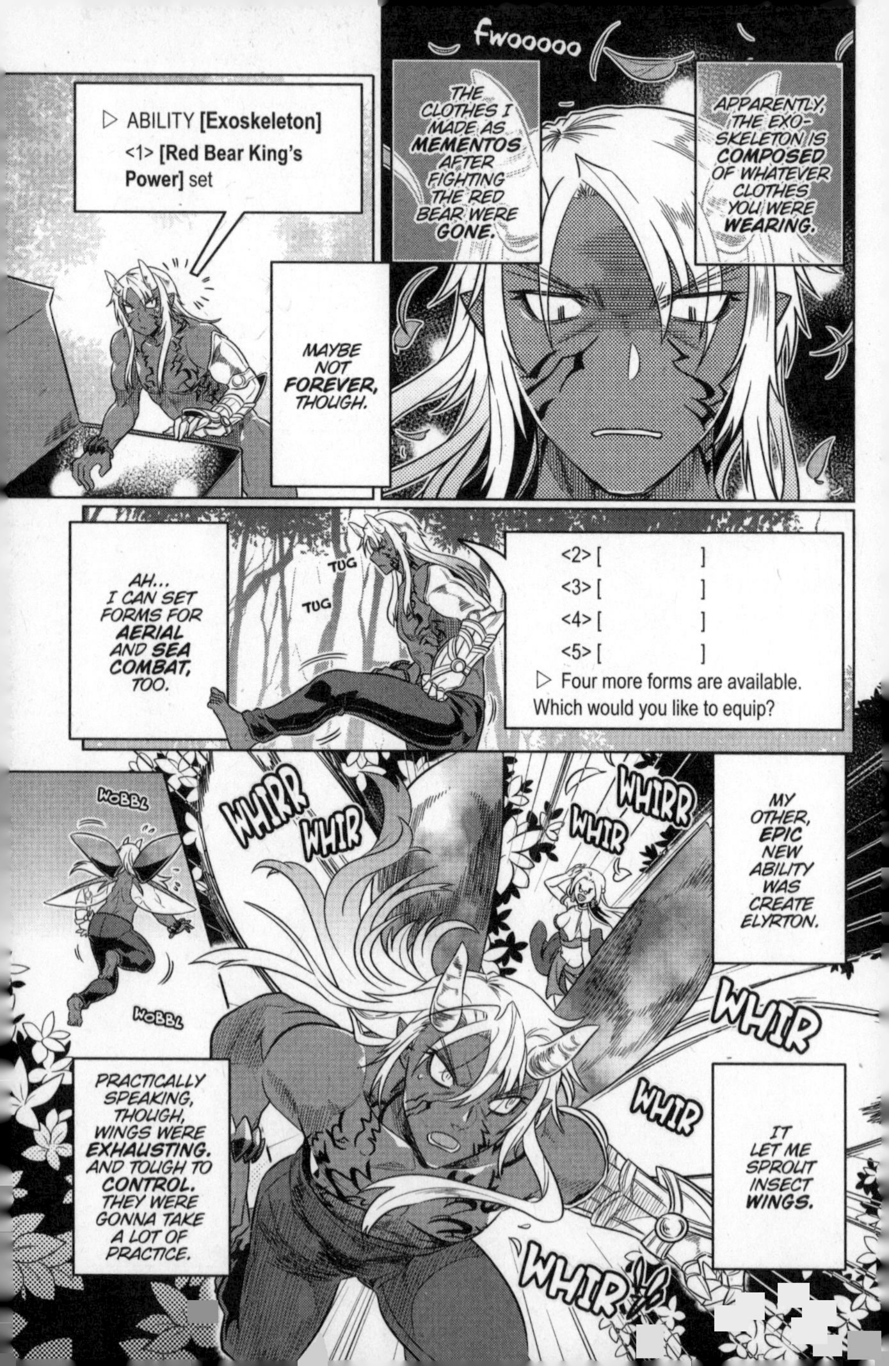
FWOOOOO
APPARENTLY, THE EXO-SKELETON IS COMPOSED OF WHATEVER CLOTHES YOU WERE WEARING.
THE CLOTHES I MADE AS MEMENTOS AFTER FIGHTING THE RED BEAR WERE GONE.
MAYBE NOT FOREVER, THOUGH.
▷ ABILITY [Exoskeleton]
<1> [Red Bear King's Power] set
<2> [ ]
<3> [ ]
<4> [ ]
<5> [ ]
▷ Four more forms are available. Which would you like to equip?
TUG
TUG
AH... I CAN SET FORMS FOR AERIAL AND SEA COMBAT, TOO.
MY OTHER, EPIC NEW ABILITY WAS CREATE ELYRTON.
WHIRR
WHIR
WHIRR
WHIR
WHIR
WHIR
IT LET ME SPROUT INSECT WINGS.
WHIR
PRACTICALLY SPEAKING, THOUGH, WINGS WERE EXHAUSTING. AND TOUGH TO CONTROL. THEY WERE GONNA TAKE A LOT OF PRACTICE.
WOBBL
WOBBL

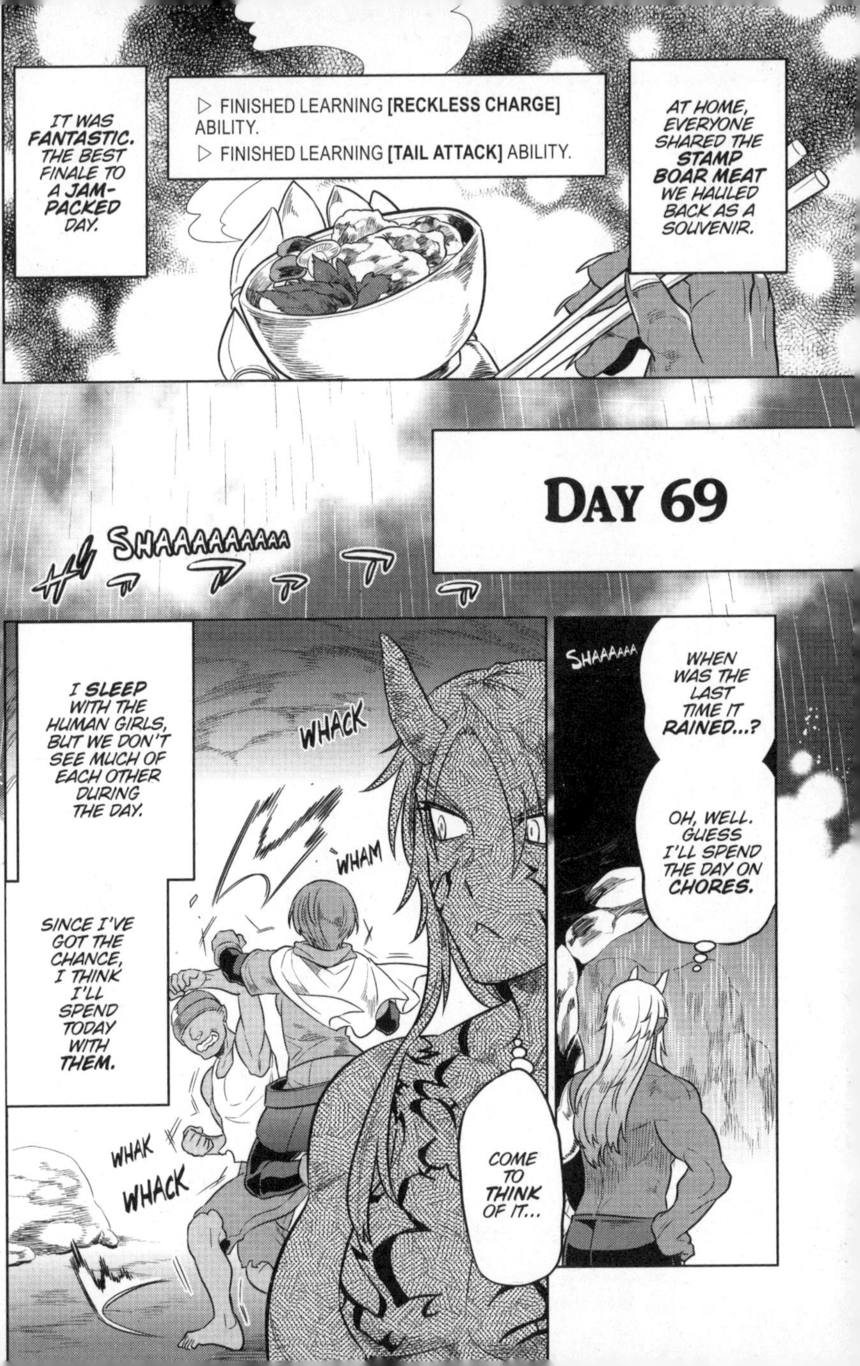
AT HOME, EVERYONE SHARED THE STAMP BOAR MEAT WE HAULED BACK AS A SOUVENIR.
▷ FINISHED LEARNING [RECKLESS CHARGE] ABILITY.
▷ FINISHED LEARNING [TAIL ATTACK] ABILITY.
IT WAS FANTASTIC. THE BEST FINALE TO A JAM-PACKED DAY.
DAY 69
SHAAAAAAAAA
SHAAAAAA
COME TO THINK OF IT...
WHEN WAS THE LAST TIME IT RAINED...?
OH, WELL. GUESS I'LL SPEND THE DAY ON CHORES.
I SLEEP WITH THE HUMAN GIRLS, BUT WE DON'T SEE MUCH OF EACH OTHER DURING THE DAY.
WHACK
WHAM
SINCE I'VE GOT THE CHANCE, I THINK I'LL SPEND TODAY WITH THEM.
WHAK
WHACK

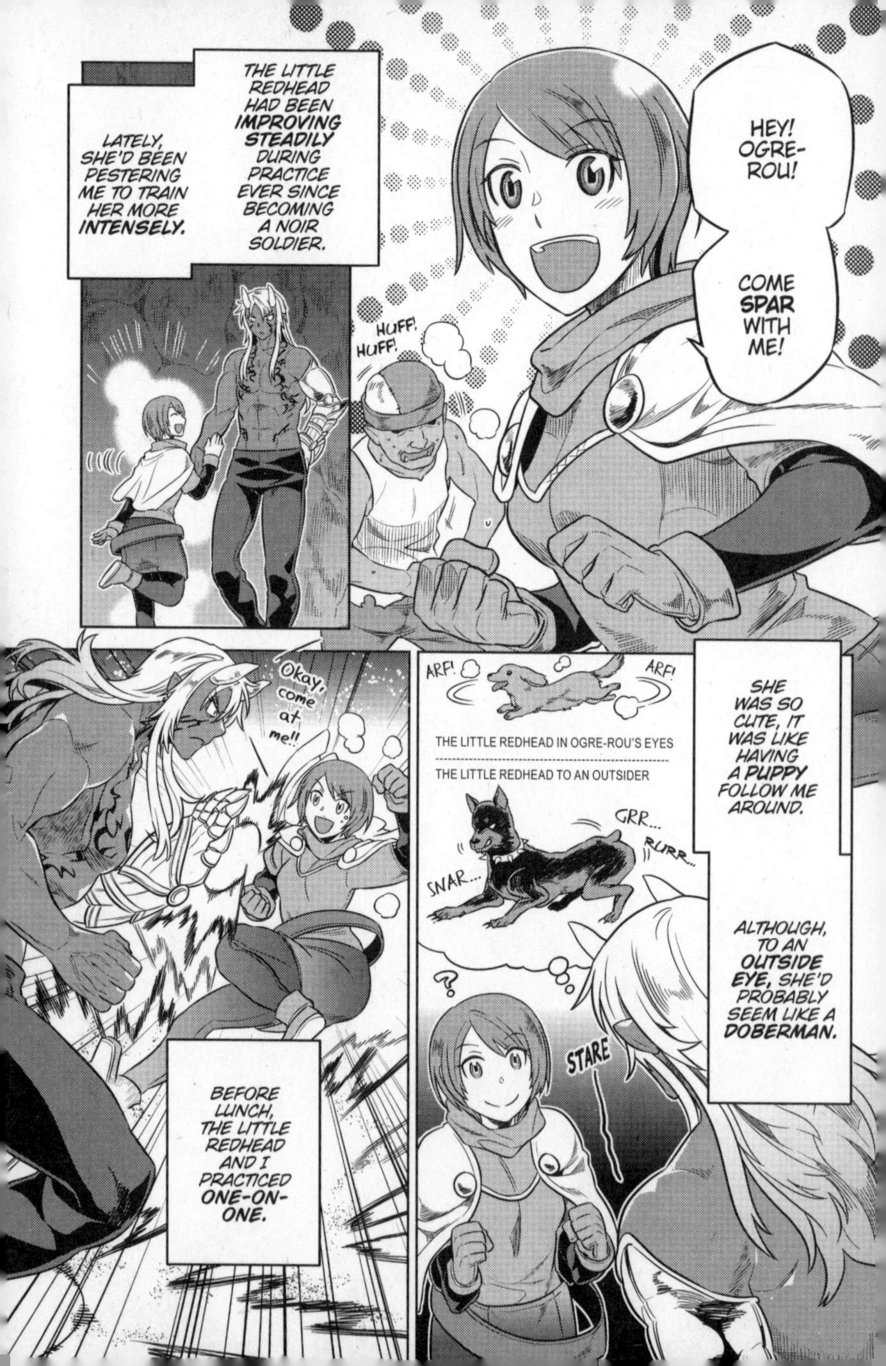
HEY! OGRE-ROU!
COME SPAR WITH ME!
HUFF! HUFF!
THE LITTLE REDHEAD HAD BEEN IMPROVING STEADILY DURING PRACTICE EVER SINCE BECOMING A NOIR SOLDIER.
LATELY, SHE'D BEEN PESTERING ME TO TRAIN HER MORE INTENSELY.
SHE WAS SO CUTE, IT WAS LIKE HAVING A PUPPY FOLLOW ME AROUND.
ARF! ARF!
THE LITTLE REDHEAD IN OGRE-ROU'S EYES
THE LITTLE REDHEAD TO AN OUTSIDER
GRR... RURR...
SNAR...
ALTHOUGH, TO AN OUTSIDE EYE, SHE'D PROBABLY SEEM LIKE A DOBERMAN.
?
STARE
Okay, come at me!!
BEFORE LUNCH, THE LITTLE REDHEAD AND I PRACTICED ONE-ON-ONE.

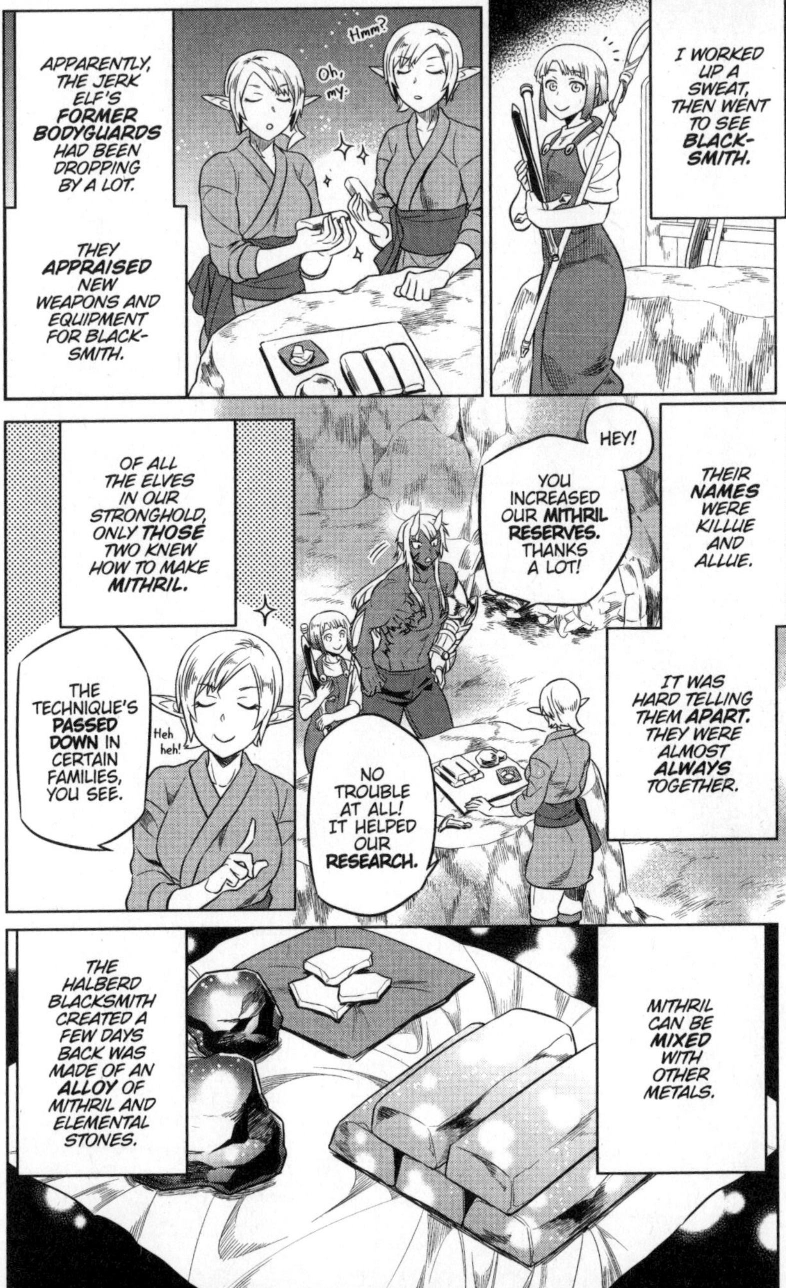
I WORKED UP A SWEAT, THEN WENT TO SEE BLACKSMITH.
APPARENTLY, THE JERK ELF'S FORMER BODYGUARDS HAD BEEN DROPPING BY A LOT.
Hmm?
Oh, my.
THEY APPRAISED NEW WEAPONS AND EQUIPMENT FOR BLACKSMITH.
THEIR NAMES WERE KILLUE AND ALLUE.
HEY!
YOU INCREASED OUR MITHRIL RESERVES. THANKS A LOT!
OF ALL THE ELVES IN OUR STRONGHOLD, ONLY THOSE TWO KNEW HOW TO MAKE MITHRIL.
IT WAS HARD TELLING THEM APART. THEY WERE ALMOST ALWAYS TOGETHER.
NO TROUBLE AT ALL! IT HELPED OUR RESEARCH.
THE TECHNIQUE'S PASSED DOWN IN CERTAIN FAMILIES, YOU SEE.
Heh heh!
MITHRIL CAN BE MIXED WITH OTHER METALS.
THE HALBERD BLACKSMITH CREATED A FEW DAYS BACK WAS MADE OF AN ALLOY OF MITHRIL AND ELEMENTAL STONES.

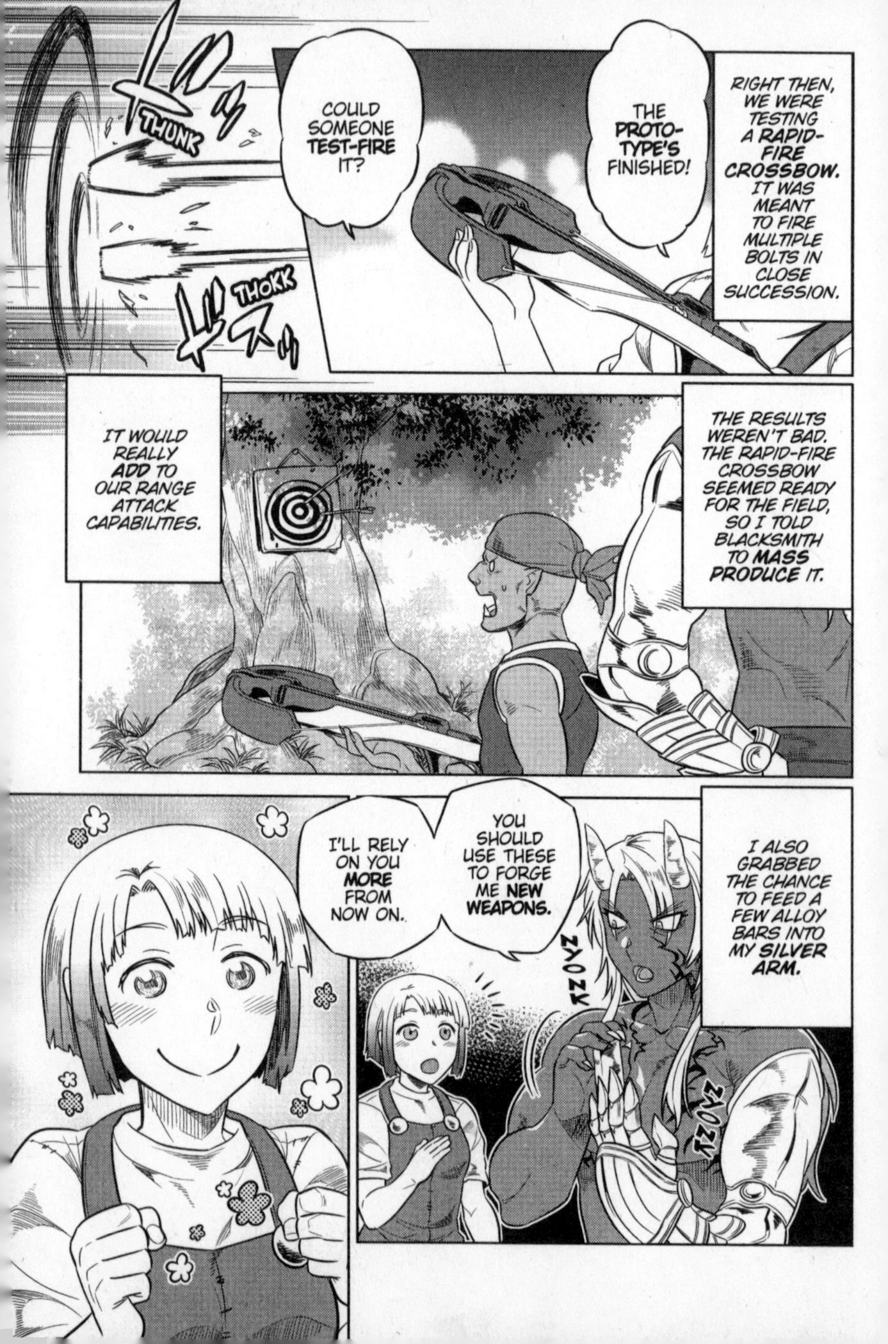
RIGHT THEN, WE WERE TESTING A RAPID-FIRE CROSSBOW. IT WAS MEANT TO FIRE MULTIPLE BOLTS IN CLOSE SUCCESSION.
THE PROTO-TYPE'S FINISHED!
COULD SOMEONE TEST-FIRE IT?
THUNK
THOKK
THE RESULTS WEREN'T BAD. THE RAPID-FIRE CROSSBOW SEEMED READY FOR THE FIELD, SO I TOLD BLACKSMITH TO MASS PRODUCE IT.
IT WOULD REALLY ADD TO OUR RANGE ATTACK CAPABILITIES.
I ALSO GRABBED THE CHANCE TO FEED A FEW ALLOY BARS INTO MY SILVER ARM.
YOU SHOULD USE THESE TO FORGE ME NEW WEAPONS.
ZYONK
ZYONK
I'LL RELY ON YOU MORE FROM NOW ON.

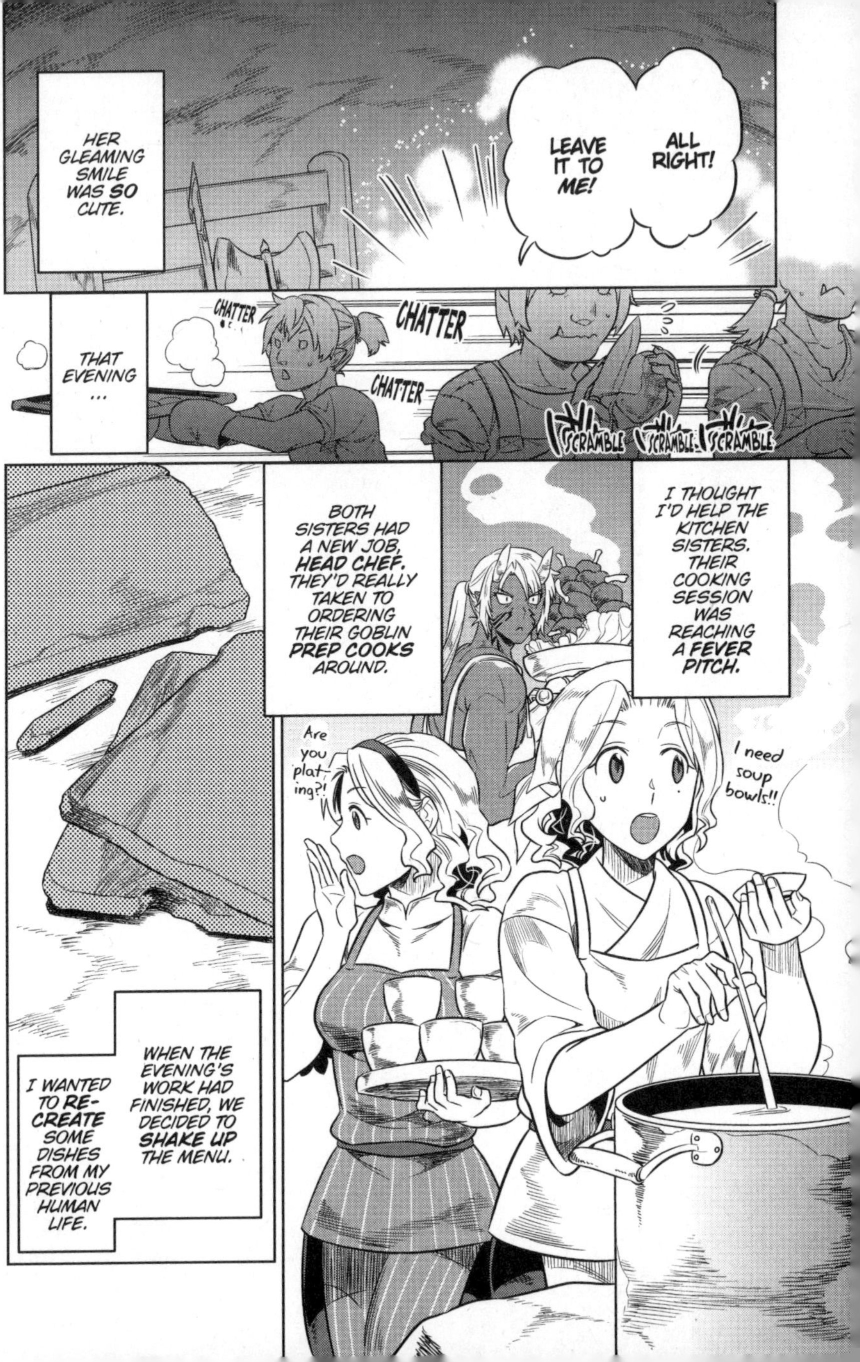
ALL RIGHT!
LEAVE IT TO ME!
HER GLEAMING SMILE WAS SO CUTE.
SCRAMBLE
SCRAMBLE
SCRAMBLE
CHATTER
CHATTER
CHATTER
THAT EVENING...
I THOUGHT I'D HELP THE KITCHEN SISTERS. THEIR COOKING SESSION WAS REACHING A FEVER PITCH.
BOTH SISTERS HAD A NEW JOB, HEAD CHEF. THEY'D REALLY TAKEN TO ORDERING THEIR GOBLIN PREP COOKS AROUND.
I need soup bowls!!
Are you plat-ing?!
WHEN THE EVENING'S WORK HAD FINISHED, WE DECIDED TO SHAKE UP THE MENU.
I WANTED TO RE-CREATE SOME DISHES FROM MY PREVIOUS HUMAN LIFE.

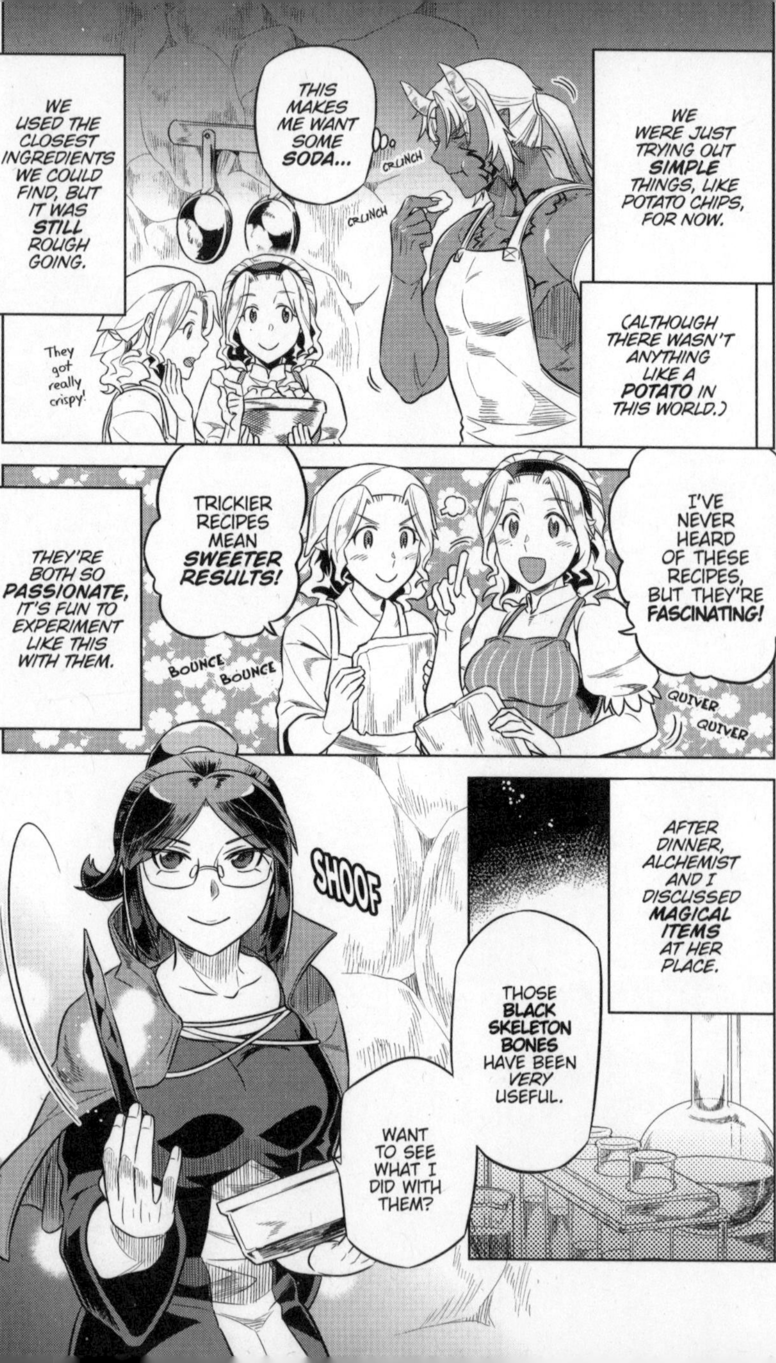
WE WERE JUST TRYING OUT SIMPLE THINGS, LIKE POTATO CHIPS, FOR NOW.
(ALTHOUGH THERE WASN'T ANYTHING LIKE A POTATO IN THIS WORLD.)
THIS MAKES ME WANT SOME SODA...
CRUNCH
CRUNCH
WE USED THE CLOSEST INGREDIENTS WE COULD FIND, BUT IT WAS STILL ROUGH GOING.
They got really crispy!
I'VE NEVER HEARD OF THESE RECIPES, BUT THEY'RE FASCINATING!
QUIVER QUIVER
TRICKIER RECIPES MEAN SWEETER RESULTS!
BOUNCE BOUNCE
THEY'RE BOTH SO PASSIONATE, IT'S FUN TO EXPERIMENT LIKE THIS WITH THEM.
AFTER DINNER, ALCHEMIST AND I DISCUSSED MAGICAL ITEMS AT HER PLACE.
THOSE BLACK SKELETON BONES HAVE BEEN VERY USEFUL.
WANT TO SEE WHAT I DID WITH THEM?
SHOOF

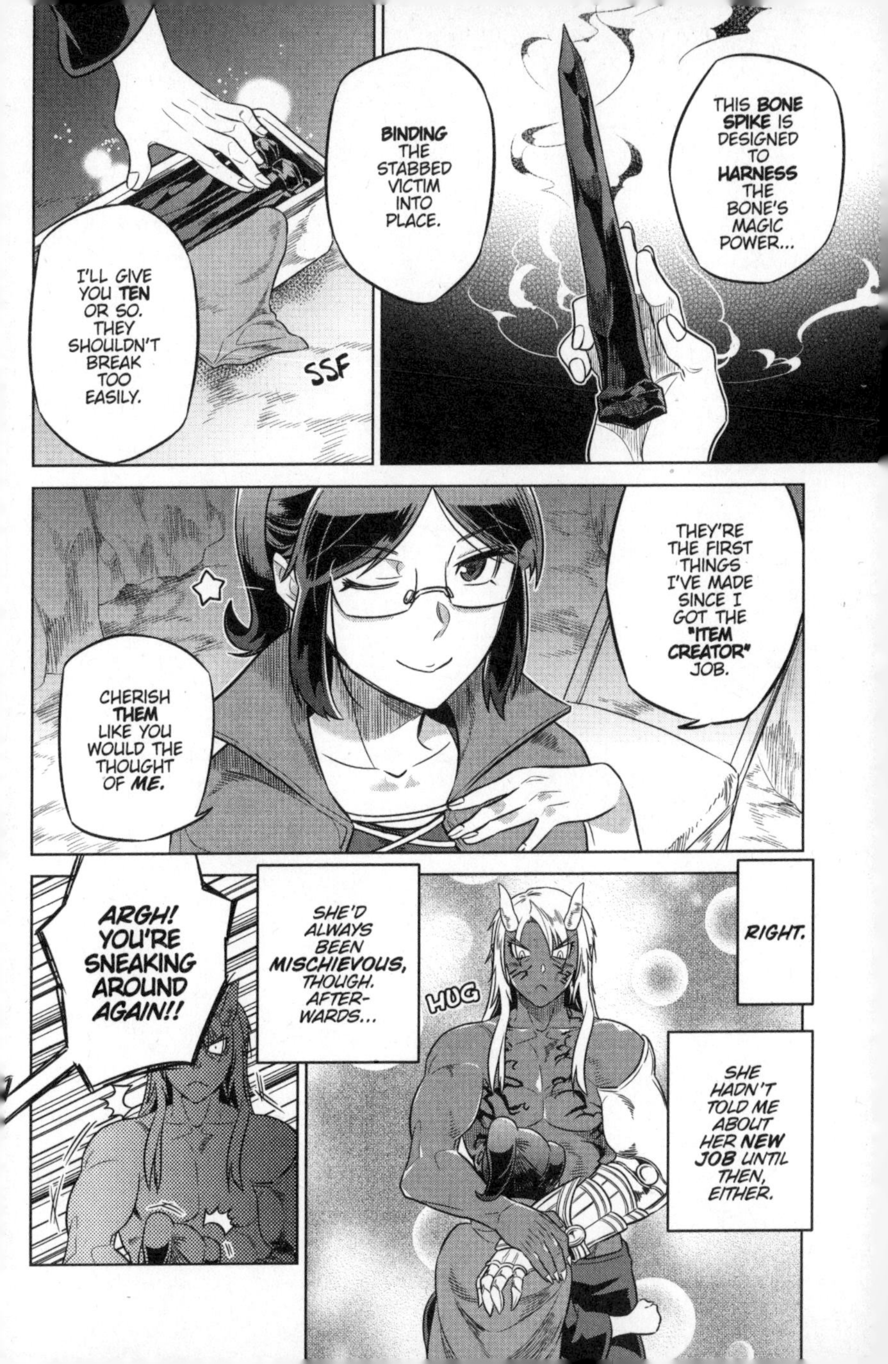
THIS BONE SPIKE IS DESIGNED TO HARNESS THE BONE'S MAGIC POWER...
BINDING THE STABBED VICTIM INTO PLACE.
I'LL GIVE YOU TEN OR SO. THEY SHOULDN'T BREAK TOO EASILY.
SSF
THEY'RE THE FIRST THINGS I'VE MADE SINCE I GOT THE "ITEM CREATOR" JOB.
CHERISH THEM LIKE YOU WOULD THE THOUGHT OF ME.
RIGHT.
SHE'D ALWAYS BEEN MISCHIEVOUS, THOUGH. AFTER-WARDS...
HUG
SHE HADN'T TOLD ME ABOUT HER NEW JOB UNTIL THEN, EITHER.
ARGH! YOU'RE SNEAKING AROUND AGAIN!!

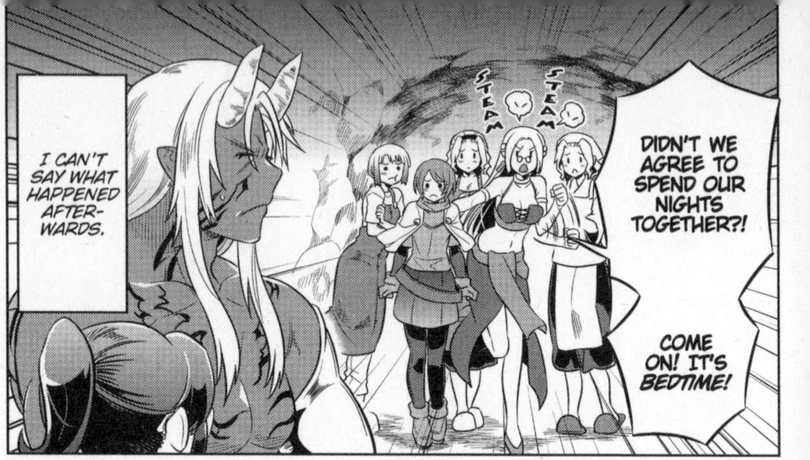
STEAM
STEAM
DIDN'T WE AGREE TO SPEND OUR NIGHTS TOGETHER?!
COME ON! IT'S BEDTIME!
I CAN'T SAY WHAT HAPPENED AFTER-WARDS.

DAY 70

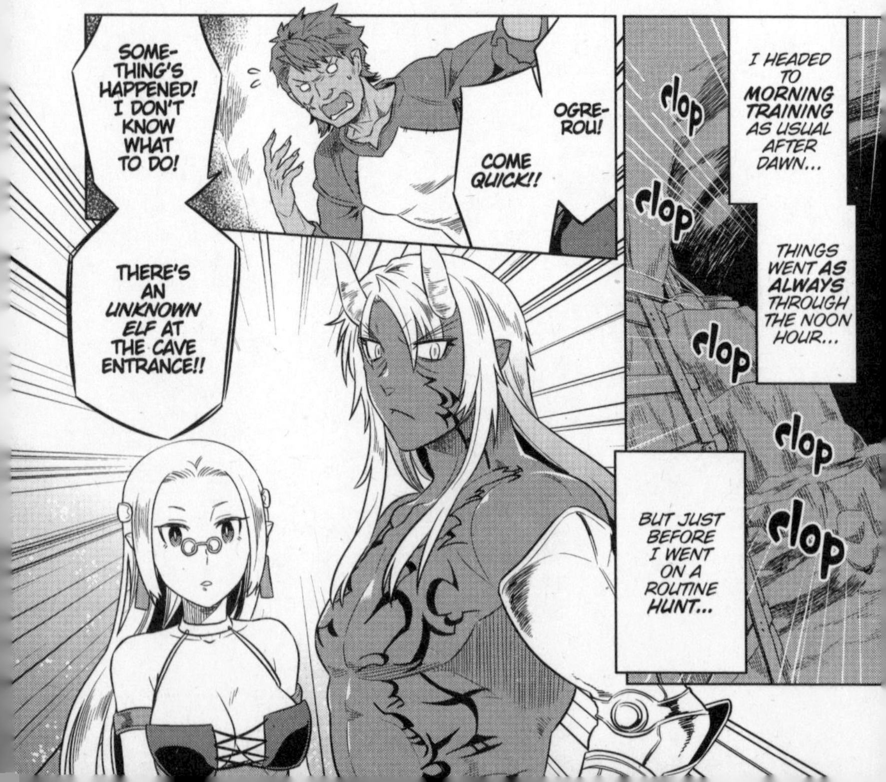
I HEADED TO MORNING TRAINING AS USUAL AFTER DAWN...
THINGS WENT AS ALWAYS THROUGH THE NOON HOUR...
clop
clop
clop
clop
clop
BUT JUST BEFORE I WENT ON A ROUTINE HUNT...
OGRE-ROU!
COME QUICK!!
SOME-THING'S HAPPENED! I DON'T KNOW WHAT TO DO!
THERE'S AN UNKNOWN ELF AT THE CAVE ENTRANCE!!

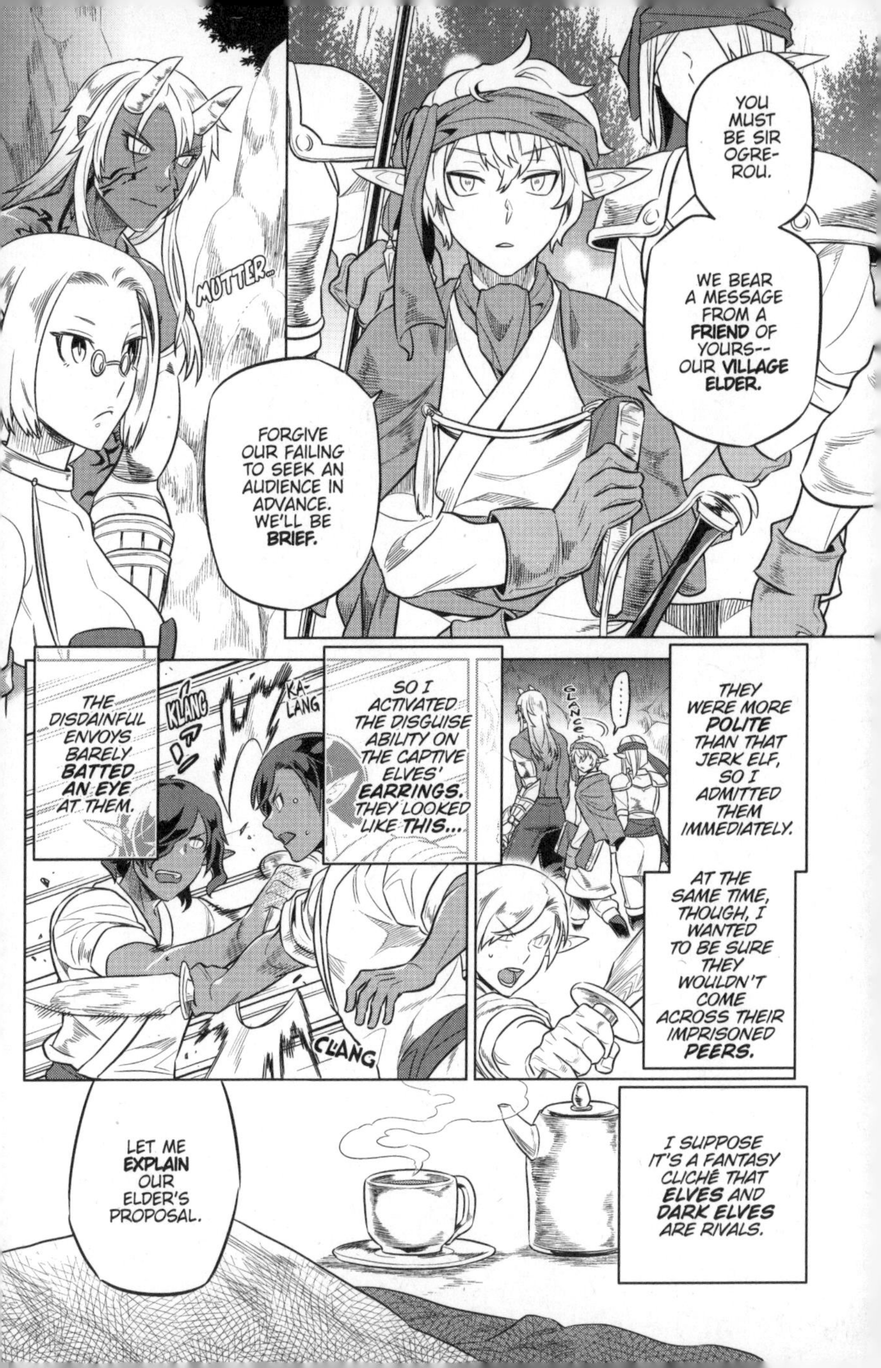
YOU MUST BE SIR OGRE-ROU.
WE BEAR A MESSAGE FROM A **FRIEND** OF YOURS-- OUR **VILLAGE ELDER.**
FORGIVE OUR FAILING TO SEEK AN AUDIENCE IN ADVANCE. WE'LL BE **BRIEF.**
MUTTER...
THEY WERE MORE **POLITE** THAN THAT JERK ELF, SO I ADMITTED THEM IMMEDIATELY.
AT THE SAME TIME, THOUGH, I WANTED TO BE SURE THEY WOULDN'T COME ACROSS THEIR IMPRISONED **PEERS.**
GLANCE
......
SO I ACTIVATED THE DISGUISE ABILITY ON THE CAPTIVE ELVES' **EARRINGS.** THEY LOOKED LIKE **THIS...**
THE DISDAINFUL ENVOYS BARELY **BATTED AN EYE** AT THEM.
KA-LANG
KLANG
CLANG
I SUPPOSE IT'S A FANTASY CLICHÉ THAT **ELVES** AND **DARK ELVES** ARE RIVALS.
LET ME **EXPLAIN** OUR ELDER'S PROPOSAL.

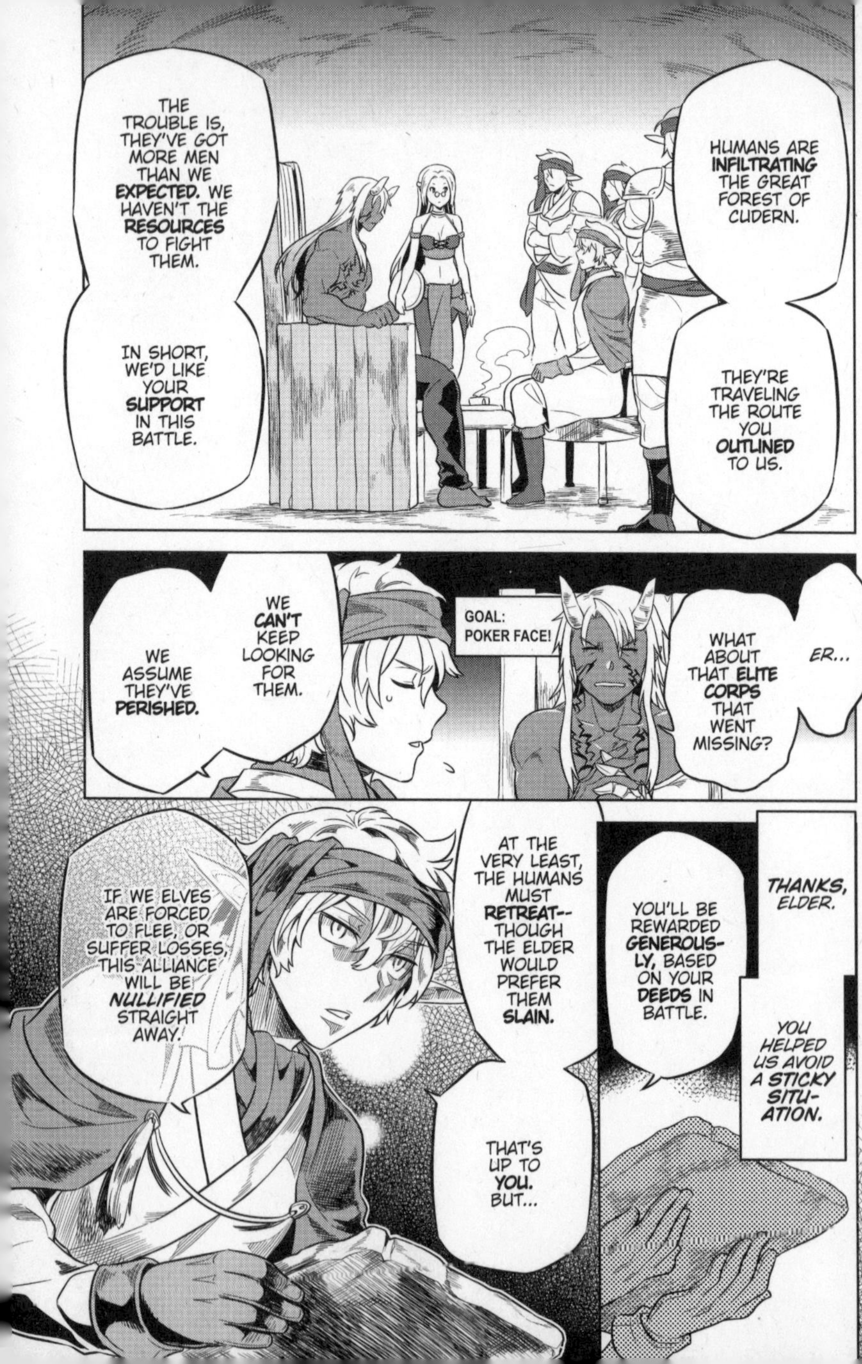
HUMANS ARE INFILTRATING THE GREAT FOREST OF CUDERN.
THEY'RE TRAVELING THE ROUTE YOU OUTLINED TO US.
THE TROUBLE IS, THEY'VE GOT MORE MEN THAN WE EXPECTED. WE HAVEN'T THE RESOURCES TO FIGHT THEM.
IN SHORT, WE'D LIKE YOUR SUPPORT IN THIS BATTLE.
ER...
WHAT ABOUT THAT ELITE CORPS THAT WENT MISSING?
GOAL: POKER FACE!
WE CAN'T KEEP LOOKING FOR THEM.
WE ASSUME THEY'VE PERISHED.
THANKS, ELDER.
YOU HELPED US AVOID A STICKY SITU-ATION.
YOU'LL BE REWARDED GENEROUS-LY, BASED ON YOUR DEEDS IN BATTLE.
AT THE VERY LEAST, THE HUMANS MUST RETREAT-- THOUGH THE ELDER WOULD PREFER THEM SLAIN.
THAT'S UP TO YOU. BUT...
IF WE ELVES ARE FORCED TO FLEE, OR SUFFER LOSSES, THIS ALLIANCE WILL BE NULLIFIED STRAIGHT AWAY.

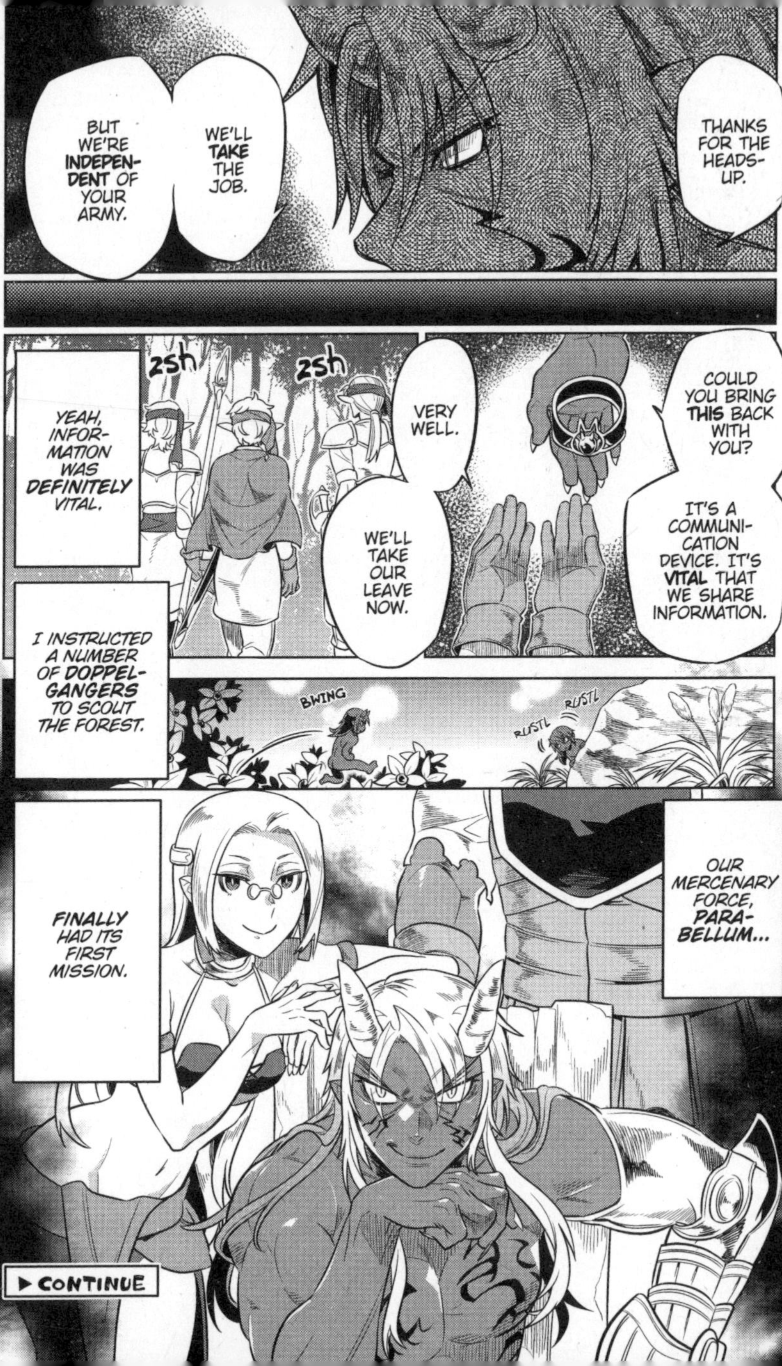
THANKS FOR THE HEADS-UP.
WE'LL TAKE THE JOB.
BUT WE'RE INDEPENDENT OF YOUR ARMY.
COULD YOU BRING THIS BACK WITH YOU?
IT'S A COMMUNICATION DEVICE. IT'S VITAL THAT WE SHARE INFORMATION.
VERY WELL.
WE'LL TAKE OUR LEAVE NOW.
ZSH
ZSH
YEAH, INFORMATION WAS DEFINITELY VITAL.
I INSTRUCTED A NUMBER OF DOPPELGANGERS TO SCOUT THE FOREST.
RUSTL
RUSTL
BWING
OUR MERCENARY FORCE, PARABELLUM...
FINALLY HAD ITS FIRST MISSION.
▶ CONTINUE

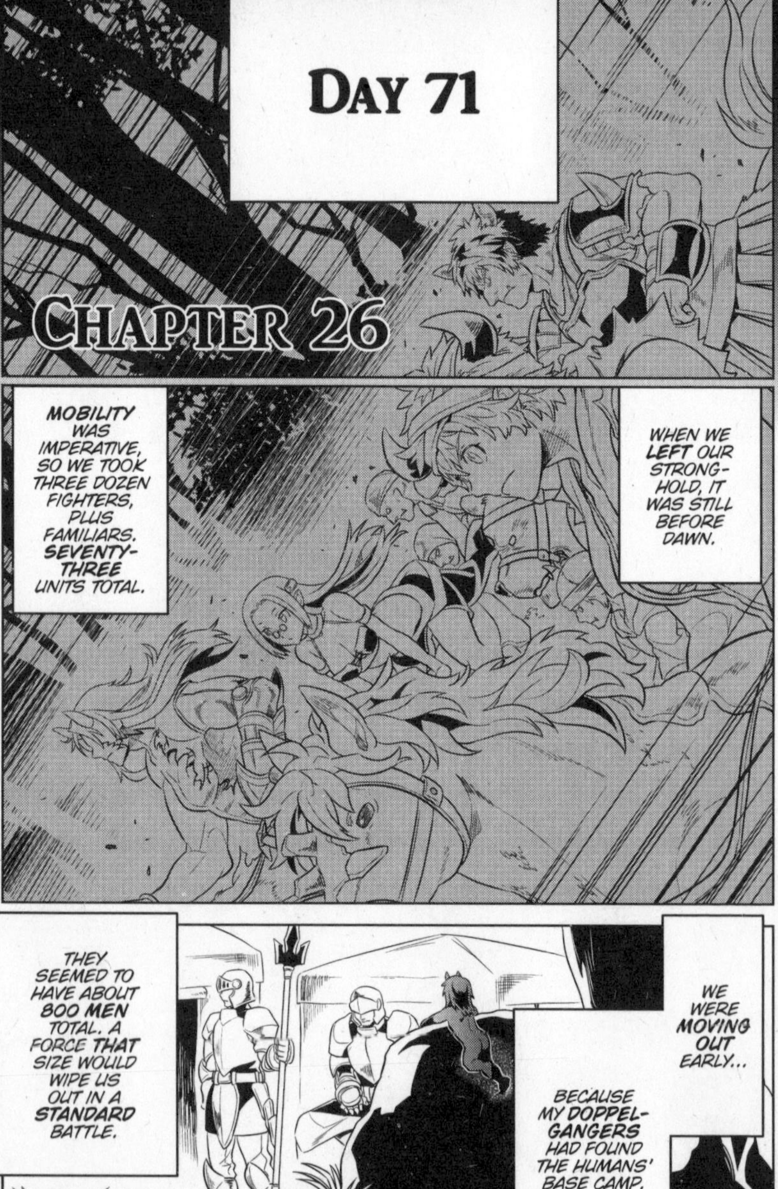
DAY 71
CHAPTER 26
WHEN WE LEFT OUR STRONGHOLD, IT WAS STILL BEFORE DAWN.
MOBILITY WAS IMPERATIVE, SO WE TOOK THREE DOZEN FIGHTERS, PLUS FAMILIARS. SEVENTY-THREE UNITS TOTAL.
WE WERE MOVING OUT EARLY...
BECAUSE MY DOPPELGANGERS HAD FOUND THE HUMANS' BASE CAMP.
THEY SEEMED TO HAVE ABOUT 800 MEN TOTAL. A FORCE THAT SIZE WOULD WIPE US OUT IN A STANDARD BATTLE.

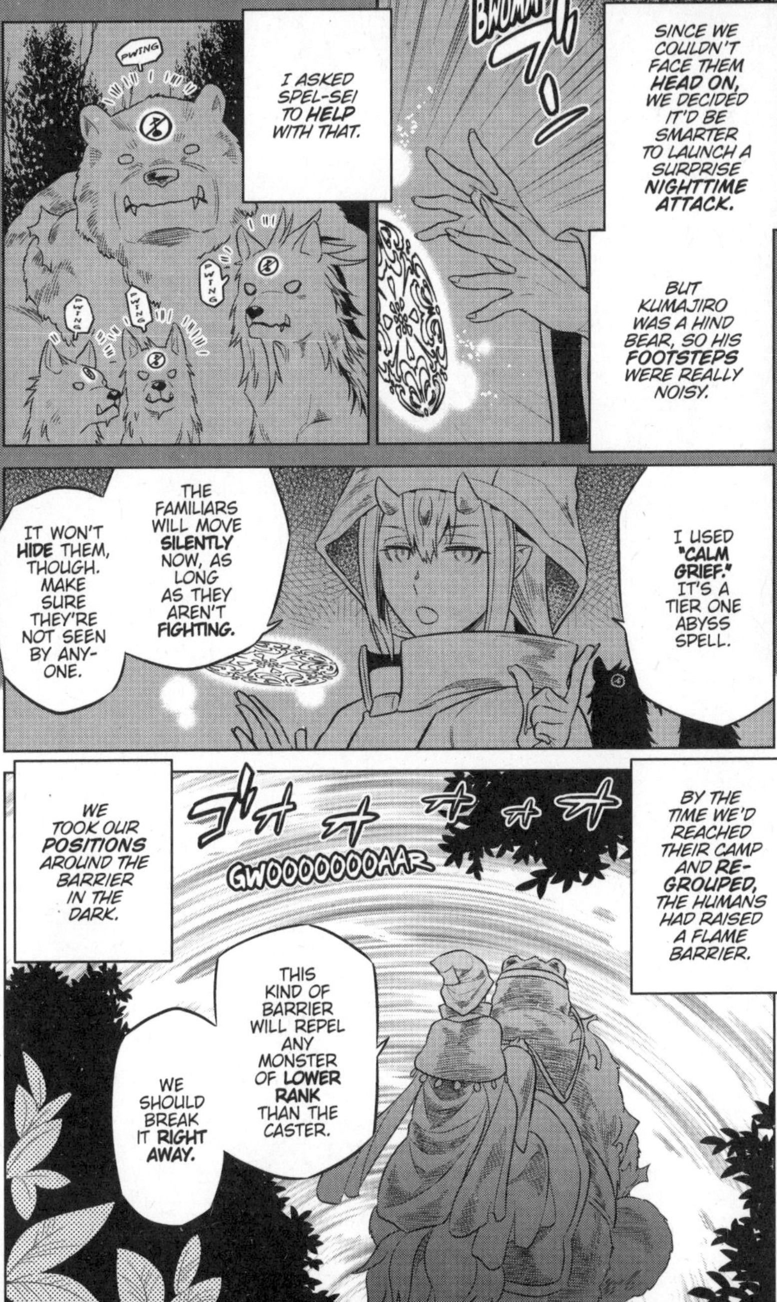
BWUMM
SINCE WE COULDN'T FACE THEM HEAD ON, WE DECIDED IT'D BE SMARTER TO LAUNCH A SURPRISE NIGHTTIME ATTACK.
BUT KUMAJIRO WAS A HIND BEAR, SO HIS FOOTSTEPS WERE REALLY NOISY.
I ASKED SPEL-SEI TO HELP WITH THAT.
PWING
PWING
PWING
PWING
I USED "CALM GRIEF." IT'S A TIER ONE ABYSS SPELL.
THE FAMILIARS WILL MOVE SILENTLY NOW, AS LONG AS THEY AREN'T FIGHTING.
IT WON'T HIDE THEM, THOUGH. MAKE SURE THEY'RE NOT SEEN BY ANYONE.
BY THE TIME WE'D REACHED THEIR CAMP AND REGROUPED, THE HUMANS HAD RAISED A FLAME BARRIER.
GWOOOOOOOAAR
WE TOOK OUR POSITIONS AROUND THE BARRIER IN THE DARK.
THIS KIND OF BARRIER WILL REPEL ANY MONSTER OF LOWER RANK THAN THE CASTER.
WE SHOULD BREAK IT RIGHT AWAY.

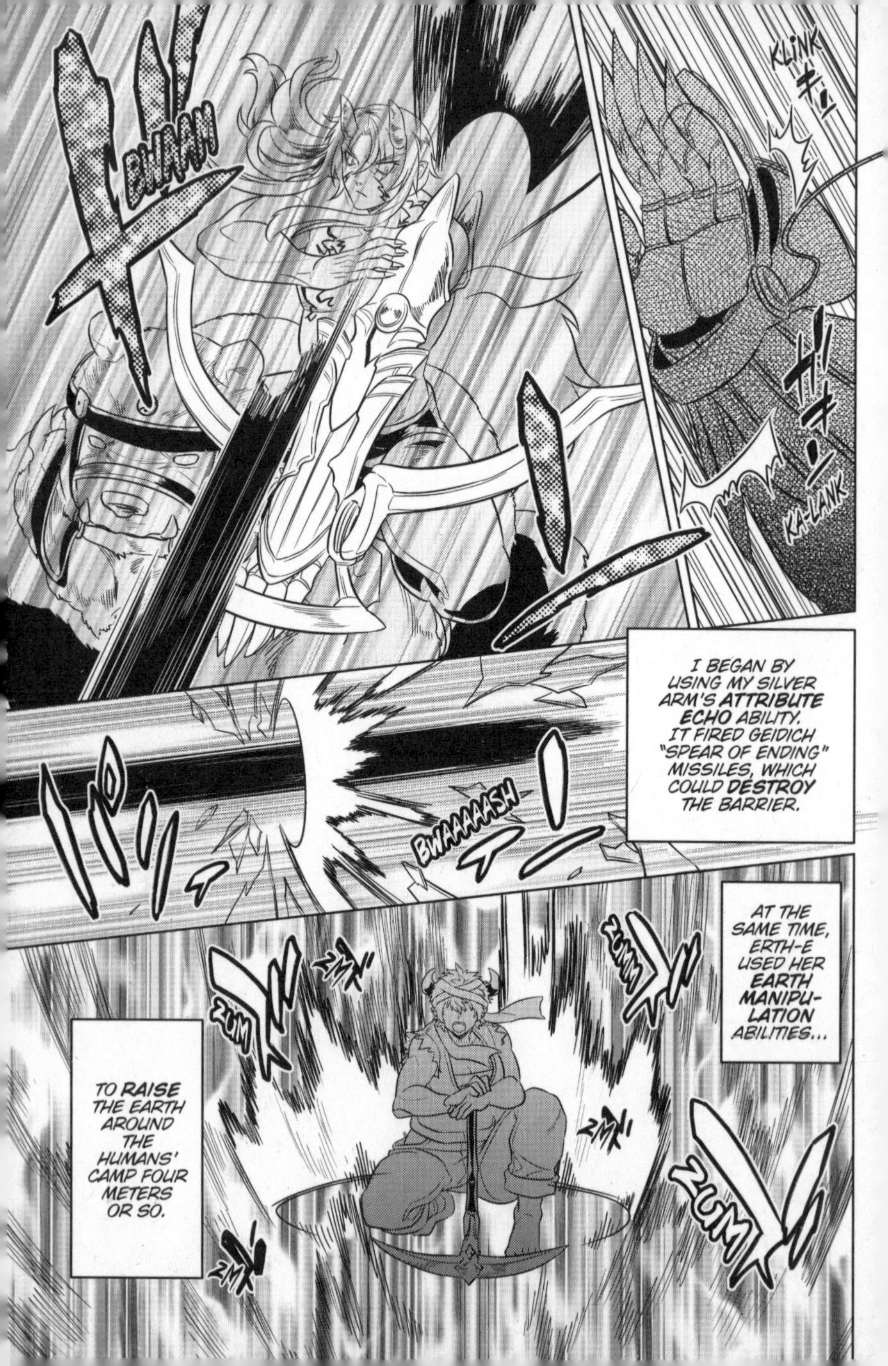
KLINK
KA-LANK
BWAAM
I BEGAN BY USING MY SILVER ARM'S **ATTRIBUTE ECHO** ABILITY. IT FIRED GEIDICH "SPEAR OF ENDING" MISSILES, WHICH COULD **DESTROY** THE BARRIER.
BWAAAAASH
AT THE SAME TIME, ERTH-E USED HER **EARTH MANIPULATION** ABILITIES...
ZUM
ZUM
ZM
ZUM
ZM
ZM
TO **RAISE** THE EARTH AROUND THE HUMANS' CAMP FOUR METERS OR SO.

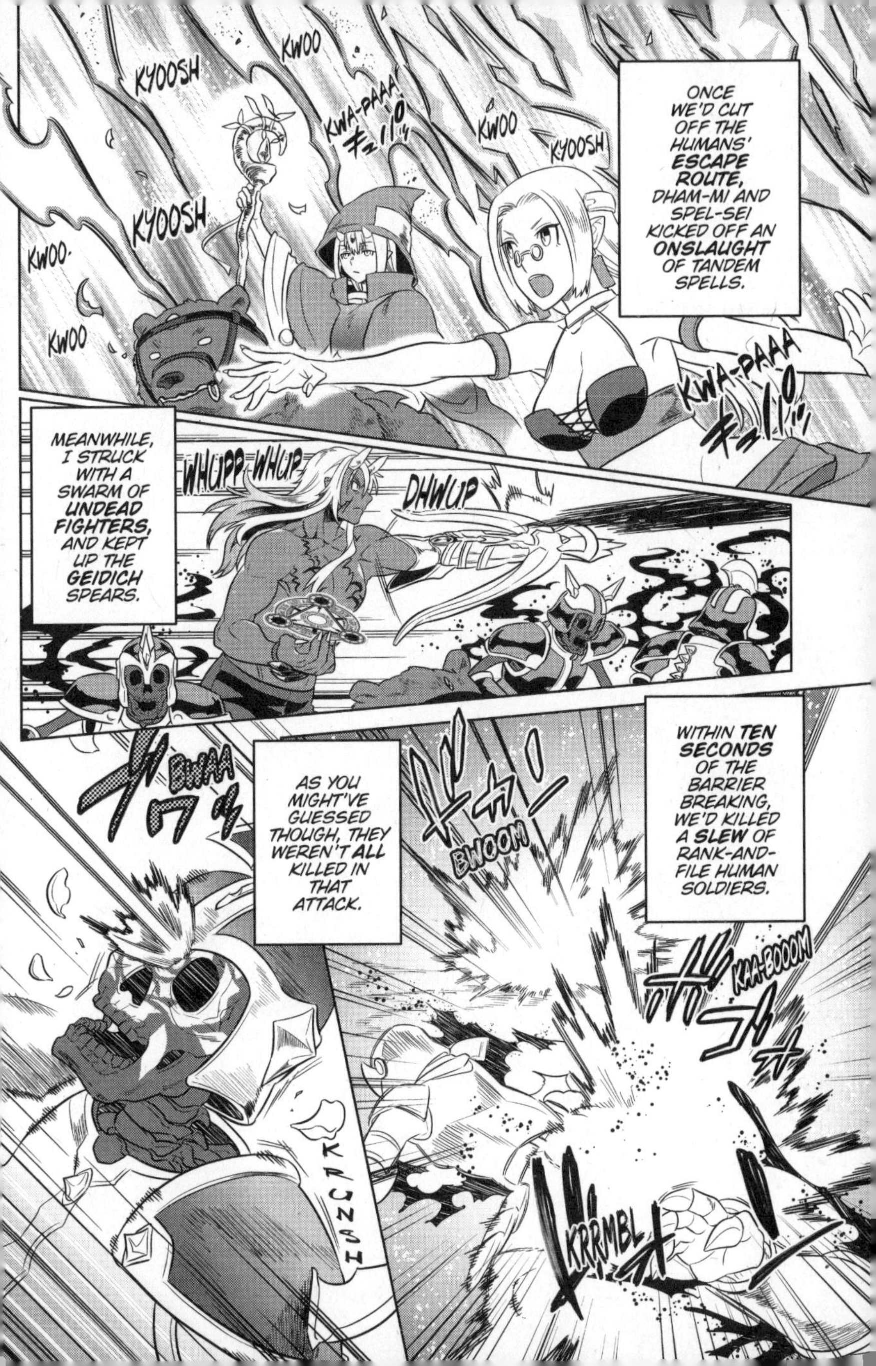
ONCE WE'D CUT OFF THE HUMANS' **ESCAPE ROUTE,** DHAM-MI AND SPEL-SEI KICKED OFF AN **ONSLAUGHT** OF TANDEM SPELLS.
KYOOSH
KWOO
KWA-PAAA
KWOO
KYOOSH
KYOOSH
KWOO
KWOO
KWA-PAAA
DHWUP
WHUPP WHUP
MEANWHILE, I STRUCK WITH A SWARM OF **UNDEAD FIGHTERS,** AND KEPT UP THE **GEIDICH** SPEARS.
WITHIN **TEN SECONDS** OF THE BARRIER BREAKING, WE'D KILLED A **SLEW** OF RANK-AND-FILE HUMAN SOLDIERS.
BWOOM
KAA-BOOOM
KRRMBL
AS YOU MIGHT'VE GUESSED THOUGH, THEY WEREN'T **ALL** KILLED IN THAT **ATTACK.**
BWAA
KRUNSH

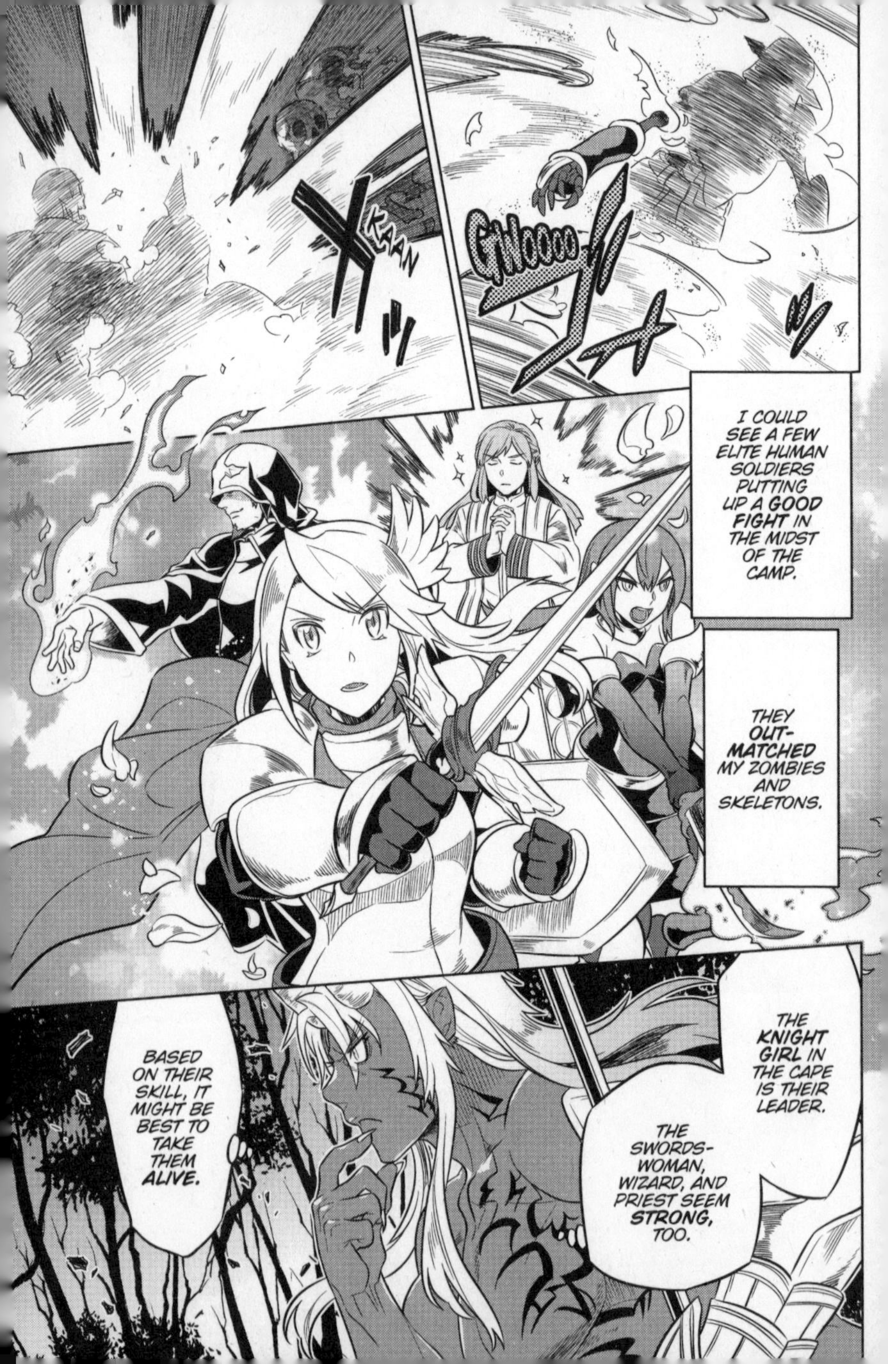
GWOOOO
KAAN
I COULD SEE A FEW ELITE HUMAN SOLDIERS PUTTING UP A **GOOD FIGHT** IN THE MIDST OF THE CAMP.
THEY **OUT-MATCHED** MY ZOMBIES AND SKELETONS.
THE **KNIGHT GIRL** IN THE CAPE IS THEIR LEADER.
THE SWORDS-WOMAN, WIZARD, AND PRIEST SEEM **STRONG,** TOO.
BASED ON THEIR SKILL, IT MIGHT BE BEST TO TAKE THEM **ALIVE.**

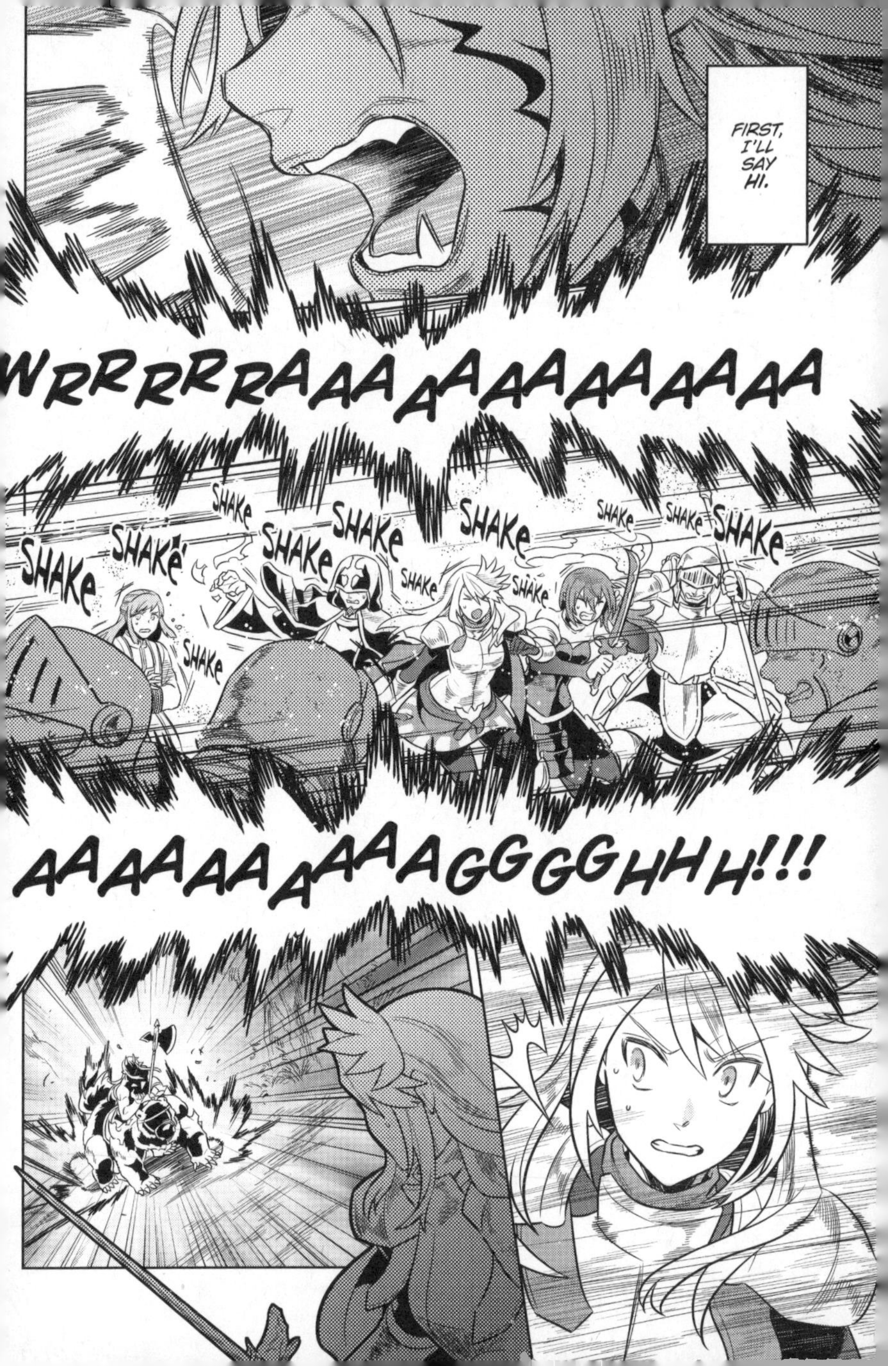
FIRST, I'LL SAY HI.
WRRRRRRAAAAAAAAAAAA
SHAKE
SHAKE
SHAKE
SHAKE
SHAKE
SHAKE
SHAKE
SHAKE
SHAKE
SHAKE
SHAKE
SHAKE
AAAAAAAAAAGGGGHHHH!!!

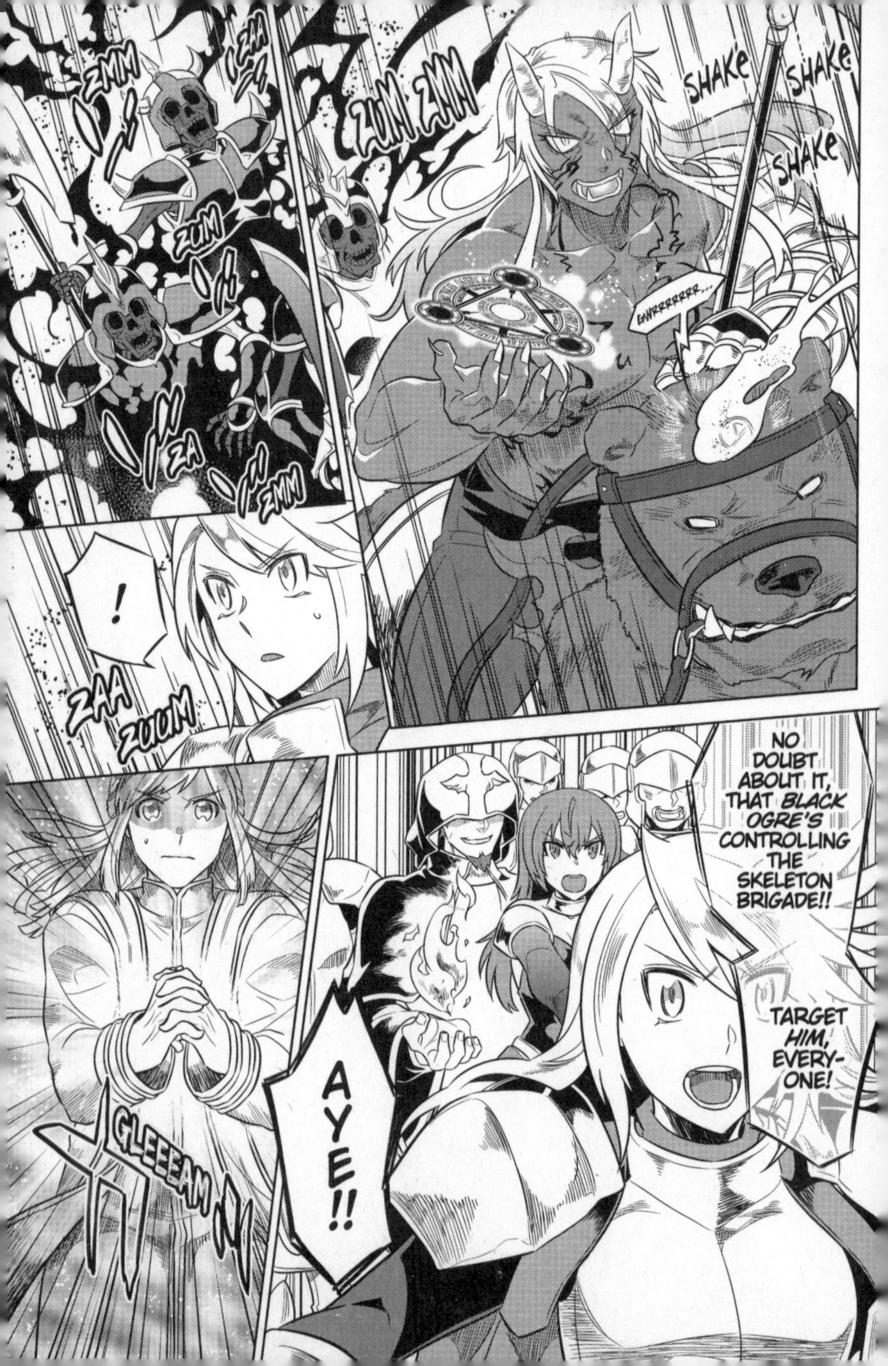
ZUM ZMM
SHAKE
SHAKE
SHAKE
GNRRRRRRR...
ZMM
ZAA
ZUM
ZA
ZMM
!
ZAA ZUUM
NO DOUBT ABOUT IT, THAT BLACK OGRE'S CONTROLLING THE SKELETON BRIGADE!!
TARGET HIM, EVERY-ONE!
AYE!!
GLEEEAM

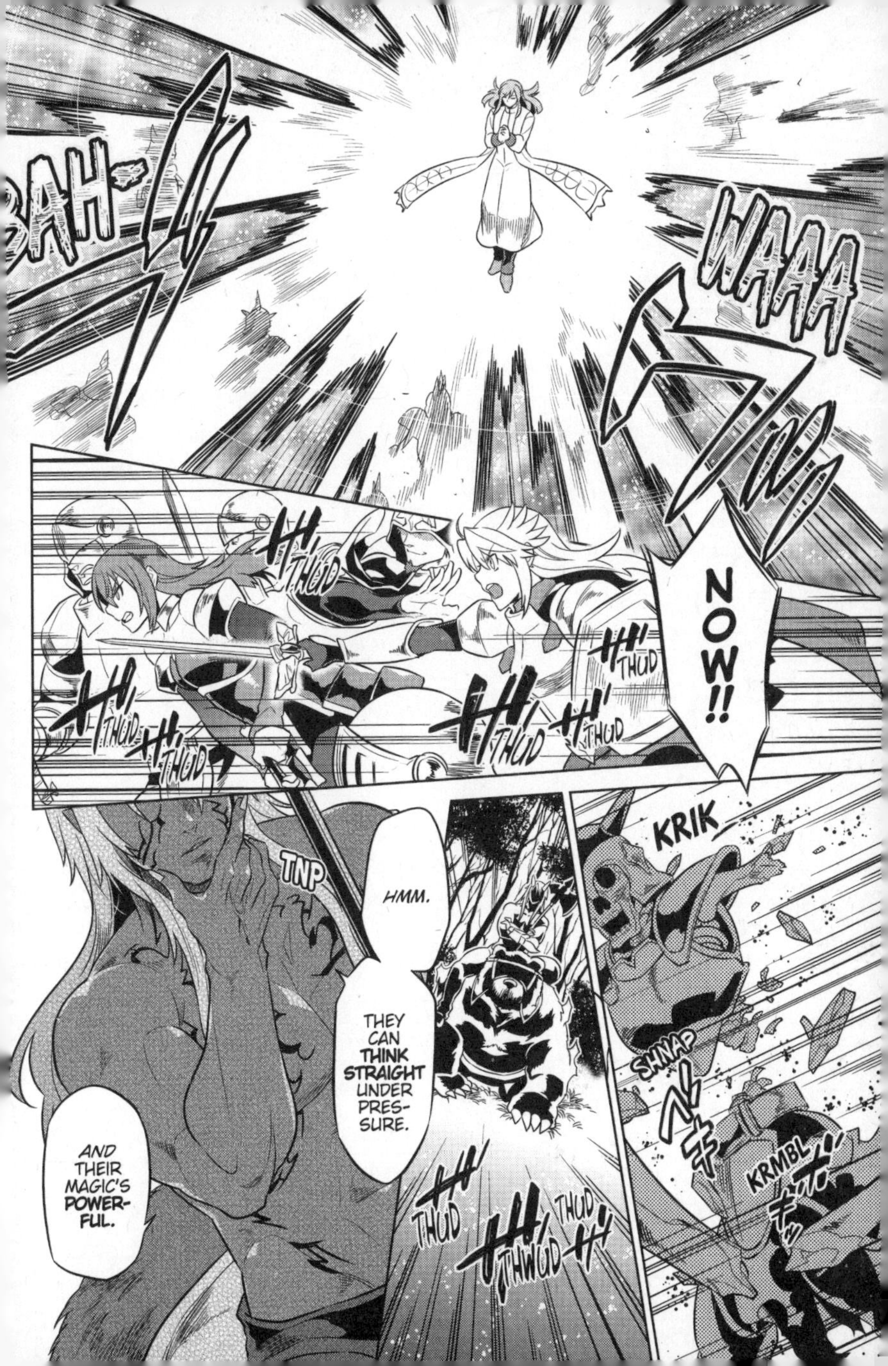
WAAA
BAH-
NOW!!
THUD
THUD
THUD
THUD
THUD
THUD
KRIK
SHNAP
KRMBL
HMM.
THEY CAN THINK STRAIGHT UNDER PRES-SURE.
TNP
AND THEIR MAGIC'S POWER-FUL.
THUD
THUD
THWUD

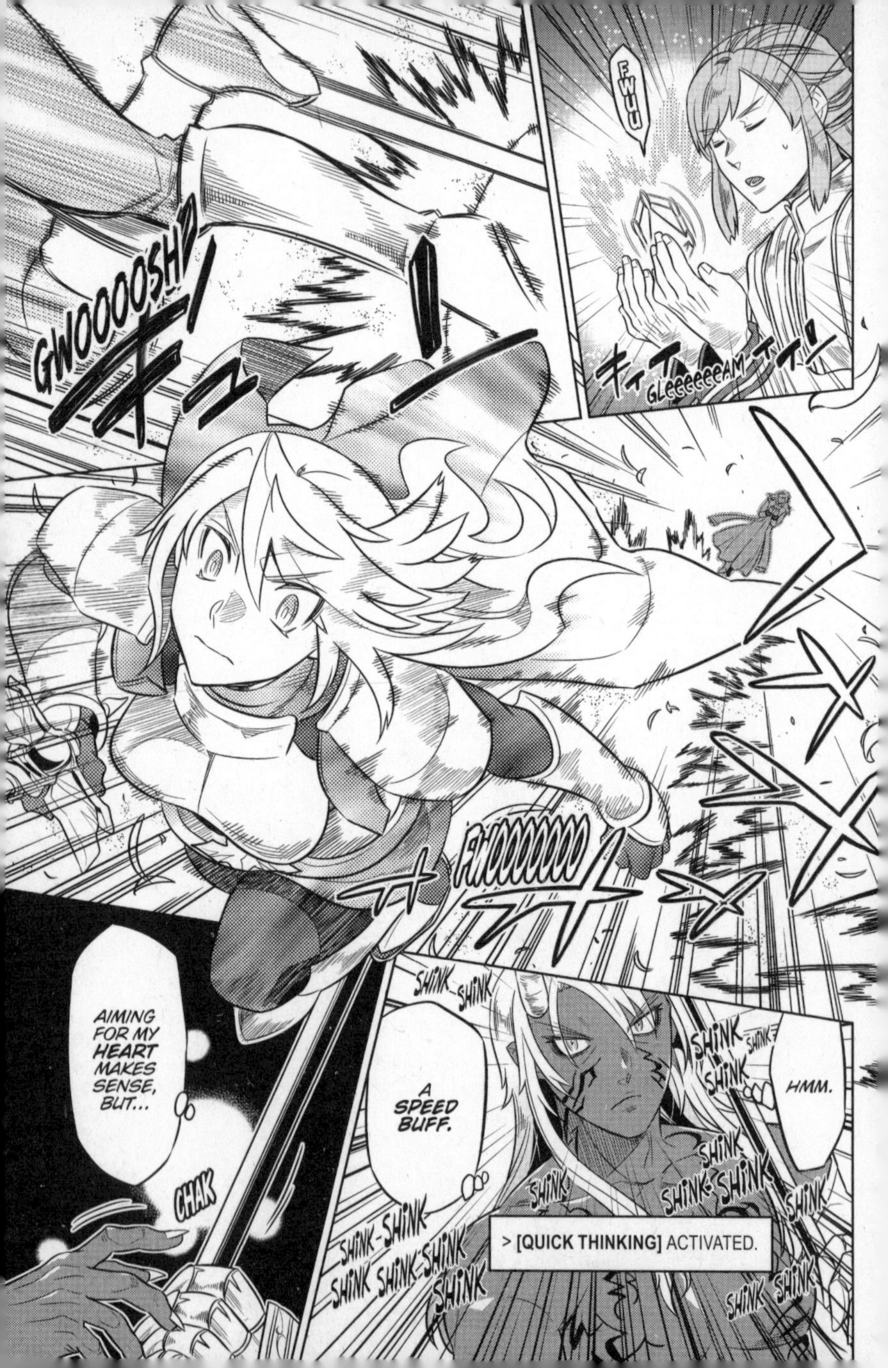
FWUU
GLEEEEEEAM
GWOOOOSH
FWOOOOOOOO
SHINK SHINK
SHINK SHINK SHINK
HMM.
A SPEED BUFF.
SHINK SHINK-SHINK
SHINK
SHINK
SHINK SHINK
SHINK-SHINK SHINK SHINK-SHINK SHINK
> [QUICK THINKING] ACTIVATED.
AIMING FOR MY HEART MAKES SENSE, BUT...
CHAK

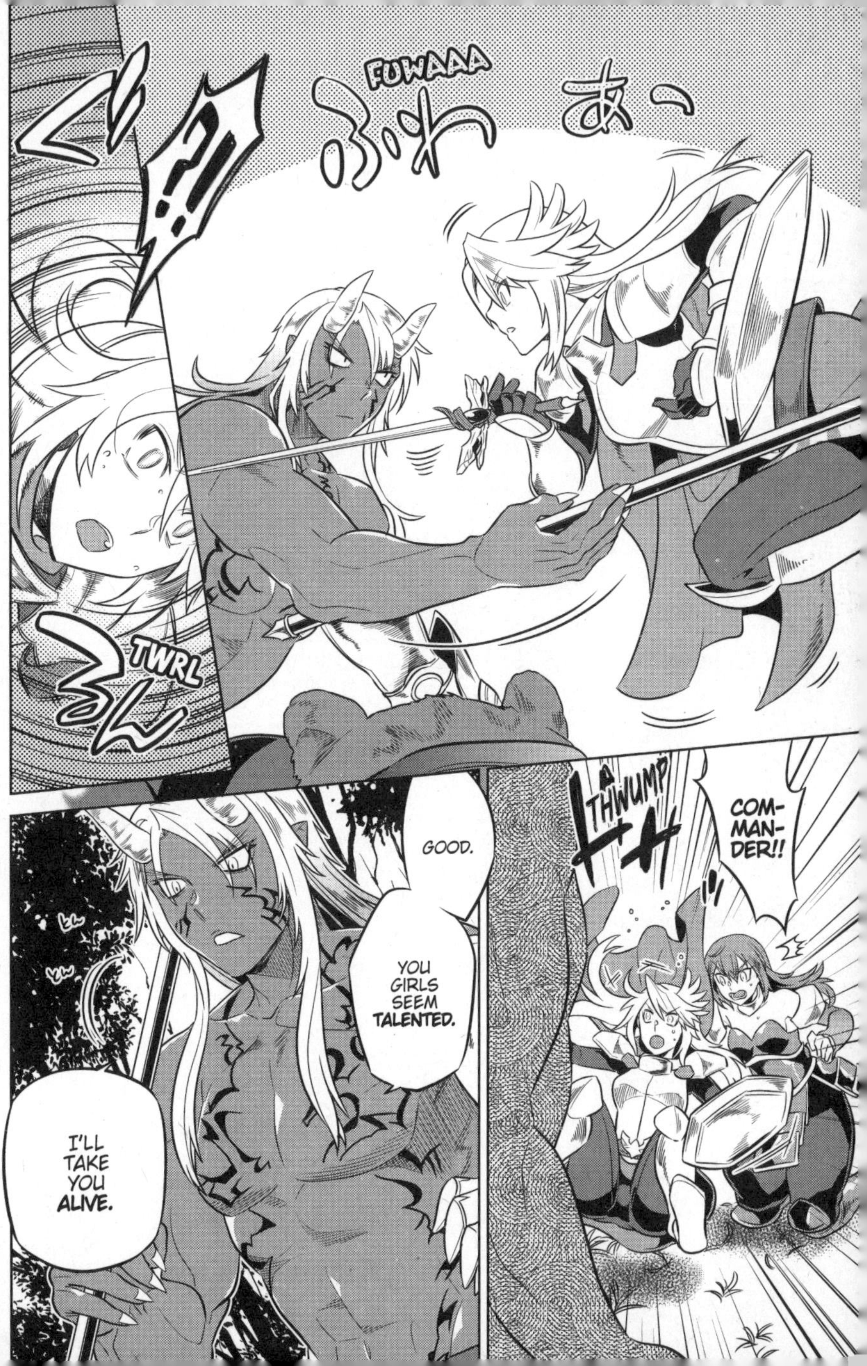
FUWAAA
ふわ あっ
?!
TWRL
THWUMP
COM-
MAN-
DER!!
GOOD.
YOU GIRLS SEEM TALENTED.
I'LL TAKE YOU ALIVE.

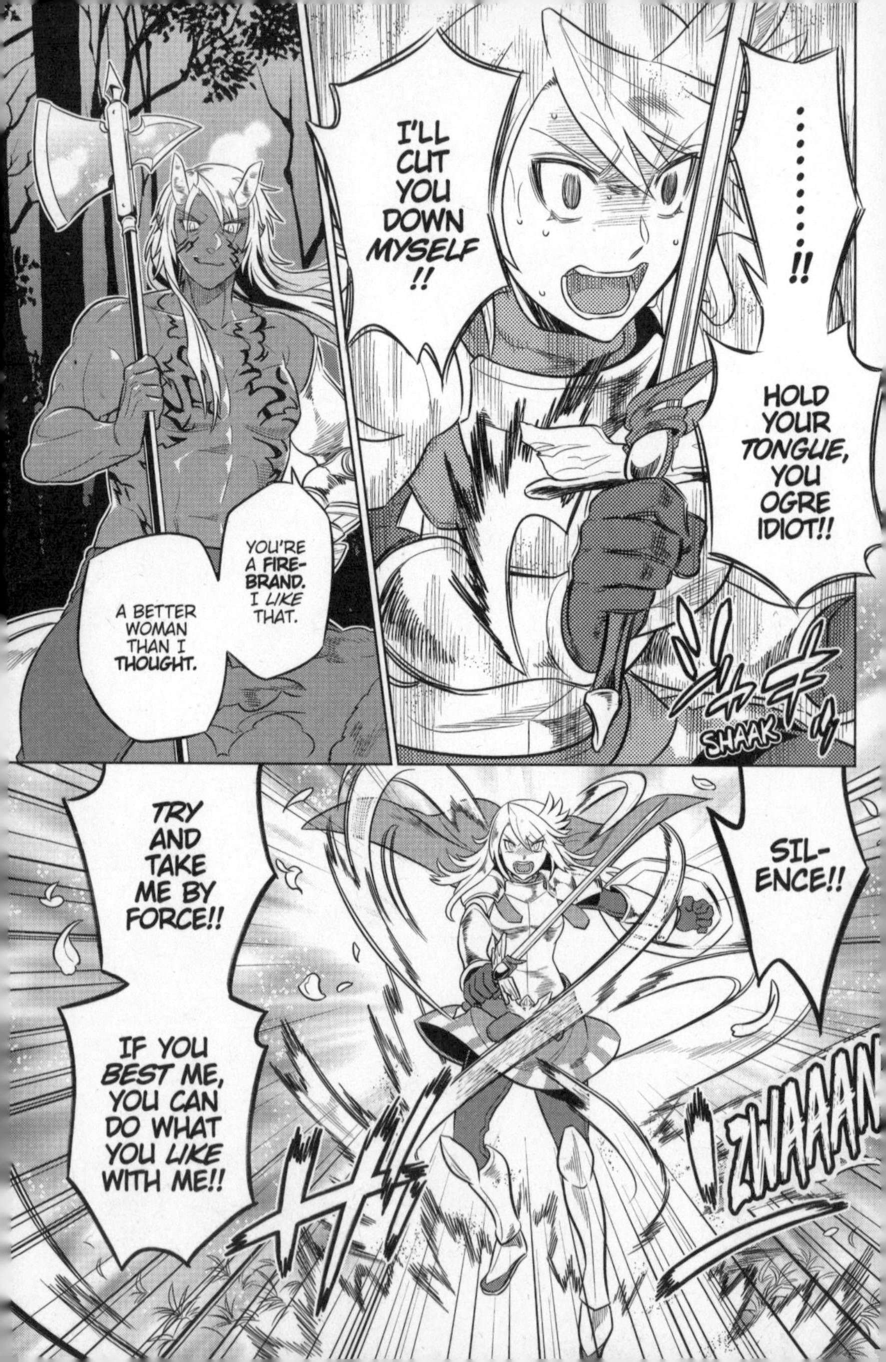
……!!
I'LL CUT YOU DOWN MYSELF!!
HOLD YOUR TONGUE, YOU OGRE IDIOT!!
SHAAK
YOU'RE A FIRE-BRAND. I LIKE THAT.
A BETTER WOMAN THAN I THOUGHT.
SIL-ENCE!!
TRY AND TAKE ME BY FORCE!!
IF YOU BEST ME, YOU CAN DO WHAT YOU LIKE WITH ME!!
ZWAAAN

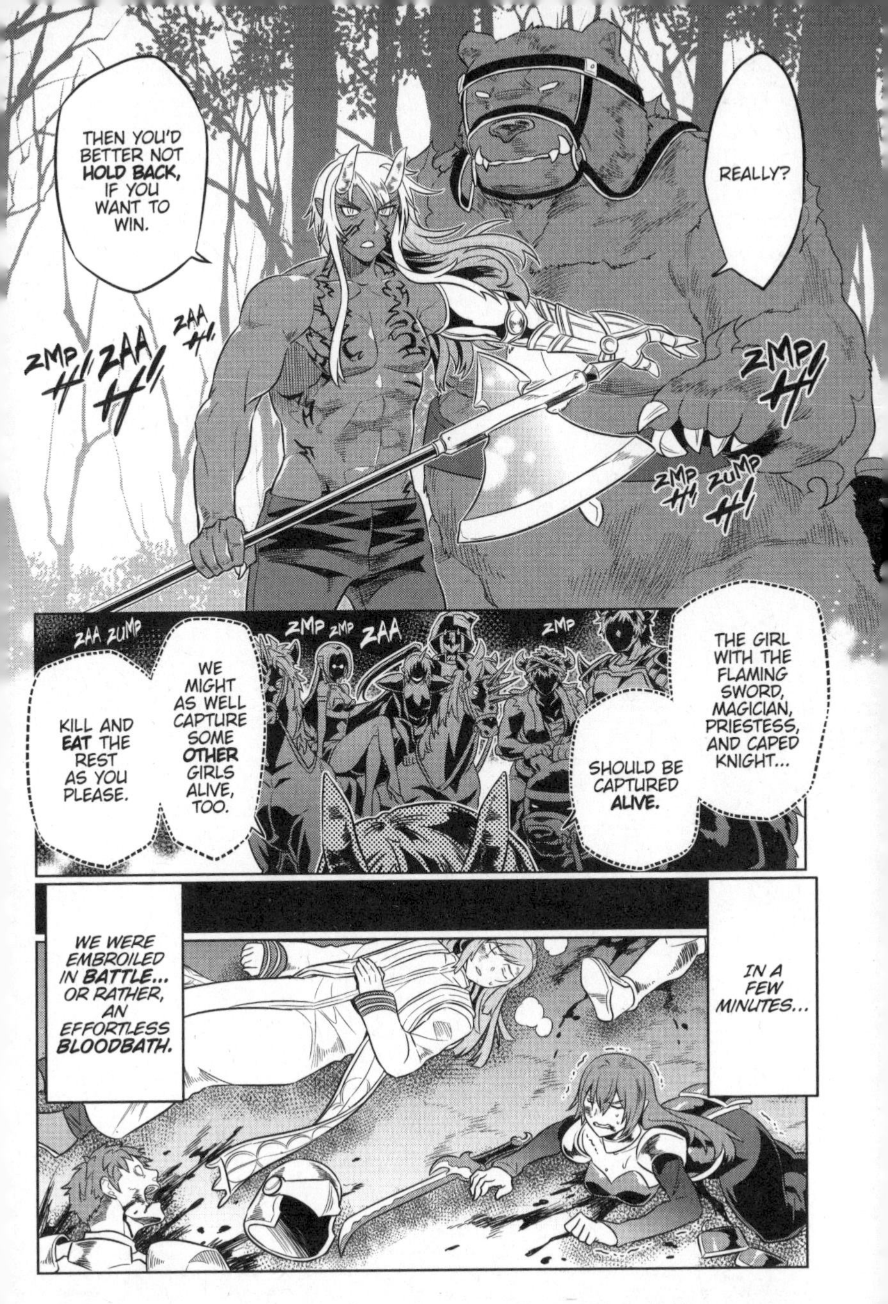
REALLY?
THEN YOU'D BETTER NOT **HOLD BACK,** IF YOU WANT TO WIN.
ZMP
ZAA
ZAA
ZMP
ZMP ZUMP
THE GIRL WITH THE FLAMING SWORD, MAGICIAN, PRIESTESS, AND CAPED KNIGHT...
SHOULD BE CAPTURED **ALIVE.**
ZMP
ZMP ZMP ZAA
WE MIGHT AS WELL CAPTURE SOME **OTHER** GIRLS ALIVE, TOO.
ZAA ZUMP
KILL AND **EAT** THE REST AS YOU PLEASE.
IN A FEW MINUTES...
WE WERE EMBROILED IN **BATTLE...** OR RATHER, AN EFFORTLESS **BLOODBATH.**

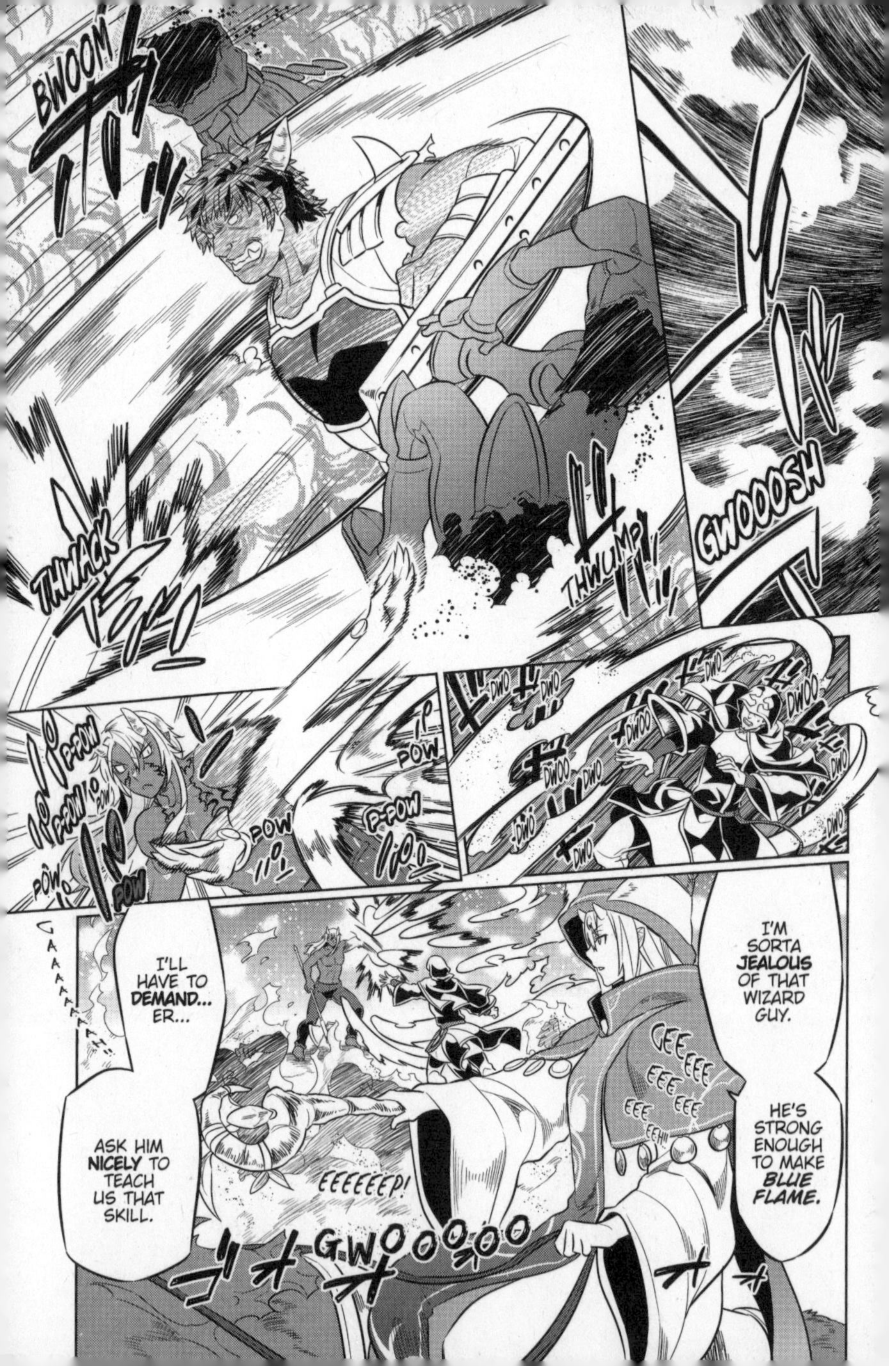
GWOOOSH
BWOOM
THWUMP
THWACK
DWO
DWOO
POW
P-POW
I'M SORTA JEALOUS OF THAT WIZARD GUY.
HE'S STRONG ENOUGH TO MAKE BLUE FLAME.
GEEEEEEEEEEEEEEEEH!!
I'LL HAVE TO DEMAND... ER...
ASK HIM NICELY TO TEACH US THAT SKILL.
EEEEEEP!
GWOOOOOOO
GAAAAAAAAH!!

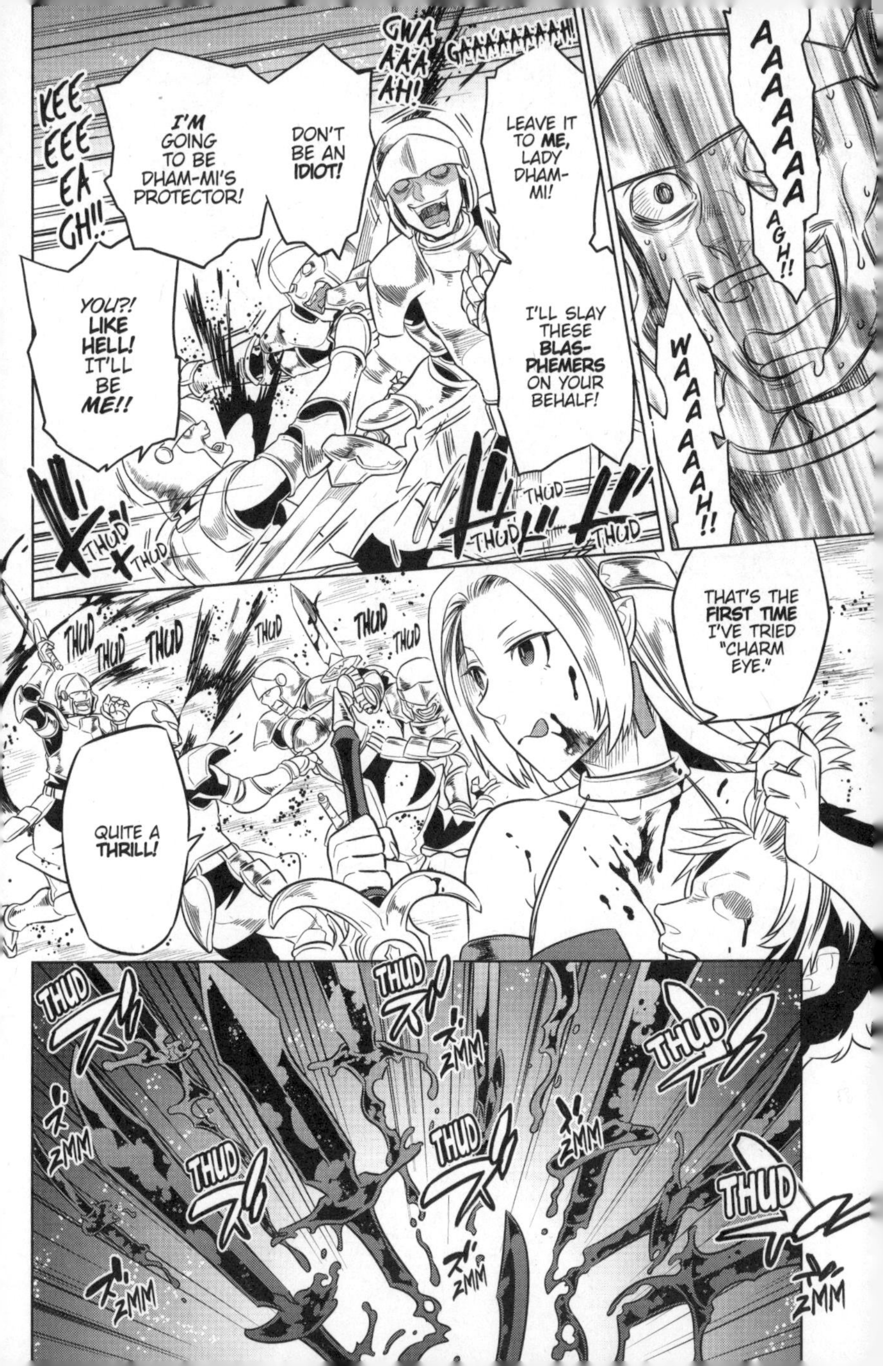
AAAAAAAAGH!!
WAAAAAAAAAH!!
GWAAAAAH!
GAAAAAAAAH!!
LEAVE IT TO ME, LADY DHAM-MI!
I'LL SLAY THESE BLASPHEMERS ON YOUR BEHALF!
DON'T BE AN IDIOT!
I'M GOING TO BE DHAM-MI'S PROTECTOR!
KEEEEEEAGH!!
YOU?! LIKE HELL! IT'LL BE ME!!
THUD
THUD
THUD
THUD
THUD
THUD
THAT'S THE FIRST TIME I'VE TRIED "CHARM EYE."
QUITE A THRILL!
THUD
THUD
THUD
THUD
THUD
THUD
THUD
THUD
ZMM
THUD
ZMM
THUD
ZMM
THUD
ZMM
THUD
ZMM
THUD
ZMM
ZMM

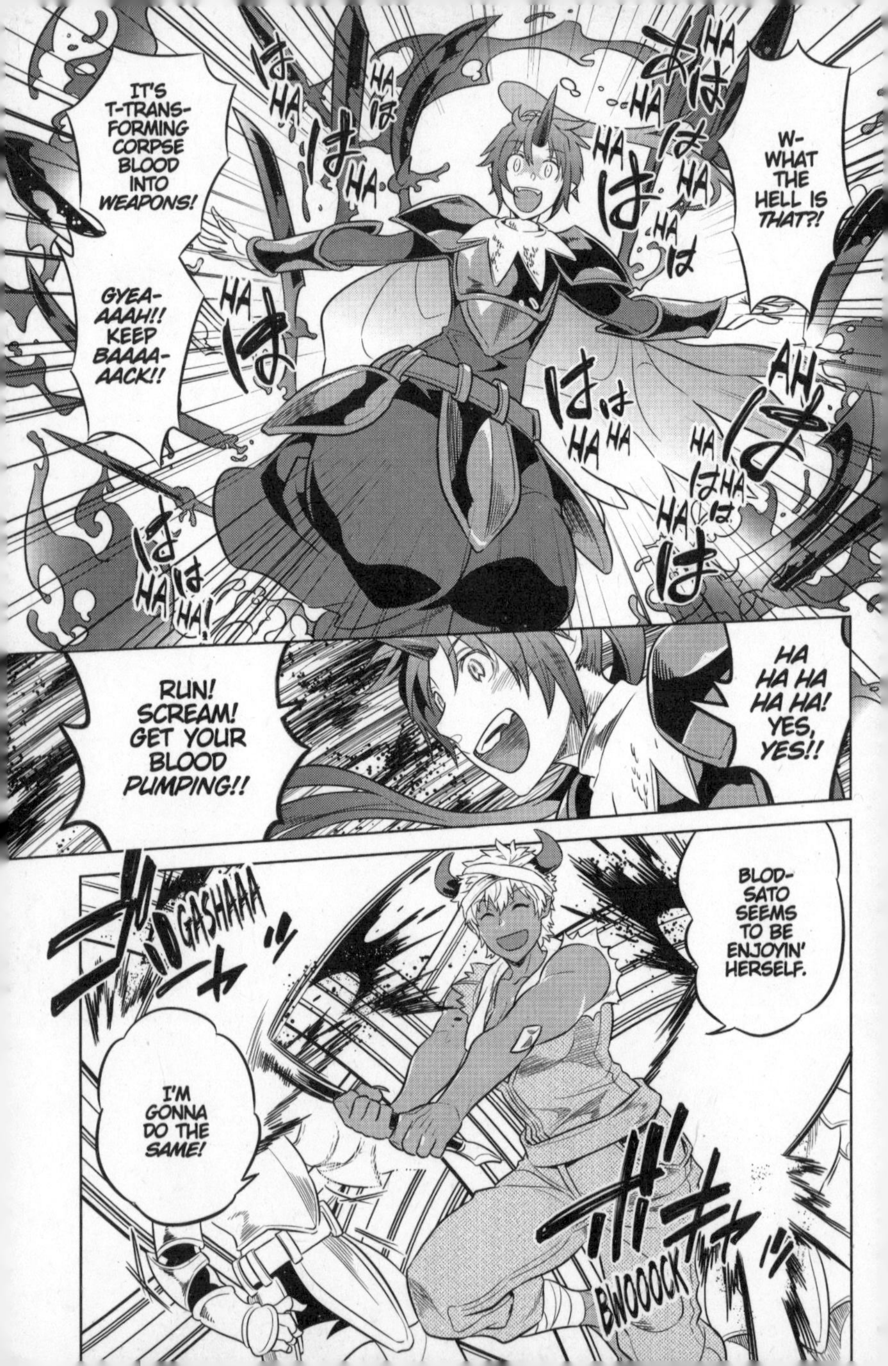
W-WHAT THE HELL IS THAT?!
AH HA HA HA HA HA HA HA HA HA
HA HA HA HA HA HA HA HA HA!
IT'S T-TRANSFORMING CORPSE BLOOD INTO WEAPONS!
GYEA-AAAH!! KEEP BAAAAACK!!
HA HA HA HA HA! YES, YES!!
RUN! SCREAM! GET YOUR BLOOD PUMPING!!
BLOD-SATO SEEMS TO BE ENJOYIN' HERSELF.
GASHAAA
I'M GONNA DO THE SAME!
BWOOOCK

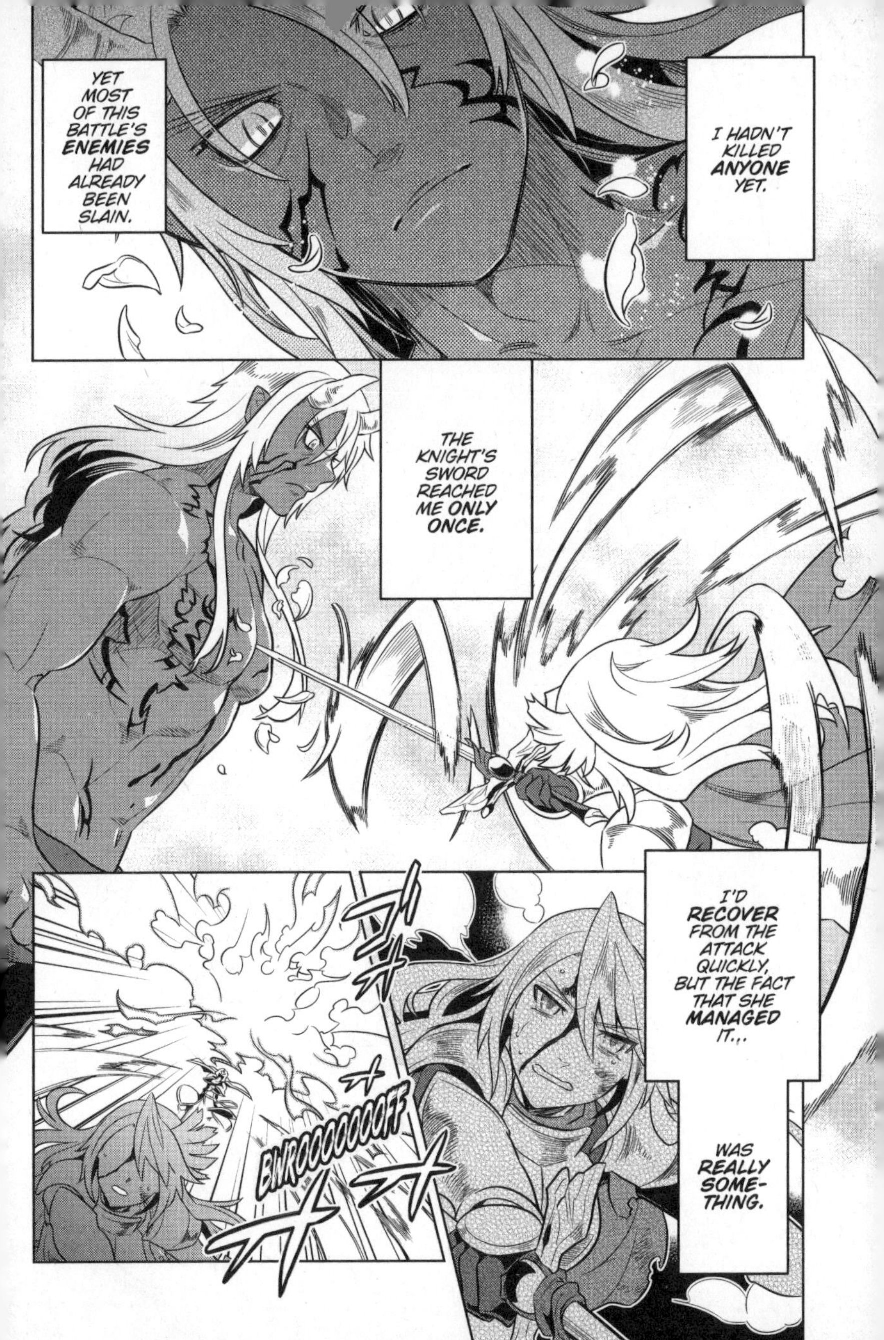
I HADN'T KILLED ANYONE YET.
YET MOST OF THIS BATTLE'S ENEMIES HAD ALREADY BEEN SLAIN.
THE KNIGHT'S SWORD REACHED ME ONLY ONCE.
I'D RECOVER FROM THE ATTACK QUICKLY, BUT THE FACT THAT SHE MANAGED IT...
WAS REALLY SOME-THING.
BWROOOOOOOOFF

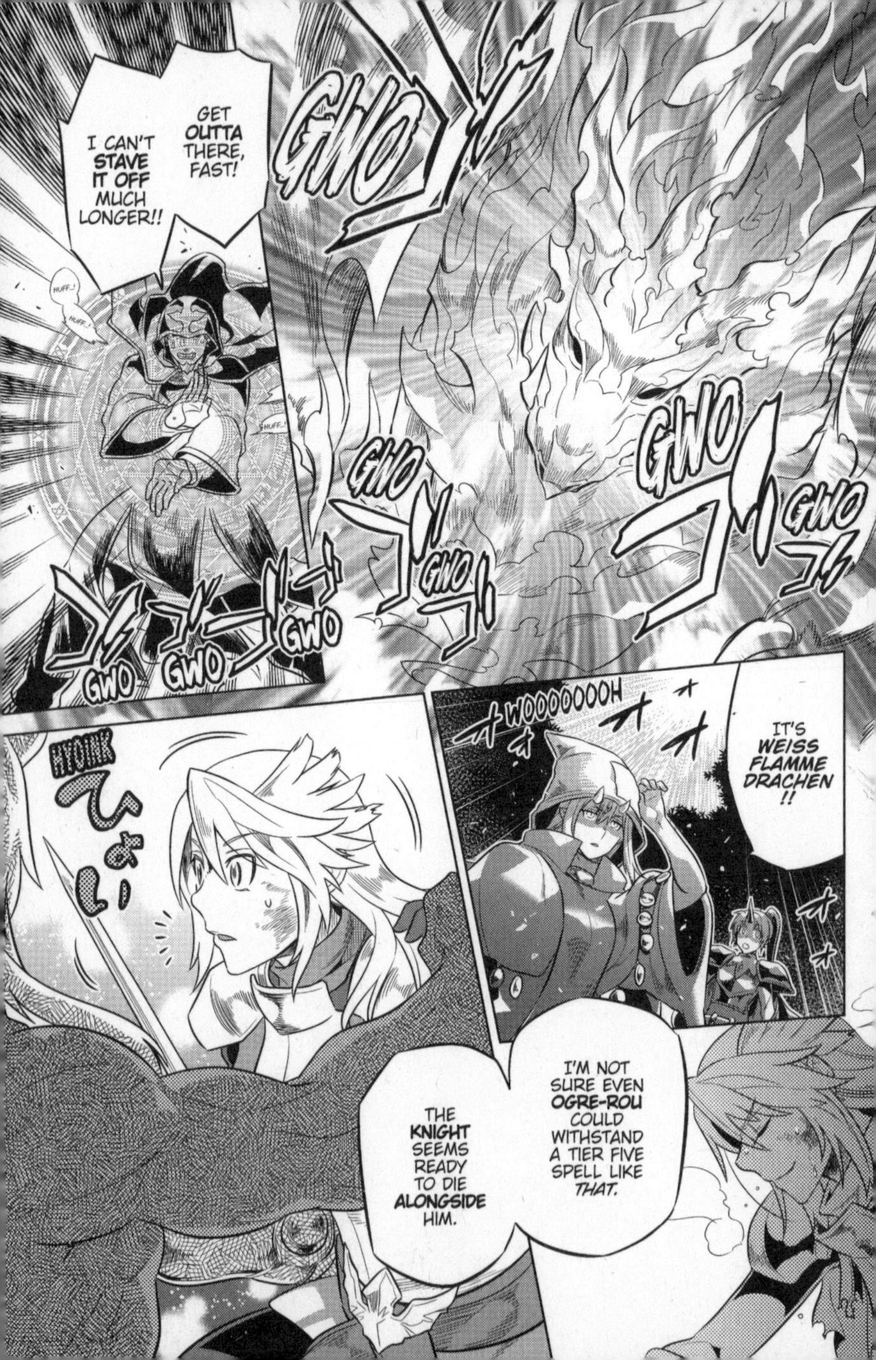
GWO
GWO GWO
GWO GWO
GWO
GET OUTTA THERE, FAST!
I CAN'T STAVE IT OFF MUCH LONGER!!
HUFF..!
HUFF..!
HUFF..!
GWO GWO GWO
WOOOOOOOH
IT'S WEISS FLAMME DRACHEN!!
HYOINK
I'M NOT SURE EVEN OGRE-ROU COULD WITHSTAND A TIER FIVE SPELL LIKE THAT.
THE KNIGHT SEEMS READY TO DIE ALONGSIDE HIM.

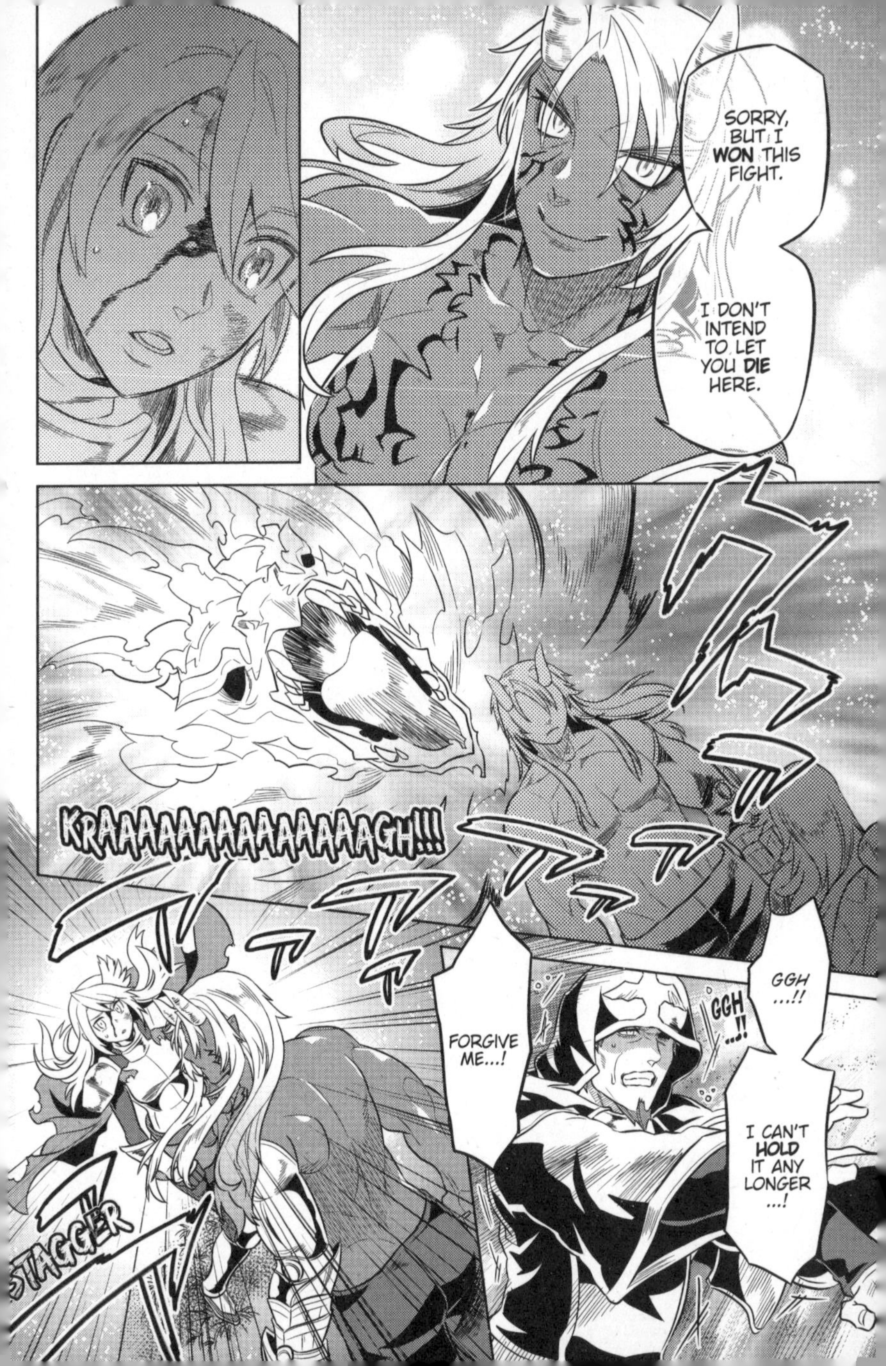
SORRY, BUT I WON THIS FIGHT.
I DON'T INTEND TO LET YOU DIE HERE.
KRAAAAAAAAAAAAAAGH!!!
GGH ...!!
GGH !! ...!!
FORGIVE ME...!
I CAN'T HOLD IT ANY LONGER ...!
STAGGER

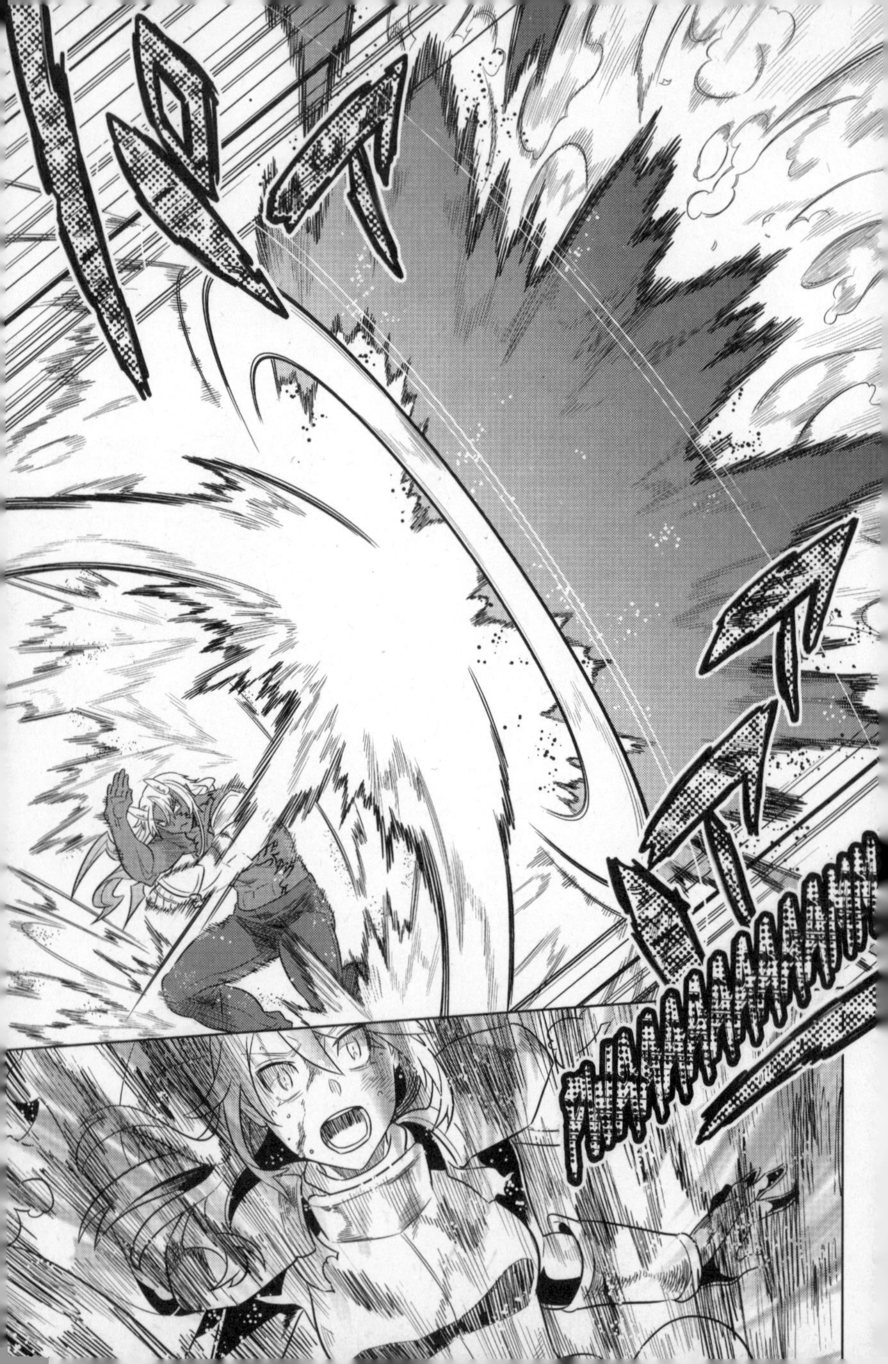

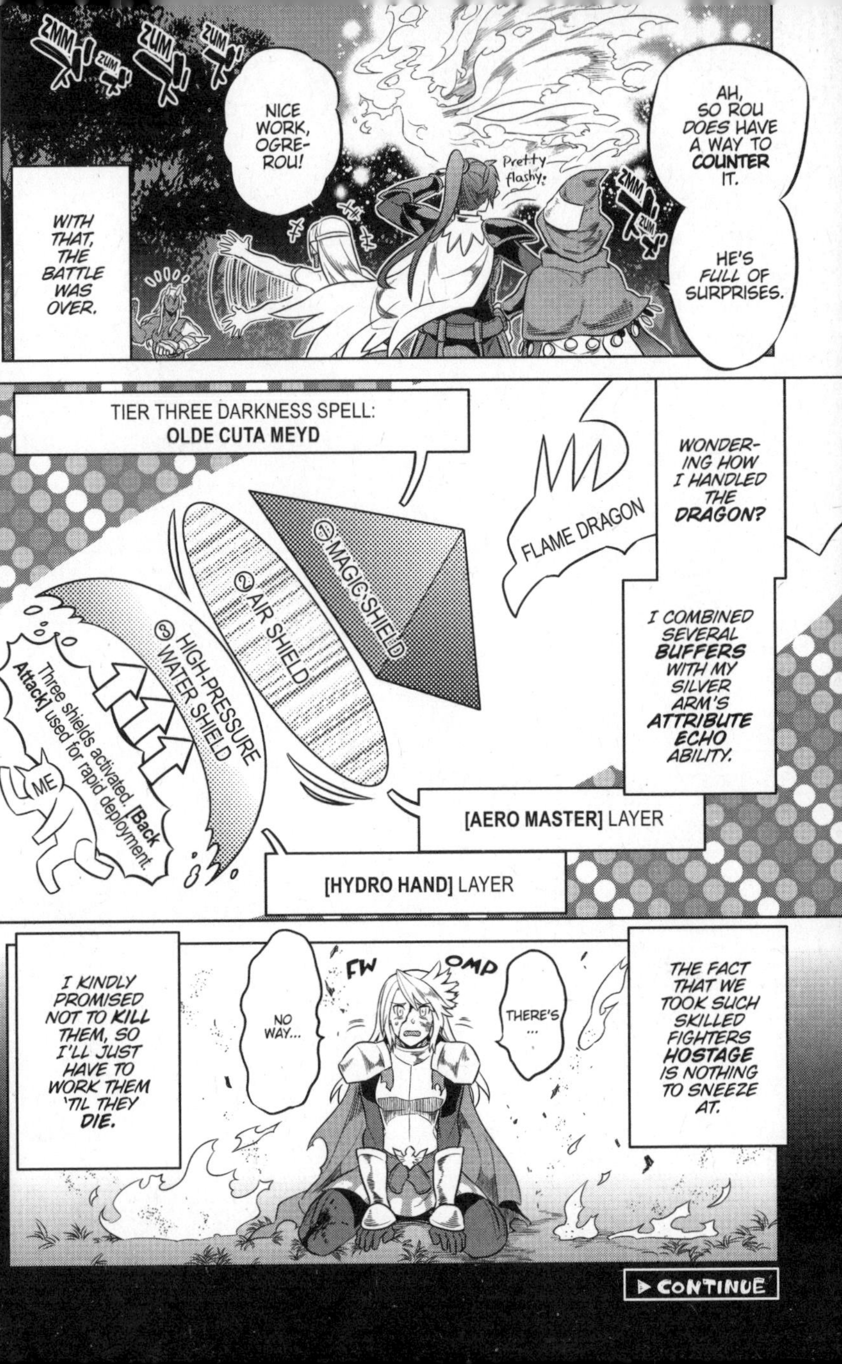
ZMM
ZUM
ZUM
ZMM
ZUM
AH, SO ROU DOES HAVE A WAY TO COUNTER IT.
HE'S FULL OF SURPRISES.
Pretty flashy.
NICE WORK, OGRE-ROU!
WITH THAT, THE BATTLE WAS OVER.
WONDERING HOW I HANDLED THE DRAGON?
I COMBINED SEVERAL BUFFERS WITH MY SILVER ARM'S ATTRIBUTE ECHO ABILITY.
FLAME DRAGON
TIER THREE DARKNESS SPELL: OLDE CUTA MEYD
① MAGIC SHIELD
② AIR SHIELD
③ HIGH-PRESSURE WATER SHIELD
[AERO MASTER] LAYER
[HYDRO HAND] LAYER
Three shields activated. [Back Attack] used for rapid deployment.
ME
THE FACT THAT WE TOOK SUCH SKILLED FIGHTERS HOSTAGE IS NOTHING TO SNEEZE AT.
THERE'S...
FWOMP
NO WAY...
I KINDLY PROMISED NOT TO KILL THEM, SO I'LL JUST HAVE TO WORK THEM 'TIL THEY DIE.
CONTINUE

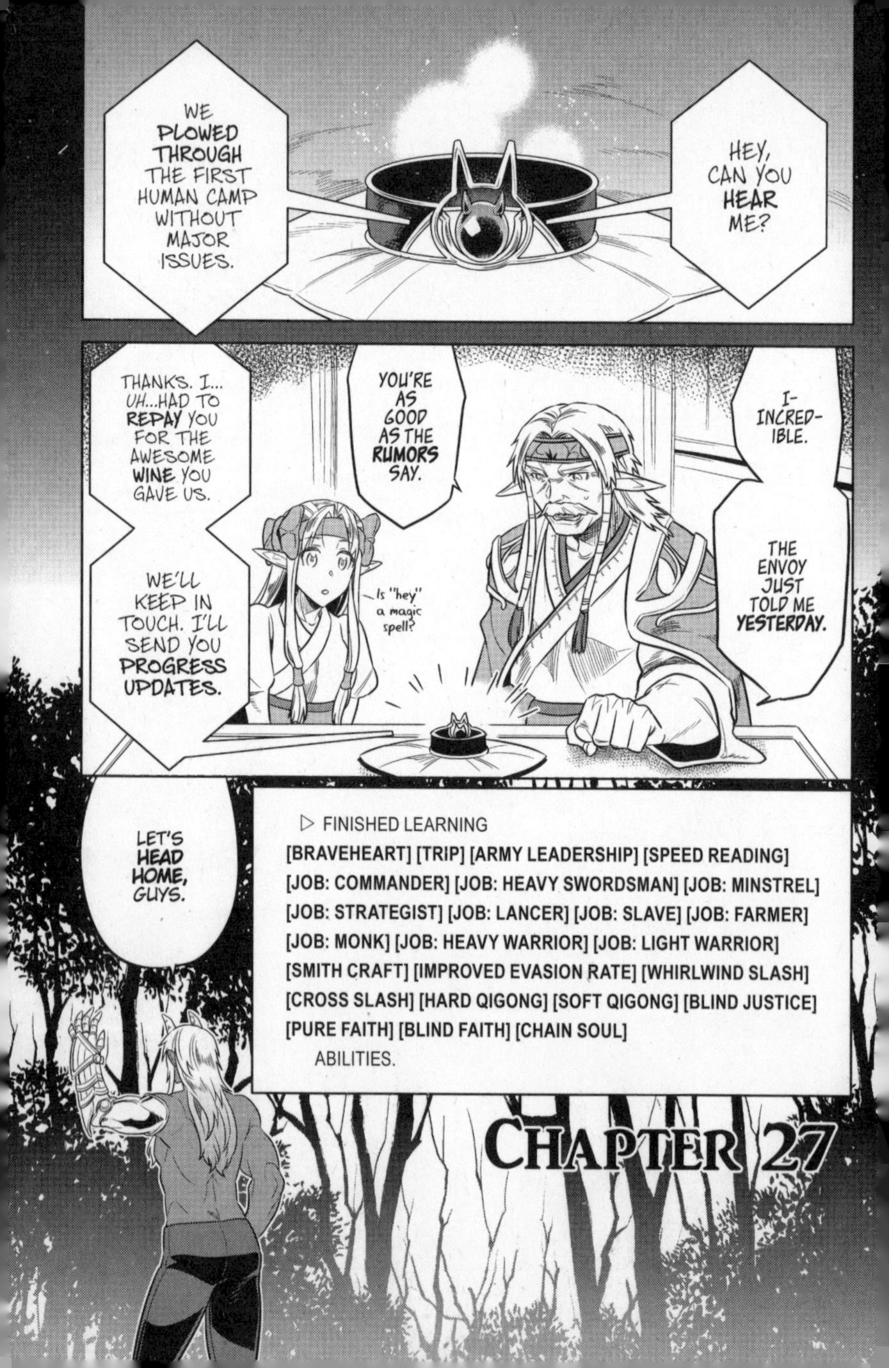
HEY, CAN YOU HEAR ME?
WE PLOWED THROUGH THE FIRST HUMAN CAMP WITHOUT MAJOR ISSUES.
I- INCREDIBLE.
THE ENVOY JUST TOLD ME YESTERDAY.
YOU'RE AS GOOD AS THE RUMORS SAY.
Is "hey" a magic spell?
THANKS. I... UH...HAD TO REPAY YOU FOR THE AWESOME WINE YOU GAVE US.
WE'LL KEEP IN TOUCH. I'LL SEND YOU PROGRESS UPDATES.
▷ FINISHED LEARNING
[BRAVEHEART] [TRIP] [ARMY LEADERSHIP] [SPEED READING] [JOB: COMMANDER] [JOB: HEAVY SWORDSMAN] [JOB: MINSTREL] [JOB: STRATEGIST] [JOB: LANCER] [JOB: SLAVE] [JOB: FARMER] [JOB: MONK] [JOB: HEAVY WARRIOR] [JOB: LIGHT WARRIOR] [SMITH CRAFT] [IMPROVED EVASION RATE] [WHIRLWIND SLASH] [CROSS SLASH] [HARD QIGONG] [SOFT QIGONG] [BLIND JUSTICE] [PURE FAITH] [BLIND FAITH] [CHAIN SOUL]
ABILITIES.
LET'S HEAD HOME, GUYS.
CHAPTER 27

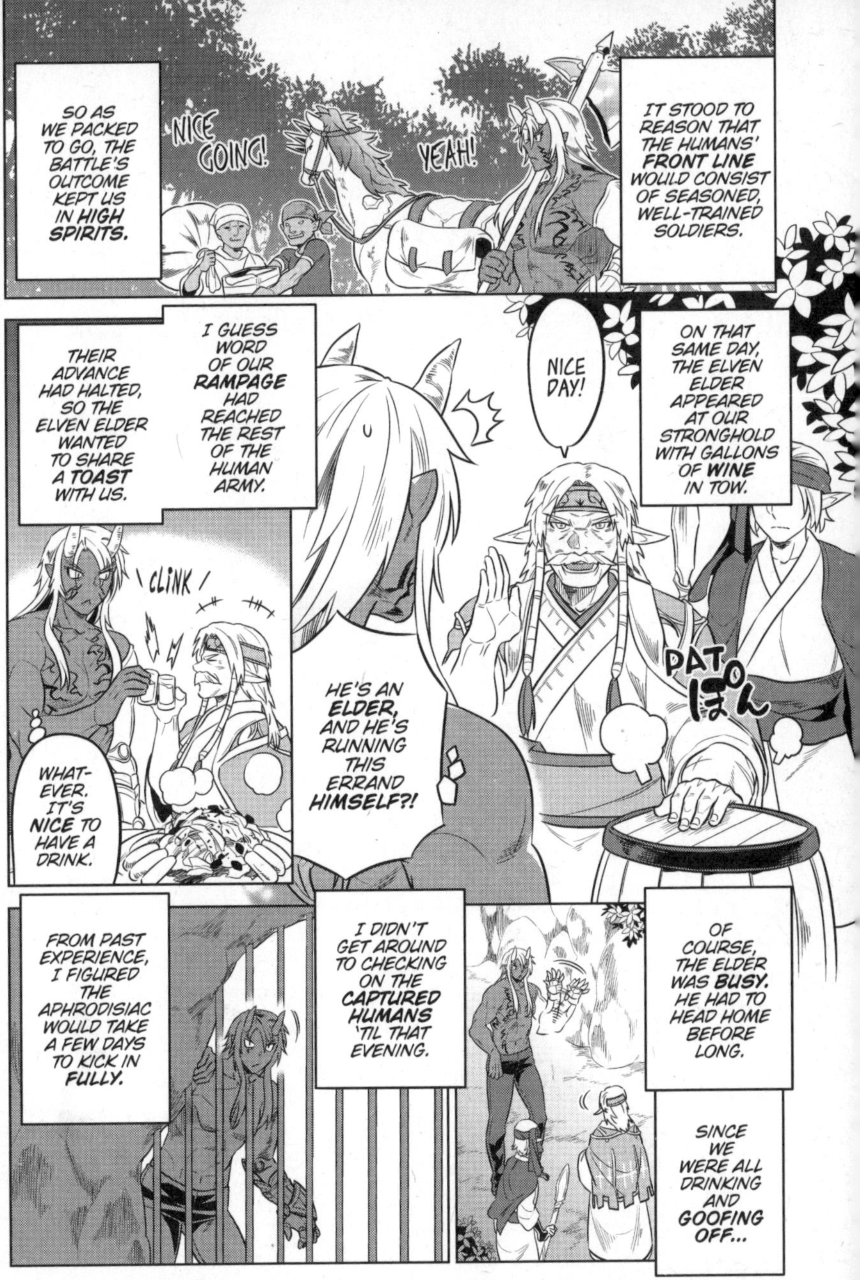
IT STOOD TO REASON THAT THE HUMANS' **FRONT LINE** WOULD CONSIST OF SEASONED, WELL-TRAINED SOLDIERS.
YEAH!
NICE GOING!
SO AS WE PACKED TO GO, THE BATTLE'S OUTCOME KEPT US IN **HIGH SPIRITS.**
ON THAT SAME DAY, THE ELVEN ELDER APPEARED AT OUR STRONGHOLD WITH GALLONS OF **WINE** IN TOW.
NICE DAY!
PAT
ぽん
HE'S AN **ELDER,** AND HE'S RUNNING THIS ERRAND **HIMSELF?!**
I GUESS WORD OF OUR **RAMPAGE** HAD REACHED THE REST OF THE HUMAN ARMY.
THEIR ADVANCE HAD HALTED, SO THE ELVEN ELDER WANTED TO SHARE A **TOAST** WITH US.
CLINK
WHAT-EVER. IT'S **NICE** TO HAVE A DRINK.
OF COURSE, THE ELDER WAS **BUSY.** HE HAD TO HEAD HOME BEFORE LONG.
SINCE WE WERE ALL DRINKING AND **GOOFING OFF...**
I DIDN'T GET AROUND TO CHECKING ON THE **CAPTURED HUMANS** 'TIL THAT EVENING.
FROM PAST EXPERIENCE, I FIGURED THE APHRODISIAC WOULD TAKE A FEW DAYS TO KICK IN **FULLY.**

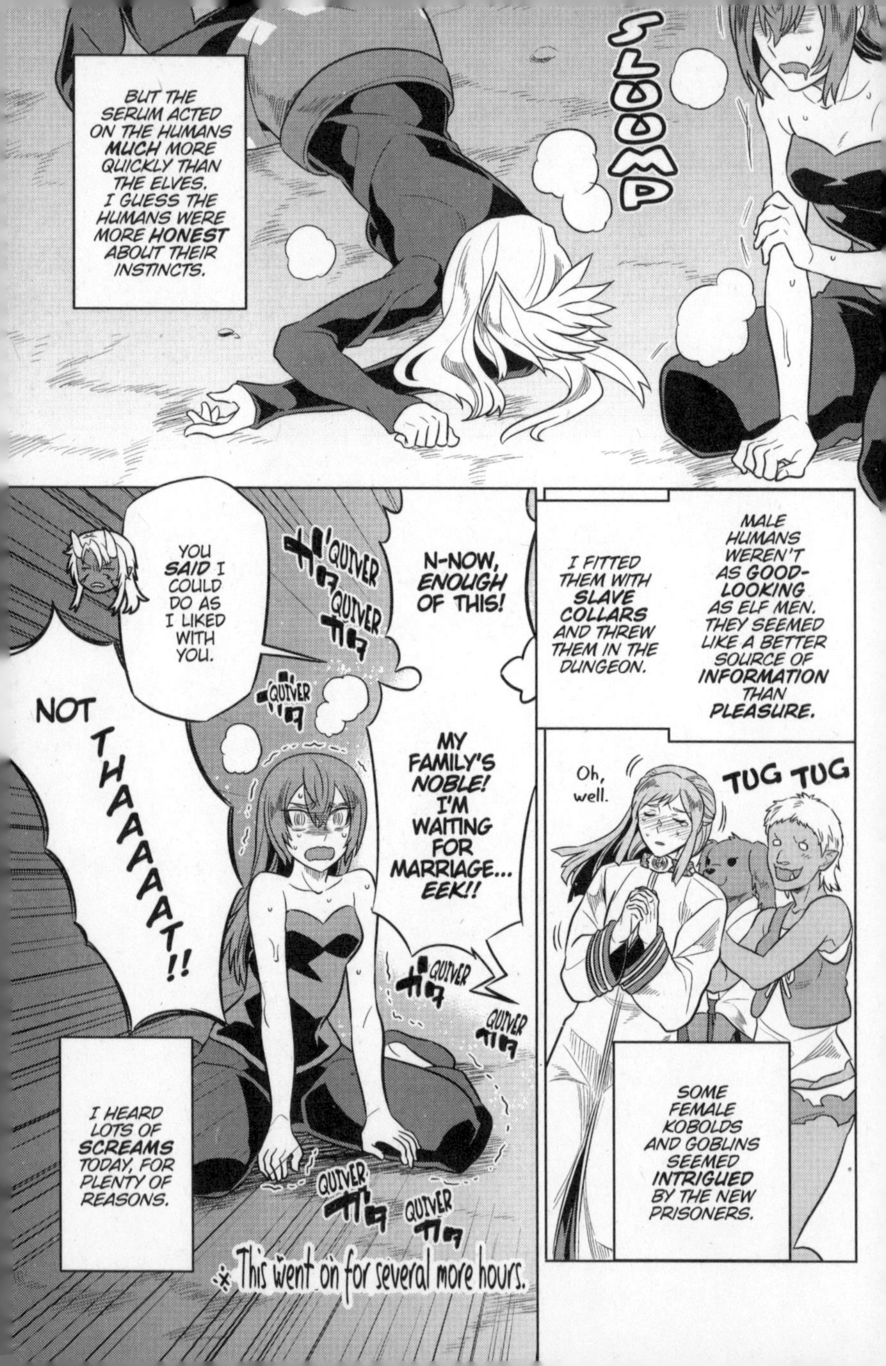
SLUUOMP
BUT THE SERUM ACTED ON THE HUMANS MUCH MORE QUICKLY THAN THE ELVES. I GUESS THE HUMANS WERE MORE HONEST ABOUT THEIR INSTINCTS.
MALE HUMANS WEREN'T AS GOOD-LOOKING AS ELF MEN. THEY SEEMED LIKE A BETTER SOURCE OF INFORMATION THAN PLEASURE.
I FITTED THEM WITH SLAVE COLLARS AND THREW THEM IN THE DUNGEON.
TUG TUG
Oh, well.
SOME FEMALE KOBOLDS AND GOBLINS SEEMED INTRIGUED BY THE NEW PRISONERS.
N-NOW, ENOUGH OF THIS!
QUIVER QUIVER
YOU SAID I COULD DO AS I LIKED WITH YOU.
QUIVER
MY FAMILY'S NOBLE! I'M WAITING FOR MARRIAGE... EEK!!
NOT THAAAAAT!!
QUIVER QUIVER
I HEARD LOTS OF SCREAMS TODAY, FOR PLENTY OF REASONS.
QUIVER QUIVER
※ This went on for several more hours.

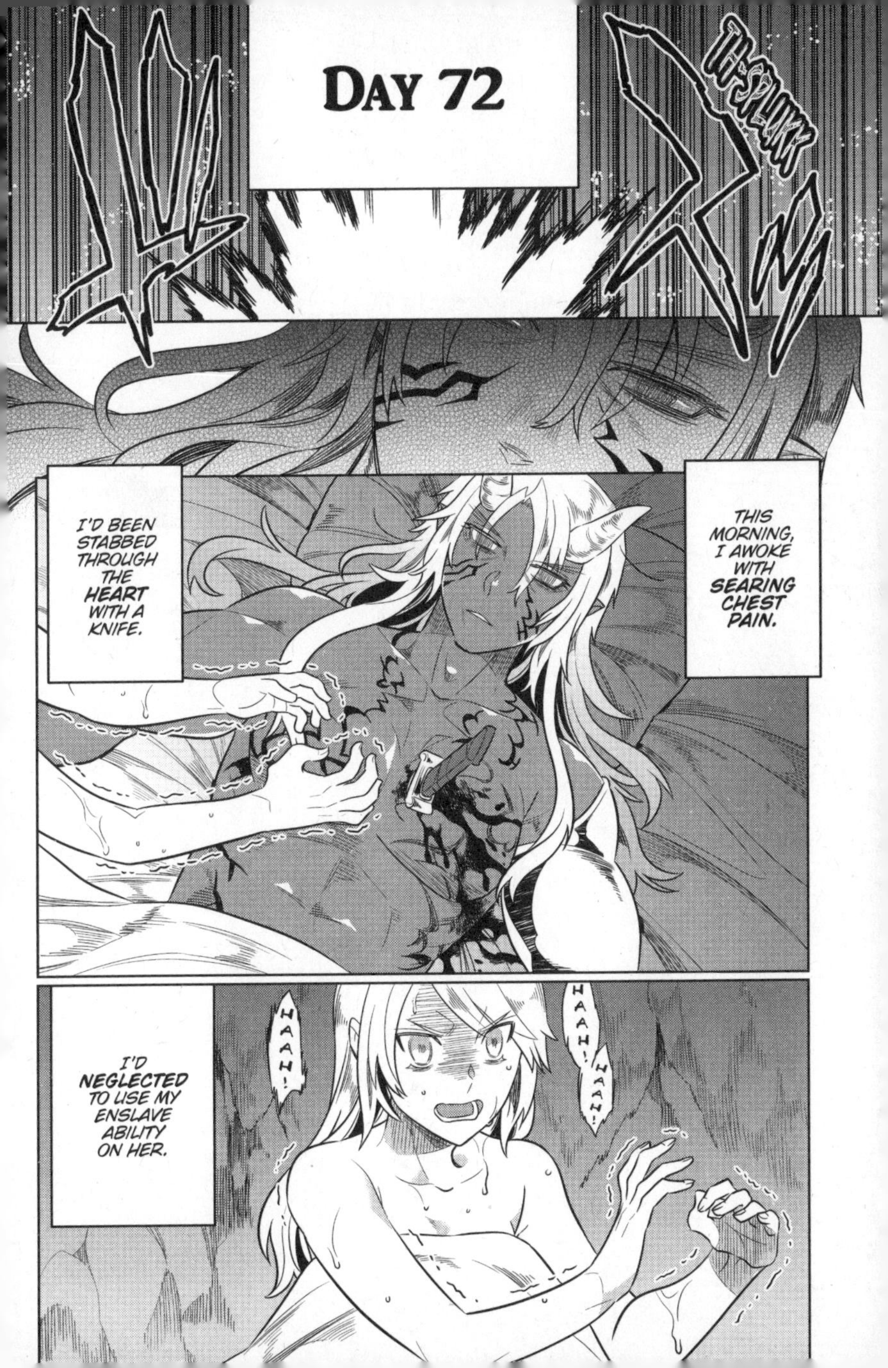

DAY 72
THIS MORNING, I AWOKE WITH SEARING CHEST PAIN.
I'D BEEN STABBED THROUGH THE HEART WITH A KNIFE.
HAAH!
HAAH!
HAAH!
I'D NEGLECTED TO USE MY ENSLAVE ABILITY ON HER.

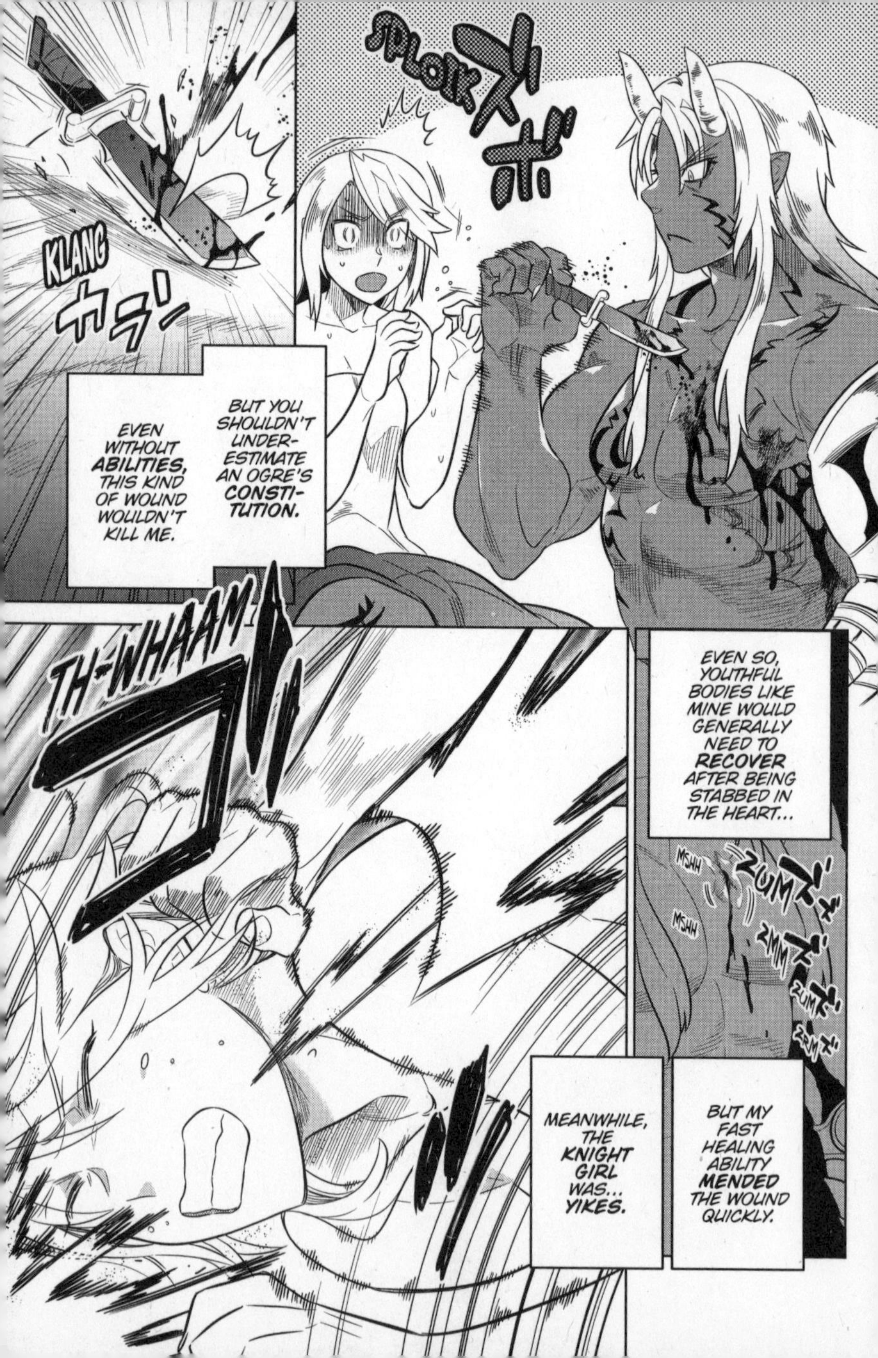
SPLOICK
ズボ
EVEN WITHOUT ABILITIES, THIS KIND OF WOUND WOULDN'T KILL ME.
BUT YOU SHOULDN'T UNDER-ESTIMATE AN OGRE'S CONSTI-TUTION.
KLANG
カラン
EVEN SO, YOUTHFUL BODIES LIKE MINE WOULD GENERALLY NEED TO RECOVER AFTER BEING STABBED IN THE HEART...
MSHH
ZUMM
MSHH
ZMM
ZUM
ZRM
BUT MY FAST HEALING ABILITY MENDED THE WOUND QUICKLY.
TH-WHAAM
MEANWHILE, THE KNIGHT GIRL WAS... YIKES.

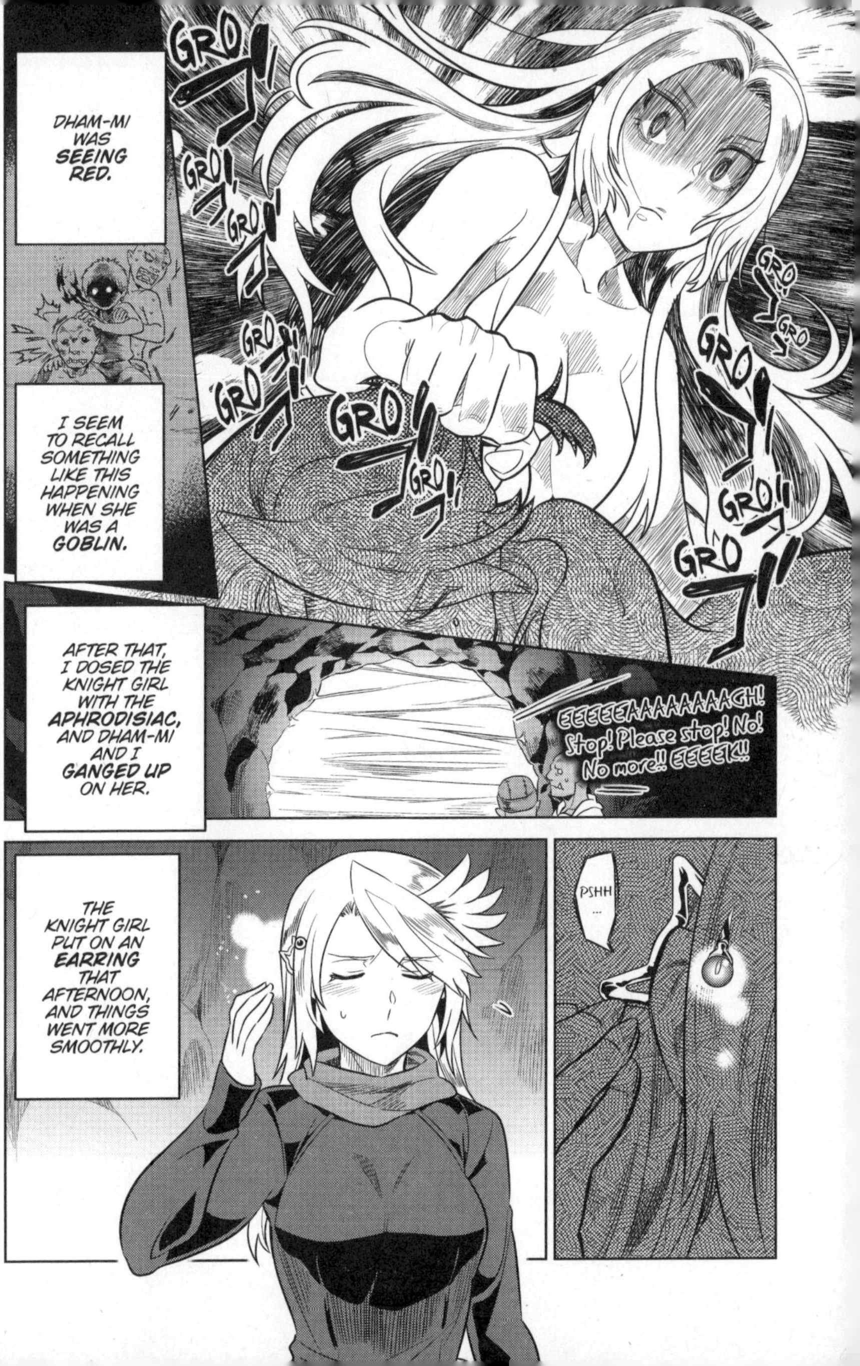
GRO
GRO
GRO
GRO
GRO
GRO
GRO
GRO
GRO
GRO
GRO
GRO
DHAM-MI WAS SEEING RED.
I SEEM TO RECALL SOMETHING LIKE THIS HAPPENING WHEN SHE WAS A GOBLIN.
EEEEEEAAAAAAAAAGH! Stop! Please stop! No! No more!! EEEEEK!!
AFTER THAT, I DOSED THE KNIGHT GIRL WITH THE APHRODISIAC, AND DHAM-MI AND I GANGED UP ON HER.
PSHH ...
THE KNIGHT GIRL PUT ON AN EARRING THAT AFTERNOON, AND THINGS WENT MORE SMOOTHLY.

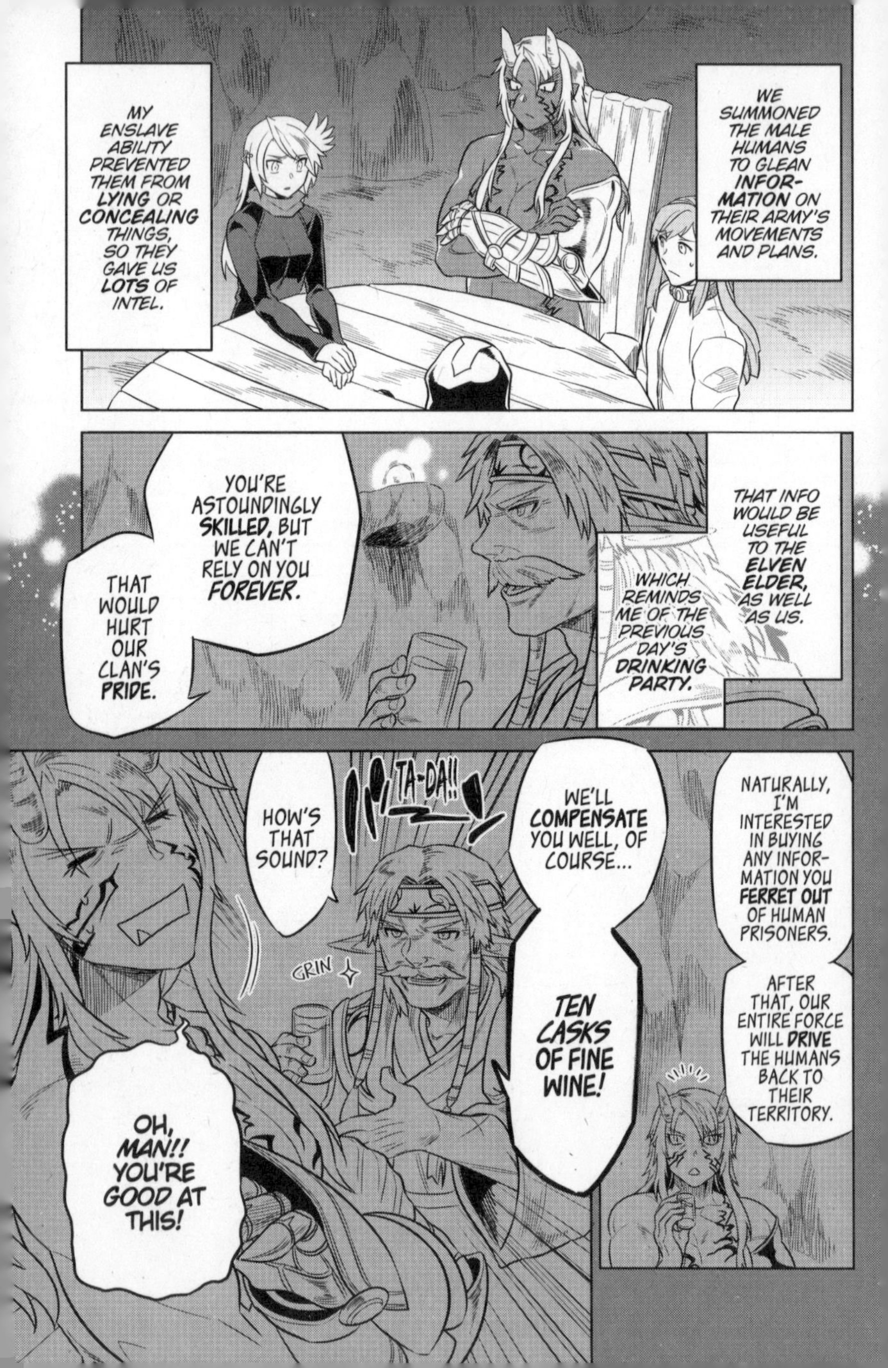
WE SUMMONED THE MALE HUMANS TO GLEAN **INFORMATION** ON THEIR ARMY'S MOVEMENTS AND PLANS.
MY ENSLAVE ABILITY PREVENTED THEM FROM **LYING** OR **CONCEALING** THINGS, SO THEY GAVE US **LOTS** OF INTEL.
THAT INFO WOULD BE USEFUL TO THE **ELVEN ELDER,** AS WELL AS US.
WHICH REMINDS ME OF THE PREVIOUS DAY'S **DRINKING PARTY.**
YOU'RE ASTOUNDINGLY **SKILLED,** BUT WE CAN'T RELY ON YOU **FOREVER.**
THAT WOULD HURT OUR CLAN'S **PRIDE.**
NATURALLY, I'M INTERESTED IN BUYING ANY INFORMATION YOU **FERRET OUT** OF HUMAN PRISONERS.
AFTER THAT, OUR ENTIRE FORCE WILL **DRIVE** THE HUMANS BACK TO THEIR TERRITORY.
WE'LL **COMPENSATE** YOU WELL, OF COURSE...
TEN CASKS OF FINE WINE!
TA-DA!!
HOW'S THAT SOUND?
GRIN
OH, MAN!! YOU'RE GOOD AT THIS!

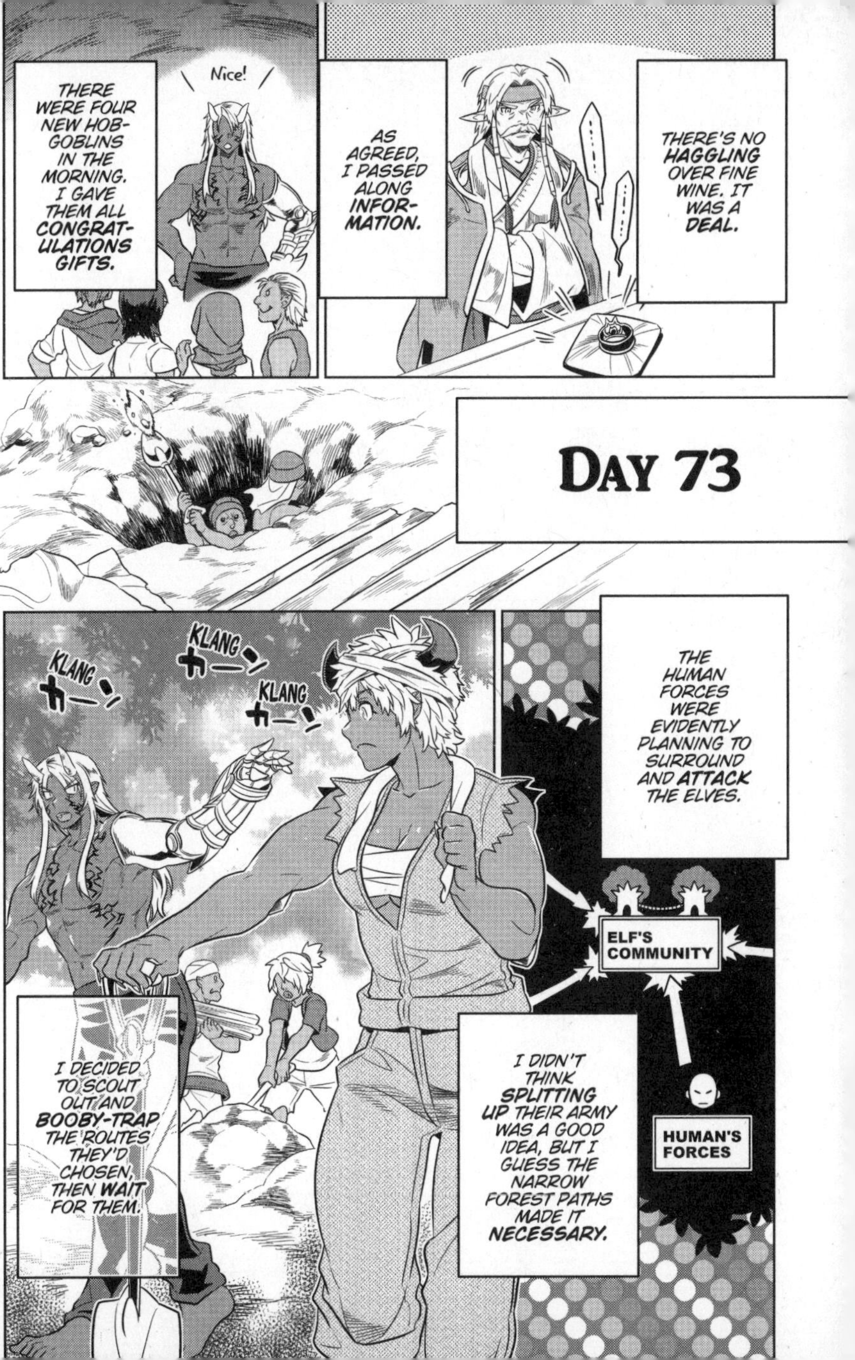
THERE'S NO HAGGLING OVER FINE WINE. IT WAS A DEAL.
AS AGREED, I PASSED ALONG INFORMATION.
Nice!
THERE WERE FOUR NEW HOBGOBLINS IN THE MORNING. I GAVE THEM ALL CONGRATULATIONS GIFTS.
DAY 73
THE HUMAN FORCES WERE EVIDENTLY PLANNING TO SURROUND AND ATTACK THE ELVES.
ELF'S COMMUNITY
HUMAN'S FORCES
KLANG カーン
KLANG カーン
KLANG カーン
I DIDN'T THINK SPLITTING UP THEIR ARMY WAS A GOOD IDEA, BUT I GUESS THE NARROW FOREST PATHS MADE IT NECESSARY.
I DECIDED TO SCOUT OUT AND BOOBY-TRAP THE ROUTES THEY'D CHOSEN, THEN WAIT FOR THEM.

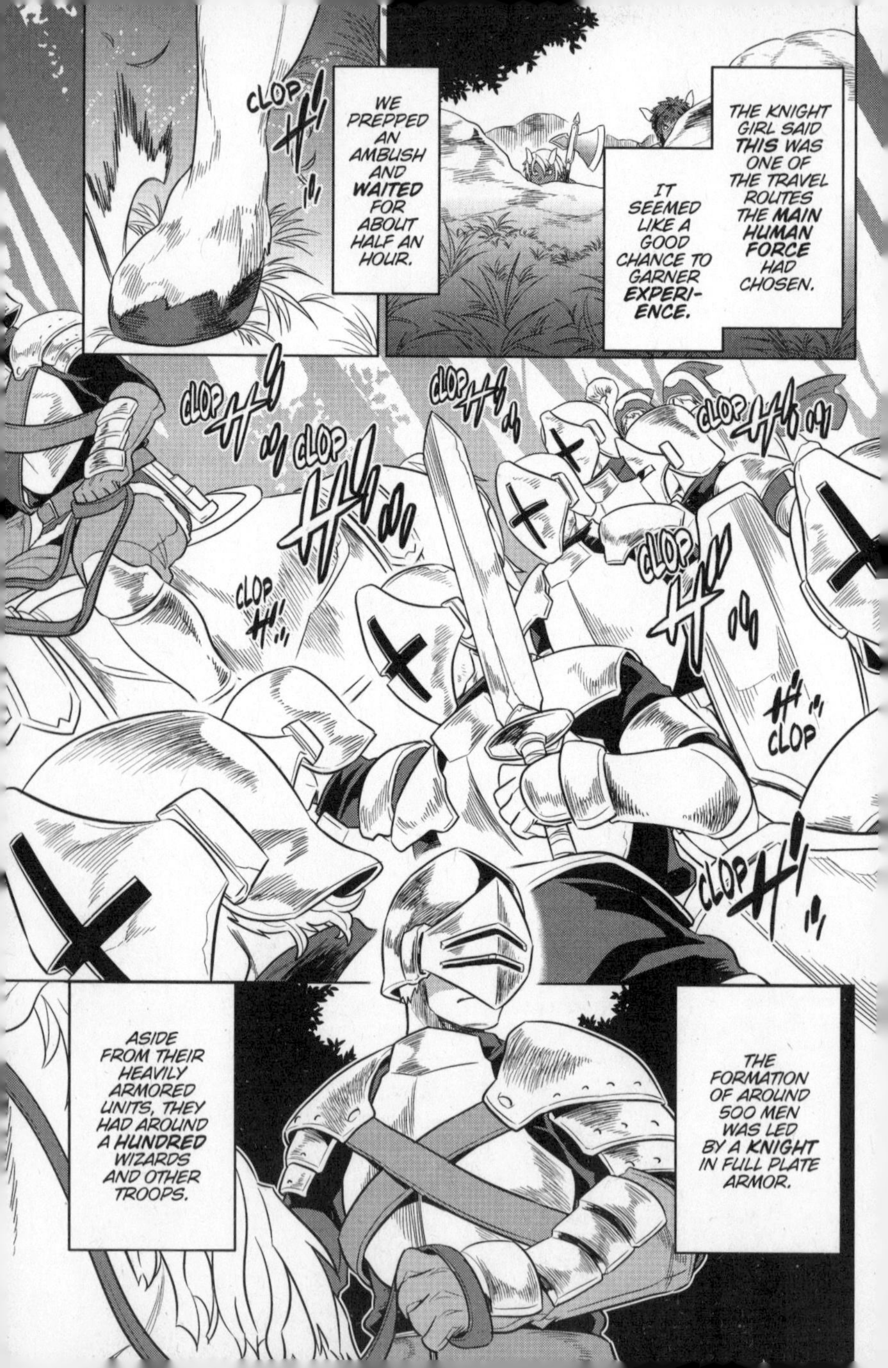
THE KNIGHT GIRL SAID THIS WAS ONE OF THE TRAVEL ROUTES THE MAIN HUMAN FORCE HAD CHOSEN.
IT SEEMED LIKE A GOOD CHANCE TO GARNER EXPERI- ENCE.
WE PREPPED AN AMBUSH AND WAITED FOR ABOUT HALF AN HOUR.
CLOP
CLOP
CLOP
CLOP
CLOP
CLOP
CLOP
CLOP
CLOP
THE FORMATION OF AROUND 500 MEN WAS LED BY A KNIGHT IN FULL PLATE ARMOR.
ASIDE FROM THEIR HEAVILY ARMORED UNITS, THEY HAD AROUND A HUNDRED WIZARDS AND OTHER TROOPS.

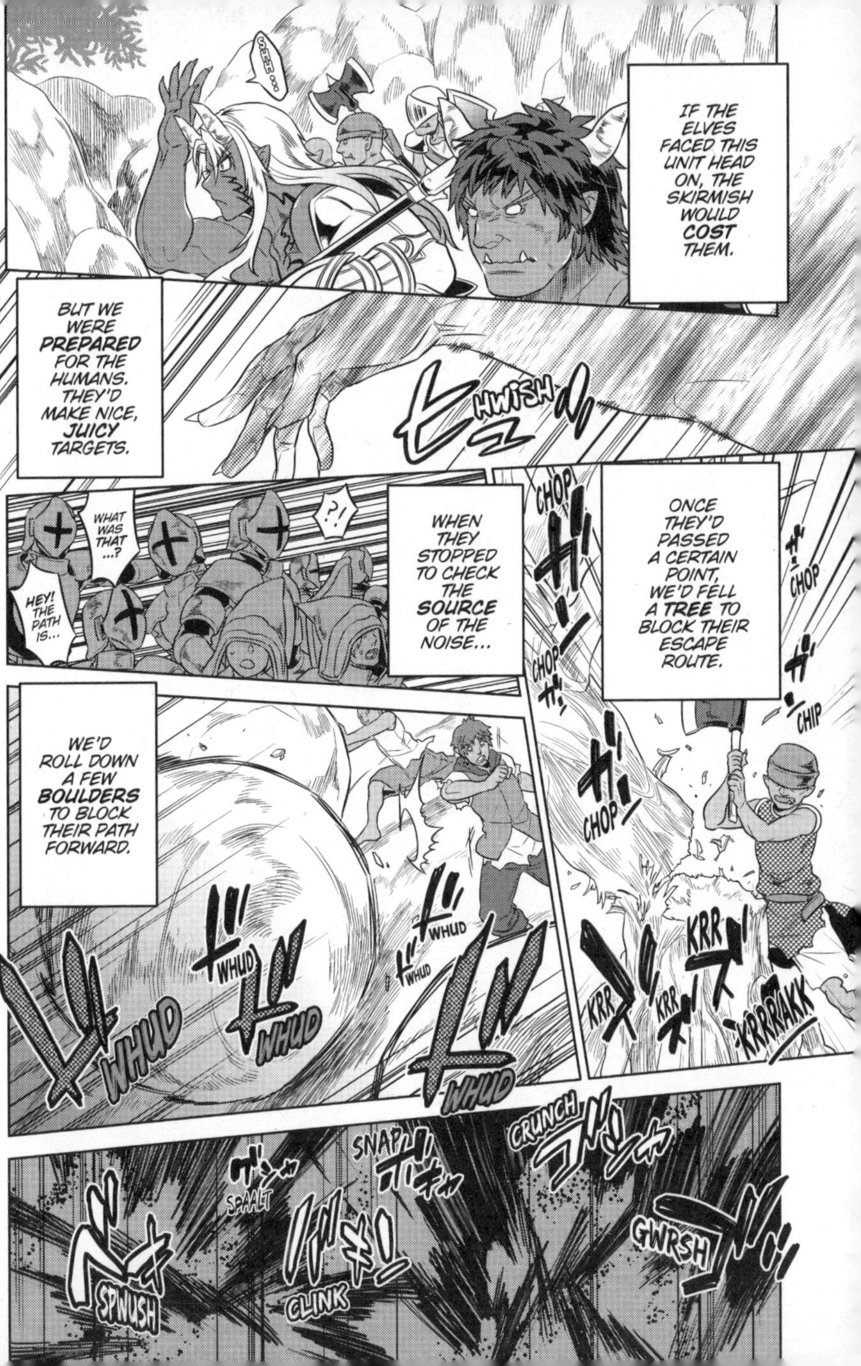

IF THE ELVES FACED THIS UNIT HEAD ON, THE SKIRMISH WOULD COST THEM.
SHHH...
BUT WE WERE PREPARED FOR THE HUMANS. THEY'D MAKE NICE, JUICY TARGETS.
HWISH
ONCE THEY'D PASSED A CERTAIN POINT, WE'D FELL A TREE TO BLOCK THEIR ESCAPE ROUTE.
CHOP
CHOP
CHOP
CHOP
WHEN THEY STOPPED TO CHECK THE SOURCE OF THE NOISE...
?!
WHAT WAS THAT ...?
HEY! THE PATH IS...
CHIP
KRR
KRR
KRR
KRRRAKK
WE'D ROLL DOWN A FEW BOULDERS TO BLOCK THEIR PATH FORWARD.
WHUD
WHUD
WHUD
WHUD
WHUD
WHUD
CRUNCH
SNAP
SPAALT
GWRSH
CLINK
SPWUSH

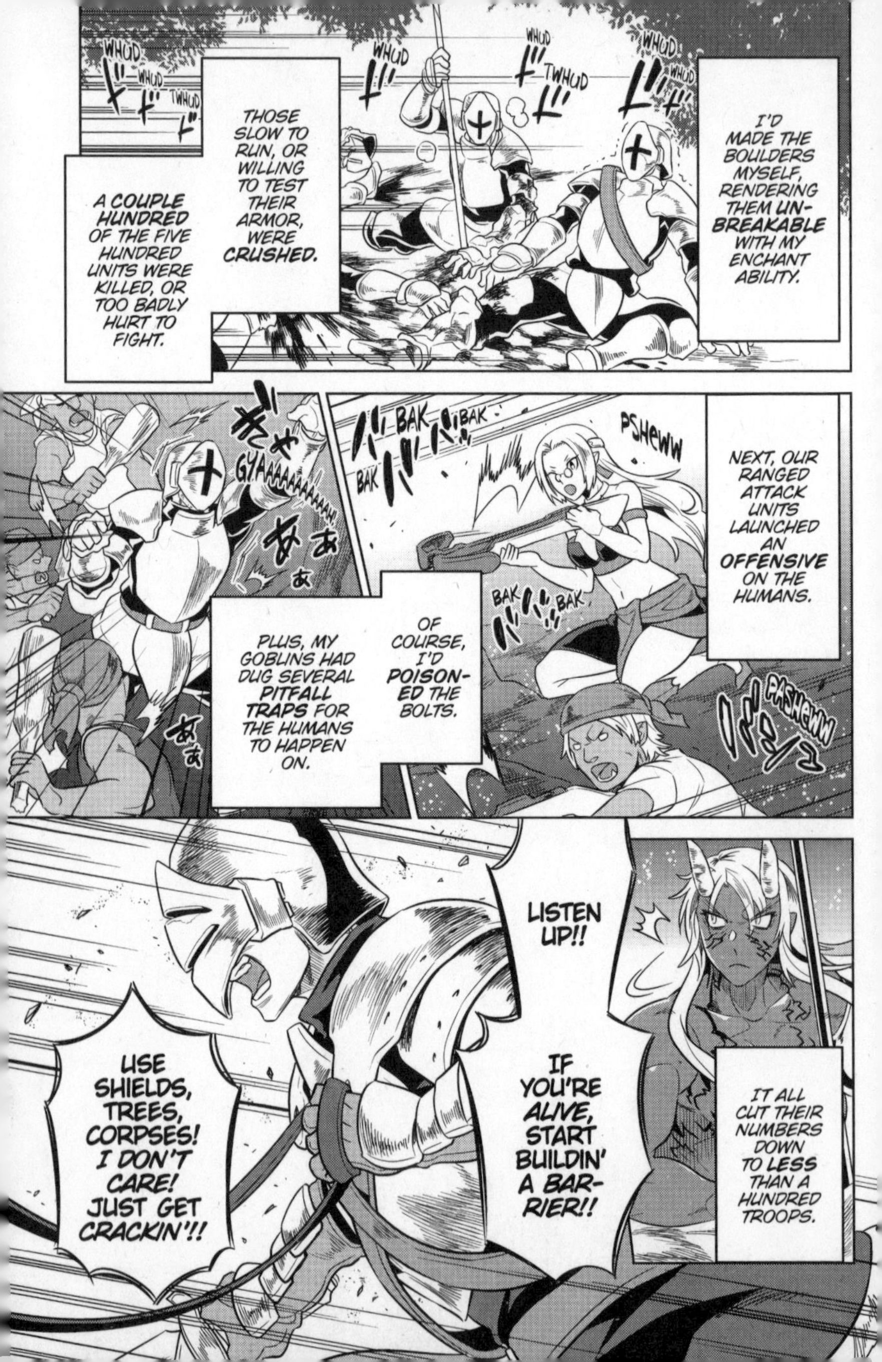
WHUD
WHUD
TWHUD
I'D MADE THE BOULDERS MYSELF, RENDERING THEM UN-BREAKABLE WITH MY ENCHANT ABILITY.
WHUD
WHUD
TWHUD
THOSE SLOW TO RUN, OR WILLING TO TEST THEIR ARMOR, WERE CRUSHED.
A COUPLE HUNDRED OF THE FIVE HUNDRED UNITS WERE KILLED, OR TOO BADLY HURT TO FIGHT.
NEXT, OUR RANGED ATTACK UNITS LAUNCHED AN OFFENSIVE ON THE HUMANS.
PSHEWW
BAK BAK BAK
BAK BAK
PASHEWW
OF COURSE, I'D POISON-ED THE BOLTS.
PLUS, MY GOBLINS HAD DUG SEVERAL PITFALL TRAPS FOR THE HUMANS TO HAPPEN ON.
GYAAAAAAAAAAH!
IT ALL CUT THEIR NUMBERS DOWN TO LESS THAN A HUNDRED TROOPS.
LISTEN UP!!
IF YOU'RE ALIVE, START BUILDIN' A BAR-RIER!!
USE SHIELDS, TREES, CORPSES! I DON'T CARE! JUST GET CRACKIN'!!

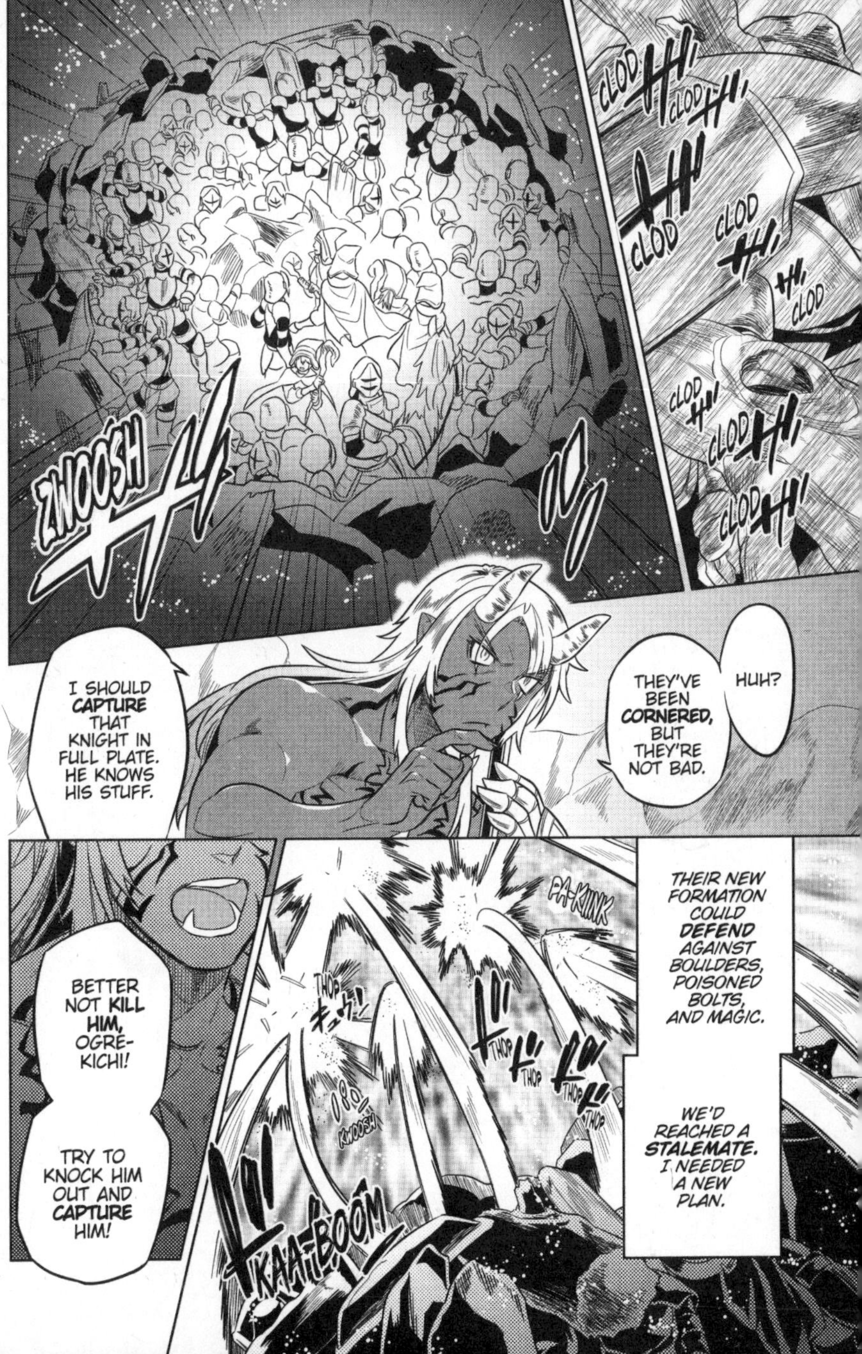
CLOD
CLOD
CLOD
CLOD
CLOD
CLOD
CLOD
CLOD
ZWOOSH
HUH?
THEY'VE BEEN **CORNERED,** BUT THEY'RE NOT BAD.
I SHOULD **CAPTURE** THAT KNIGHT IN FULL PLATE. HE KNOWS HIS STUFF.
THEIR NEW FORMATION COULD **DEFEND** AGAINST BOULDERS, POISONED BOLTS, AND MAGIC.
WE'D REACHED A **STALEMATE.** I NEEDED A NEW PLAN.
PA-KIINK
THOP
THOP
THOP
THOP
THOP
THOP
KWOOSH
KAA-BOOM
BETTER NOT **KILL HIM,** OGRE-KICHI!
TRY TO KNOCK HIM OUT AND **CAPTURE** HIM!

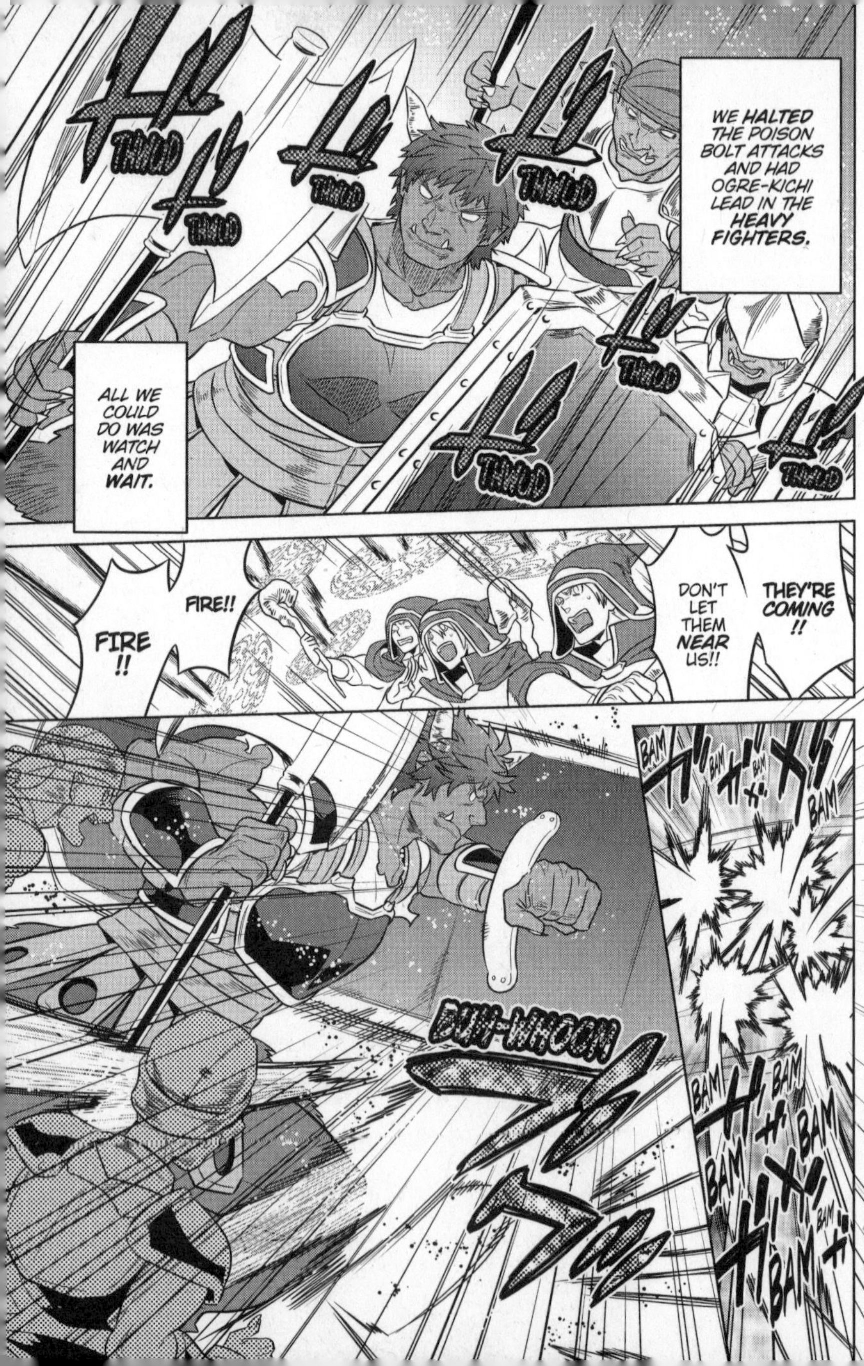
WE HALTED THE POISON BOLT ATTACKS AND HAD OGRE-KICHI LEAD IN THE HEAVY FIGHTERS.
THWUD
THWUD
THWUD
THWUD
THWUD
THWUD
THWUD
THWUD
ALL WE COULD DO WAS WATCH AND WAIT.
THEY'RE COMING!!
DON'T LET THEM NEAR US!!
FIRE!!
FIRE!!
BAM
BAM
BAM
BAM
DUN-WHOOM
BAM
BAM
BAM
BAM
BAM
BAM
BAM

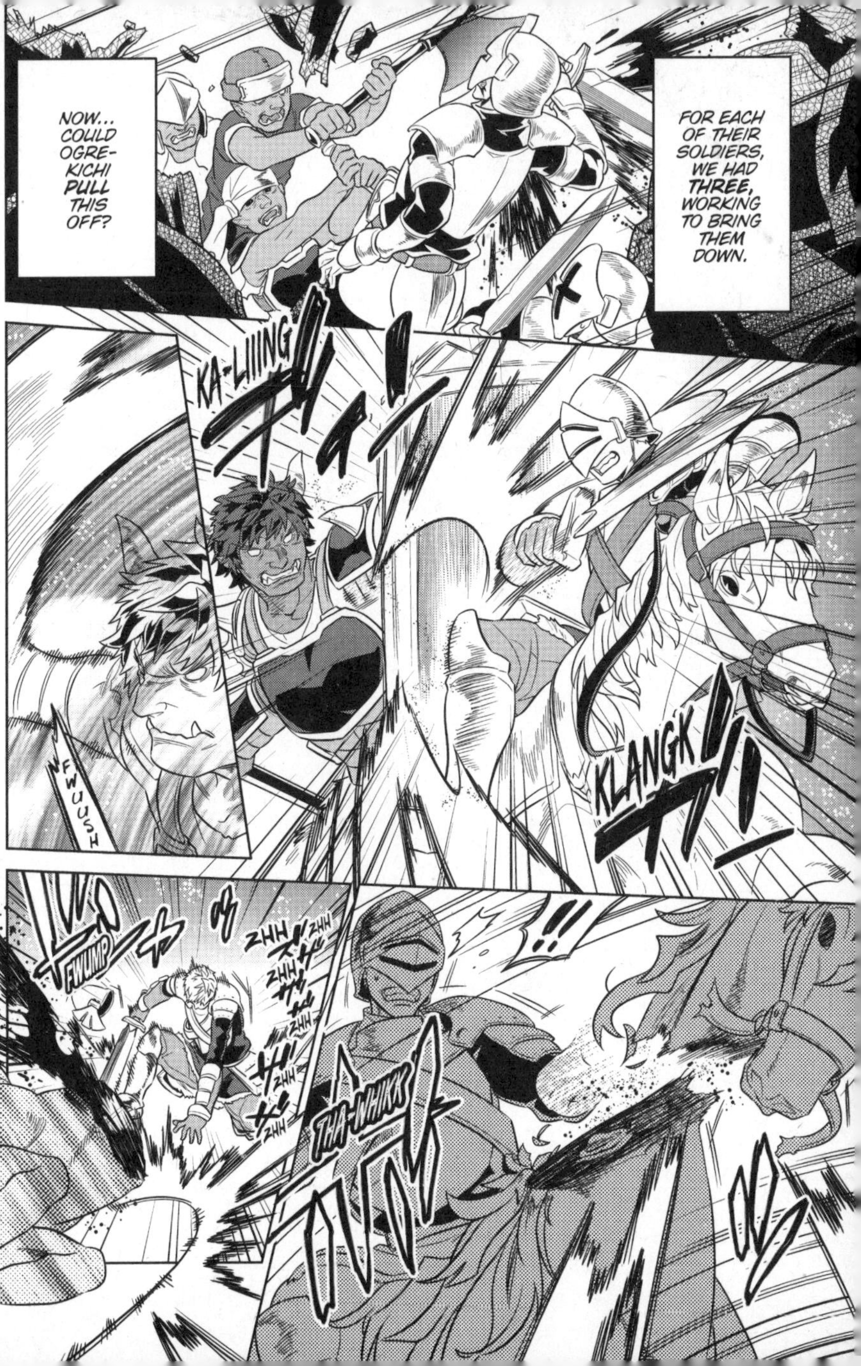
FOR EACH OF THEIR SOLDIERS, WE HAD **THREE**, WORKING TO BRING THEM DOWN.
NOW... COULD OGRE-KICHI **PULL** THIS OFF?
KA-LIIING
KLANGK
FWUUSH
!!
THA-WHIKK
ZHH ZHH ZHH ZHH ZHH ZHH
FWUMP

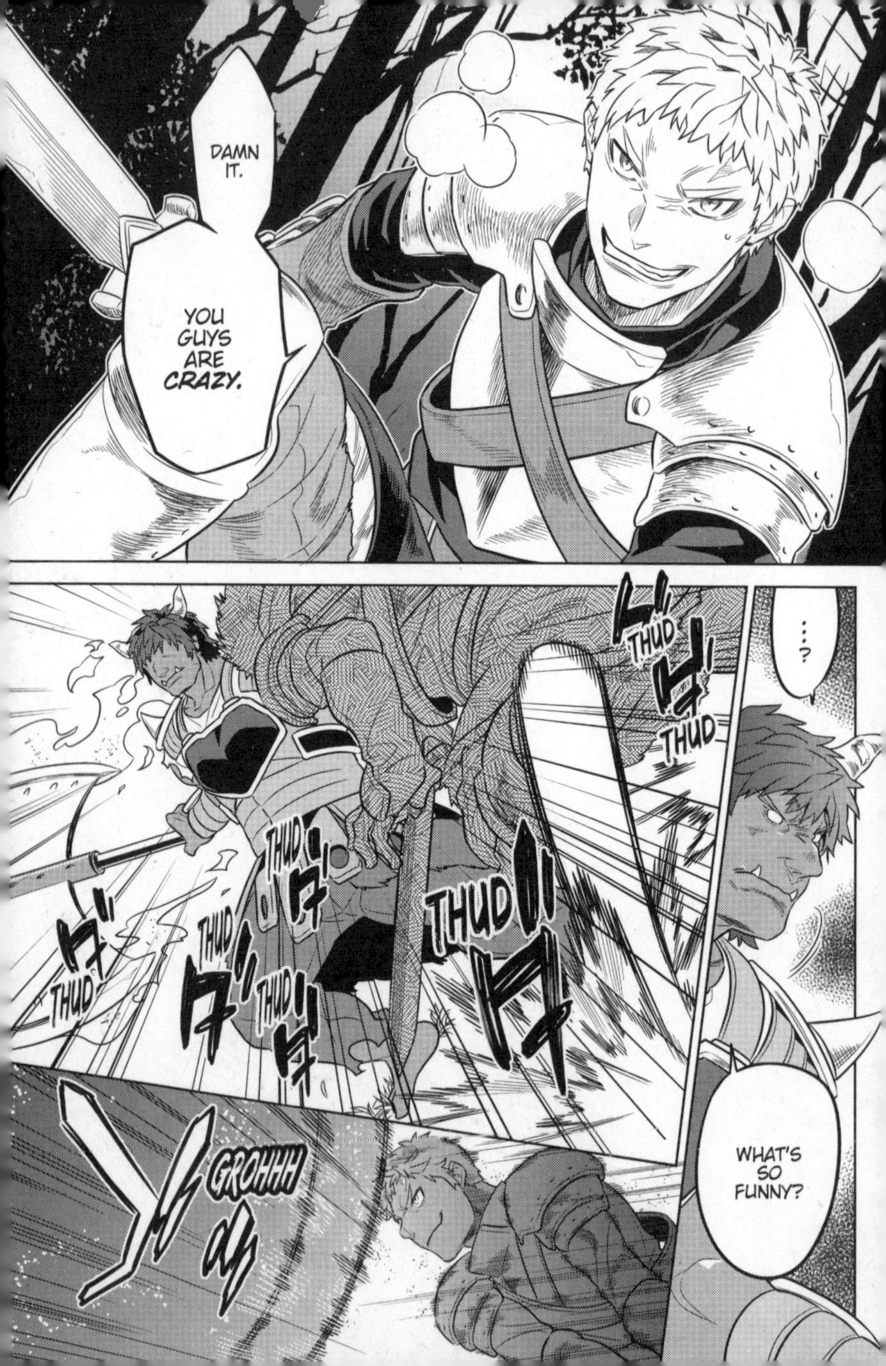
DAMN IT.
YOU GUYS ARE CRAZY.
...?
WHAT'S SO FUNNY?
THUD
THUD
THUD
THUD
THUD
THUD
THUD
THUD
GROHHH

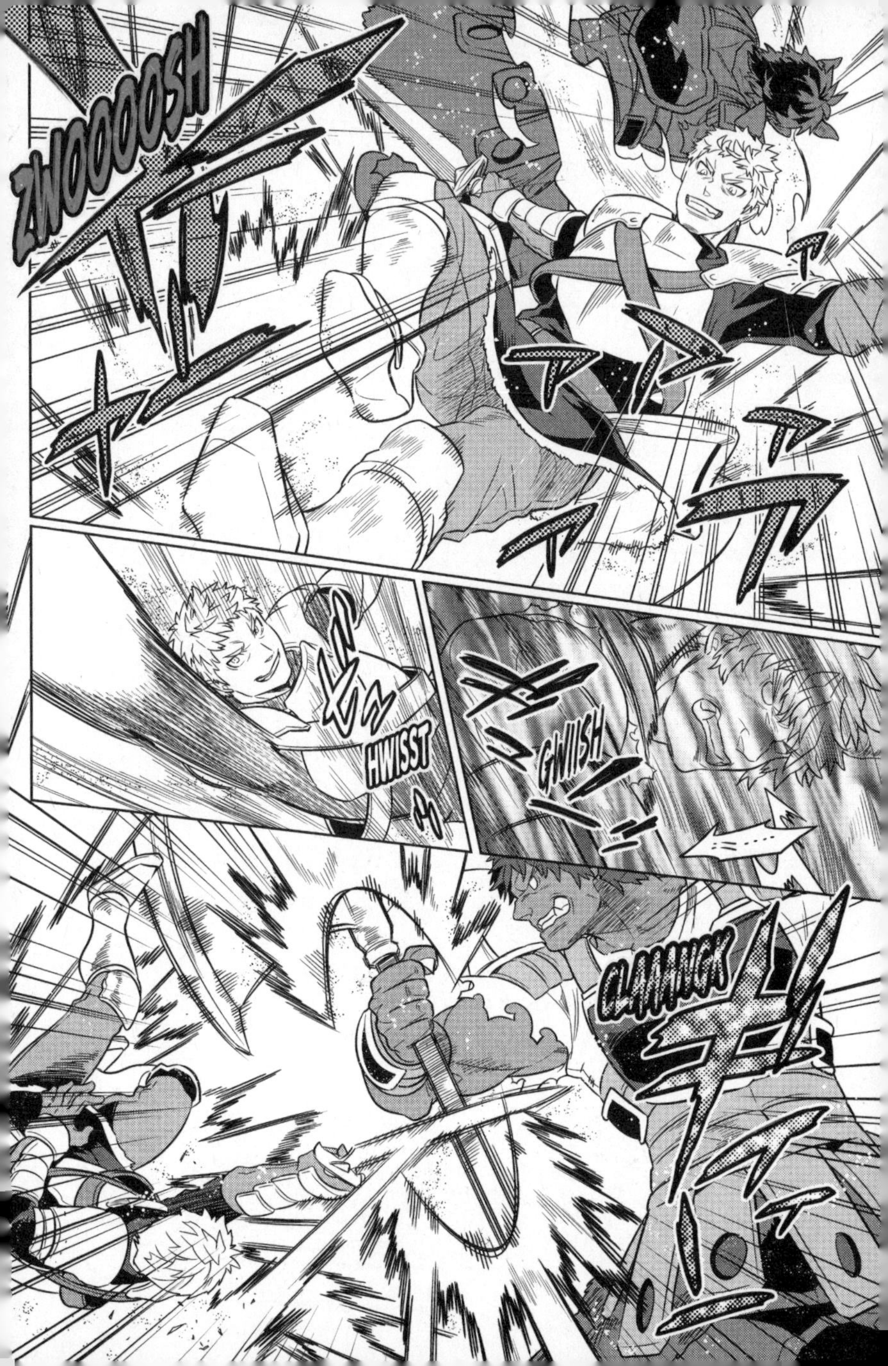
ZWOOOOSH
GWIISH
HWISST
CLAANGK

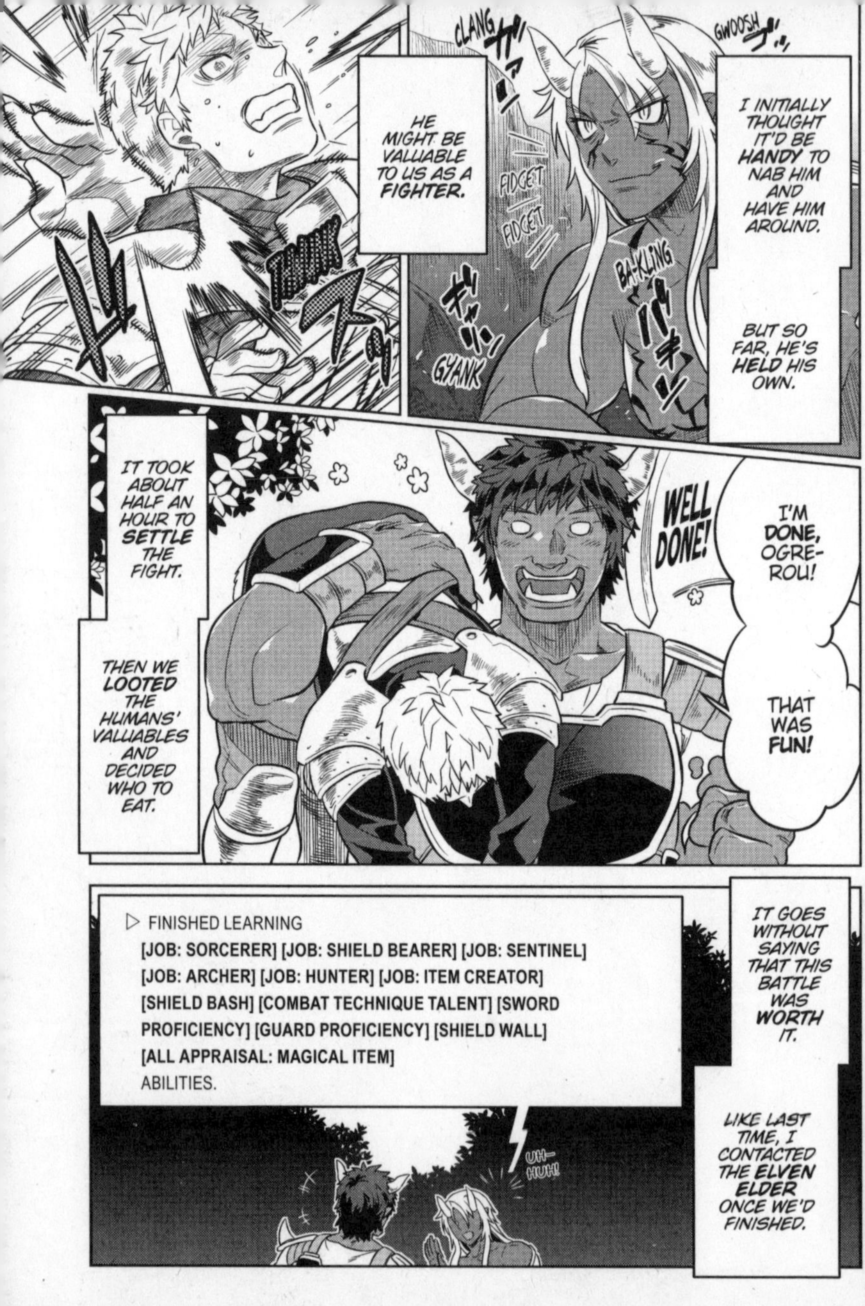
GWOOSH
I INITIALLY THOUGHT IT'D BE HANDY TO NAB HIM AND HAVE HIM AROUND.
CLANG
HE MIGHT BE VALUABLE TO US AS A FIGHTER.
FIDGET FIDGET
BA-KLING
BUT SO FAR, HE'S HELD HIS OWN.
GYANK
THUNK
I'M DONE, OGRE-ROU!
THAT WAS FUN!
WELL DONE!
IT TOOK ABOUT HALF AN HOUR TO SETTLE THE FIGHT.
THEN WE LOOTED THE HUMANS' VALUABLES AND DECIDED WHO TO EAT.
IT GOES WITHOUT SAYING THAT THIS BATTLE WAS WORTH IT.
▷ FINISHED LEARNING
[JOB: SORCERER] [JOB: SHIELD BEARER] [JOB: SENTINEL]
[JOB: ARCHER] [JOB: HUNTER] [JOB: ITEM CREATOR]
[SHIELD BASH] [COMBAT TECHNIQUE TALENT] [SWORD
PROFICIENCY] [GUARD PROFICIENCY] [SHIELD WALL]
[ALL APPRAISAL: MAGICAL ITEM]
ABILITIES.
LIKE LAST TIME, I CONTACTED THE ELVEN ELDER ONCE WE'D FINISHED.
UH-HUH!

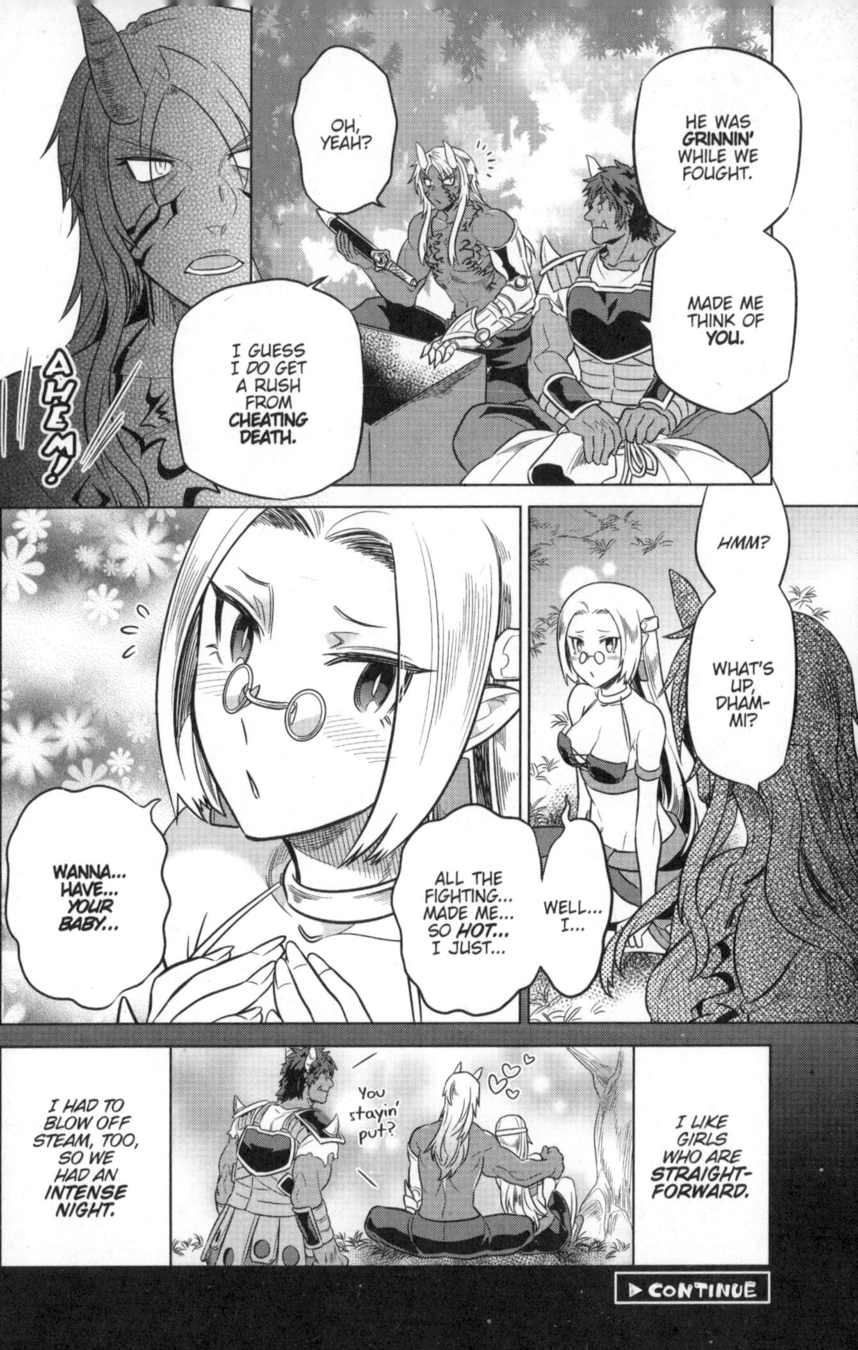
HE WAS GRINNIN' WHILE WE FOUGHT.
MADE ME THINK OF YOU.
OH, YEAH?
I GUESS I DO GET A RUSH FROM CHEATING DEATH.
AHEM!
HMM?
WHAT'S UP, DHAM-MI?
WELL... I...
ALL THE FIGHTING... MADE ME... SO HOT... I JUST...
WANNA... HAVE... YOUR BABY...
I LIKE GIRLS WHO ARE STRAIGHT-FORWARD.
You stayin' put?
I HAD TO BLOW OFF STEAM, TOO, SO WE HAD AN INTENSE NIGHT.
CONTINUE

DAY 74

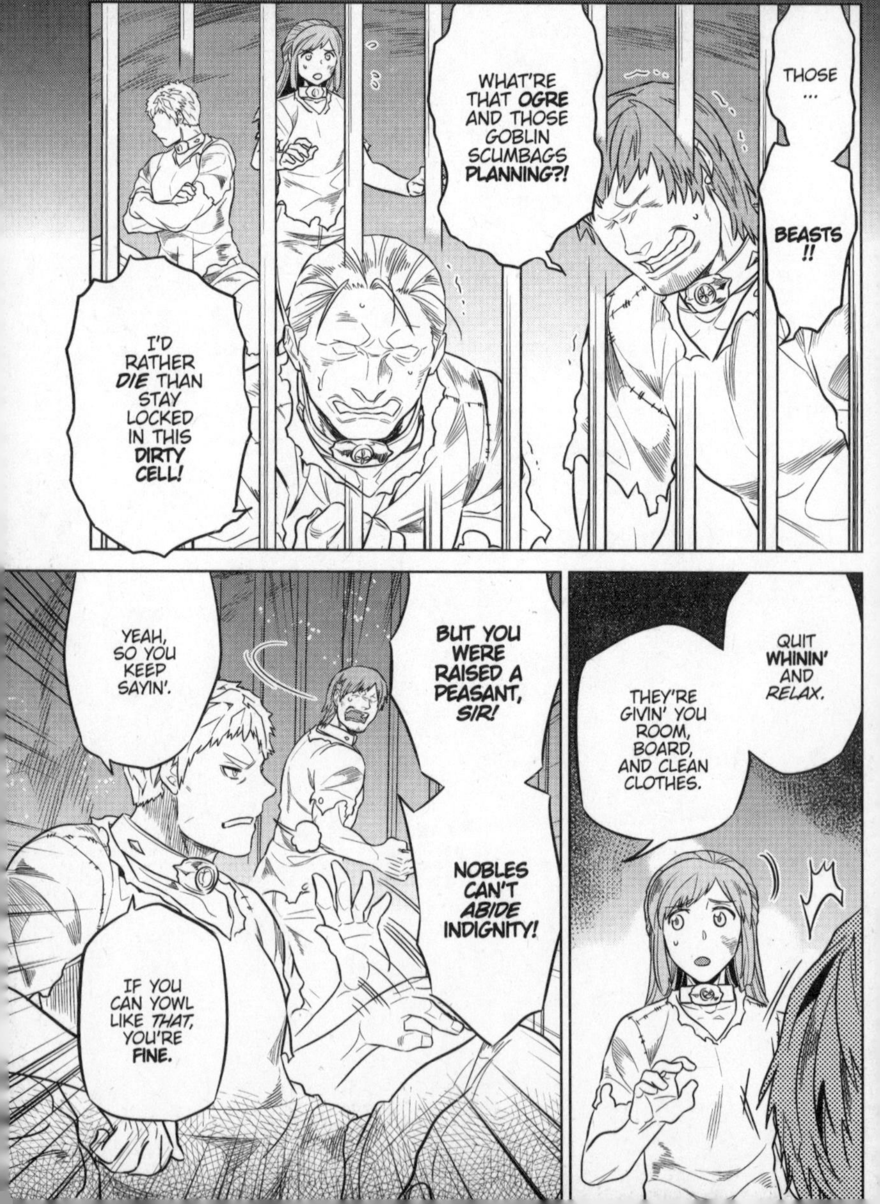
THOSE ...
BEASTS !!
WHAT'RE THAT OGRE AND THOSE GOBLIN SCUMBAGS PLANNING?!
I'D RATHER DIE THAN STAY LOCKED IN THIS DIRTY CELL!
QUIT WHININ' AND RELAX.
THEY'RE GIVIN' YOU ROOM, BOARD, AND CLEAN CLOTHES.
BUT YOU WERE RAISED A PEASANT, SIR!
YEAH, SO YOU KEEP SAYIN'.
NOBLES CAN'T ABIDE INDIGNITY!
IF YOU CAN YOWL LIKE THAT, YOU'RE FINE.

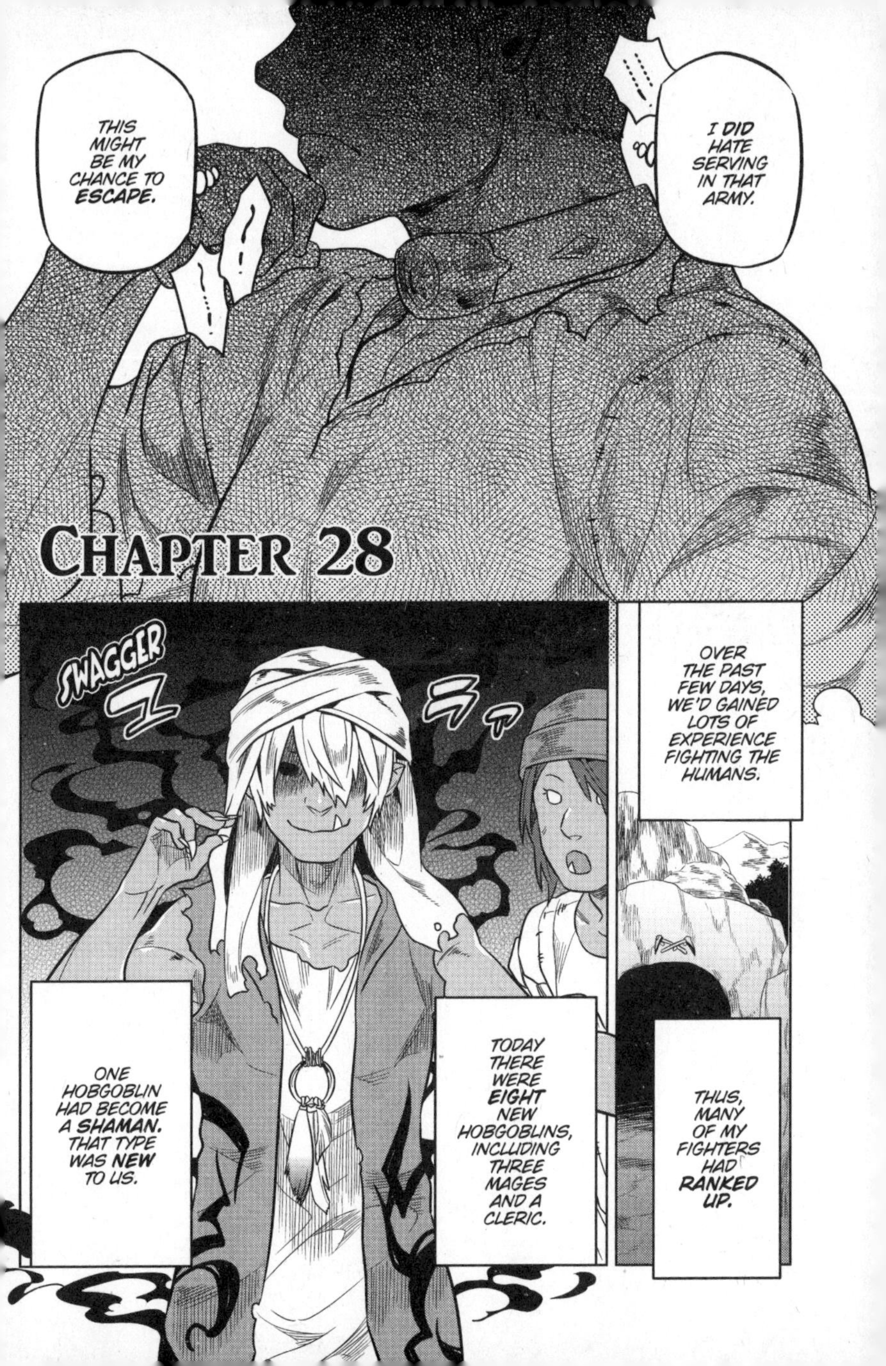
......
I DID HATE SERVING IN THAT ARMY.
......
THIS MIGHT BE MY CHANCE TO ESCAPE.
CHAPTER 28
OVER THE PAST FEW DAYS, WE'D GAINED LOTS OF EXPERIENCE FIGHTING THE HUMANS.
THUS, MANY OF MY FIGHTERS HAD RANKED UP.
SWAGGER
TODAY THERE WERE EIGHT NEW HOBGOBLINS, INCLUDING THREE MAGES AND A CLERIC.
ONE HOBGOBLIN HAD BECOME A SHAMAN. THAT TYPE WAS NEW TO US.

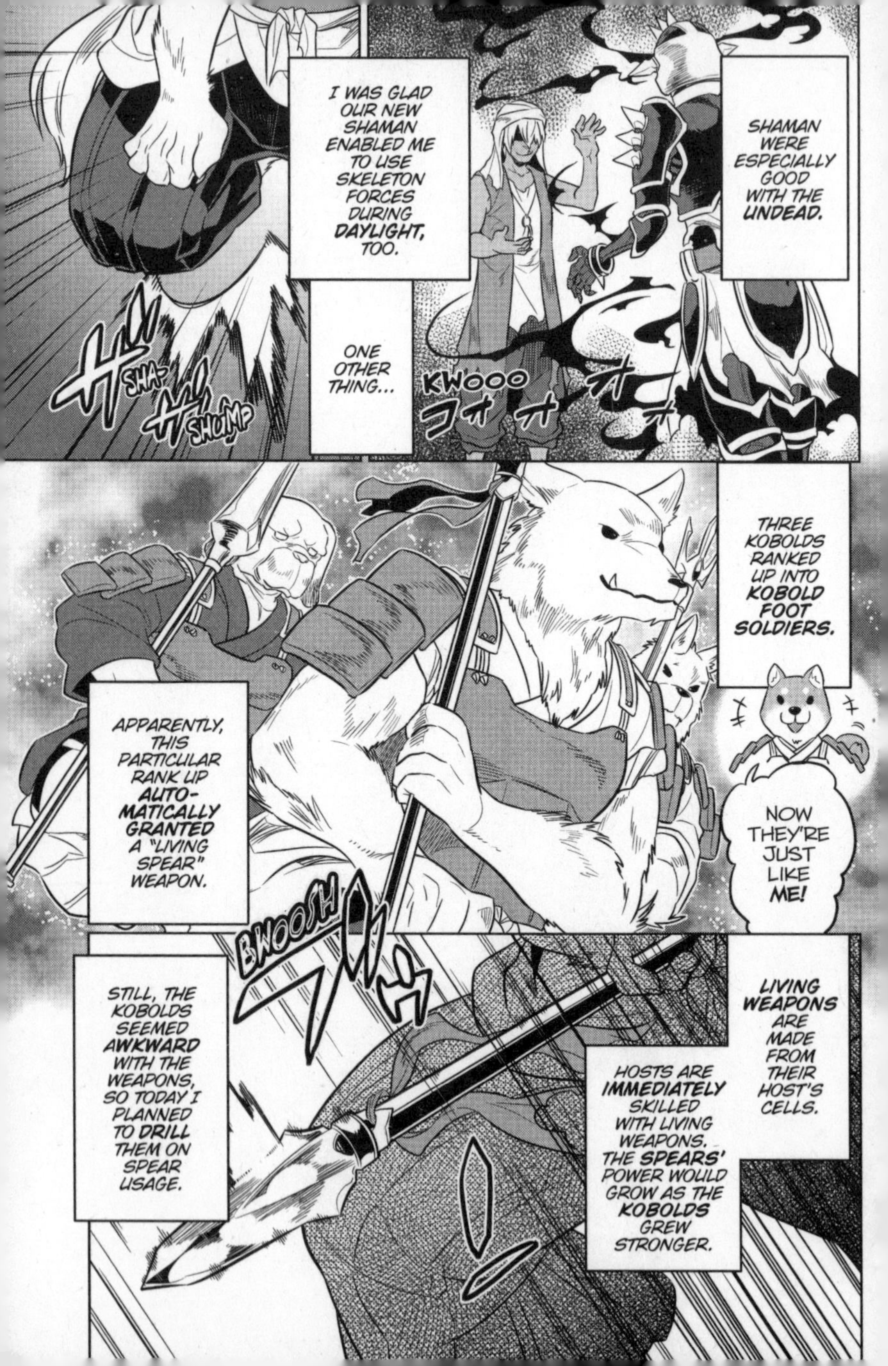
SHAMAN WERE ESPECIALLY GOOD WITH THE UNDEAD.
I WAS GLAD OUR NEW SHAMAN ENABLED ME TO USE SKELETON FORCES DURING DAYLIGHT, TOO.
KWOOO
ONE OTHER THING...
SHA-
SHOMP
THREE KOBOLDS RANKED UP INTO KOBOLD FOOT SOLDIERS.
NOW THEY'RE JUST LIKE ME!
APPARENTLY, THIS PARTICULAR RANK UP AUTOMATICALLY GRANTED A "LIVING SPEAR" WEAPON.
LIVING WEAPONS ARE MADE FROM THEIR HOST'S CELLS.
HOSTS ARE IMMEDIATELY SKILLED WITH LIVING WEAPONS. THE SPEARS' POWER WOULD GROW AS THE KOBOLDS GREW STRONGER.
BWOOSH
STILL, THE KOBOLDS SEEMED AWKWARD WITH THE WEAPONS, SO TODAY I PLANNED TO DRILL THEM ON SPEAR USAGE.

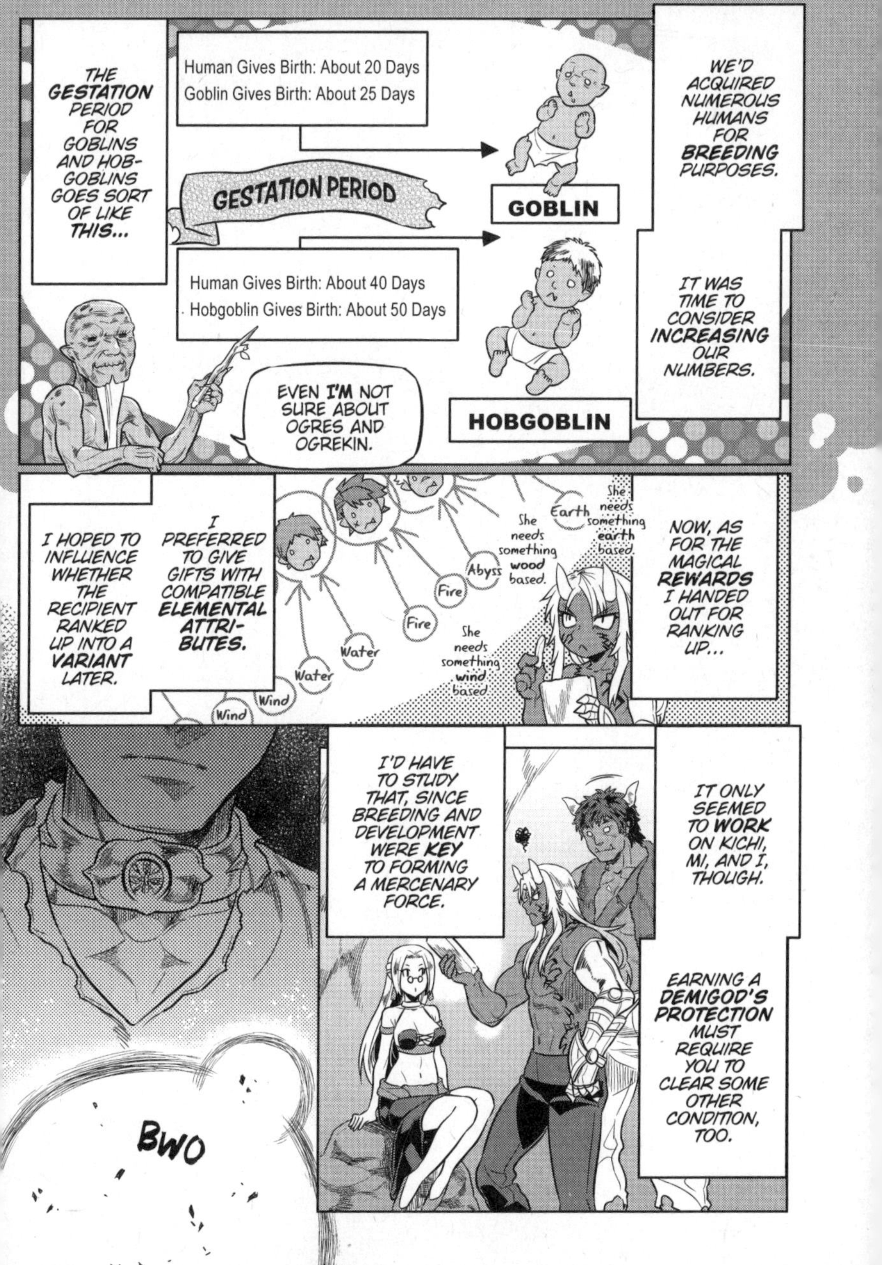
WE'D ACQUIRED NUMEROUS HUMANS FOR BREEDING PURPOSES.
IT WAS TIME TO CONSIDER INCREASING OUR NUMBERS.
THE GESTATION PERIOD FOR GOBLINS AND HOB-GOBLINS GOES SORT OF LIKE THIS...
GESTATION PERIOD
Human Gives Birth: About 20 Days
Goblin Gives Birth: About 25 Days
GOBLIN
Human Gives Birth: About 40 Days
Hobgoblin Gives Birth: About 50 Days
HOBGOBLIN
EVEN I'M NOT SURE ABOUT OGRES AND OGREKIN.
NOW, AS FOR THE MAGICAL REWARDS I HANDED OUT FOR RANKING UP...
She needs something earth based.
Earth
She needs something wood based.
Abyss
Fire
Fire
She needs something wind based.
Water
Water
Wind
Wind
I PREFERRED TO GIVE GIFTS WITH COMPATIBLE ELEMENTAL ATTRIBUTES.
I HOPED TO INFLUENCE WHETHER THE RECIPIENT RANKED UP INTO A VARIANT LATER.
IT ONLY SEEMED TO WORK ON KICHI, MI, AND I, THOUGH.
EARNING A DEMIGOD'S PROTECTION MUST REQUIRE YOU TO CLEAR SOME OTHER CONDITION, TOO.
I'D HAVE TO STUDY THAT, SINCE BREEDING AND DEVELOPMENT WERE KEY TO FORMING A MERCENARY FORCE.
BWO

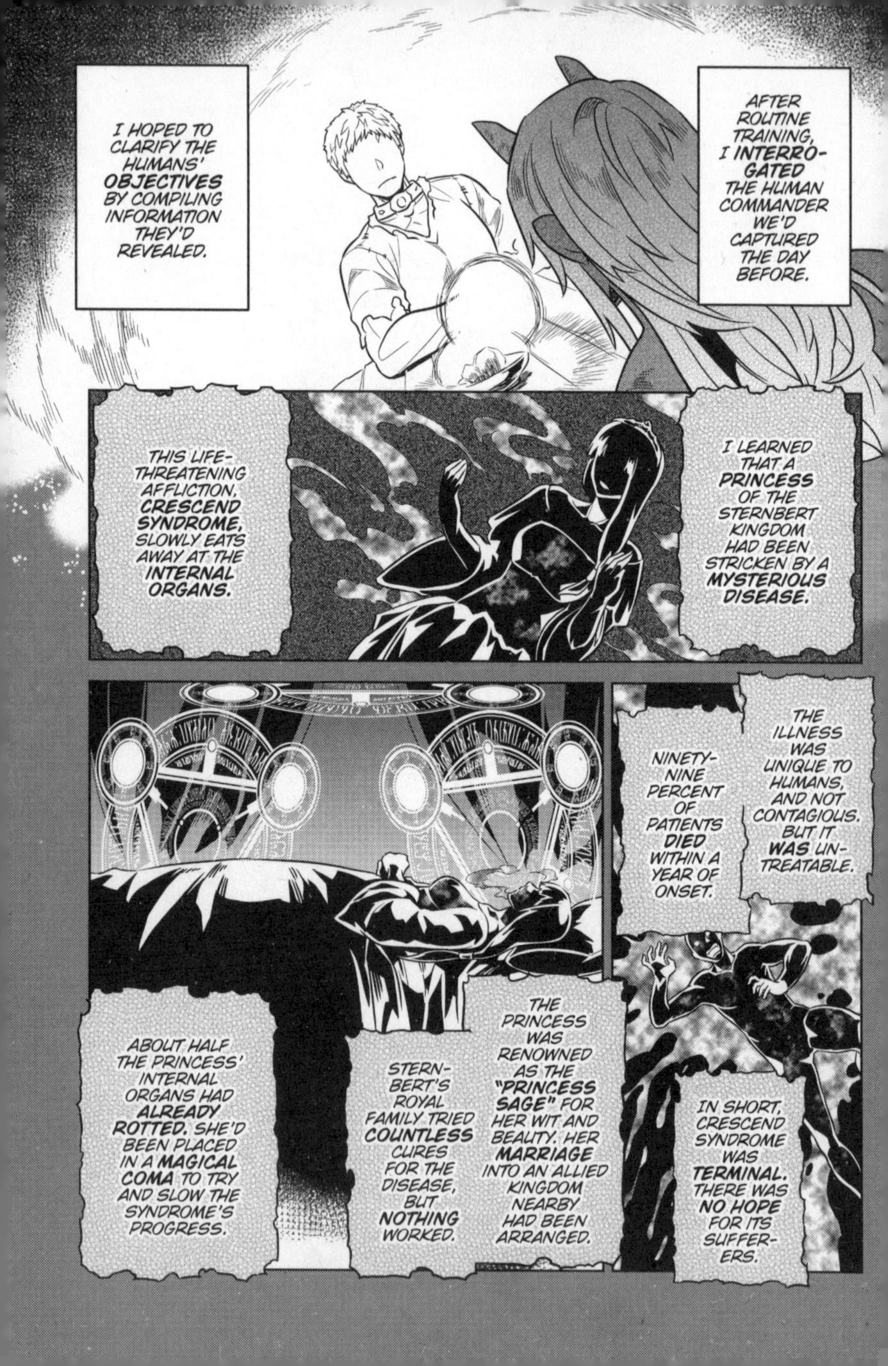
AFTER ROUTINE TRAINING, I INTERROGATED THE HUMAN COMMANDER WE'D CAPTURED THE DAY BEFORE.
I HOPED TO CLARIFY THE HUMANS' OBJECTIVES BY COMPILING INFORMATION THEY'D REVEALED.
I LEARNED THAT A PRINCESS OF THE STERNBERT KINGDOM HAD BEEN STRICKEN BY A MYSTERIOUS DISEASE.
THIS LIFE-THREATENING AFFLICTION, CRESCEND SYNDROME, SLOWLY EATS AWAY AT THE INTERNAL ORGANS.
THE ILLNESS WAS UNIQUE TO HUMANS, AND NOT CONTAGIOUS. BUT IT WAS UNTREATABLE.
NINETY-NINE PERCENT OF PATIENTS DIED WITHIN A YEAR OF ONSET.
IN SHORT, CRESCEND SYNDROME WAS TERMINAL. THERE WAS NO HOPE FOR ITS SUFFERERS.
THE PRINCESS WAS RENOWNED AS THE "PRINCESS SAGE" FOR HER WIT AND BEAUTY. HER MARRIAGE INTO AN ALLIED KINGDOM NEARBY HAD BEEN ARRANGED.
STERNBERT'S ROYAL FAMILY TRIED COUNTLESS CURES FOR THE DISEASE, BUT NOTHING WORKED.
ABOUT HALF THE PRINCESS' INTERNAL ORGANS HAD ALREADY ROTTED. SHE'D BEEN PLACED IN A MAGICAL COMA TO TRY AND SLOW THE SYNDROME'S PROGRESS.

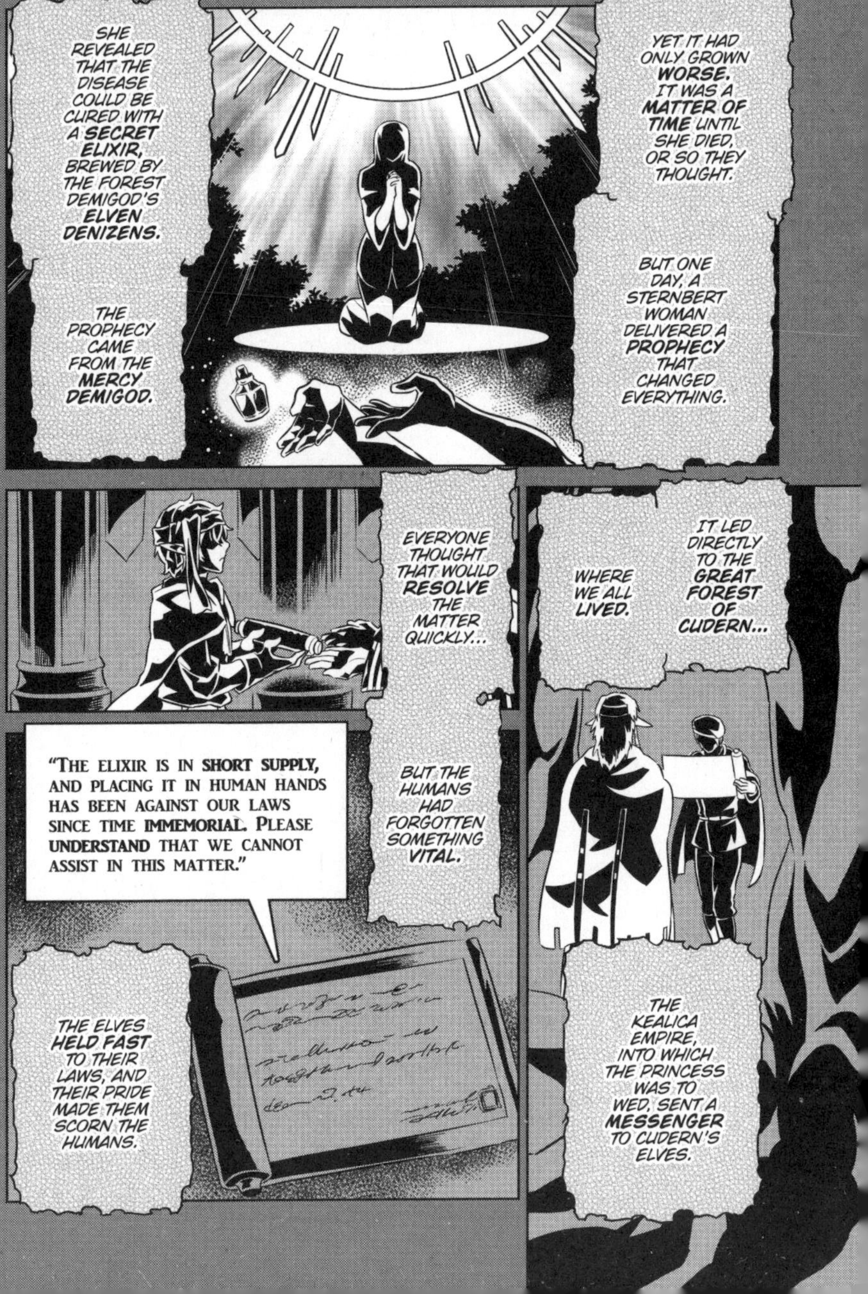
YET IT HAD ONLY GROWN WORSE. IT WAS A MATTER OF TIME UNTIL SHE DIED, OR SO THEY THOUGHT.
BUT ONE DAY, A STERNBERT WOMAN DELIVERED A PROPHECY THAT CHANGED EVERYTHING.
THE PROPHECY CAME FROM THE MERCY DEMIGOD.
SHE REVEALED THAT THE DISEASE COULD BE CURED WITH A SECRET ELIXIR, BREWED BY THE FOREST DEMIGOD'S ELVEN DENIZENS.
IT LED DIRECTLY TO THE GREAT FOREST OF CUDERN...
WHERE WE ALL LIVED.
THE KEALICA EMPIRE, INTO WHICH THE PRINCESS WAS TO WED, SENT A MESSENGER TO CUDERN'S ELVES.
EVERYONE THOUGHT THAT WOULD RESOLVE THE MATTER QUICKLY...
BUT THE HUMANS HAD FORGOTTEN SOMETHING VITAL.
"THE ELIXIR IS IN SHORT SUPPLY, AND PLACING IT IN HUMAN HANDS HAS BEEN AGAINST OUR LAWS SINCE TIME IMMEMORIAL. PLEASE UNDERSTAND THAT WE CANNOT ASSIST IN THIS MATTER."
THE ELVES HELD FAST TO THEIR LAWS, AND THEIR PRIDE MADE THEM SCORN THE HUMANS.

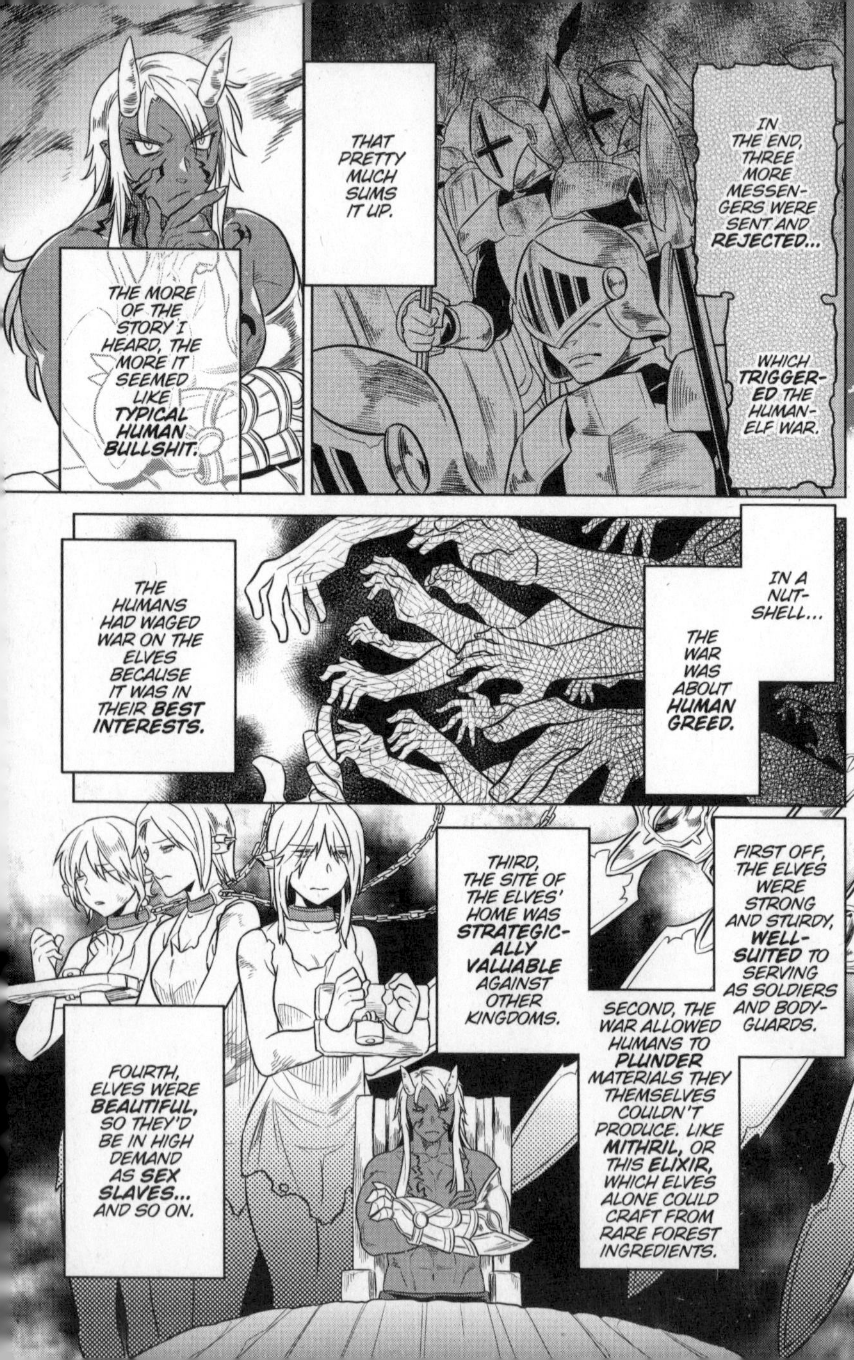

IN THE END, THREE MORE MESSENGERS WERE SENT AND REJECTED...
WHICH TRIGGERED THE HUMAN-ELF WAR.
THAT PRETTY MUCH SUMS IT UP.
THE MORE OF THE STORY I HEARD, THE MORE IT SEEMED LIKE TYPICAL HUMAN BULLSHIT.
IN A NUTSHELL...
THE WAR WAS ABOUT HUMAN GREED.
THE HUMANS HAD WAGED WAR ON THE ELVES BECAUSE IT WAS IN THEIR BEST INTERESTS.
FIRST OFF, THE ELVES WERE STRONG AND STURDY, WELL-SUITED TO SERVING AS SOLDIERS AND BODYGUARDS.
SECOND, THE WAR ALLOWED HUMANS TO PLUNDER MATERIALS THEY THEMSELVES COULDN'T PRODUCE. LIKE MITHRIL, OR THIS ELIXIR, WHICH ELVES ALONE COULD CRAFT FROM RARE FOREST INGREDIENTS.
THIRD, THE SITE OF THE ELVES' HOME WAS STRATEGICALLY VALUABLE AGAINST OTHER KINGDOMS.
FOURTH, ELVES WERE BEAUTIFUL, SO THEY'D BE IN HIGH DEMAND AS SEX SLAVES... AND SO ON.

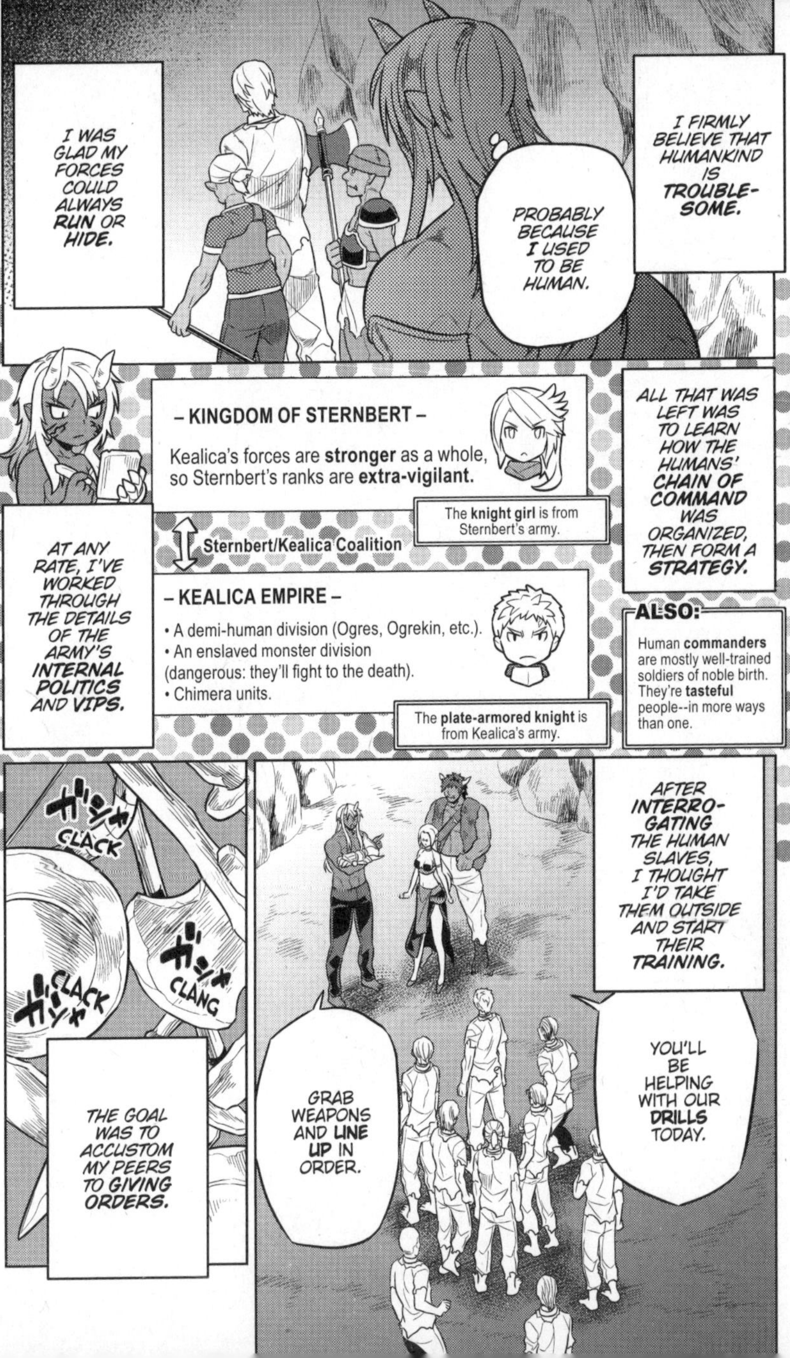
I FIRMLY BELIEVE THAT HUMANKIND IS TROUBLESOME.
PROBABLY BECAUSE I USED TO BE HUMAN.
I WAS GLAD MY FORCES COULD ALWAYS RUN OR HIDE.
ALL THAT WAS LEFT WAS TO LEARN HOW THE HUMANS' CHAIN OF COMMAND WAS ORGANIZED, THEN FORM A STRATEGY.
ALSO:
Human commanders are mostly well-trained soldiers of noble birth. They're tasteful people--in more ways than one.
– KINGDOM OF STERNBERT –
Kealica's forces are stronger as a whole, so Sternbert's ranks are extra-vigilant.
The knight girl is from Sternbert's army.
Sternbert/Kealica Coalition
– KEALICA EMPIRE –
• A demi-human division (Ogres, Ogrekin, etc.).
• An enslaved monster division (dangerous: they'll fight to the death).
• Chimera units.
The plate-armored knight is from Kealica's army.
AT ANY RATE, I'VE WORKED THROUGH THE DETAILS OF THE ARMY'S INTERNAL POLITICS AND VIPS.
AFTER INTERROGATING THE HUMAN SLAVES, I THOUGHT I'D TAKE THEM OUTSIDE AND START THEIR TRAINING.
YOU'LL BE HELPING WITH OUR DRILLS TODAY.
GRAB WEAPONS AND LINE UP IN ORDER.
CLACK
CLANG
CLACK
THE GOAL WAS TO ACCUSTOM MY PEERS TO GIVING ORDERS.

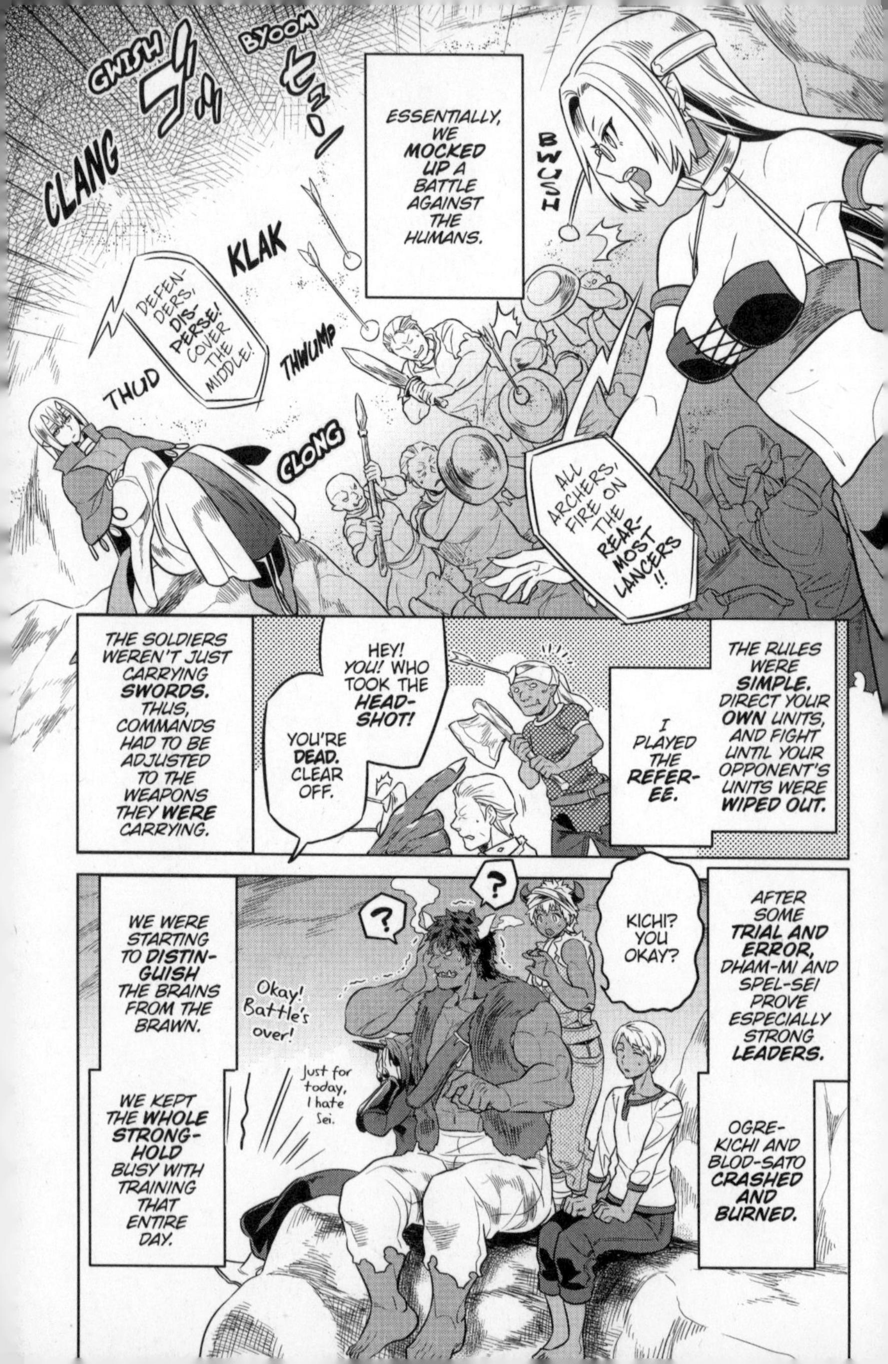
ESSENTIALLY, WE MOCKED UP A BATTLE AGAINST THE HUMANS.
BWUSH
BYOOM
GWISH
CLANG
KLAK
ALL ARCHERS, FIRE ON THE REAR-MOST LANCERS!!
DEFEN-DERS, DIS-PERSE! COVER THE MIDDLE!
THWUMP
THUD
CLONG
THE RULES WERE SIMPLE. DIRECT YOUR OWN UNITS, AND FIGHT UNTIL YOUR OPPONENT'S UNITS WERE WIPED OUT.
I PLAYED THE REFER-EE.
HEY! YOU! WHO TOOK THE HEAD-SHOT!
YOU'RE DEAD. CLEAR OFF.
THE SOLDIERS WEREN'T JUST CARRYING SWORDS. THUS, COMMANDS HAD TO BE ADJUSTED TO THE WEAPONS THEY WERE CARRYING.
AFTER SOME TRIAL AND ERROR, DHAM-MI AND SPEL-SEI PROVE ESPECIALLY STRONG LEADERS.
OGRE-KICHI AND BLOD-SATO CRASHED AND BURNED.
KICHI? YOU OKAY?
?
?
Okay! Battle's over!
Just for today, I hate Sei.
WE WERE STARTING TO DISTIN-GUISH THE BRAINS FROM THE BRAWN.
WE KEPT THE WHOLE STRONG-HOLD BUSY WITH TRAINING THAT ENTIRE DAY.

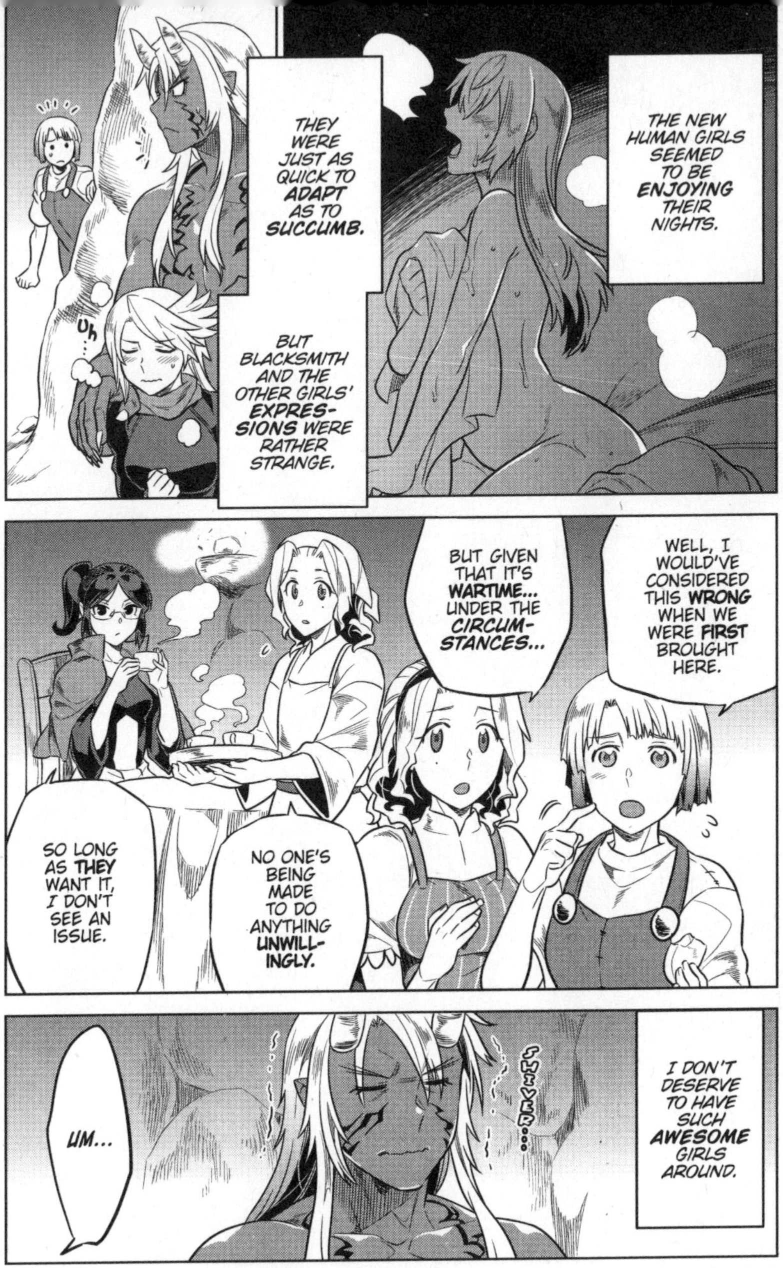
THE NEW HUMAN GIRLS SEEMED TO BE ENJOYING THEIR NIGHTS.
THEY WERE JUST AS QUICK TO ADAPT AS TO SUCCUMB.
BUT BLACKSMITH AND THE OTHER GIRLS' EXPRESSIONS WERE RATHER STRANGE.
Uh...
WELL, I WOULD'VE CONSIDERED THIS WRONG WHEN WE WERE FIRST BROUGHT HERE.
BUT GIVEN THAT IT'S WARTIME... UNDER THE CIRCUMSTANCES...
NO ONE'S BEING MADE TO DO ANYTHING UNWILLINGLY.
SO LONG AS THEY WANT IT, I DON'T SEE AN ISSUE.
I DON'T DESERVE TO HAVE SUCH AWESOME GIRLS AROUND.
SHIVER...
UM...

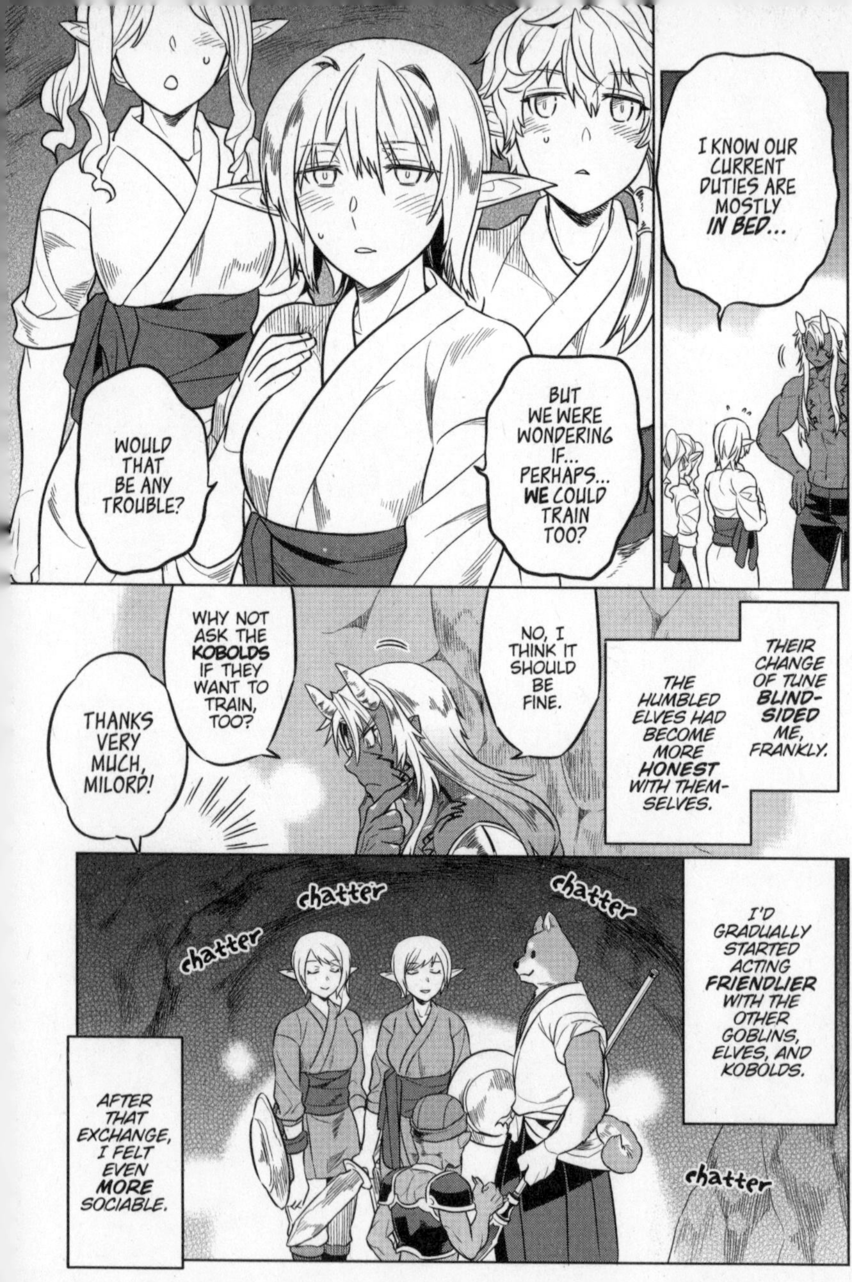
I KNOW OUR CURRENT DUTIES ARE MOSTLY IN BED...
BUT WE WERE WONDERING IF... PERHAPS... WE COULD TRAIN TOO?
WOULD THAT BE ANY TROUBLE?
THEIR CHANGE OF TUNE BLIND-SIDED ME, FRANKLY.
THE HUMBLED ELVES HAD BECOME MORE HONEST WITH THEM-SELVES.
NO, I THINK IT SHOULD BE FINE.
WHY NOT ASK THE KOBOLDS IF THEY WANT TO TRAIN, TOO?
THANKS VERY MUCH, MILORD!
I'D GRADUALLY STARTED ACTING FRIENDLIER WITH THE OTHER GOBLINS, ELVES, AND KOBOLDS.
chatter
chatter
chatter
chatter
AFTER THAT EXCHANGE, I FELT EVEN MORE SOCIABLE.

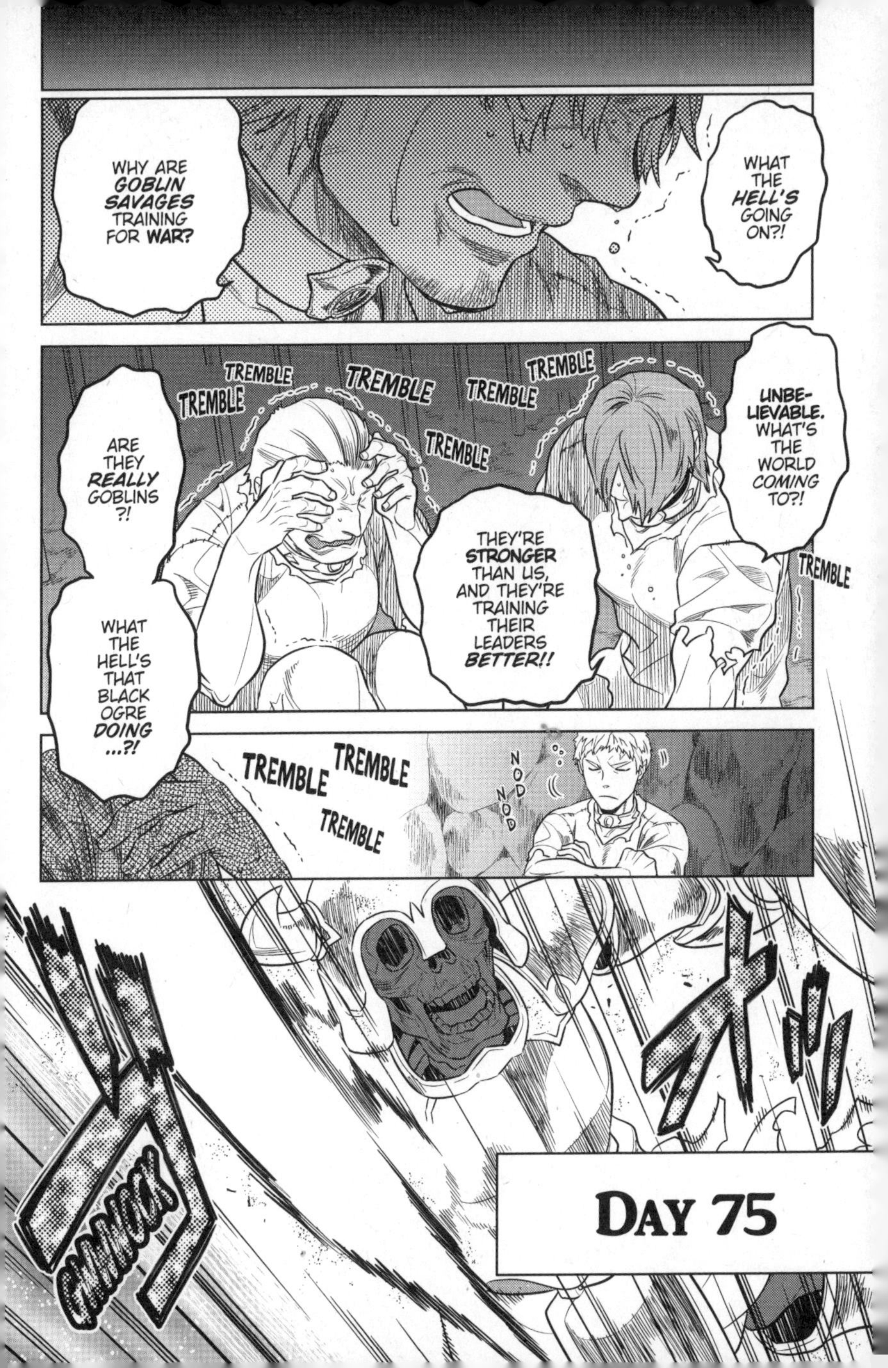
WHAT THE HELL'S GOING ON?!
WHY ARE GOBLIN SAVAGES TRAINING FOR WAR?
UNBE-LIEVABLE. WHAT'S THE WORLD COMING TO?!
TREMBLE
TREMBLE
TREMBLE
TREMBLE
TREMBLE
TREMBLE
TREMBLE
THEY'RE STRONGER THAN US, AND THEY'RE TRAINING THEIR LEADERS BETTER!!
ARE THEY REALLY GOBLINS?!
WHAT THE HELL'S THAT BLACK OGRE DOING...?!
NOD NOD
TREMBLE
TREMBLE
TREMBLE
DAY 75

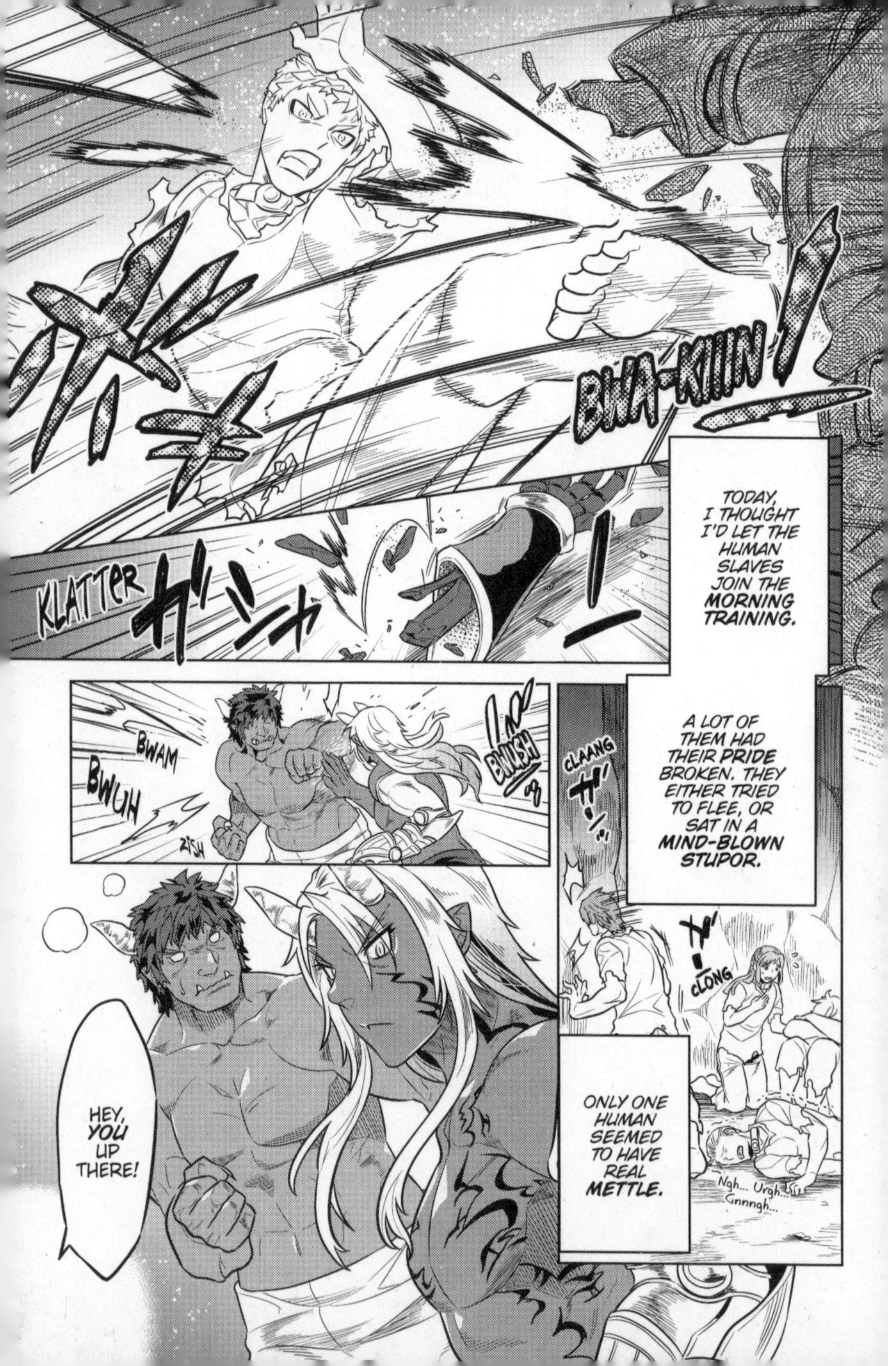
BWA-KIIN
TODAY, I THOUGHT I'D LET THE HUMAN SLAVES JOIN THE MORNING TRAINING.
KLATTER
A LOT OF THEM HAD THEIR PRIDE BROKEN. THEY EITHER TRIED TO FLEE, OR SAT IN A MIND-BLOWN STUPOR.
CLAANG
CLONG
ONLY ONE HUMAN SEEMED TO HAVE REAL METTLE.
Ngh... Urgh... Gnnnngh...
BWUSH
BWAM
BWUH
ZISH
HEY, YOU UP THERE!

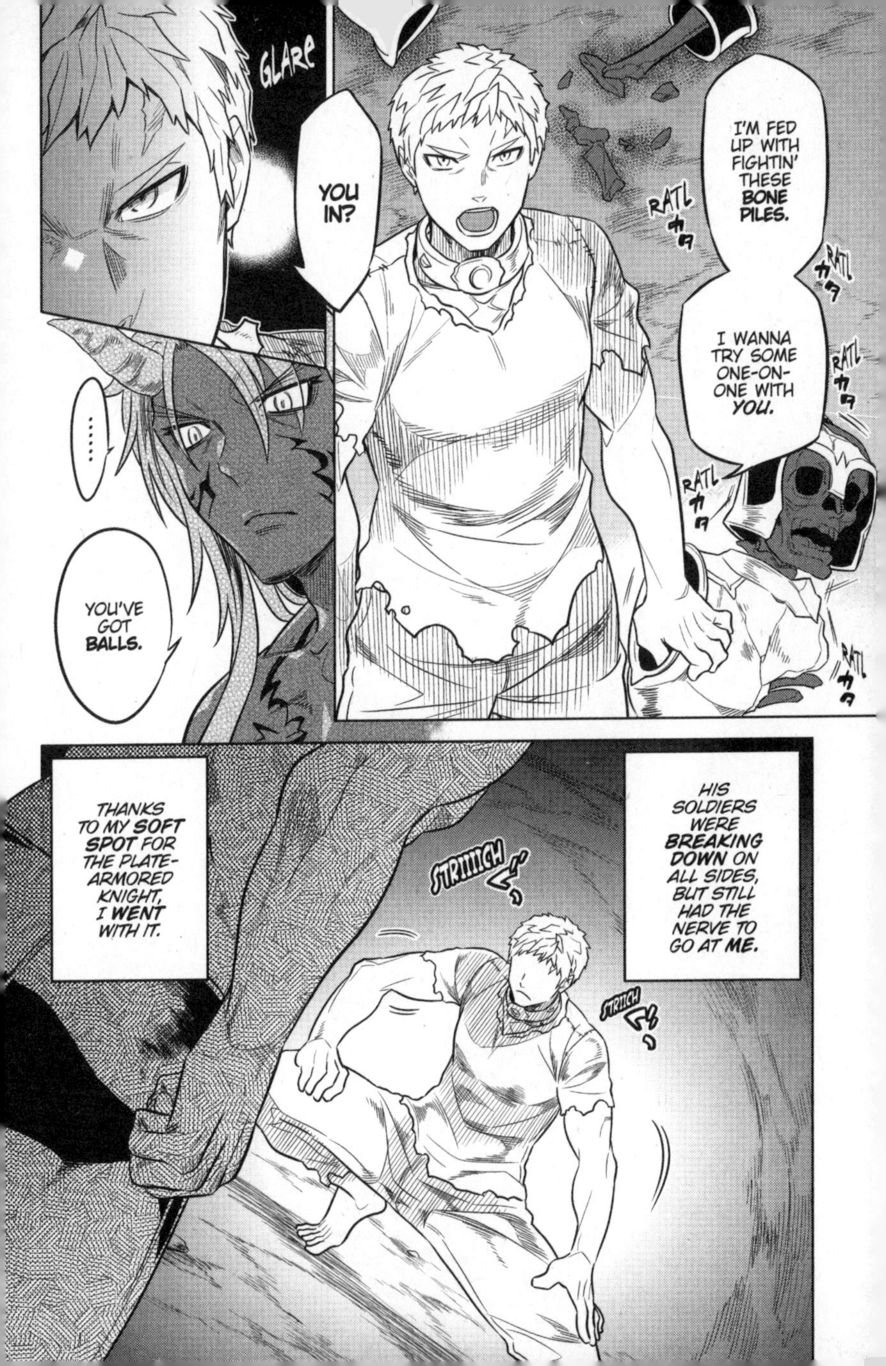
I'M FED UP WITH FIGHTIN' THESE BONE PILES.
RATL カタ
RATL カタ
I WANNA TRY SOME ONE-ON-ONE WITH YOU.
RATL カタ
RATL カタ
YOU IN?
RATL カタ
GLARE
......
YOU'VE GOT BALLS.
HIS SOLDIERS WERE BREAKING DOWN ON ALL SIDES, BUT STILL HAD THE NERVE TO GO AT ME.
STRIIIICH
THANKS TO MY SOFT SPOT FOR THE PLATE-ARMORED KNIGHT, I WENT WITH IT.
STRIICH

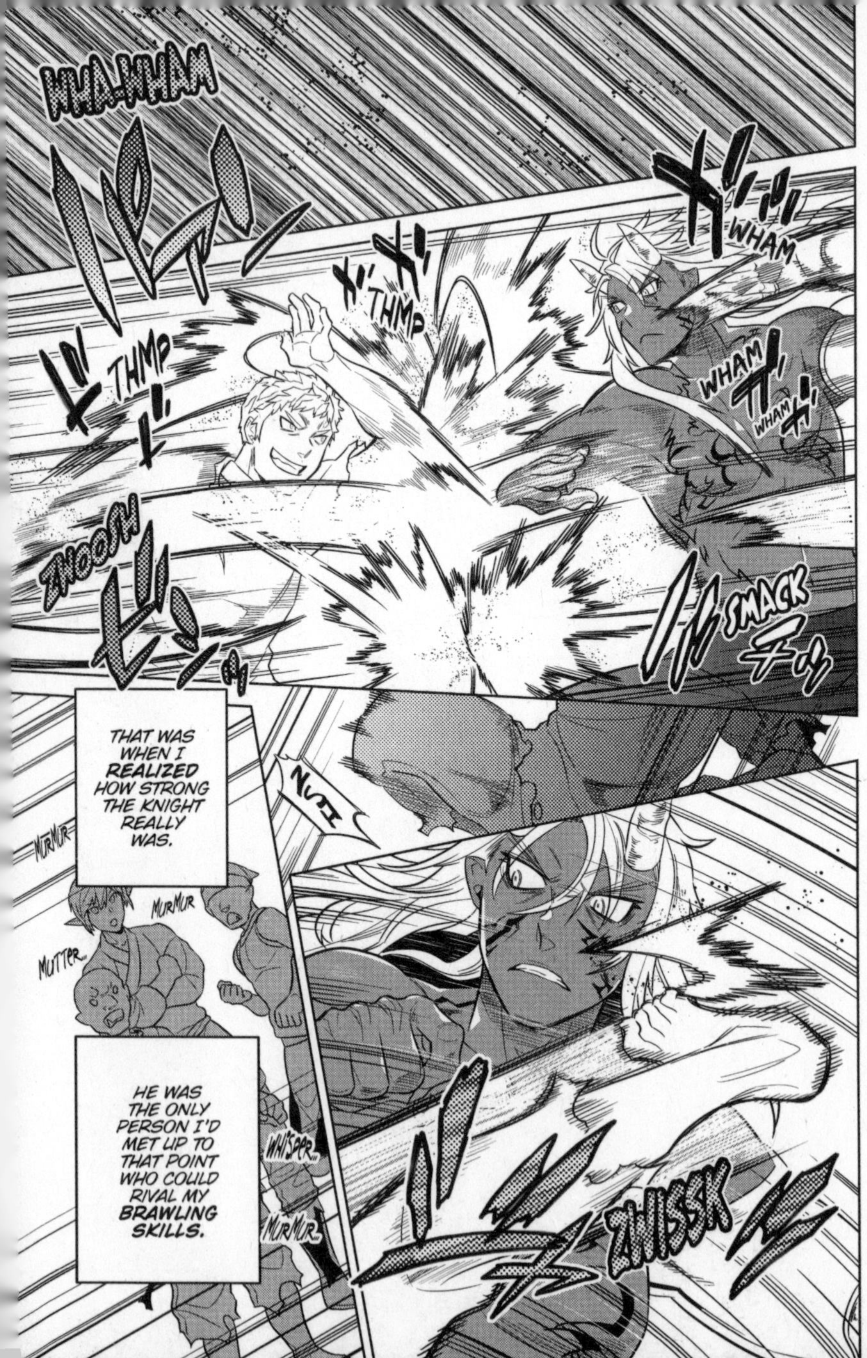

WHAM
WHA-WHAM
THMP
WHAM
WHAM
THMP
SMACK
ZWOOSH
ZWISSK
THAT WAS WHEN I REALIZED HOW STRONG THE KNIGHT REALLY WAS.
MURMUR
MURMUR
MUTTER...
HE WAS THE ONLY PERSON I'D MET UP TO THAT POINT WHO COULD RIVAL MY BRAWLING SKILLS.
WHISPER...
MURMUR...

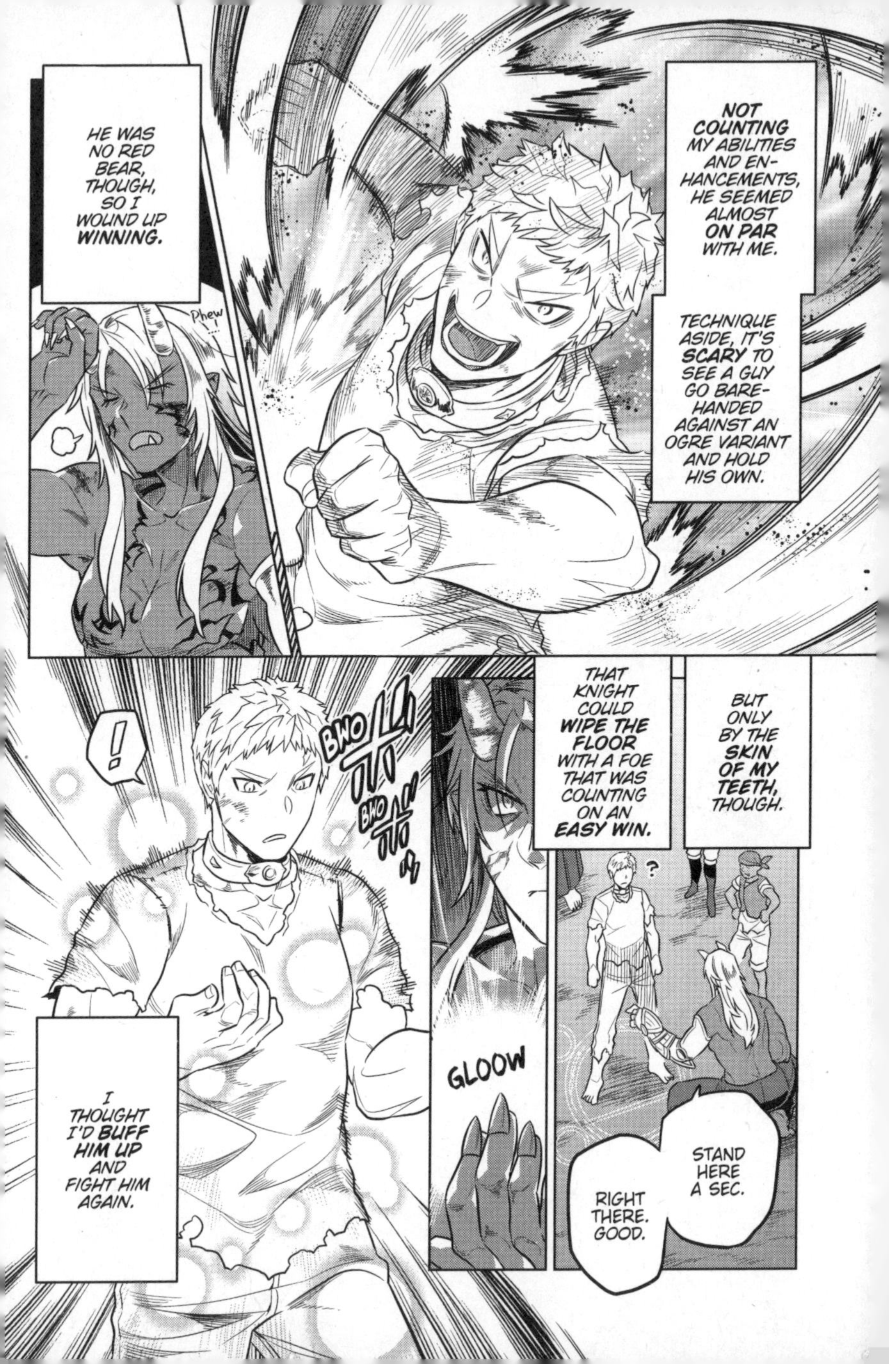
NOT COUNTING MY ABILITIES AND EN-HANCEMENTS, HE SEEMED ALMOST ON PAR WITH ME.
TECHNIQUE ASIDE, IT'S SCARY TO SEE A GUY GO BARE-HANDED AGAINST AN OGRE VARIANT AND HOLD HIS OWN.
HE WAS NO RED BEAR, THOUGH, SO I WOUND UP WINNING.
Phew
BUT ONLY BY THE SKIN OF MY TEETH, THOUGH.
THAT KNIGHT COULD WIPE THE FLOOR WITH A FOE THAT WAS COUNTING ON AN EASY WIN.
?
STAND HERE A SEC.
RIGHT THERE. GOOD.
GLOOW
!
BWO BWO
I THOUGHT I'D BUFF HIM UP AND FIGHT HIM AGAIN.

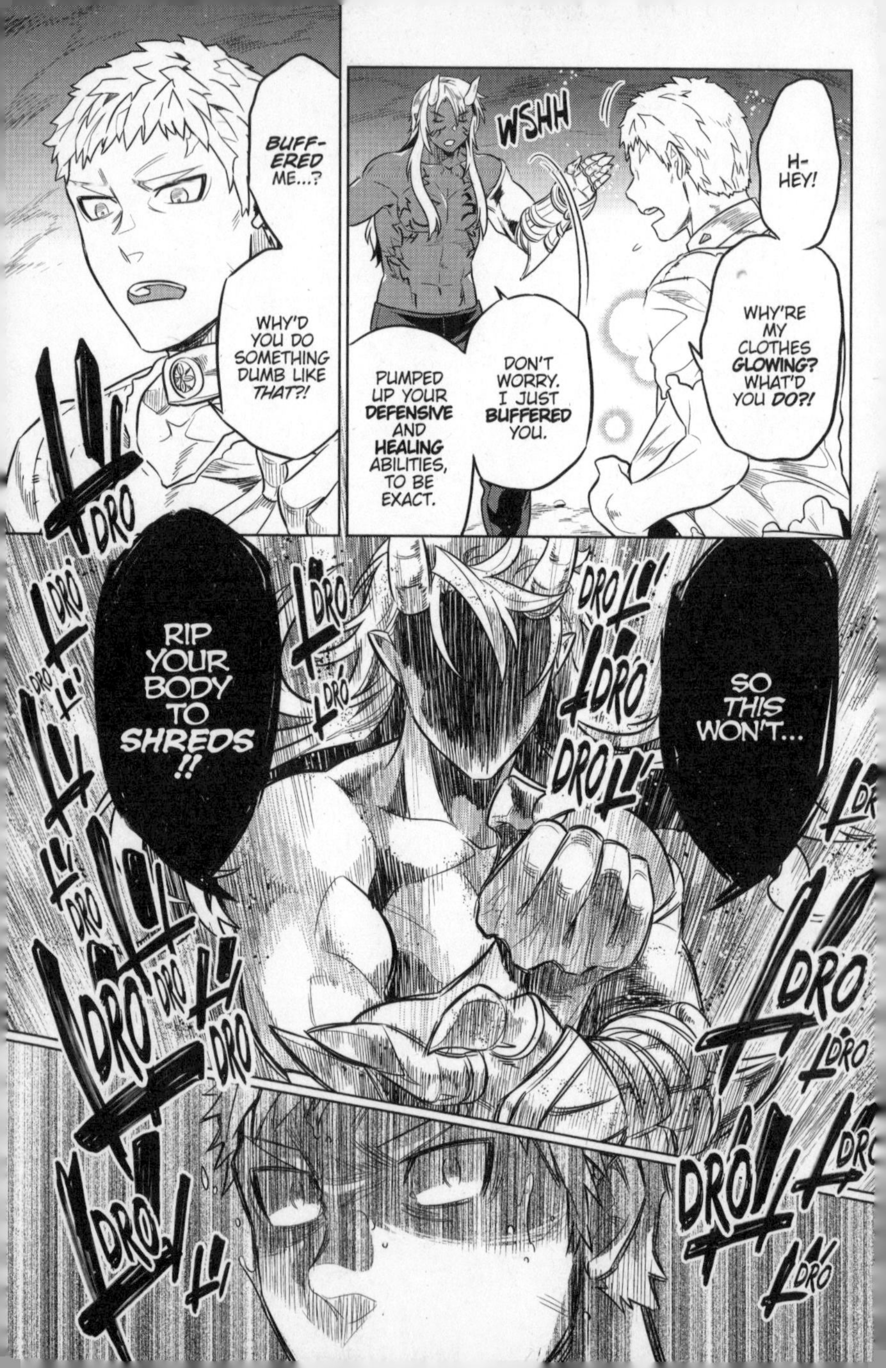
H-HEY!
WSHH
WHY'RE MY CLOTHES GLOWING? WHAT'D YOU DO?!
DON'T WORRY. I JUST BUFFERED YOU.
PUMPED UP YOUR DEFENSIVE AND HEALING ABILITIES, TO BE EXACT.
BUFF-ERED ME...?
WHY'D YOU DO SOMETHING DUMB LIKE THAT?!
DRO
SO THIS WON'T...
RIP YOUR BODY TO SHREDS!!
DRO DRO DRO DRO

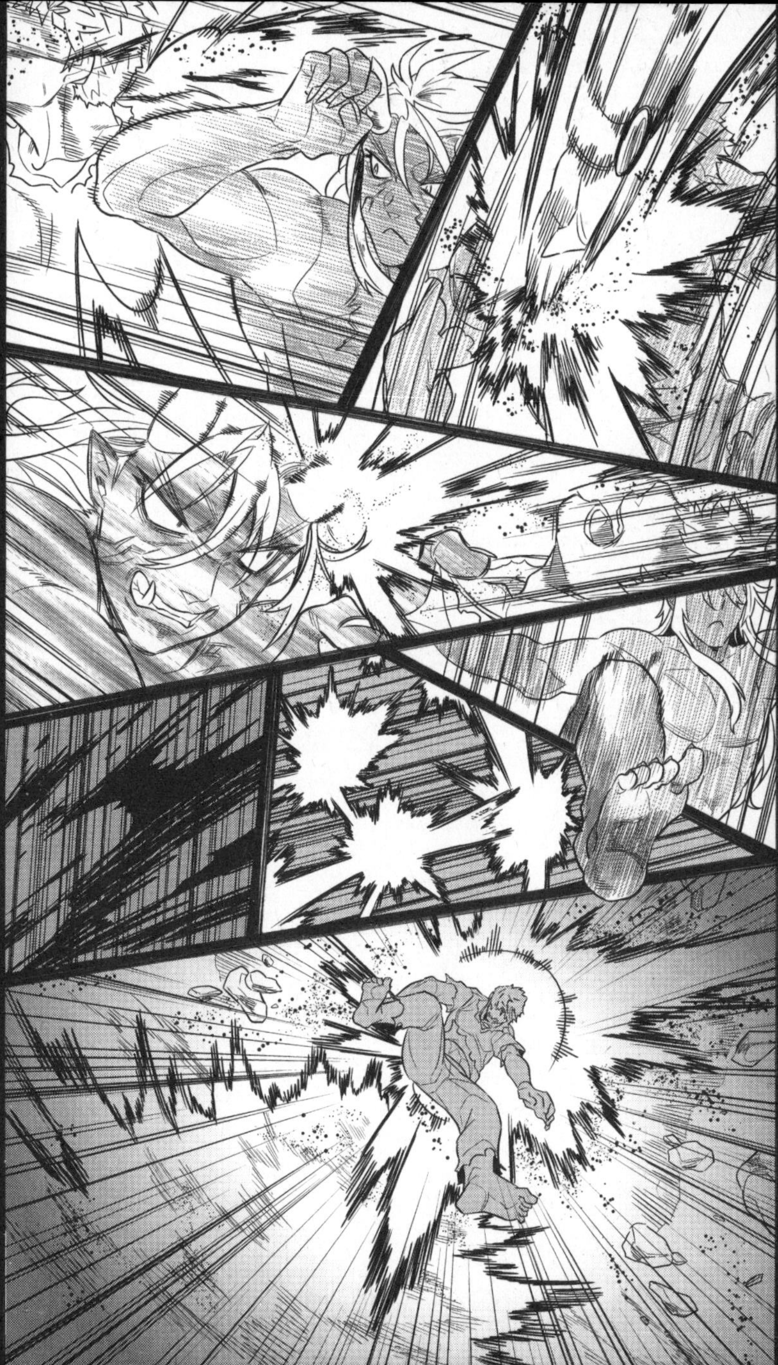

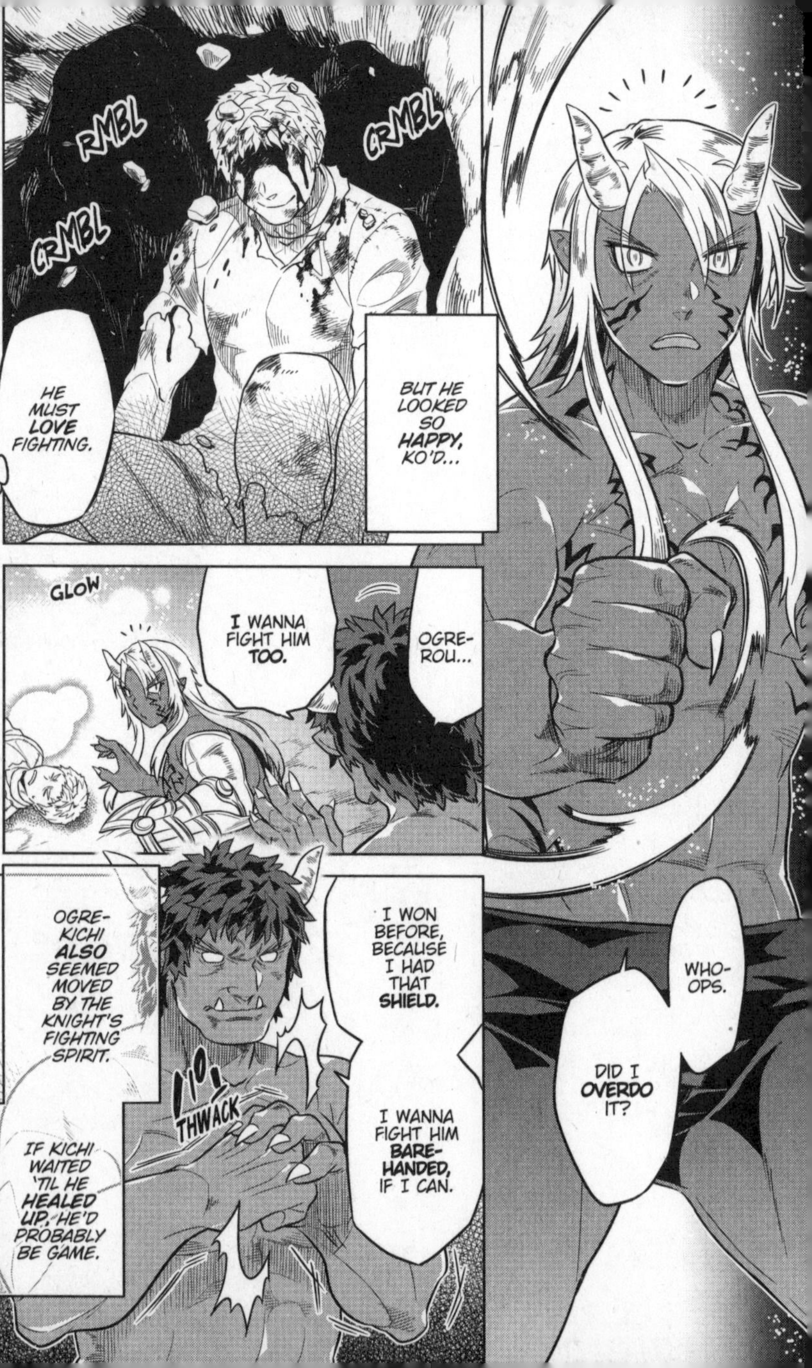
WHO-OPS.
DID I OVERDO IT?
CRMBL
RMBL
CRMBL
BUT HE LOOKED SO HAPPY, KO'D...
HE MUST LOVE FIGHTING.
OGRE-ROU...
I WANNA FIGHT HIM TOO.
GLOW
I WON BEFORE, BECAUSE I HAD THAT SHIELD.
I WANNA FIGHT HIM BARE-HANDED, IF I CAN.
OGRE-KICHI ALSO SEEMED MOVED BY THE KNIGHT'S FIGHTING SPIRIT.
THWACK
IF KICHI WAITED 'TIL HE HEALED UP, HE'D PROBABLY BE GAME.

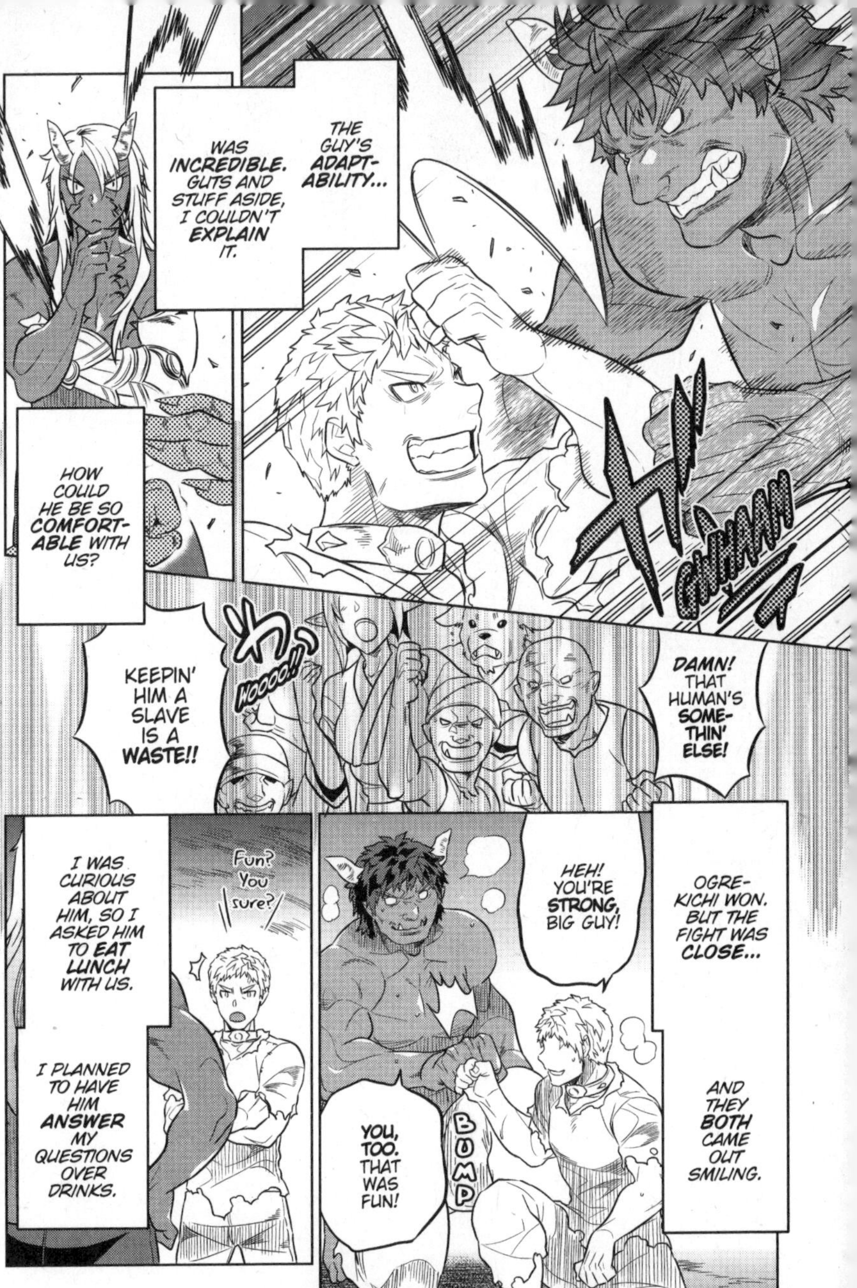
THE GUY'S ADAPTABILITY...
WAS INCREDIBLE. GUTS AND STUFF ASIDE, I COULDN'T EXPLAIN IT.
HOW COULD HE BE SO COMFORTABLE WITH US?
DAMN! THAT HUMAN'S SOMETHIN' ELSE!
WOOOO!!
KEEPIN' HIM A SLAVE IS A WASTE!!
OGRE-KICHI WON. BUT THE FIGHT WAS CLOSE...
HEH! YOU'RE STRONG, BIG GUY!
YOU, TOO. THAT WAS FUN!
BUMP
AND THEY BOTH CAME OUT SMILING.
Fun? You sure?
I WAS CURIOUS ABOUT HIM, SO I ASKED HIM TO EAT LUNCH WITH US.
I PLANNED TO HAVE HIM ANSWER MY QUESTIONS OVER DRINKS.

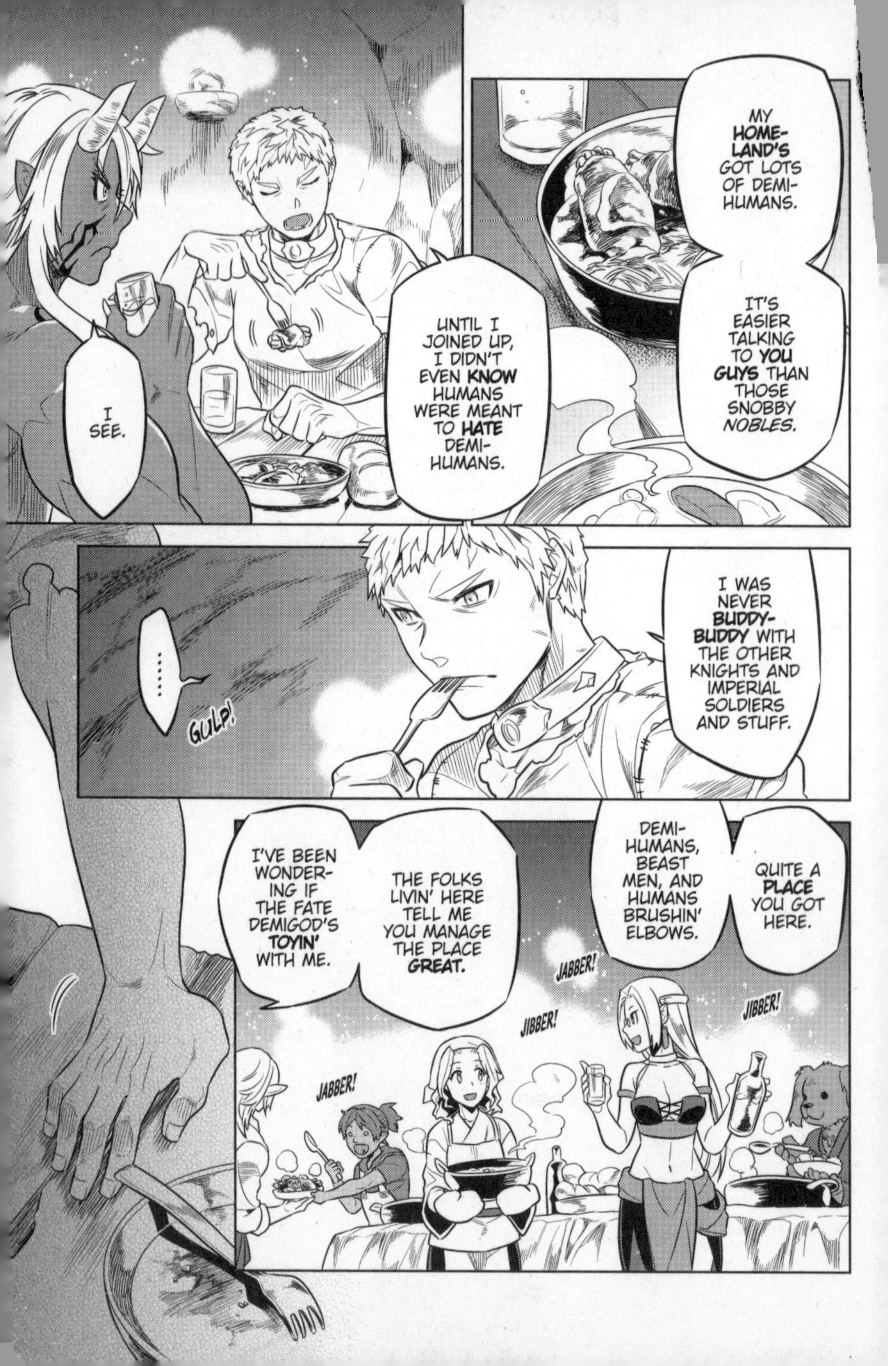
MY HOME-LAND'S GOT LOTS OF DEMI-HUMANS.
IT'S EASIER TALKING TO YOU GUYS THAN THOSE SNOBBY NOBLES.
UNTIL I JOINED UP, I DIDN'T EVEN KNOW HUMANS WERE MEANT TO HATE DEMI-HUMANS.
I SEE.
I WAS NEVER BUDDY-BUDDY WITH THE OTHER KNIGHTS AND IMPERIAL SOLDIERS AND STUFF.
......
GULP!
QUITE A PLACE YOU GOT HERE.
DEMI-HUMANS, BEAST MEN, AND HUMANS BRUSHIN' ELBOWS.
THE FOLKS LIVIN' HERE TELL ME YOU MANAGE THE PLACE GREAT.
I'VE BEEN WONDER-ING IF THE FATE DEMIGOD'S TOYIN' WITH ME.
JIBBER!
JABBER!
JIBBER!
JABBER!

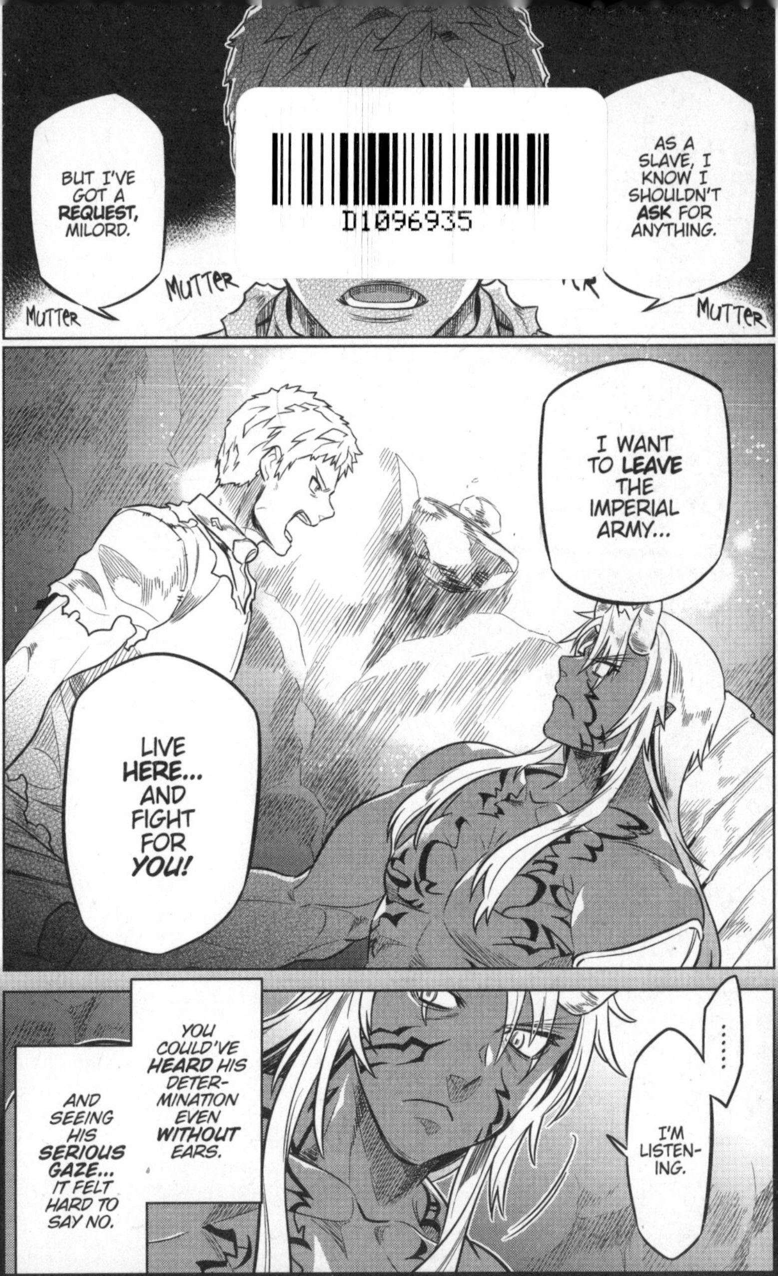
AS A SLAVE, I KNOW I SHOULDN'T ASK FOR ANYTHING.
MUTTER
BUT I'VE GOT A REQUEST, MILORD.
MUTTER
MUTTER
I WANT TO LEAVE THE IMPERIAL ARMY...
LIVE HERE... AND FIGHT FOR YOU!
......
I'M LISTEN-ING.
YOU COULD'VE HEARD HIS DETER-MINATION EVEN WITHOUT EARS.
AND SEEING HIS SERIOUS GAZE... IT FELT HARD TO SAY NO.

▶ CONTINUE